NISEKOI

False Love

vol. 15: Beauty Contest

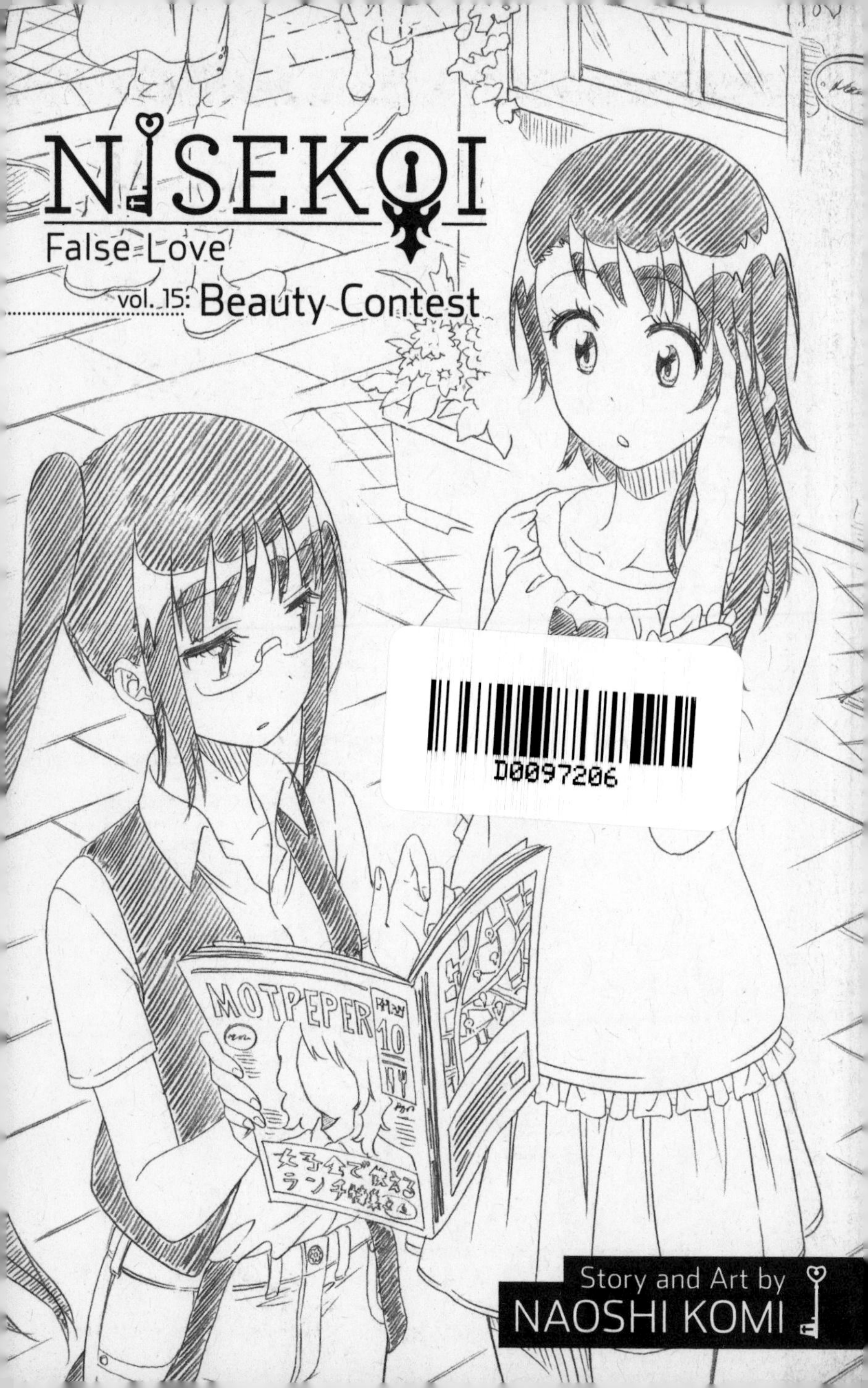
MOTPEPER

Story and Art by
NAOSHI KOMI

CHITOGE KIRISAKI

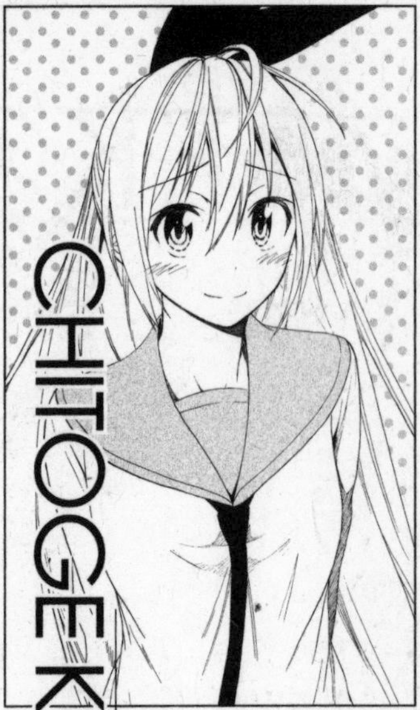

A half-Japanese bombshell with stellar athletic abilities. Short-tempered and violent. Comes from a family of gangsters.

RAKU ICHIJO

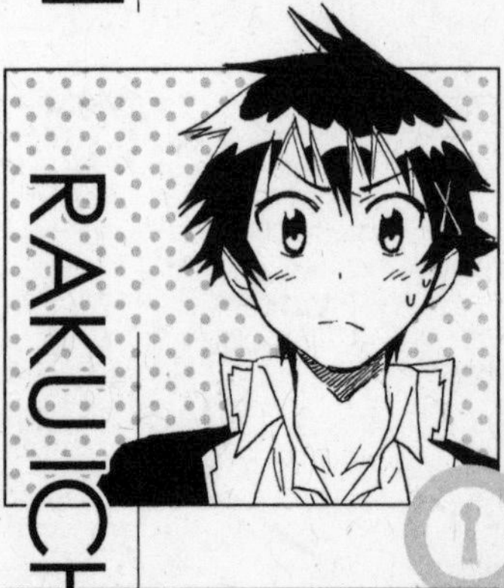

A normal teen whose family happens to be yakuza. Cherishes a pendant given to him by a girl he met ten years ago.

KOSAKI ONODERA

A girl Raku has a crush on. Beautiful and sweet, Kosaki has no shortage of admirers. She's a terrible cook but makes food that *looks* amazing.

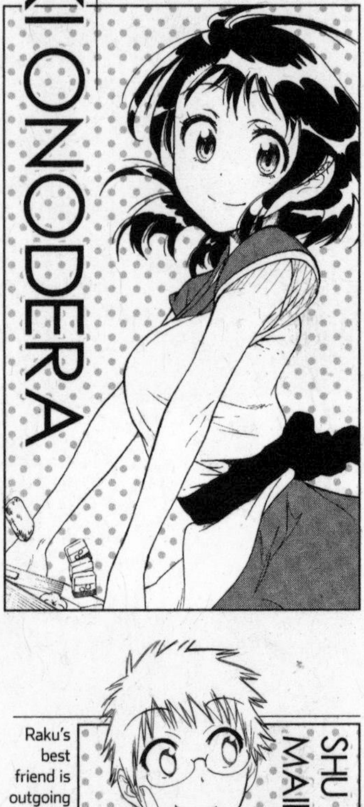

SHU MAIKO

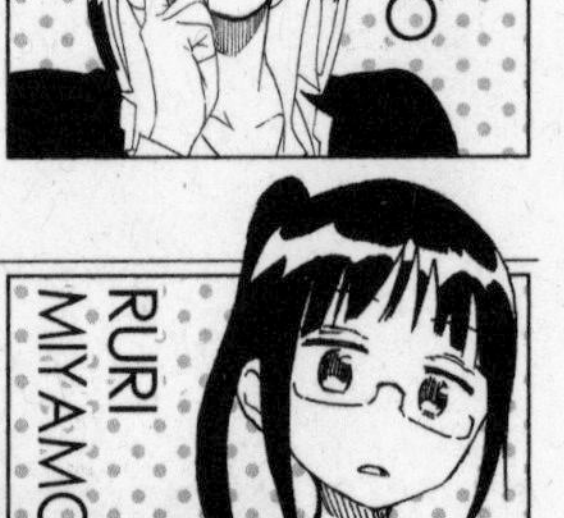

Raku's best friend is outgoing and girl-crazy.

RURI MIYAMOTO

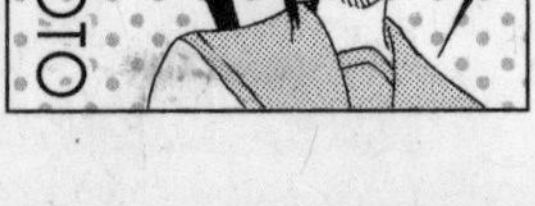

Kosaki's best gal pal. Comes off as aloof, but is actually a devoted and highly intuitive friend.

This volume includes episodes from the school festival. My memories of my own school festivals include being in the art club and publishing a manga in our club zine. It was quite an ordeal. It was my first time drawing a manga, and I had all sorts of trouble drawing it and finishing it on time... Lots of people helped me, and I finally finished it on the day of the festival! Back then, I was really discouraged, wondering if I could ever make it as a manga author. Now, it's a fond memory...

Naoshi Komi

NAOSHI KOMI was born in Kochi Prefecture, Japan, on March 28, 1986. His first serialized work in *Weekly Shonen Jump* was the series *Double Arts*. His current series, *Nisekoi*, is serialized in *Weekly Shonen Jump*.

NISEKOI:
False Love
VOLUME 15
SHONEN JUMP Manga Edition

Story and Art by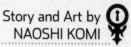
NAOSHI KOMI

Translation ✎ Camellia Nieh
Touch-Up Art & Lettering ✎ Stephen Dutro
Design ✎ Fawn Lau
Shonen Jump Series Editor ✎ John Bae
Graphic Novel Editor ✎ Amy Yu

NISEKOI © 2011 by Naoshi Komi
All rights reserved.
First published in Japan in 2011
by SHUEISHA Inc., Tokyo.
English translation rights arranged
by SHUEISHA Inc.

Printed in the U.S.A.

Published by VIZ Media, LLC
P.O. Box 77010
San Francisco, CA 94107

10 9 8 7 6 5 4 3 2 1
First printing, May 2016

www.shonenjump.com

www.viz.com

MARIKA TACHIBANA

Daughter of the chief of police, Marika is Raku's fiancée, according to an agreement made by their fathers—an agreement Marika takes very seriously! Also has a key and remembers making a promise with Raku ten years ago.

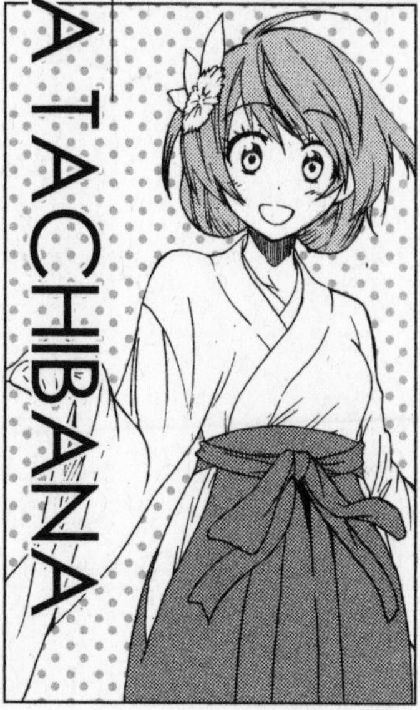

YUI KANAKURA

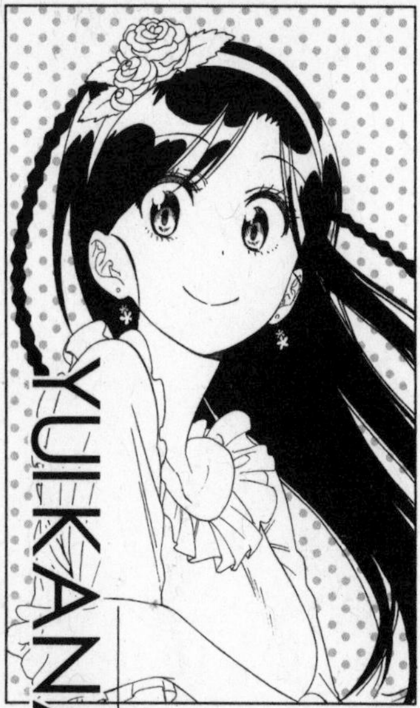

A childhood friend of Raku's, Yui is the head of a Chinese mafia gang and the homeroom teacher of Raku's class at his school. She is currently staying at Raku's house and also has a special key linked to some kind of promise...

CHARACTERS & STORY

Ten years ago, Raku Ichijo made a promise with a girl he loved that they would get married when they met again...and he still treasures the pendant she gave him to seal their pledge.

Thanks to his family's circumstances, Raku has to pretend he's dating Chitoge Kirisaki, the daughter of a rival gangster. Despite their constant spats, Raku and Chitoge manage to fool everyone. Chitoge also has a token from her first love ten years ago—an old key. Meanwhile, Raku's crush, Kosaki, also has a key, as does Marika, the girl Raku's father has arranged for him to marry. Now, Raku's childhood friend Yui has been hired as their homeroom teacher. It turns out that she, too, has a key connected to a special promise...

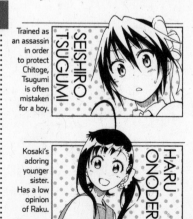

SEISHIRO TSUGUMI

Trained as an assassin in order to protect Chitoge, Tsugumi is often mistaken for a boy.

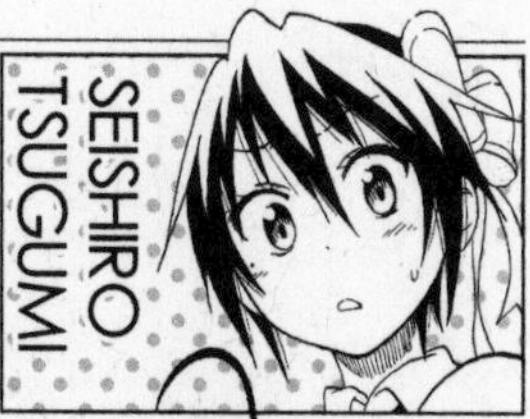

HARU ONODERA

Kosaki's adoring younger sister. Has a low opinion of Raku.

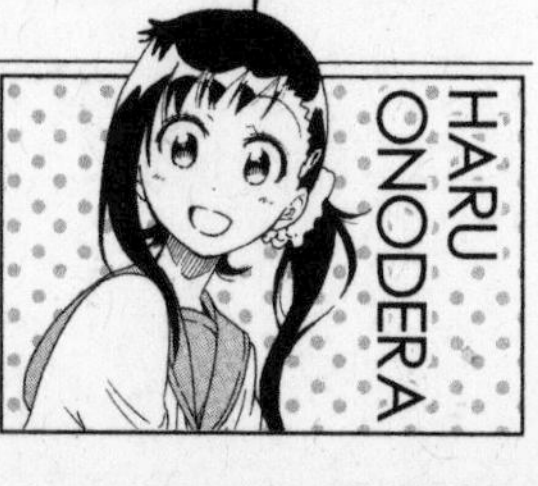

NISEKOI
False Love
vol. 15: Beauty Contest

TABLE OF CONTENTS

chapter 126: Declaration 7

chapter 127: The King 27

chapter 128: Together 47

chapter 129: Cold 67

chapter 130: Interview 87

chapter 131: Plot 107

chapter 132: Beauty Contest 127

chapter 133: One-on-One 149

chapter 134: Choice 169

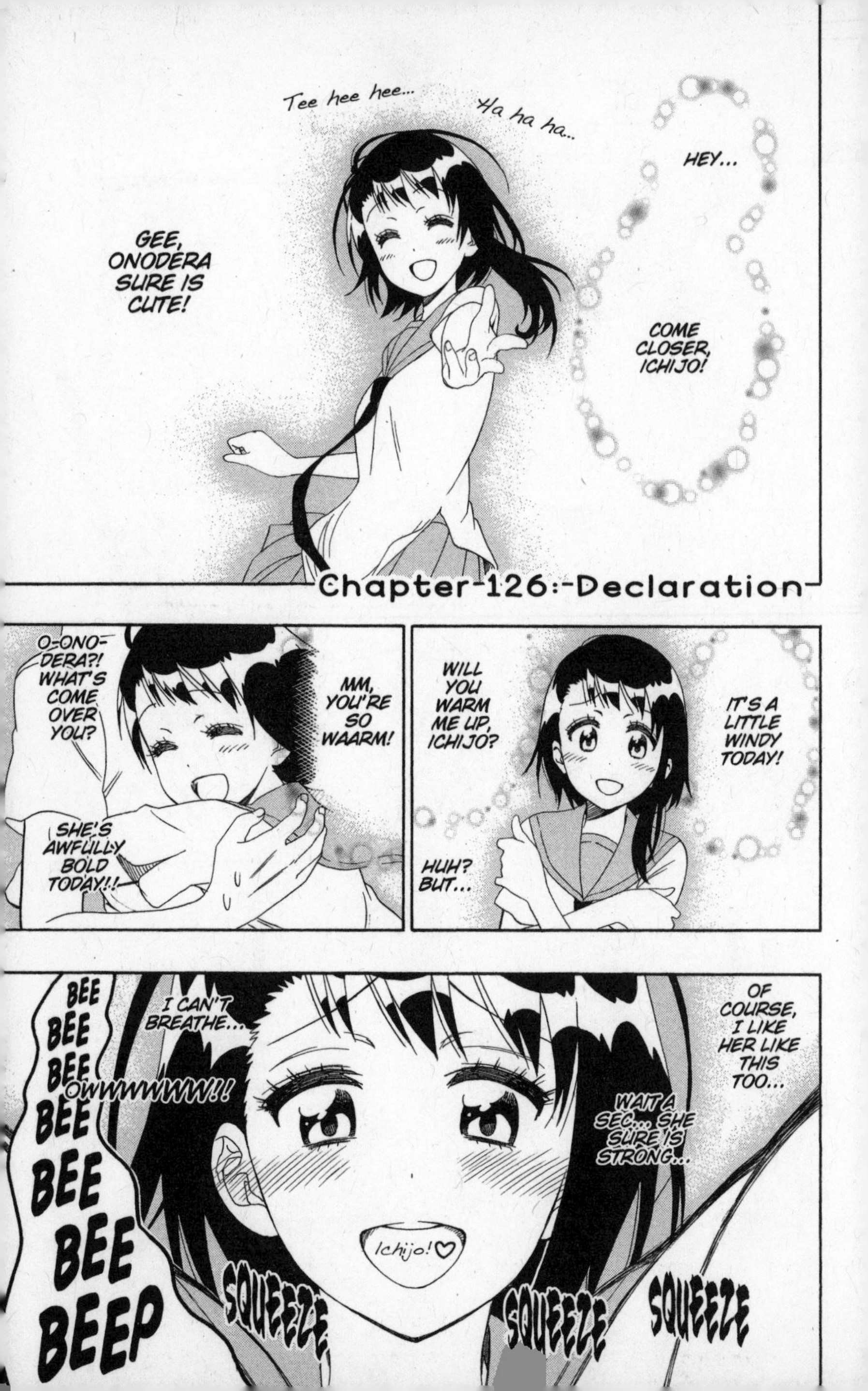
HEY...
Ha ha ha..
Tee hee hee...
COME CLOSER, ICHIJO!
GEE, ONODERA SURE IS CUTE!
Chapter 126: Declaration
IT'S A LITTLE WINDY TODAY!
WILL YOU WARM ME UP, ICHIJO?
HUH? BUT...
MM, YOU'RE SO WAARM!
O-ONODERA?! WHAT'S COME OVER YOU?
SHE'S AWFULLY BOLD TODAY!!
OF COURSE, I LIKE HER LIKE THIS TOO...
WAIT A SEC... SHE SURE IS STRONG...
I CAN'T BREATHE...
OWWWWWW!!
Ichijo!♡
SQUEEZE
SQUEEZE
SQUEEZE
BEE BEE BEE BEE BEE BEE BEEP

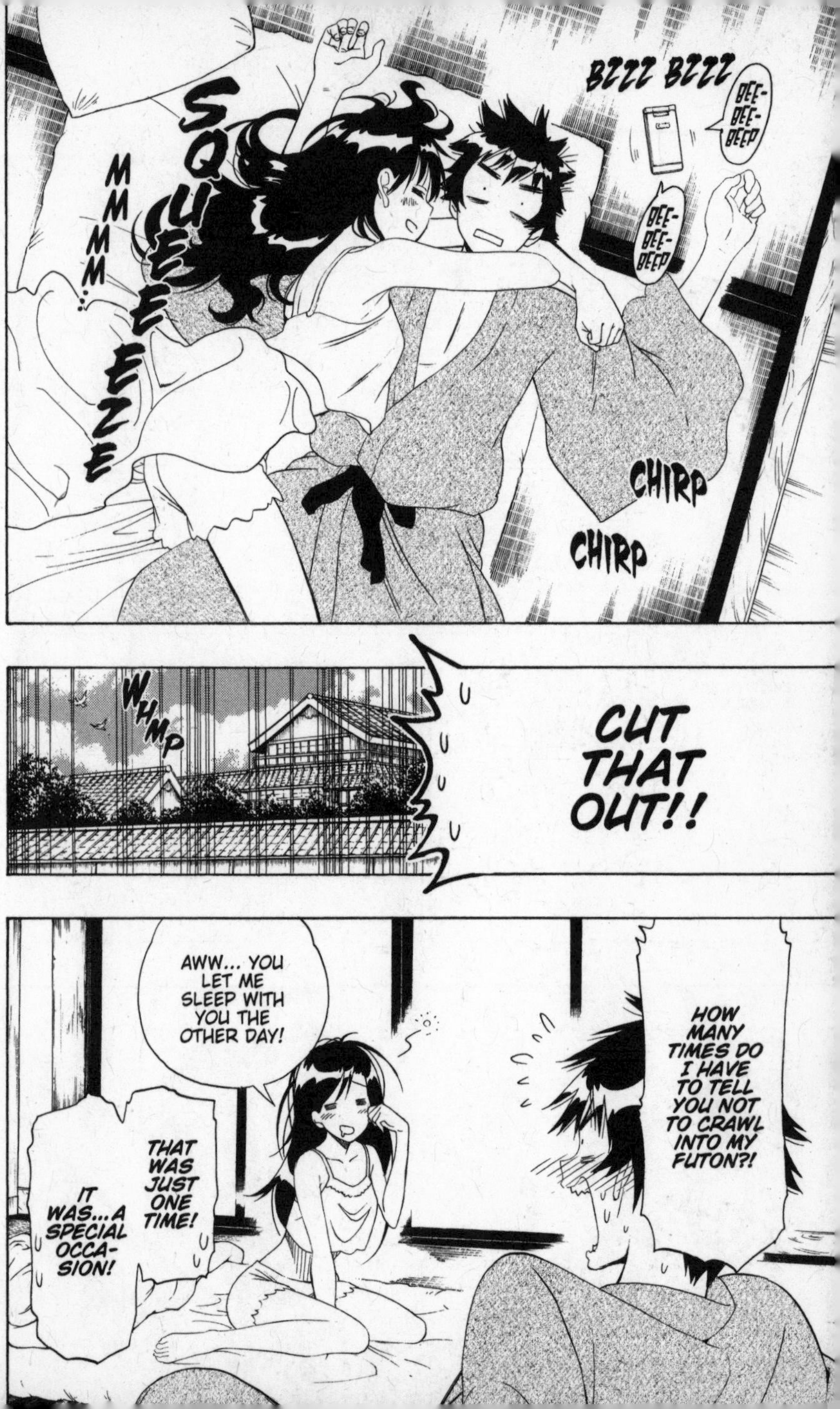
BZZZ BZZZ
BEE-BEE-BEEP
BEE-BEE-BEEP
SQUEEEEZE
MMMMM...
CHIRP
CHIRP
CUT THAT OUT!!
WHMP
HOW MANY TIMES DO I HAVE TO TELL YOU NOT TO CRAWL INTO MY FUTON?!
AWW... YOU LET ME SLEEP WITH YOU THE OTHER DAY!
THAT WAS JUST ONE TIME!
IT WAS...A SPECIAL OCCA-SION!

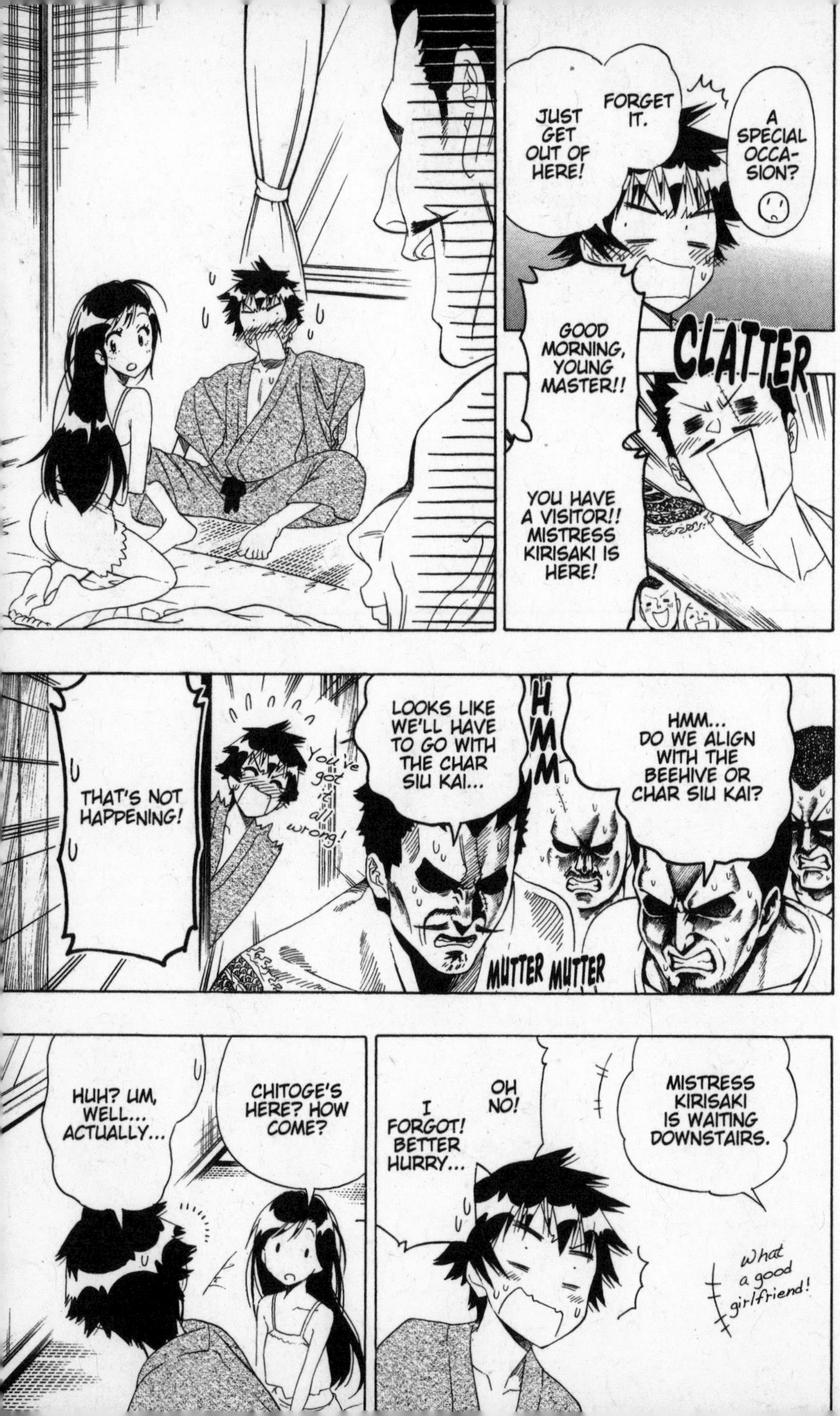
A SPECIAL OCCASION?
FORGET IT.
JUST GET OUT OF HERE!
CLATTER
GOOD MORNING, YOUNG MASTER!!
YOU HAVE A VISITOR!! MISTRESS KIRISAKI IS HERE!
HMM... DO WE ALIGN WITH THE BEEHIVE OR CHAR SIU KAI?
HMM
LOOKS LIKE WE'LL HAVE TO GO WITH THE CHAR SIU KAI...
MUTTER MUTTER
You've got it all wrong!
THAT'S NOT HAPPENING!
MISTRESS KIRISAKI IS WAITING DOWNSTAIRS.
OH NO!
I FORGOT! BETTER HURRY...
What a good girlfriend!
CHITOGE'S HERE? HOW COME?
HUH? UM, WELL... ACTUALLY...

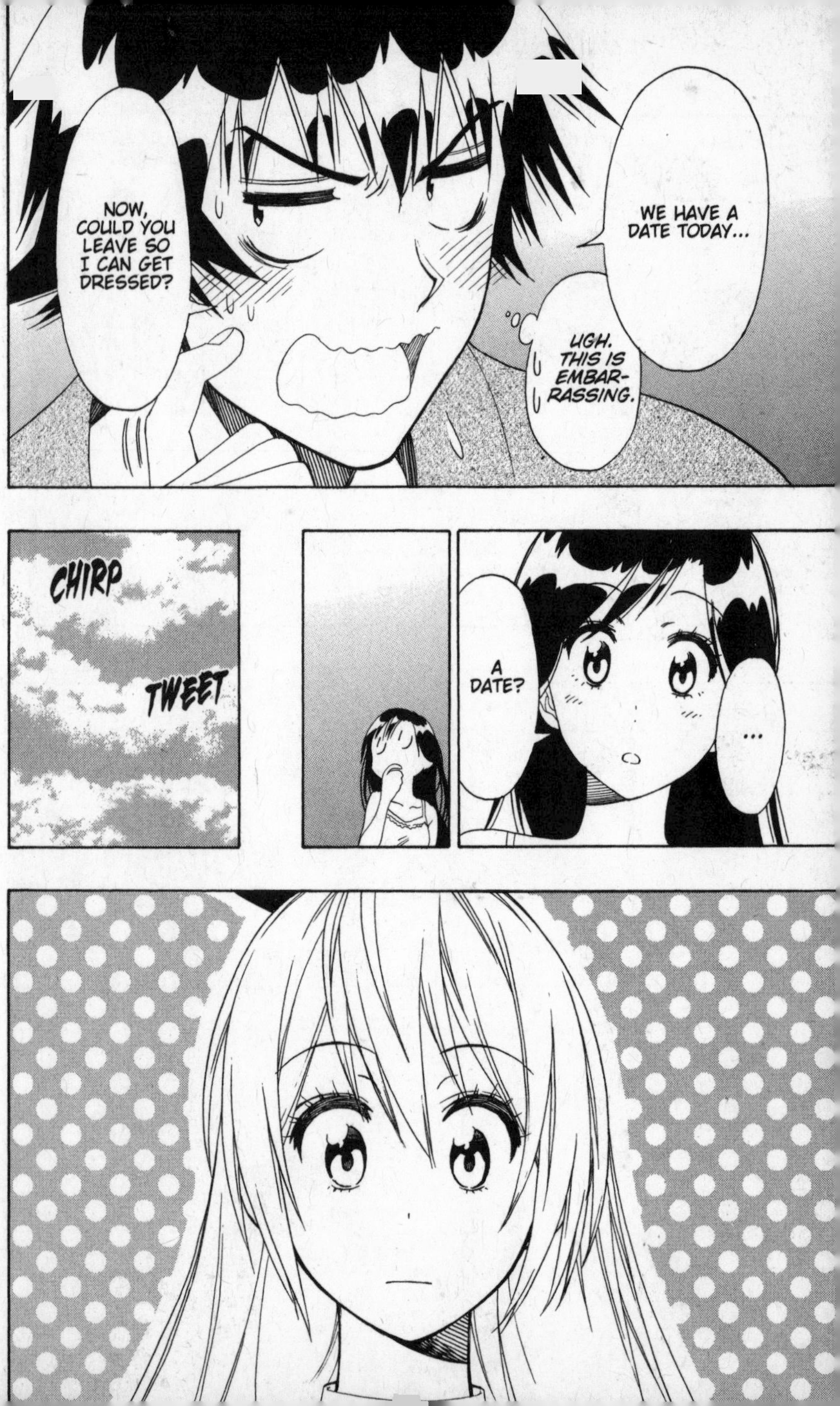
WE HAVE A DATE TODAY...
UGH. THIS IS EMBAR-RASSING.
NOW, COULD YOU LEAVE SO I CAN GET DRESSED?
...
A DATE?
TWEET
CHIRP

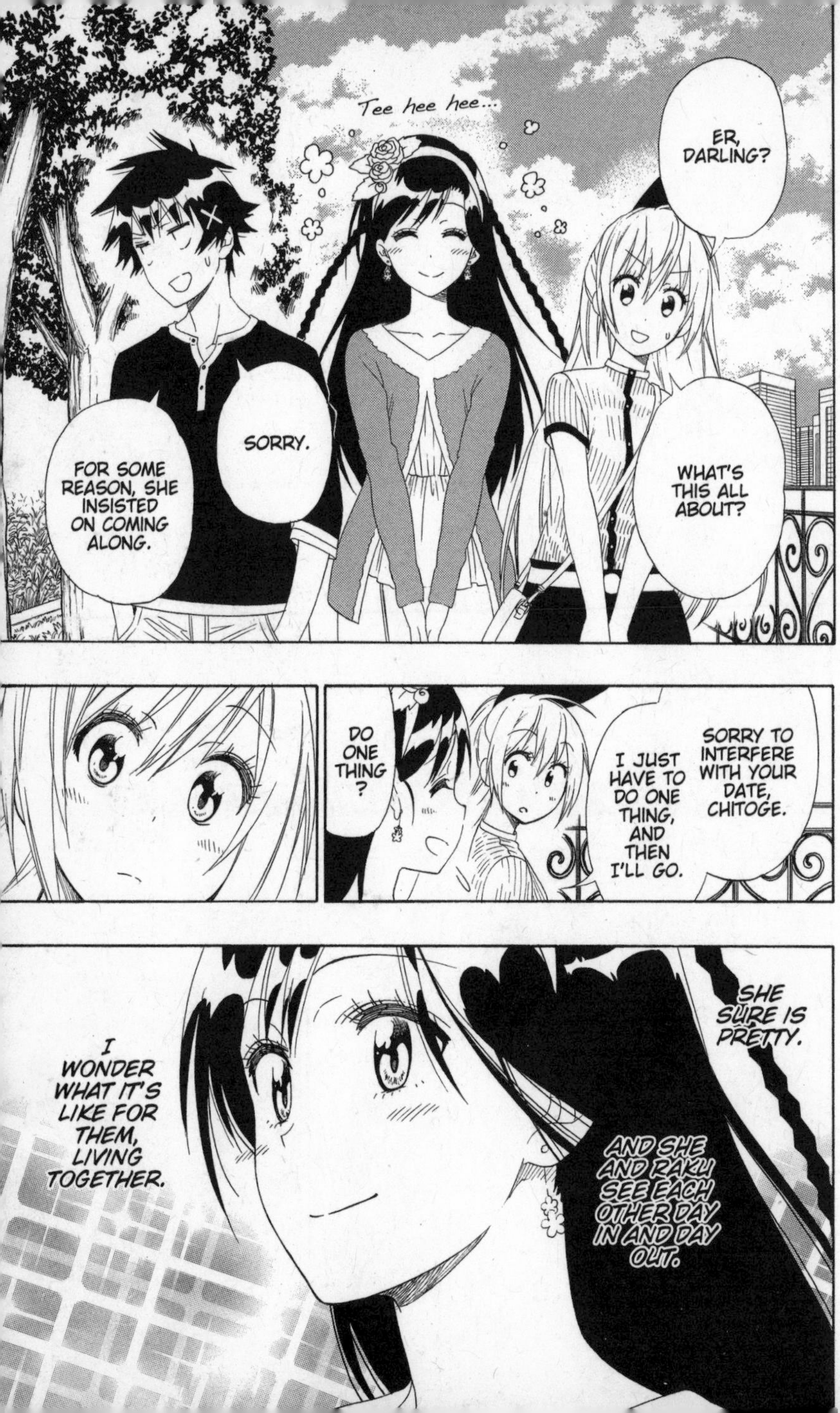
ER, DARLING?
WHAT'S THIS ALL ABOUT?
Tee hee hee...
SORRY.
FOR SOME REASON, SHE INSISTED ON COMING ALONG.
SORRY TO INTERFERE WITH YOUR DATE, CHITOGE.
I JUST HAVE TO DO ONE THING, AND THEN I'LL GO.
DO ONE THING?
SHE SURE IS PRETTY.
AND SHE AND RAKU SEE EACH OTHER DAY IN AND DAY OUT.
I WONDER WHAT IT'S LIKE FOR THEM, LIVING TOGETHER.

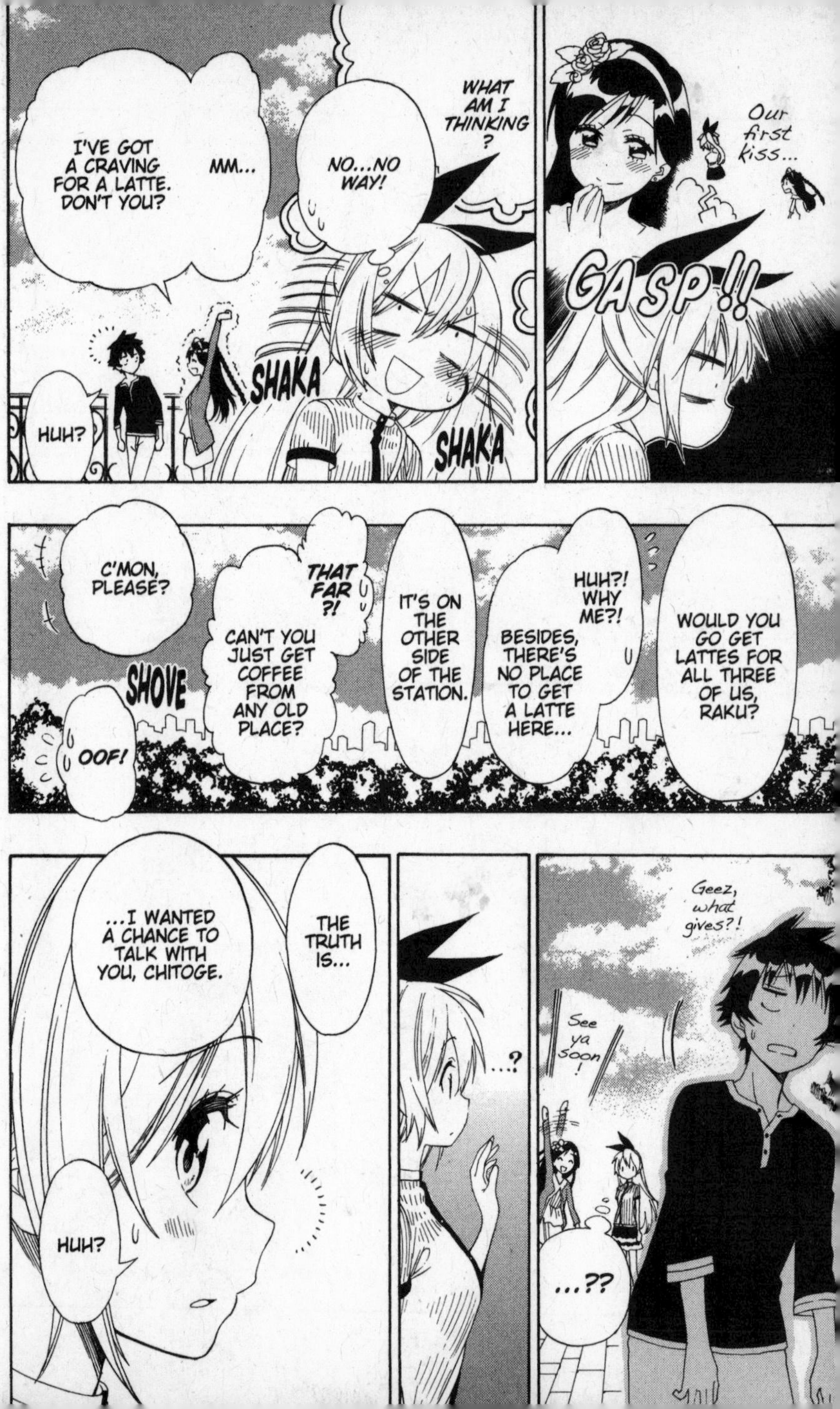
Our first kiss...
GASP!!
WHAT AM I THINKING?
NO...NO WAY!
SHAKA
SHAKA
MM...
I'VE GOT A CRAVING FOR A LATTE. DON'T YOU?
HUH?
WOULD YOU GO GET LATTES FOR ALL THREE OF US, RAKU?
HUH?! WHY ME?!
BESIDES, THERE'S NO PLACE TO GET A LATTE HERE...
IT'S ON THE OTHER SIDE OF THE STATION.
THAT FAR?!
CAN'T YOU JUST GET COFFEE FROM ANY OLD PLACE?
C'MON, PLEASE?
SHOVE
OOF!
Geez, what gives?!
See ya soon!
...??
THE TRUTH IS...
...?
...I WANTED A CHANCE TO TALK WITH YOU, CHITOGE.
HUH?

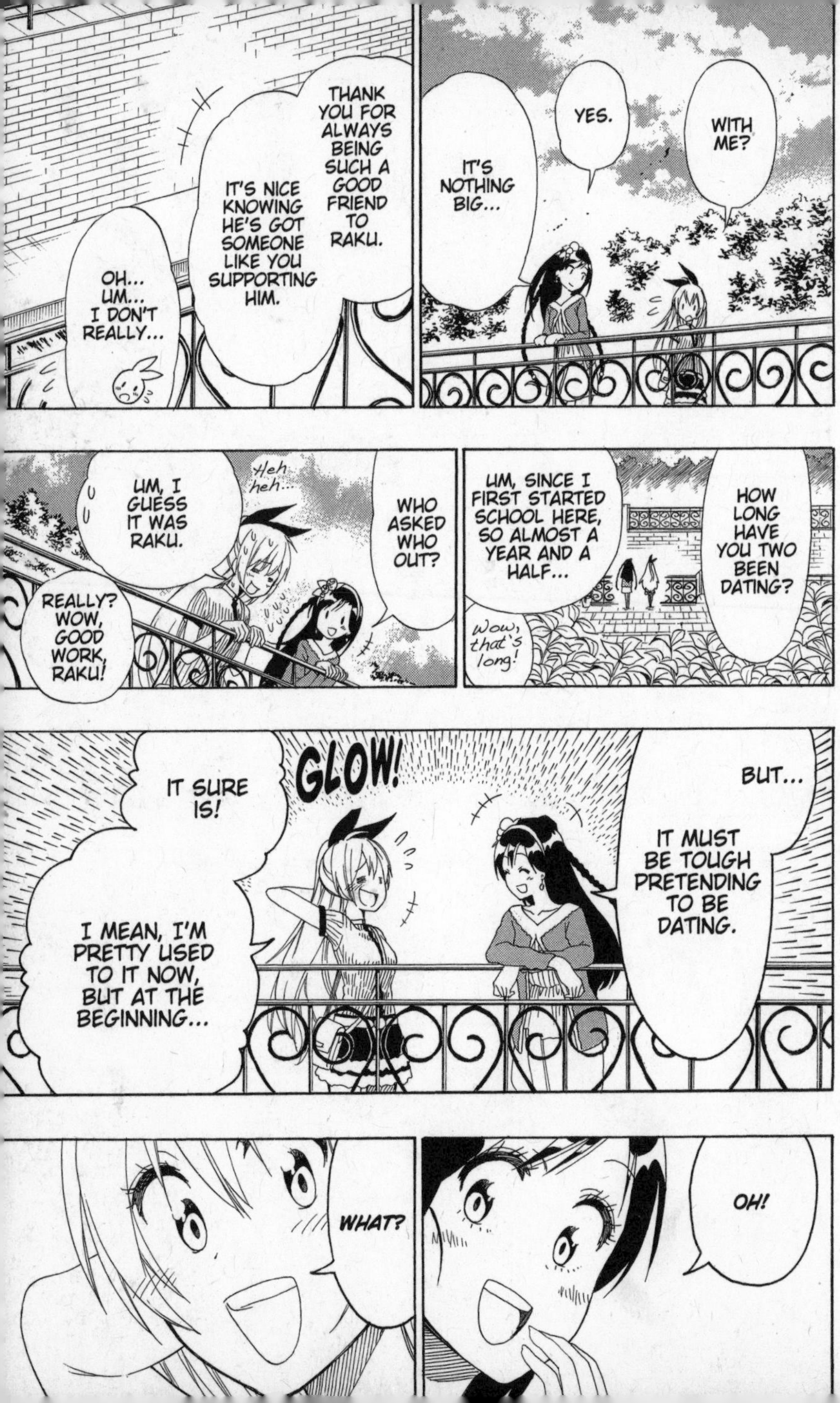
WITH ME?
YES.
IT'S NOTHING BIG...
THANK YOU FOR ALWAYS BEING SUCH A GOOD FRIEND TO RAKU.
IT'S NICE KNOWING HE'S GOT SOMEONE LIKE YOU SUPPORTING HIM.
OH... UM... I DON'T REALLY...
HOW LONG HAVE YOU TWO BEEN DATING?
UM, SINCE I FIRST STARTED SCHOOL HERE, SO ALMOST A YEAR AND A HALF...
Wow, that's long!
WHO ASKED WHO OUT?
Heh heh...
UM, I GUESS IT WAS RAKU.
REALLY? WOW, GOOD WORK, RAKU!
BUT...
IT MUST BE TOUGH PRETENDING TO BE DATING.
GLOW!
IT SURE IS!
I MEAN, I'M PRETTY USED TO IT NOW, BUT AT THE BEGINNING...
OH!
WHAT?

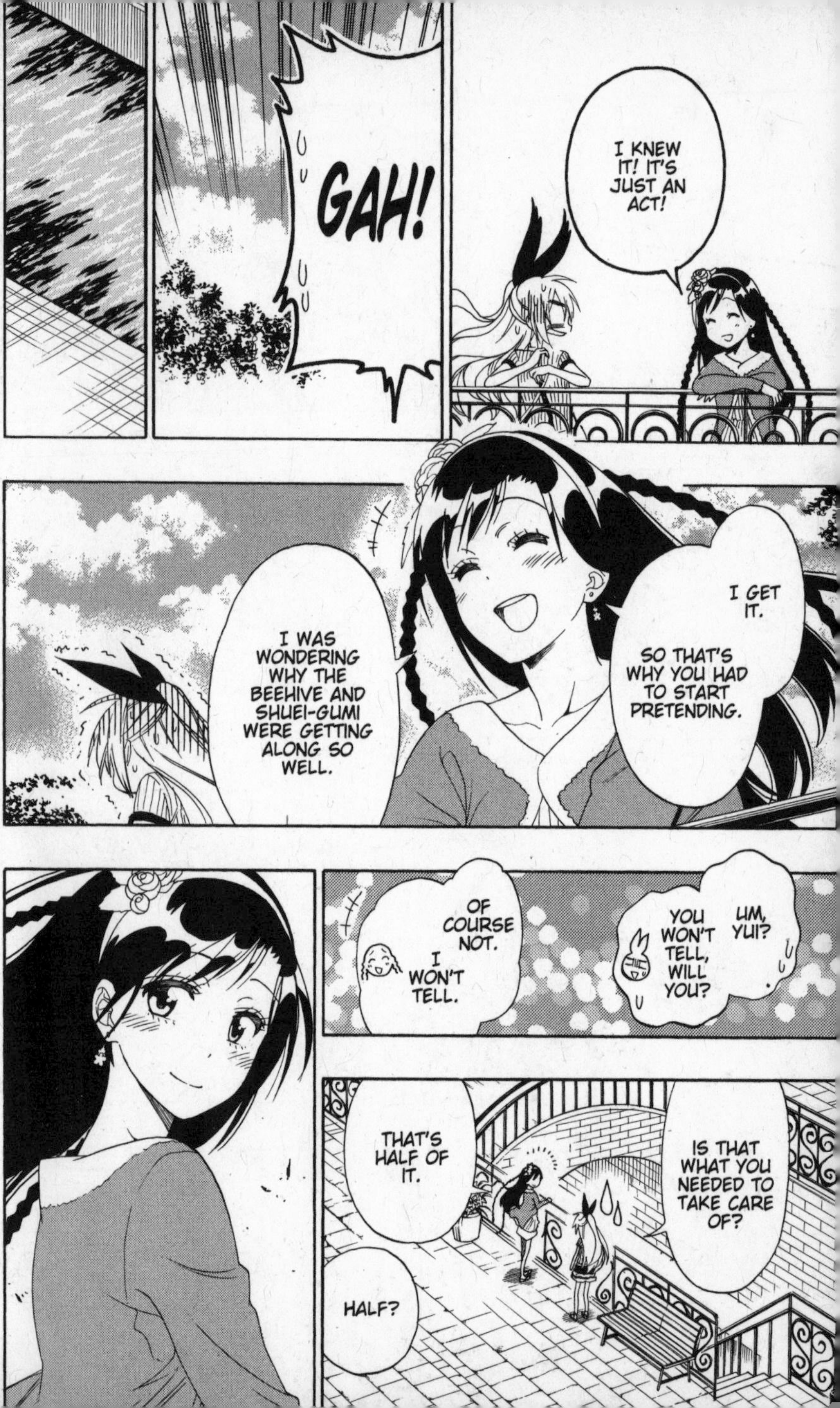
I KNEW IT! IT'S JUST AN ACT!
GAH!
I GET IT.
SO THAT'S WHY YOU HAD TO START PRETENDING.
I WAS WONDERING WHY THE BEEHIVE AND SHUEI-GUMI WERE GETTING ALONG SO WELL.
UM, YUI?
YOU WON'T TELL, WILL YOU?
OF COURSE NOT.
I WON'T TELL.
IS THAT WHAT YOU NEEDED TO TAKE CARE OF?
THAT'S HALF OF IT.
HALF?

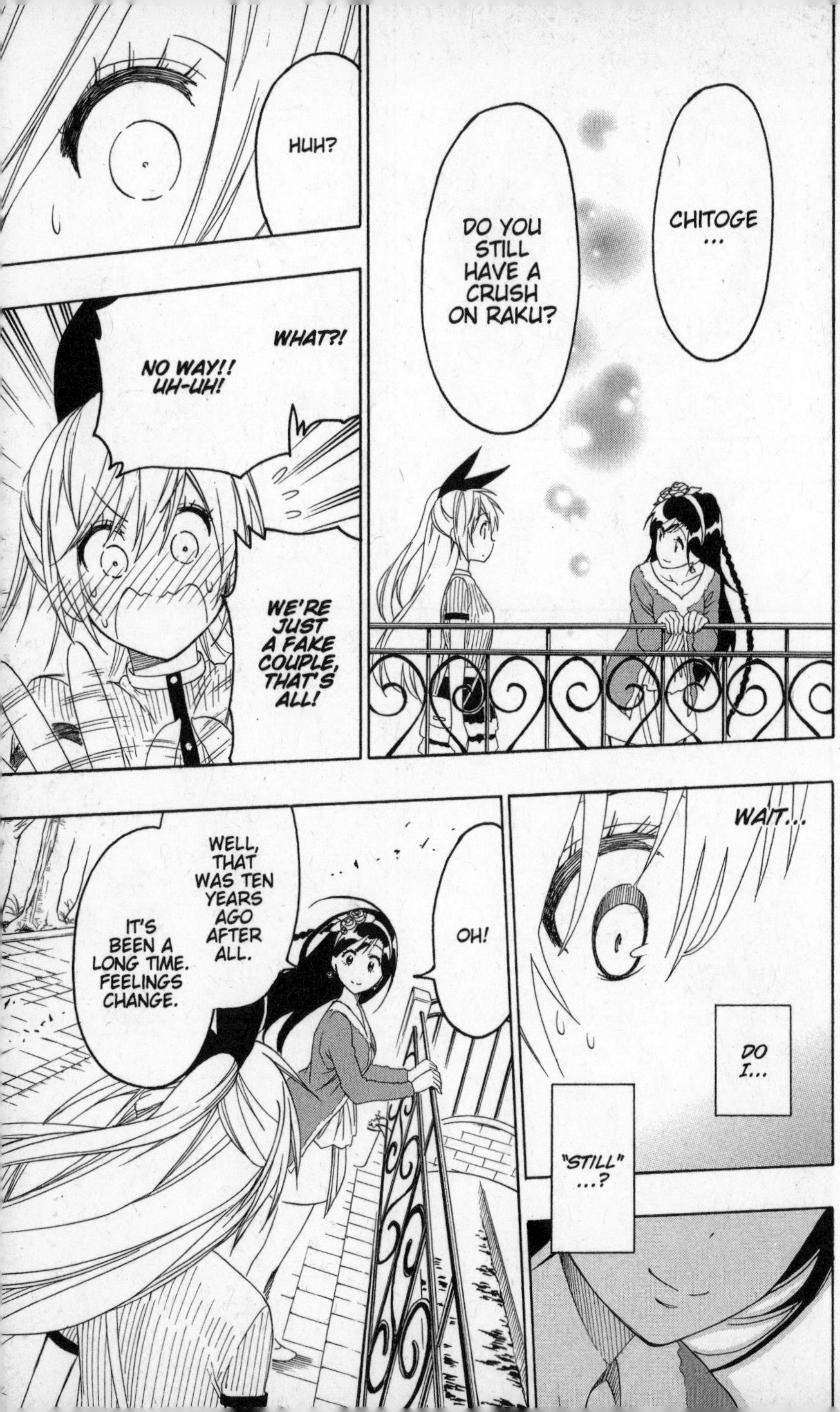
CHITOGE ...
DO YOU STILL HAVE A CRUSH ON RAKU?
HUH?
WHAT?!
NO WAY!! UH-UH!
WE'RE JUST A FAKE COUPLE, THAT'S ALL!
WAIT...
DO I...
"STILL" ...?
OH!
WELL, THAT WAS TEN YEARS AGO AFTER ALL.
IT'S BEEN A LONG TIME. FEELINGS CHANGE.

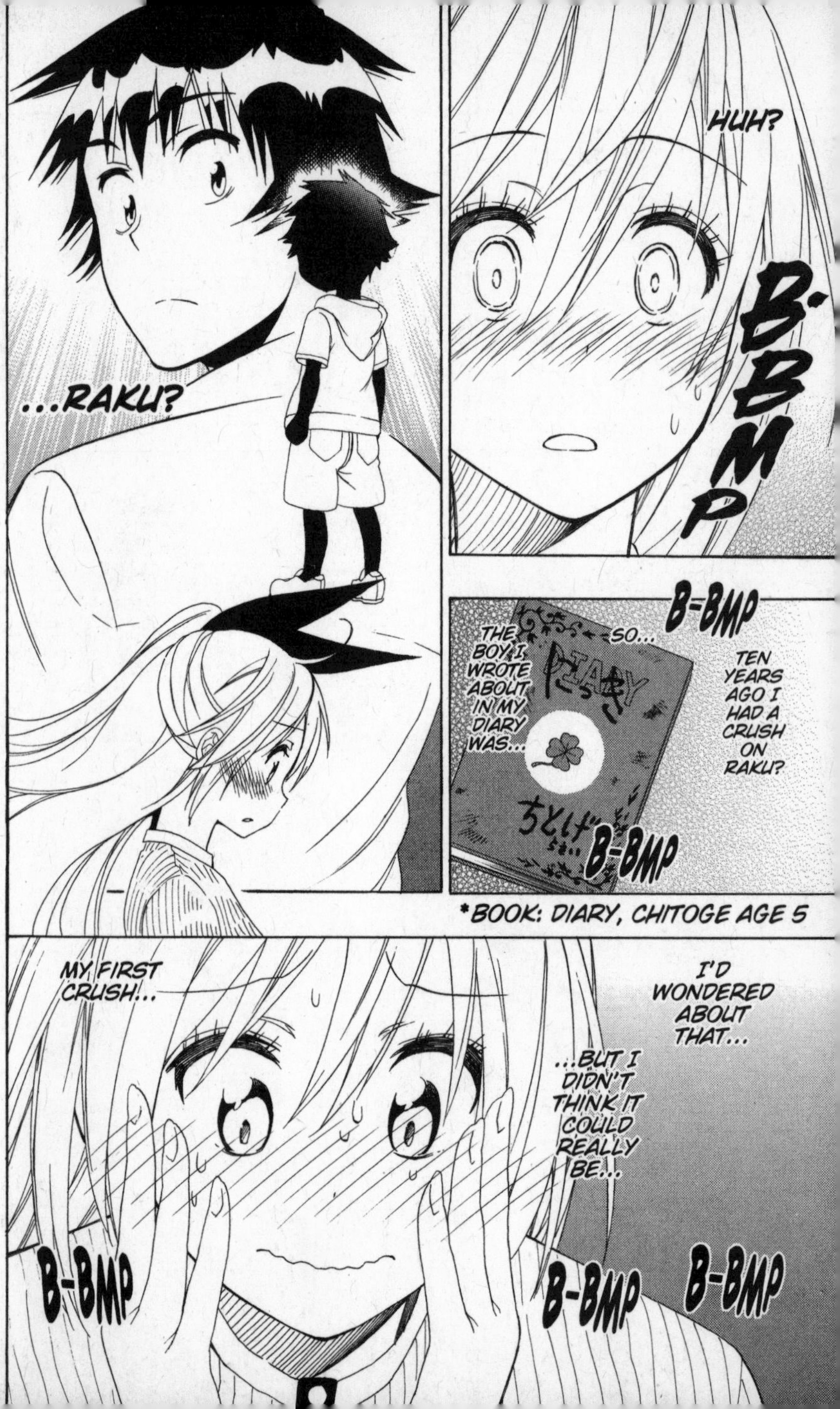
HUH?
B-BMP
B-BMP
TEN YEARS AGO I HAD A CRUSH ON RAKU?
THE BOY I WROTE ABOUT IN MY DIARY WAS...
...SO...
B-BMP
*BOOK: DIARY, CHITOGE AGE 5
...RAKU?
I'D WONDERED ABOUT THAT...
...BUT I DIDN'T THINK IT COULD REALLY BE...
MY FIRST CRUSH...
B-BMP
B-BMP
B-BMP

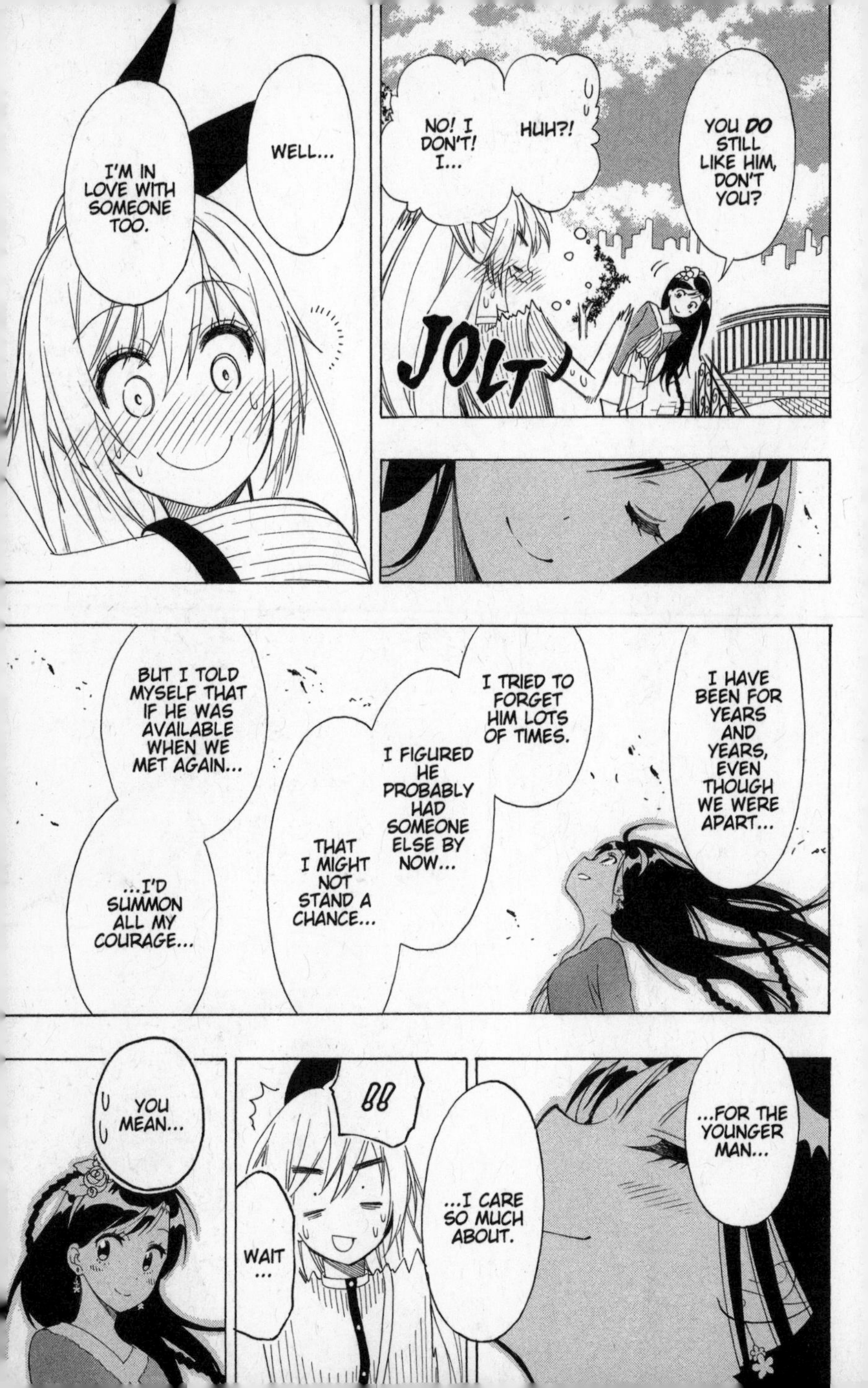

YOU DO STILL LIKE HIM, DON'T YOU?
HUH?!
NO! I DON'T! I...
JOLT
WELL...
I'M IN LOVE WITH SOMEONE TOO.
I HAVE BEEN FOR YEARS AND YEARS, EVEN THOUGH WE WERE APART...
I TRIED TO FORGET HIM LOTS OF TIMES.
I FIGURED HE PROBABLY HAD SOMEONE ELSE BY NOW...
THAT I MIGHT NOT STAND A CHANCE...
BUT I TOLD MYSELF THAT IF HE WAS AVAILABLE WHEN WE MET AGAIN...
...I'D SUMMON ALL MY COURAGE...
...FOR THE YOUNGER MAN...
...I CARE SO MUCH ABOUT.
!!
WAIT...
YOU MEAN...

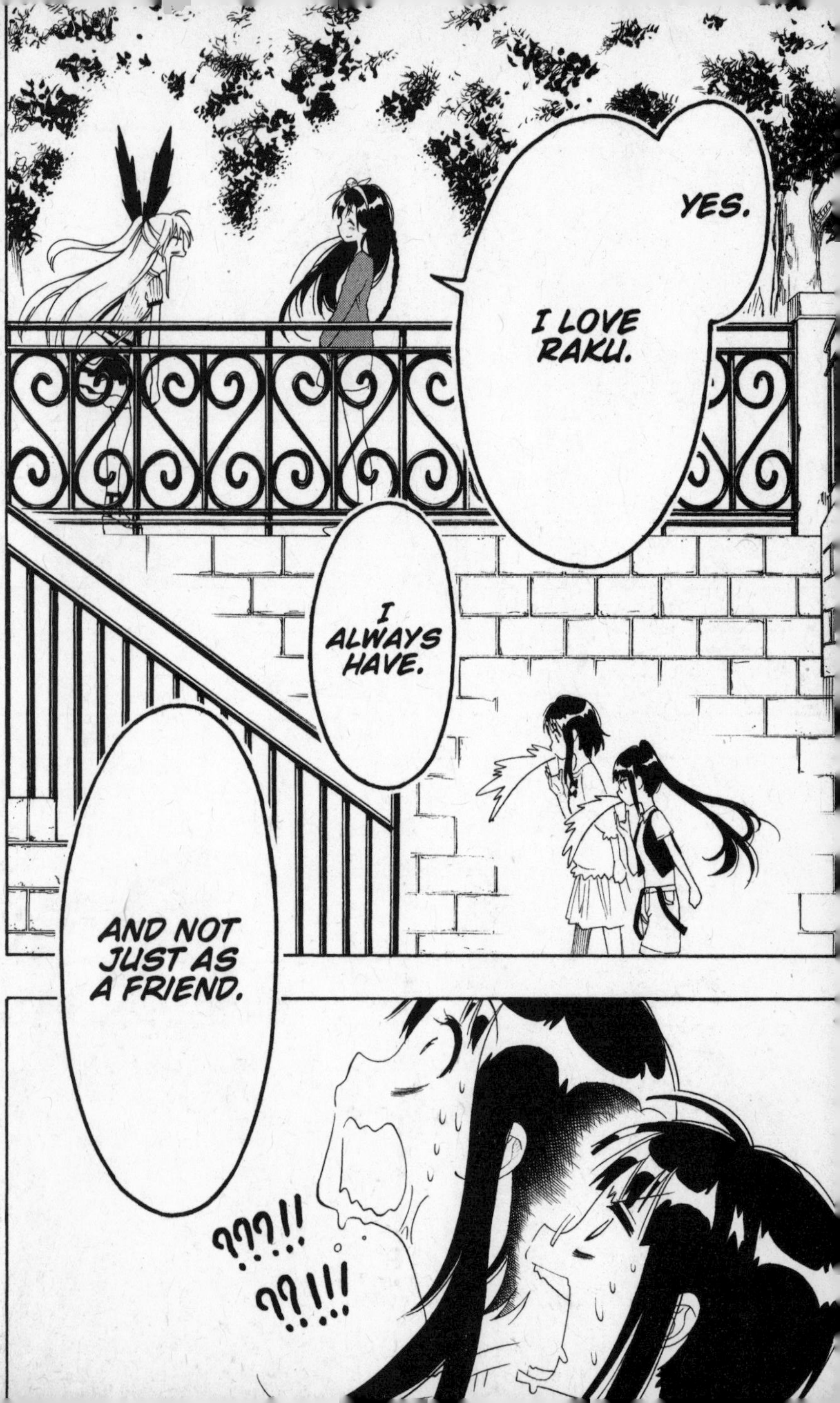
YES.
I LOVE RAKU.
I ALWAYS HAVE.
AND NOT JUST AS A FRIEND.
???!!
??!!!

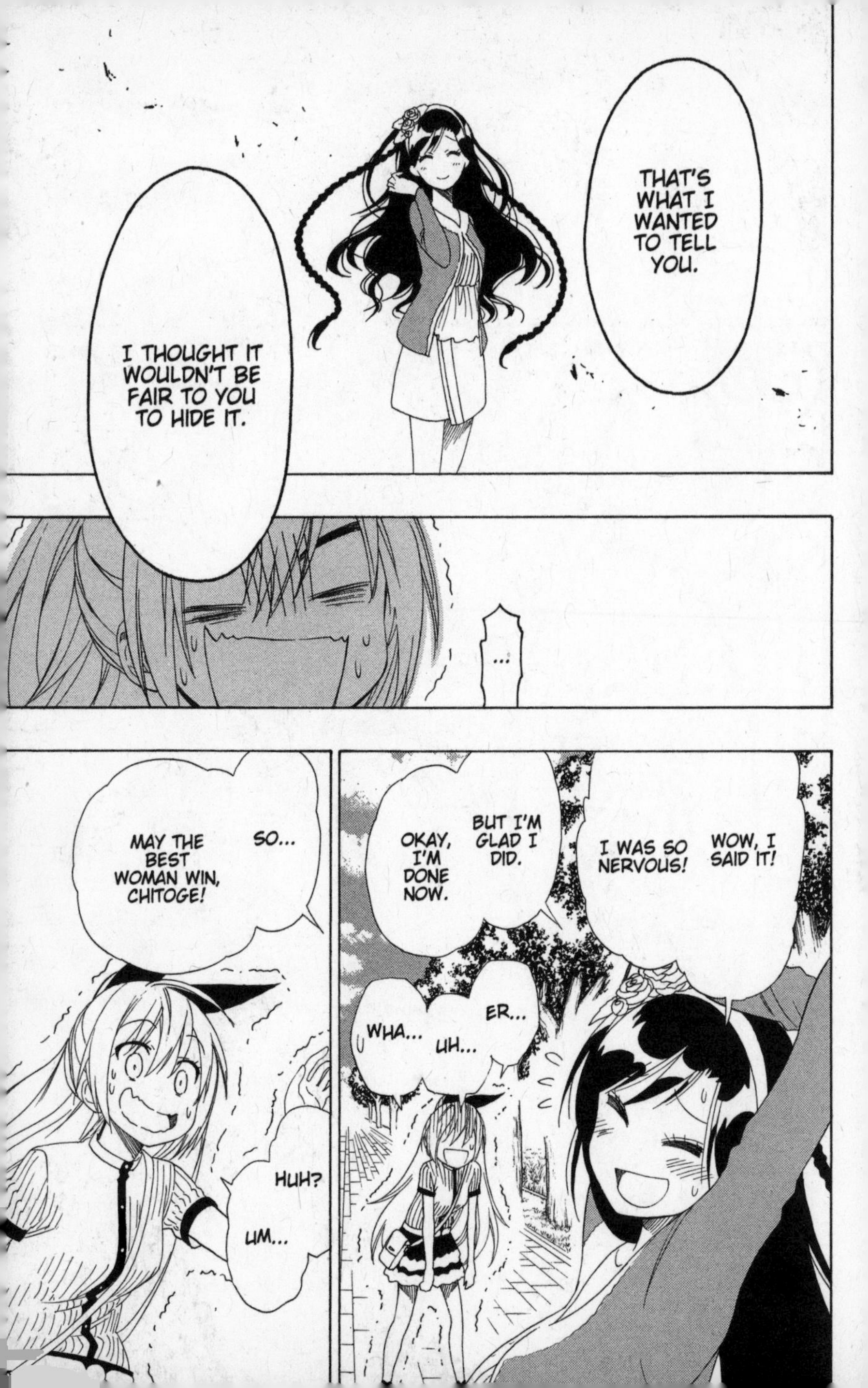
THAT'S WHAT I WANTED TO TELL YOU.
I THOUGHT IT WOULDN'T BE FAIR TO YOU TO HIDE IT.
...
WOW, I SAID IT!
I WAS SO NERVOUS!
BUT I'M GLAD I DID.
OKAY, I'M DONE NOW.
ER...
UH...
WHA...
SO...
MAY THE BEST WOMAN WIN, CHITOGE!
HUH?
UM...

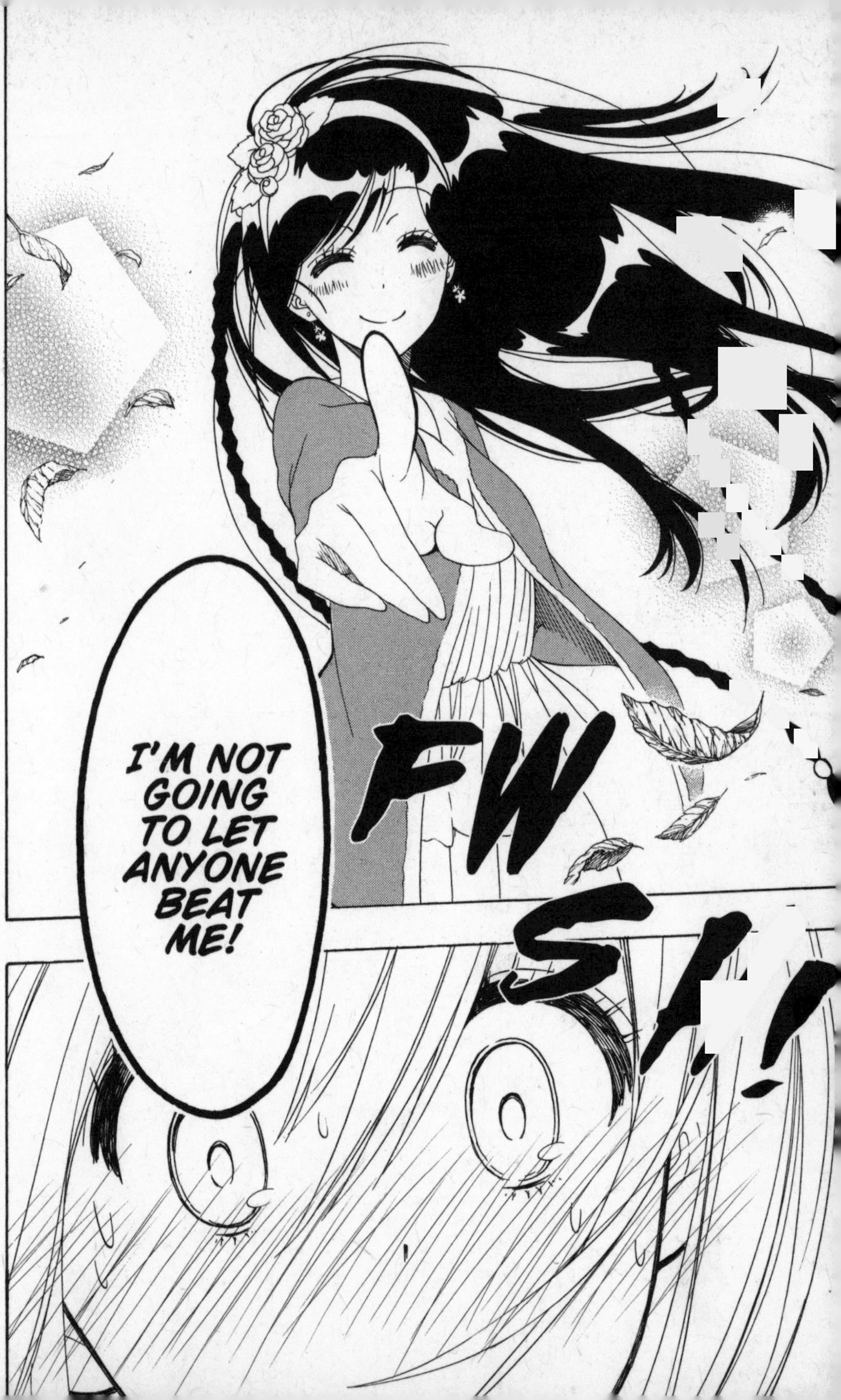
I'M NOT GOING TO LET ANYONE BEAT ME!
FWSH!!

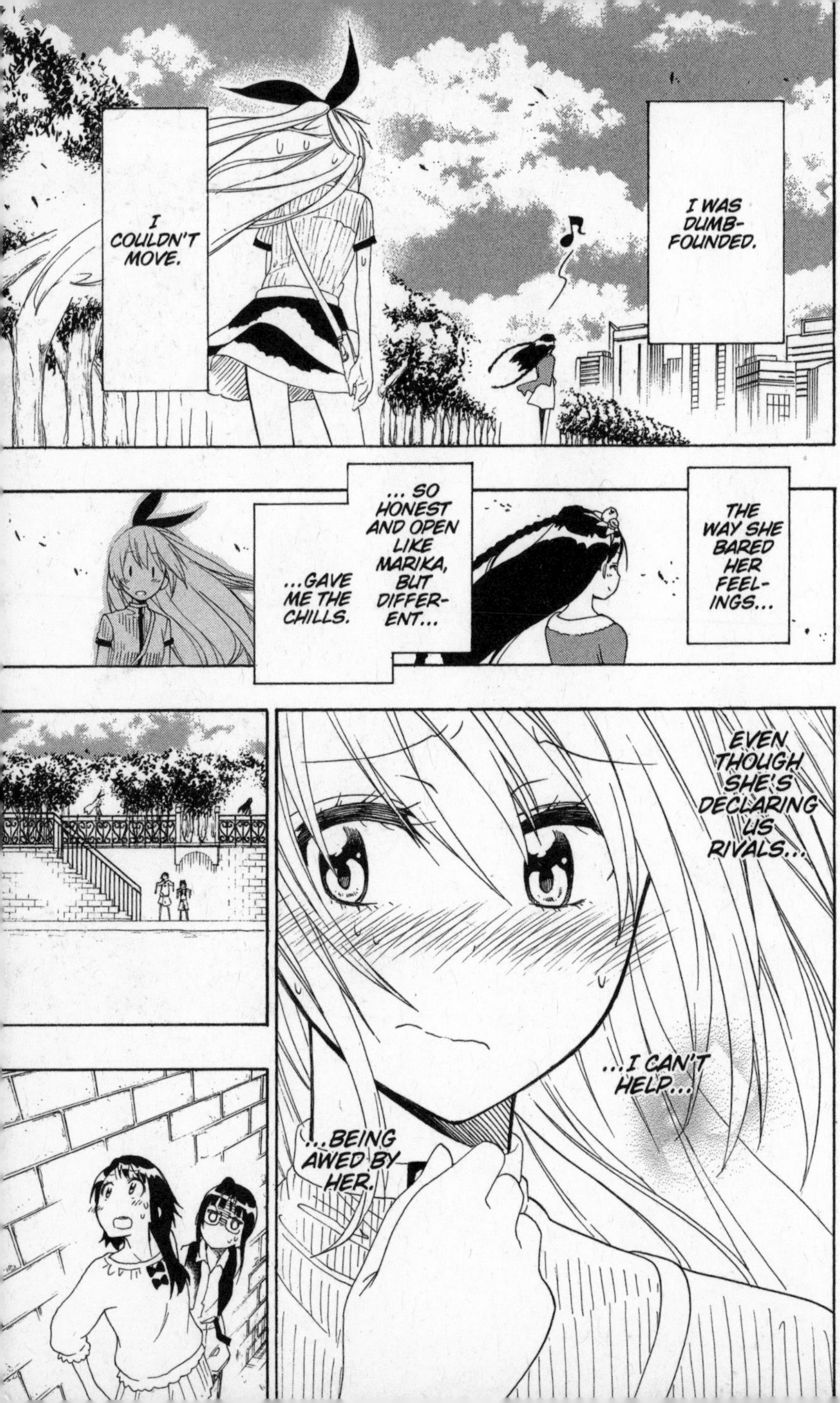
I WAS DUMB-FOUNDED.
I COULDN'T MOVE.
THE WAY SHE BARED HER FEEL-INGS...
... SO HONEST AND OPEN LIKE MARIKA, BUT DIFFER-ENT...
...GAVE ME THE CHILLS.
EVEN THOUGH SHE'S DECLARING US RIVALS...
...I CAN'T HELP...
...BEING AWED BY HER.

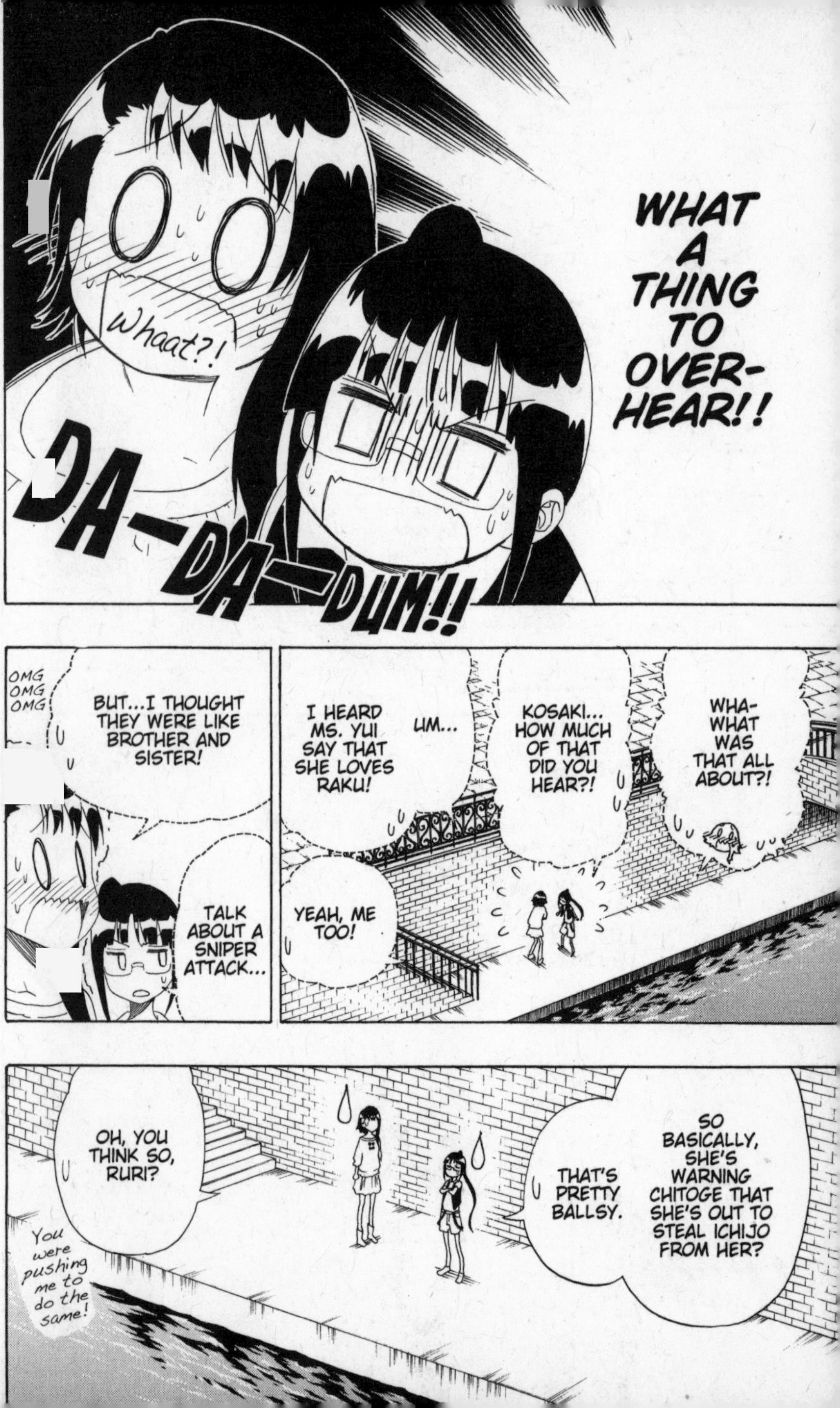

WHAT A THING TO OVER-HEAR!!
Whaat?!
DA-DA-DUM!!
WHA-WHAT WAS THAT ALL ABOUT?!
KOSAKI... HOW MUCH OF THAT DID YOU HEAR?!
UM...
I HEARD MS. YUI SAY THAT SHE LOVES RAKU!
YEAH, ME TOO!
OMG OMG OMG
BUT...I THOUGHT THEY WERE LIKE BROTHER AND SISTER!
TALK ABOUT A SNIPER ATTACK...
SO BASICALLY, SHE'S WARNING CHITOGE THAT SHE'S OUT TO STEAL ICHIJO FROM HER?
THAT'S PRETTY BALLSY.
OH, YOU THINK SO, RURI?
You were pushing me to do the same!

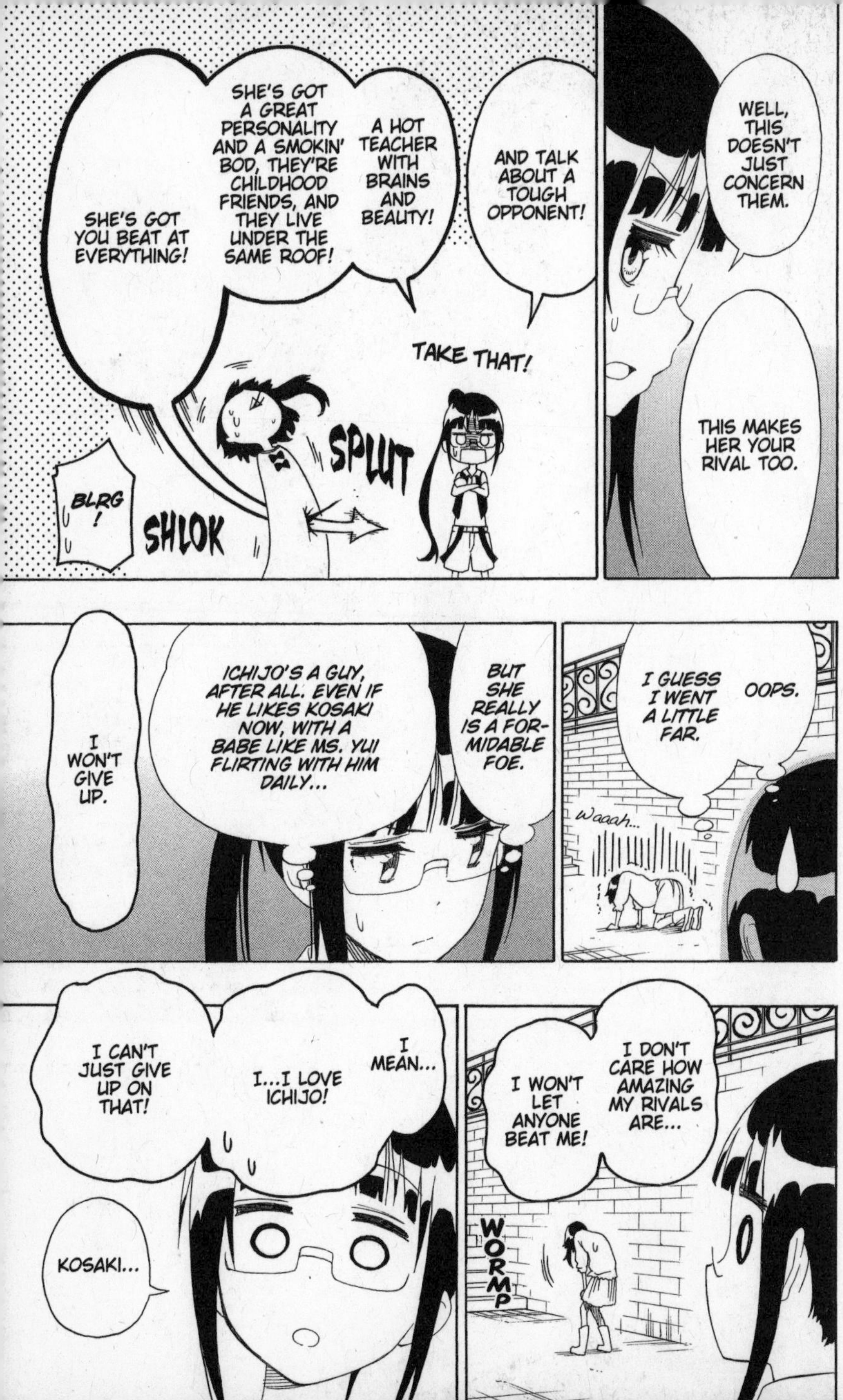
WELL, THIS DOESN'T JUST CONCERN THEM.
THIS MAKES HER YOUR RIVAL TOO.
AND TALK ABOUT A TOUGH OPPONENT!
A HOT TEACHER WITH BRAINS AND BEAUTY!
SHE'S GOT A GREAT PERSONALITY AND A SMOKIN' BOD, THEY'RE CHILDHOOD FRIENDS, AND THEY LIVE UNDER THE SAME ROOF!
SHE'S GOT YOU BEAT AT EVERYTHING!
TAKE THAT!
SPLUT
SHLOK
BLRG!
OOPS.
I GUESS I WENT A LITTLE FAR.
Waaah...
BUT SHE REALLY IS A FOR-MIDABLE FOE.
ICHIJO'S A GUY, AFTER ALL. EVEN IF HE LIKES KOSAKI NOW, WITH A BABE LIKE MS. YUI FLIRTING WITH HIM DAILY...
I WON'T GIVE UP.
I DON'T CARE HOW AMAZING MY RIVALS ARE...
I WON'T LET ANYONE BEAT ME!
WORMP
I MEAN...
I...I LOVE ICHIJO!
I CAN'T JUST GIVE UP ON THAT!
KOSAKI...

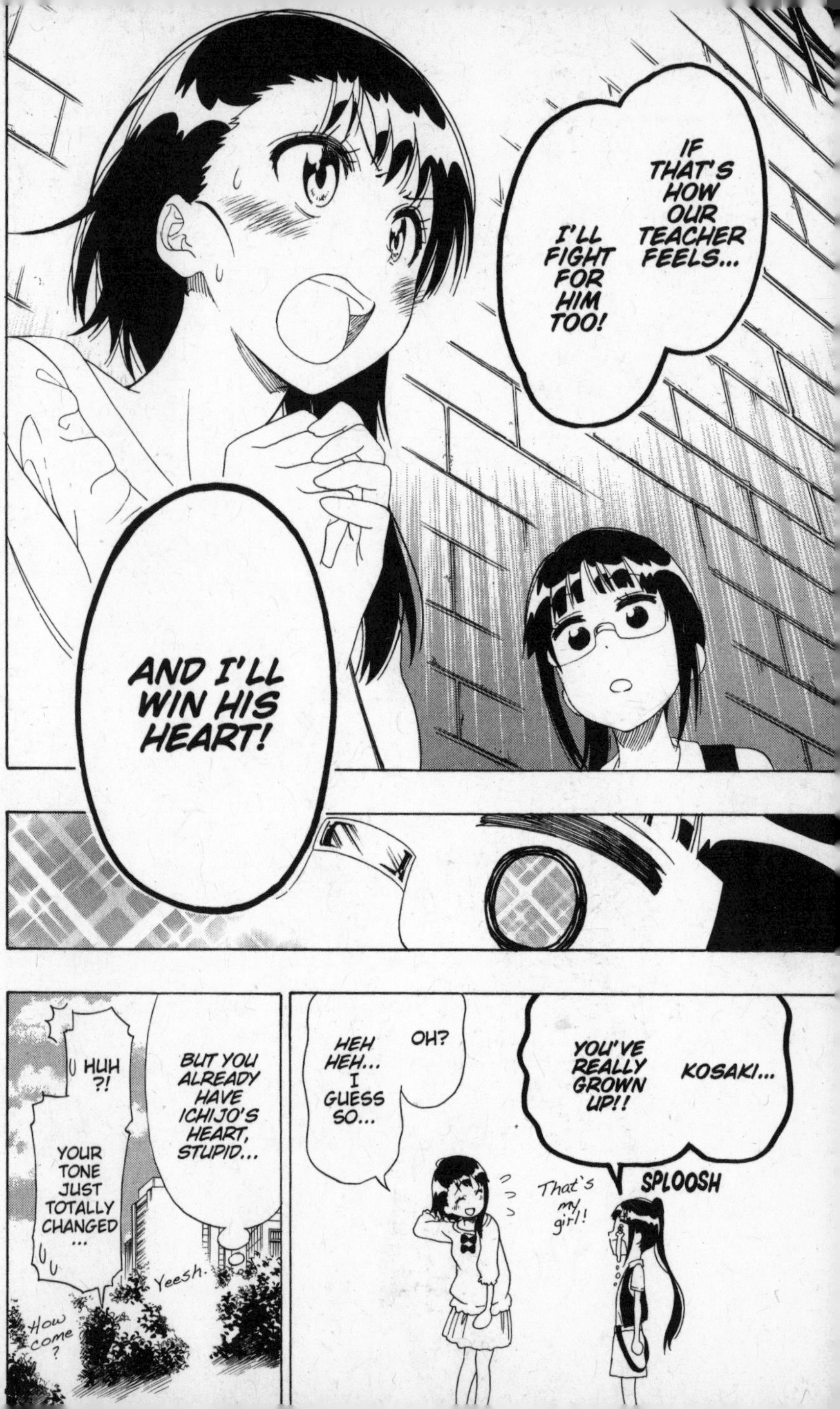
IF THAT'S HOW OUR TEACHER FEELS...
I'LL FIGHT FOR HIM TOO!
AND I'LL WIN HIS HEART!
KOSAKI...
YOU'VE REALLY GROWN UP!!
SPLOOSH
That's my girl!
OH?
HEH HEH... I GUESS SO...
BUT YOU ALREADY HAVE ICHIJO'S HEART, STUPID...
HUH?!
YOUR TONE JUST TOTALLY CHANGED...
Yeesh.
How come?

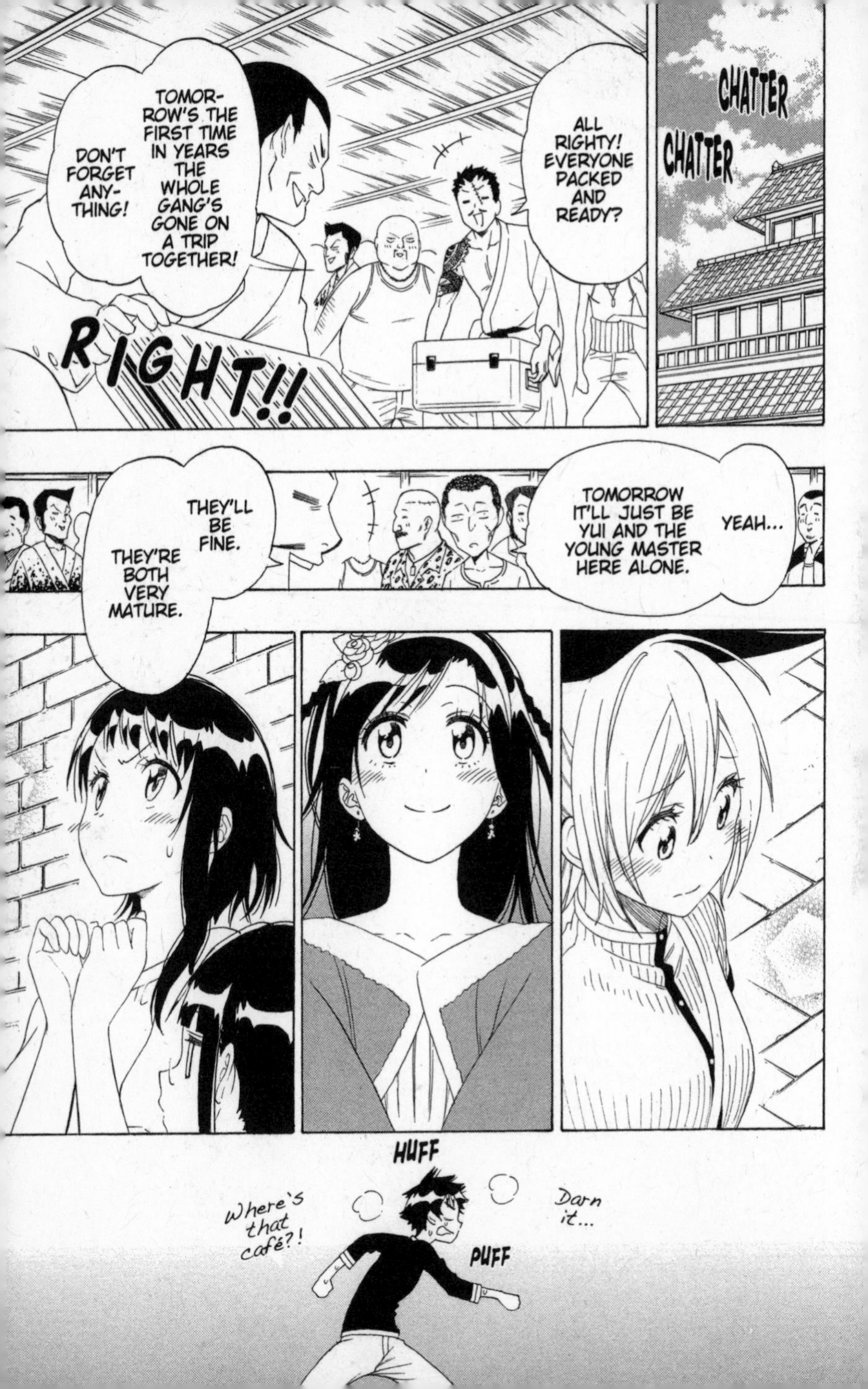
CHATTER
CHATTER
ALL RIGHTY! EVERYONE PACKED AND READY?
TOMORROW'S THE FIRST TIME IN YEARS THE WHOLE GANG'S GONE ON A TRIP TOGETHER!
DON'T FORGET ANYTHING!
RIGHT!!
TOMORROW IT'LL JUST BE YUI AND THE YOUNG MASTER HERE ALONE.
YEAH...
THEY'LL BE FINE.
THEY'RE BOTH VERY MATURE.
HUFF
Darn it...
PUFF
Where's that café?!

Starbucks
Coffee

Popular primarily
among young people
for its stylish
interior design and
ridiculously long
menu. Doesn't
sell alcohol.

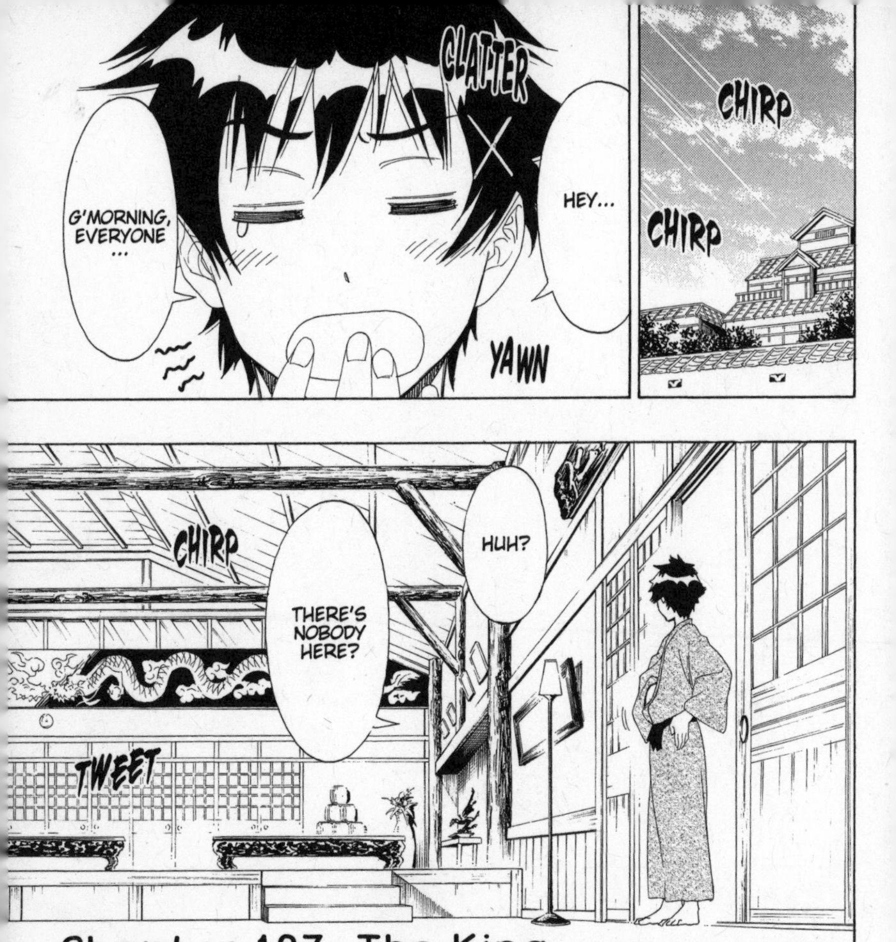
CHIRP
CHIRP
HEY...
CLATTER
G'MORNING, EVERYONE ...
YAWN
HUH?
THERE'S NOBODY HERE?
CHIRP
TWEET

Chapter 127: The King

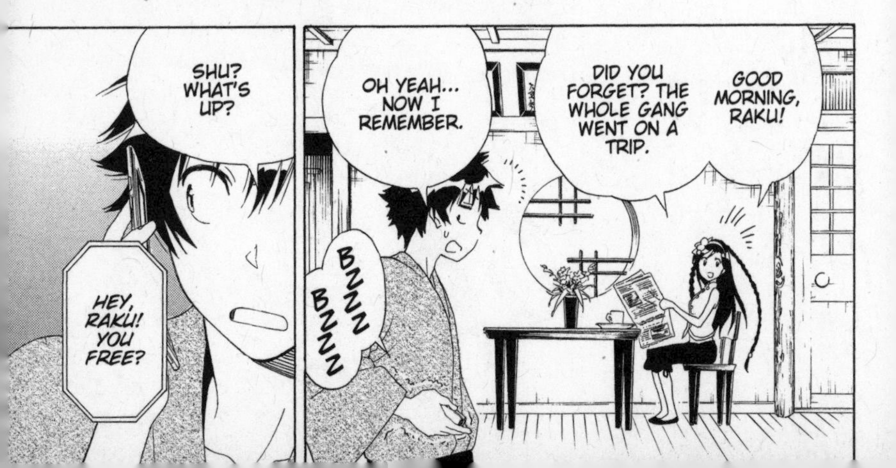
GOOD MORNING, RAKU!
DID YOU FORGET? THE WHOLE GANG WENT ON A TRIP.
OH YEAH... NOW I REMEMBER.
BZZZ BZZZ
SHU? WHAT'S UP?
HEY, RAKU! YOU FREE?

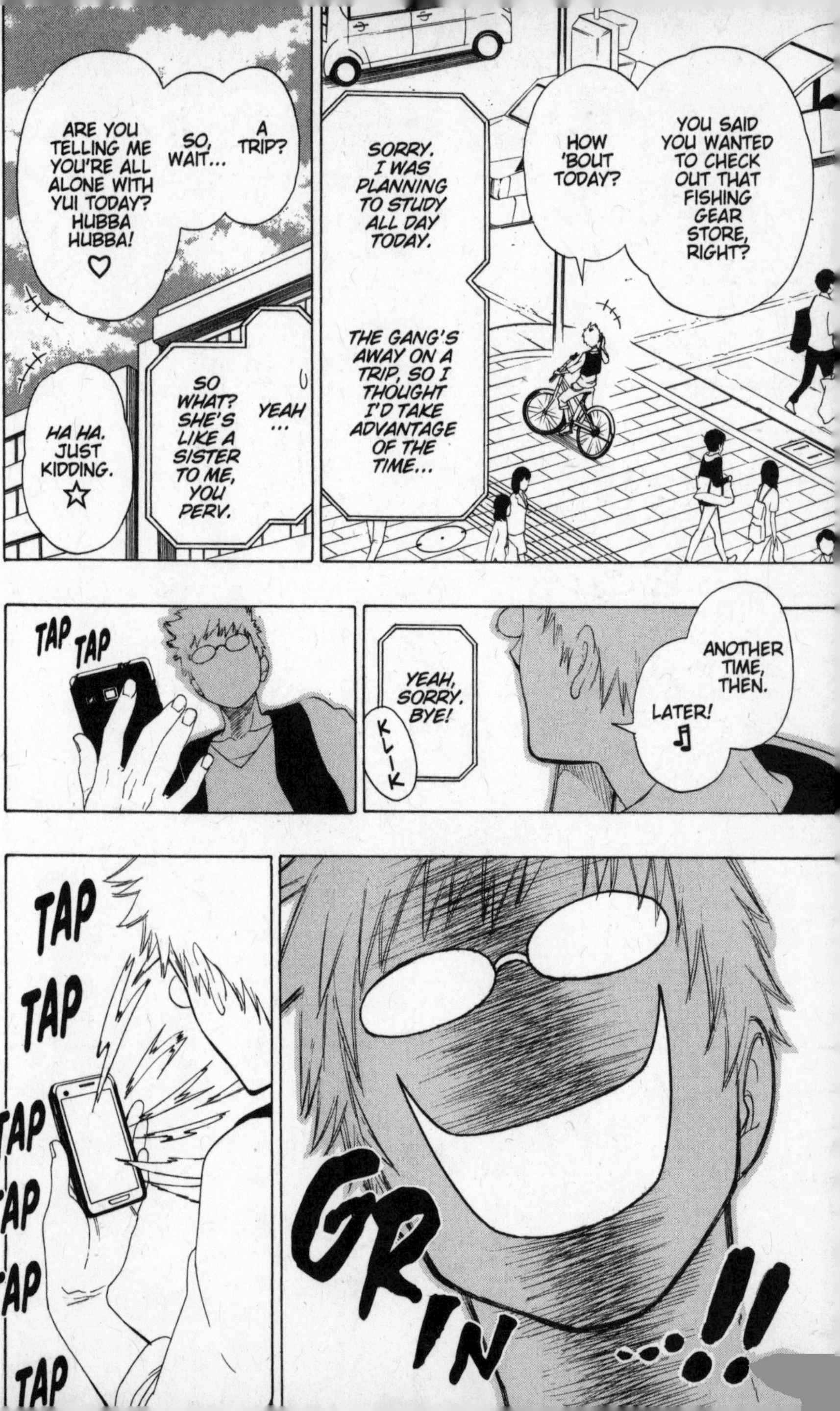
YOU SAID YOU WANTED TO CHECK OUT THAT FISHING GEAR STORE, RIGHT?
HOW 'BOUT TODAY?
SORRY. I WAS PLANNING TO STUDY ALL DAY TODAY.
THE GANG'S AWAY ON A TRIP, SO I THOUGHT I'D TAKE ADVANTAGE OF THE TIME...
A TRIP?
SO, WAIT...
ARE YOU TELLING ME YOU'RE ALL ALONE WITH YUI TODAY? HUBBA HUBBA! ♡
YEAH...
SO WHAT? SHE'S LIKE A SISTER TO ME, YOU PERV.
HA HA. JUST KIDDING. ☆
ANOTHER TIME, THEN.
LATER! ♫
YEAH, SORRY. BYE!
KLIK
TAP TAP
GRIN...!!
TAP
TAP
TAP
TAP
TAP
TAP

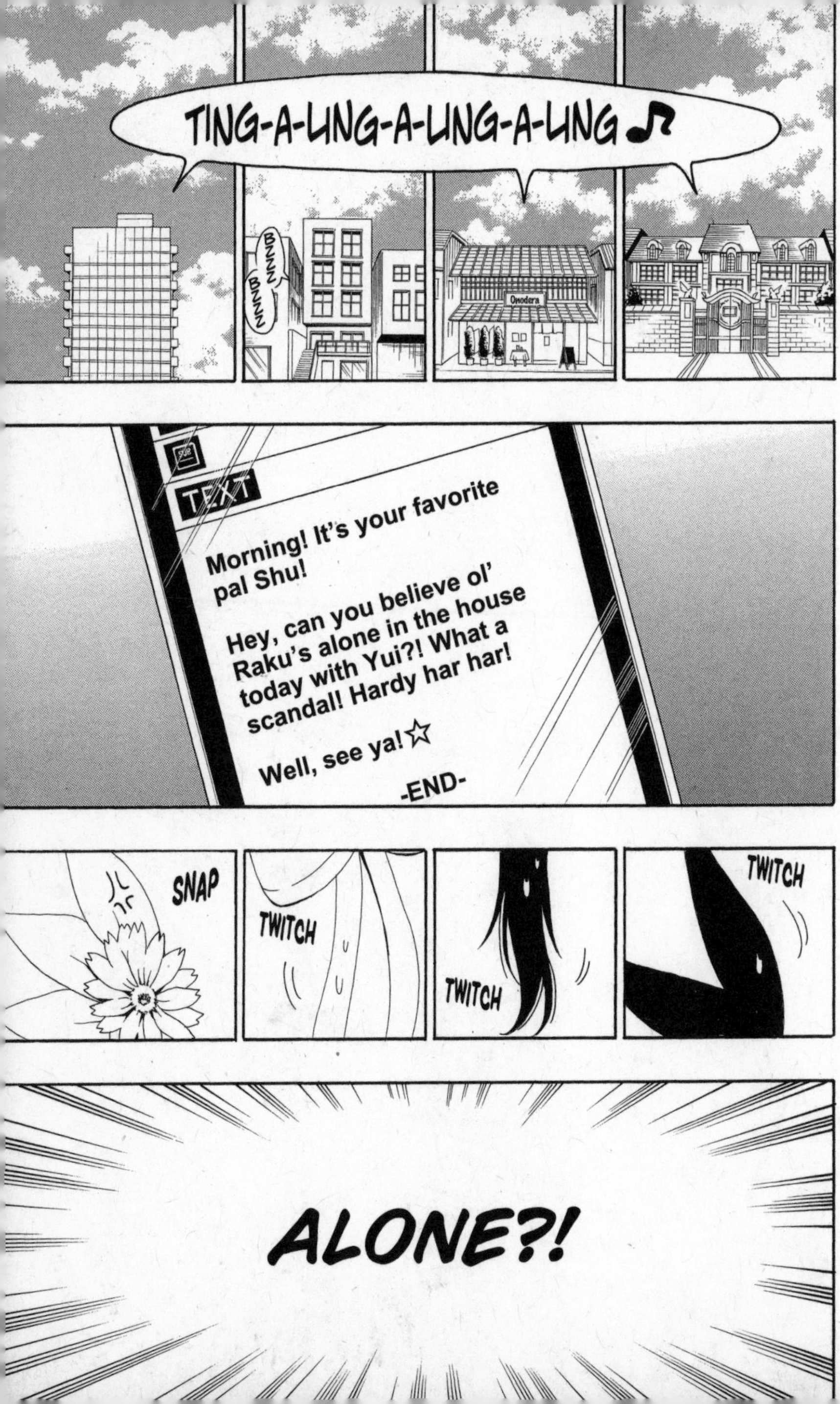
TING-A-LING-A-LING-A-LING ♪
Onodera
BZZZ
BZZZ
TEXT
Morning! It's your favorite pal Shu!
Hey, can you believe ol' Raku's alone in the house today with Yui?! What a scandal! Hardy har har!
Well, see ya! ☆
-END-
TWITCH
TWITCH
TWITCH
SNAP
ALONE?!

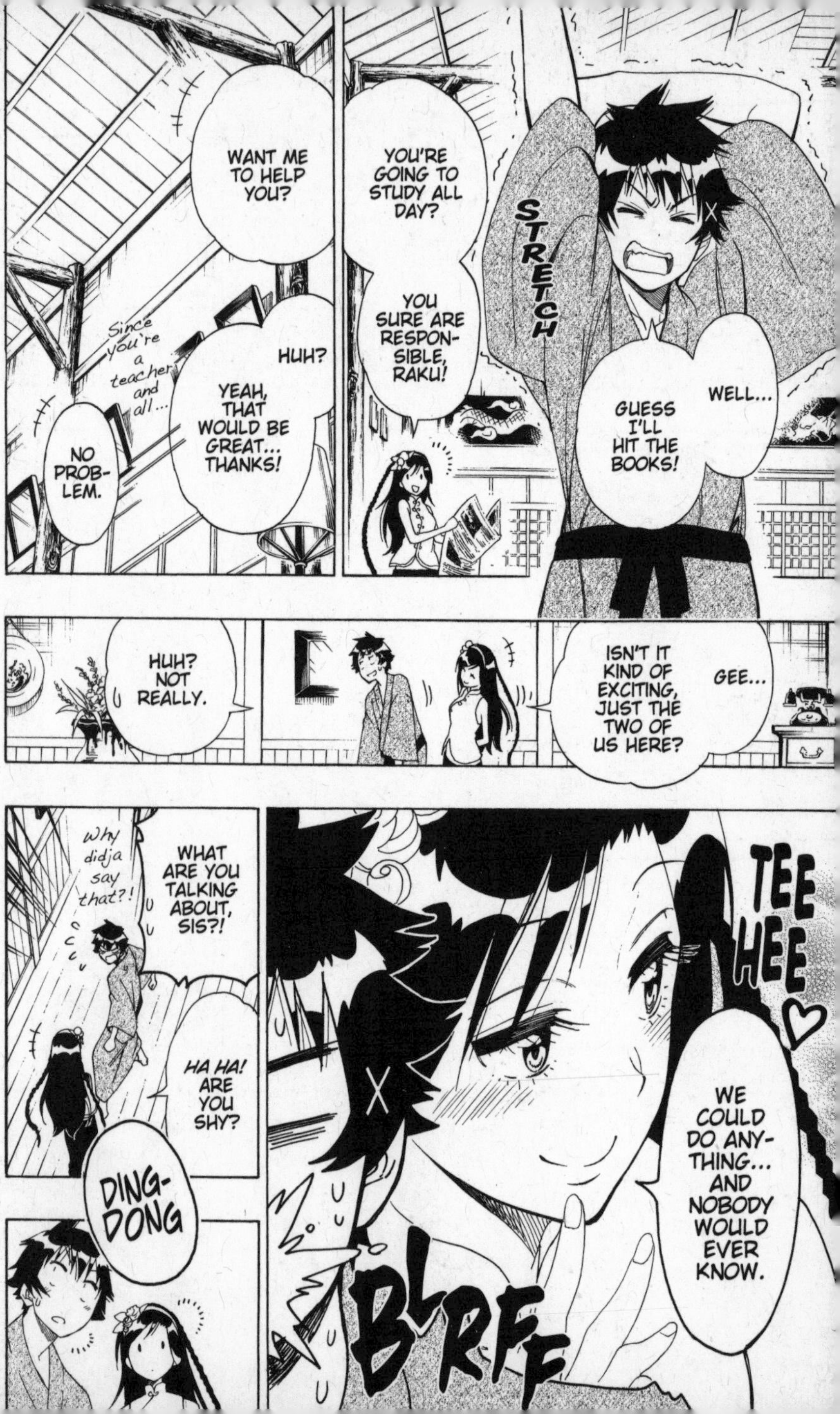
WELL...
GUESS I'LL HIT THE BOOKS!
STRETCH
YOU'RE GOING TO STUDY ALL DAY?
YOU SURE ARE RESPONSIBLE, RAKU!
WANT ME TO HELP YOU?
Since you're a teacher and all...
HUH?
YEAH, THAT WOULD BE GREAT... THANKS!
NO PROBLEM.
GEE...
ISN'T IT KIND OF EXCITING, JUST THE TWO OF US HERE?
HUH? NOT REALLY.
TEE HEE
WE COULD DO ANYTHING... AND NOBODY WOULD EVER KNOW.
BLRFF
WHAT ARE YOU TALKING ABOUT, SIS?!
Why didja say that?!
HA HA! ARE YOU SHY?
DING-DONG

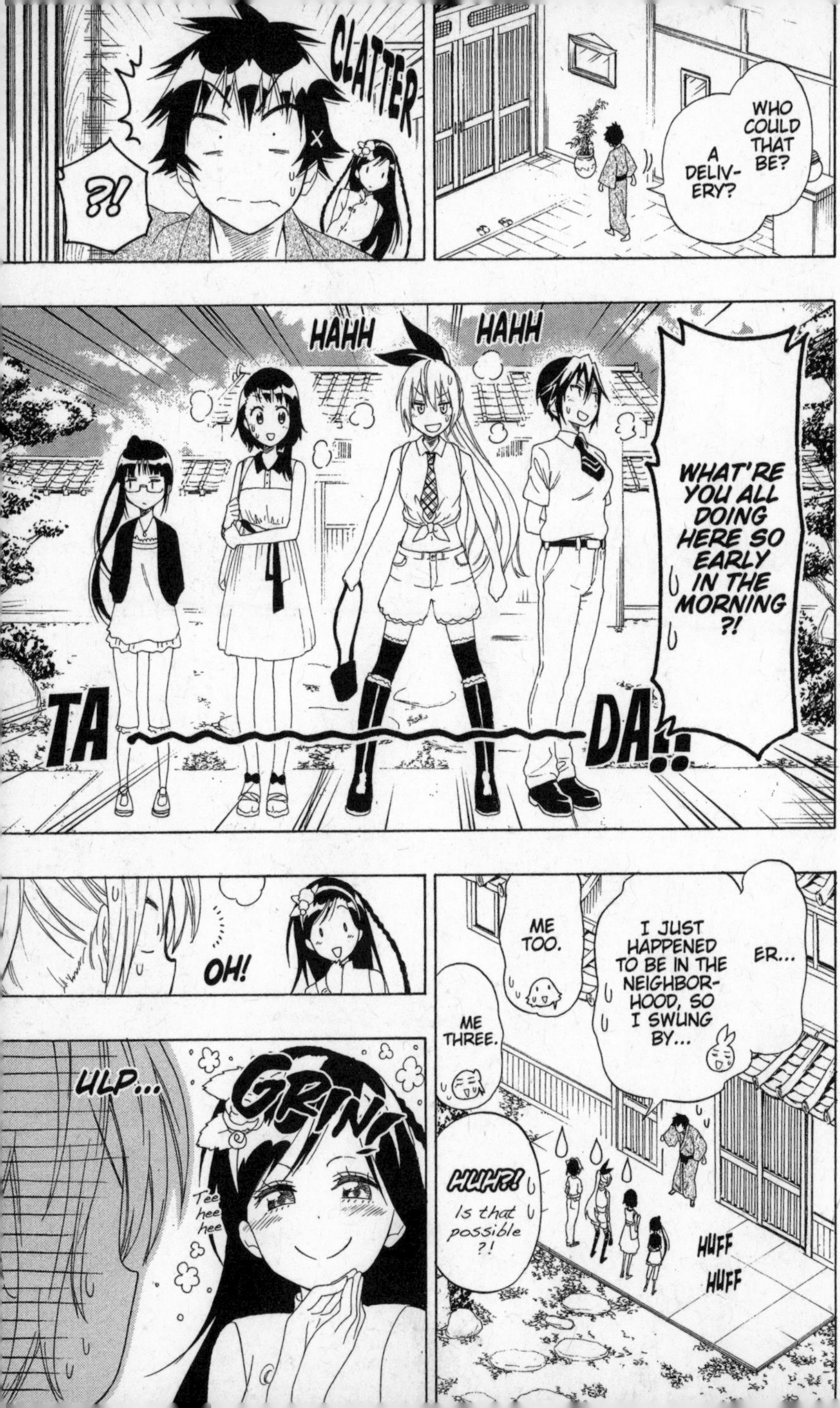
WHO COULD THAT BE?
A DELIVERY?
CLATTER
?!
WHAT'RE YOU ALL DOING HERE SO EARLY IN THE MORNING?!
HAHH
HAHH
TA~DA!!
ER...
I JUST HAPPENED TO BE IN THE NEIGHBORHOOD, SO I SWUNG BY...
ME TOO.
ME THREE.
HUH?!
Is that possible?!
HUFF
HUFF
OH!
GRIN!
ULP...
Tee hee hee

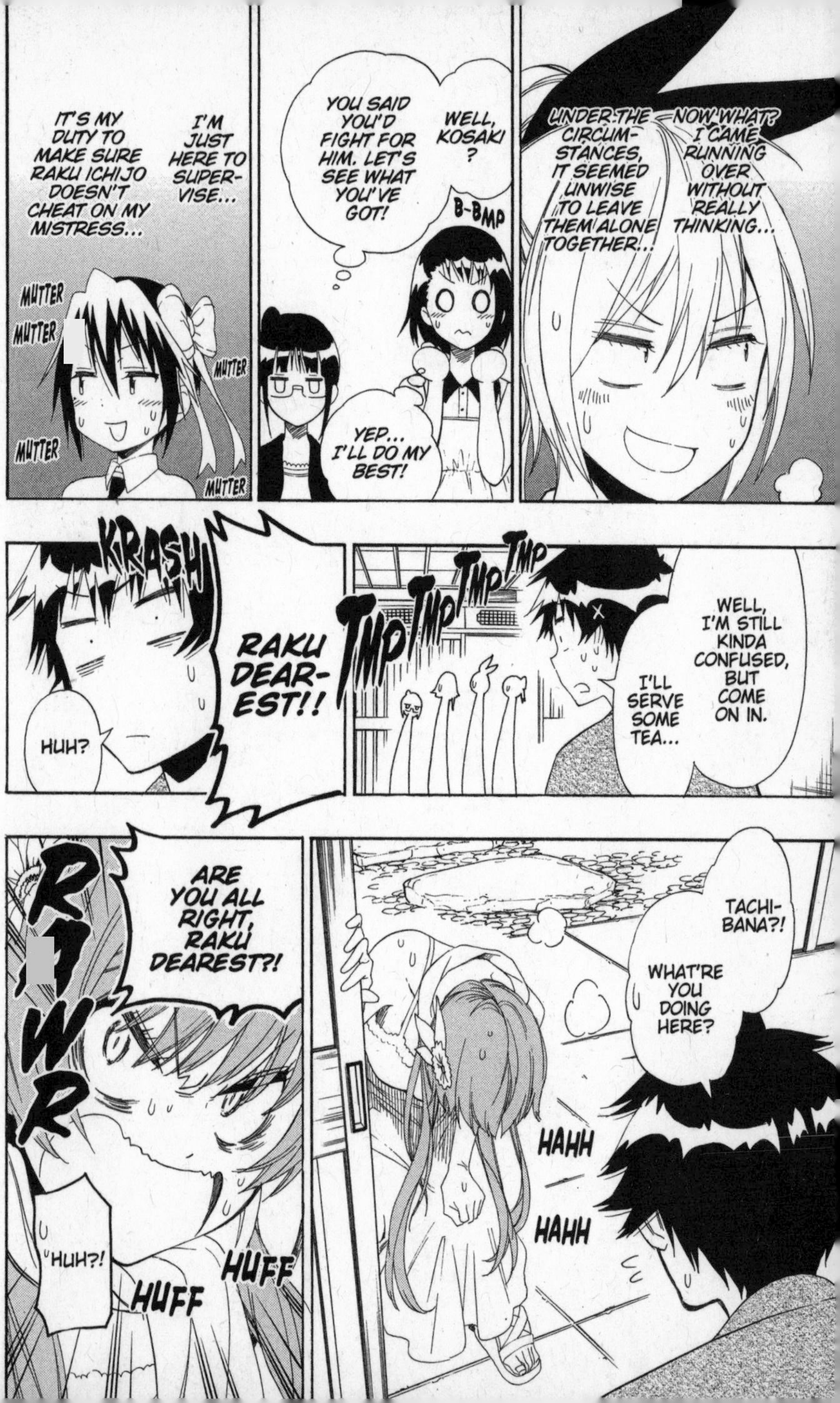
NOW WHAT? I CAME RUNNING OVER WITHOUT REALLY THINKING...
UNDER THE CIRCUMSTANCES, IT SEEMED UNWISE TO LEAVE THEM ALONE TOGETHER...
WELL, KOSAKI?
YOU SAID YOU'D FIGHT FOR HIM. LET'S SEE WHAT YOU'VE GOT!
B-BMP
YEP... I'LL DO MY BEST!
I'M JUST HERE TO SUPERVISE...
IT'S MY DUTY TO MAKE SURE RAKU ICHIJO DOESN'T CHEAT ON MY MISTRESS...
MUTTER
MUTTER
MUTTER
MUTTER
MUTTER
WELL, I'M STILL KINDA CONFUSED, BUT COME ON IN.
I'LL SERVE SOME TEA...
TMP THP THP TMP TMP
KRASH
RAKU DEAREST!!
HUH?
TACHIBANA?!
WHAT'RE YOU DOING HERE?
HAHH
HAHH
ARE YOU ALL RIGHT, RAKU DEAREST?!
HUH?!
HUFF
HUFF

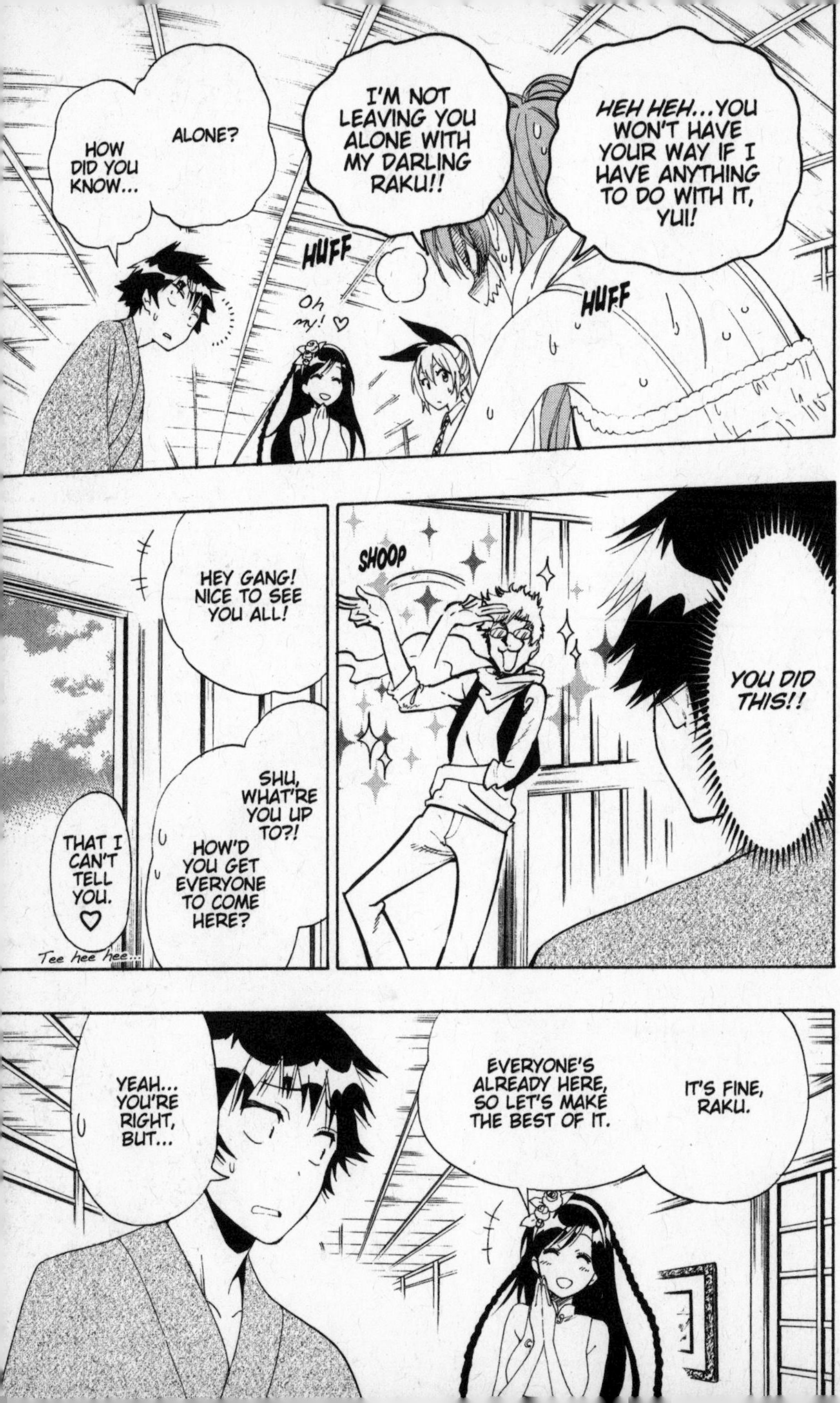
HEH HEH...YOU WON'T HAVE YOUR WAY IF I HAVE ANYTHING TO DO WITH IT, YUI!
I'M NOT LEAVING YOU ALONE WITH MY DARLING RAKU!!
HUFF
HUFF
Oh my! ♡
HOW DID YOU KNOW... ALONE?
YOU DID THIS!!
SHOOP
HEY GANG! NICE TO SEE YOU ALL!
SHU, WHAT'RE YOU UP TO?! HOW'D YOU GET EVERYONE TO COME HERE?
THAT I CAN'T TELL YOU. ♡
Tee hee hee...
IT'S FINE, RAKU. EVERYONE'S ALREADY HERE, SO LET'S MAKE THE BEST OF IT.
YEAH... YOU'RE RIGHT, BUT...

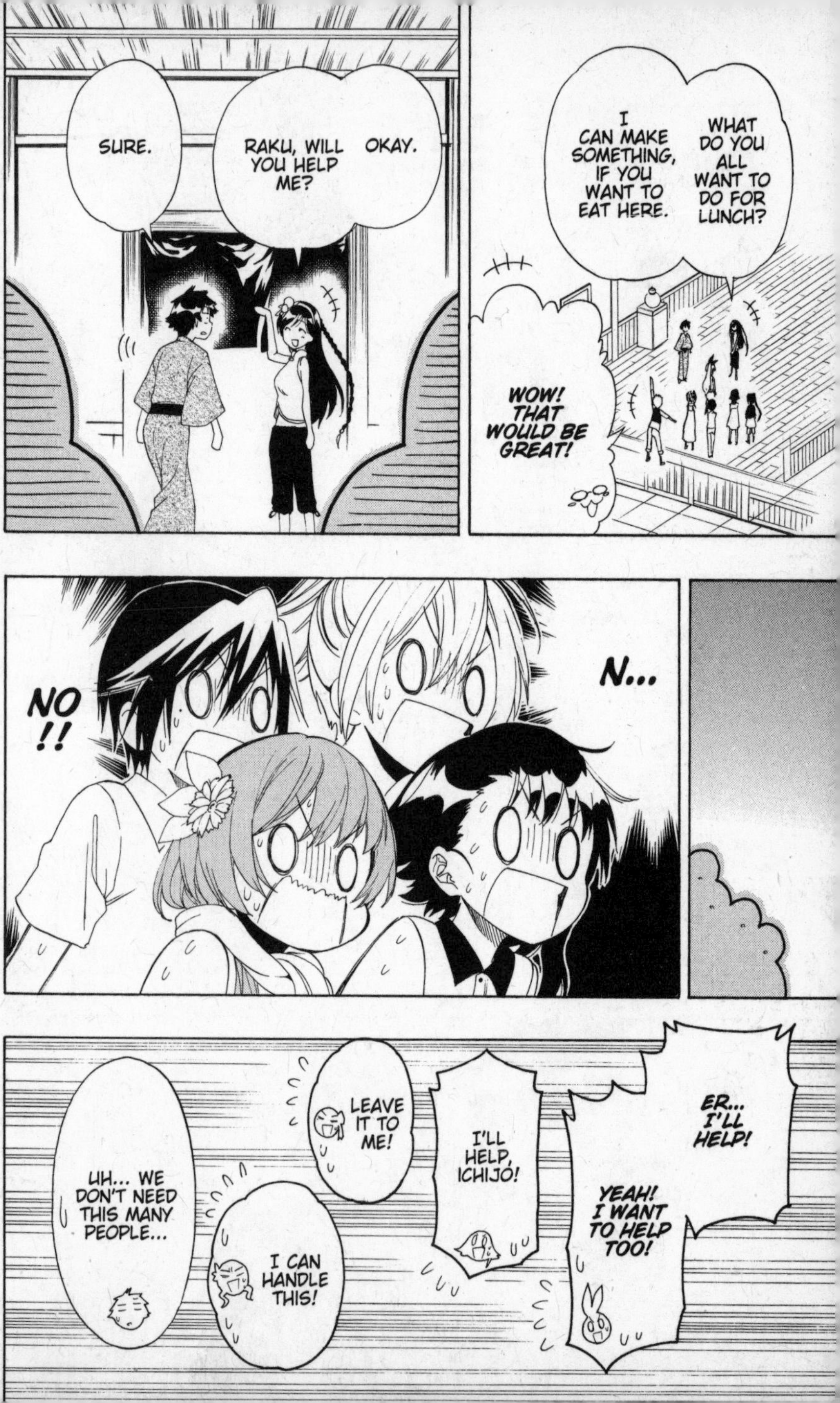
WHAT DO YOU ALL WANT TO DO FOR LUNCH?
I CAN MAKE SOMETHING, IF YOU WANT TO EAT HERE.
WOW! THAT WOULD BE GREAT!
OKAY.
RAKU, WILL YOU HELP ME?
SURE.
N...
NO!!
ER... I'LL HELP!
YEAH! I WANT TO HELP TOO!
I'LL HELP, ICHIJŌ!
LEAVE IT TO ME!
I CAN HANDLE THIS!
UH... WE DON'T NEED THIS MANY PEOPLE...

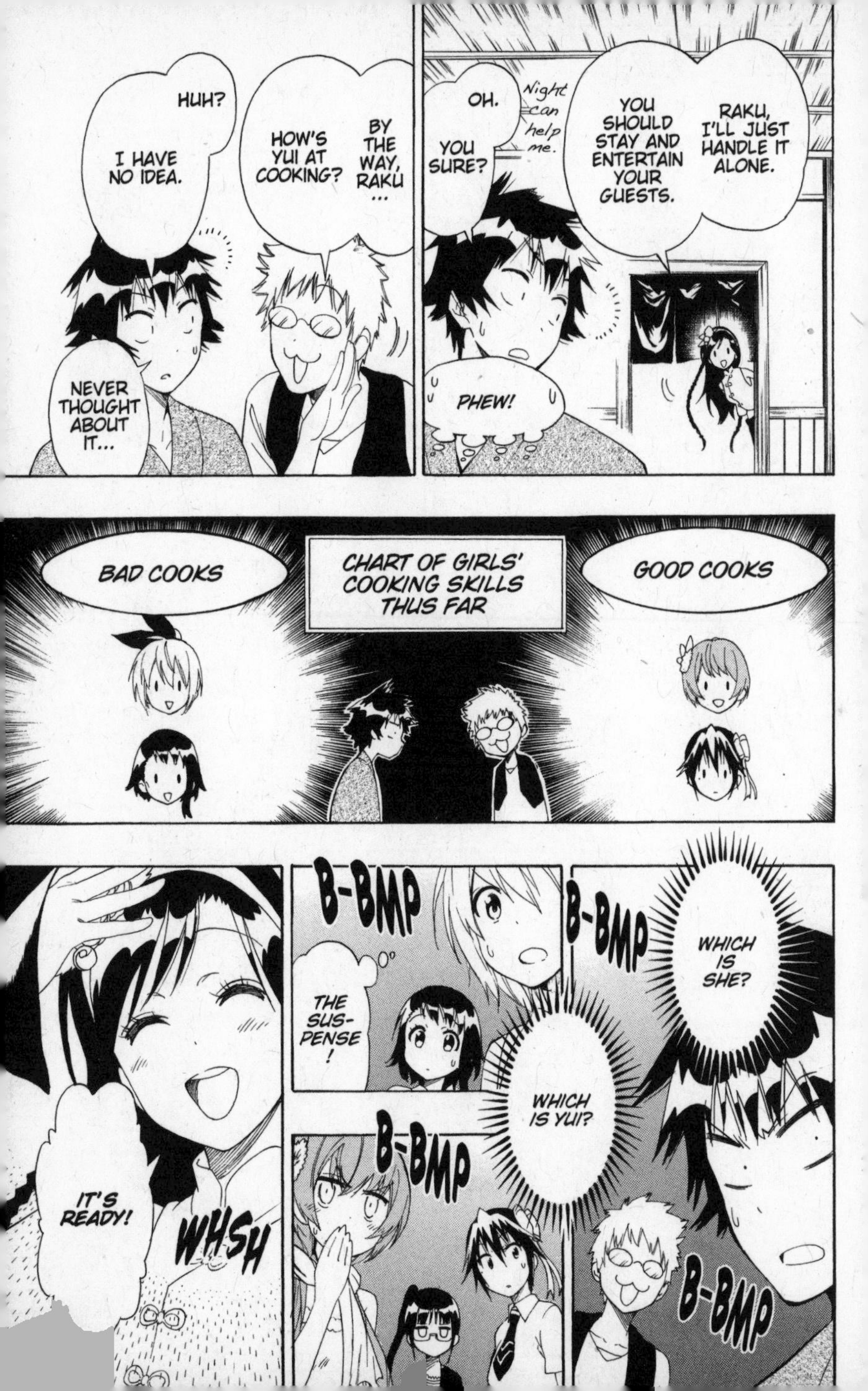
RAKU, I'LL JUST HANDLE IT ALONE.
YOU SHOULD STAY AND ENTERTAIN YOUR GUESTS.
Night can help me.
OH.
YOU SURE?
PHEW!
BY THE WAY, RAKU...
HOW'S YUI AT COOKING?
HUH?
I HAVE NO IDEA.
NEVER THOUGHT ABOUT IT...
GOOD COOKS
CHART OF GIRLS' COOKING SKILLS THUS FAR
BAD COOKS
B-BMP
WHICH IS SHE?
WHICH IS YUI?
B-BMP
B-BMP
THE SUS-PENSE!
B-BMP
IT'S READY!
WHSH

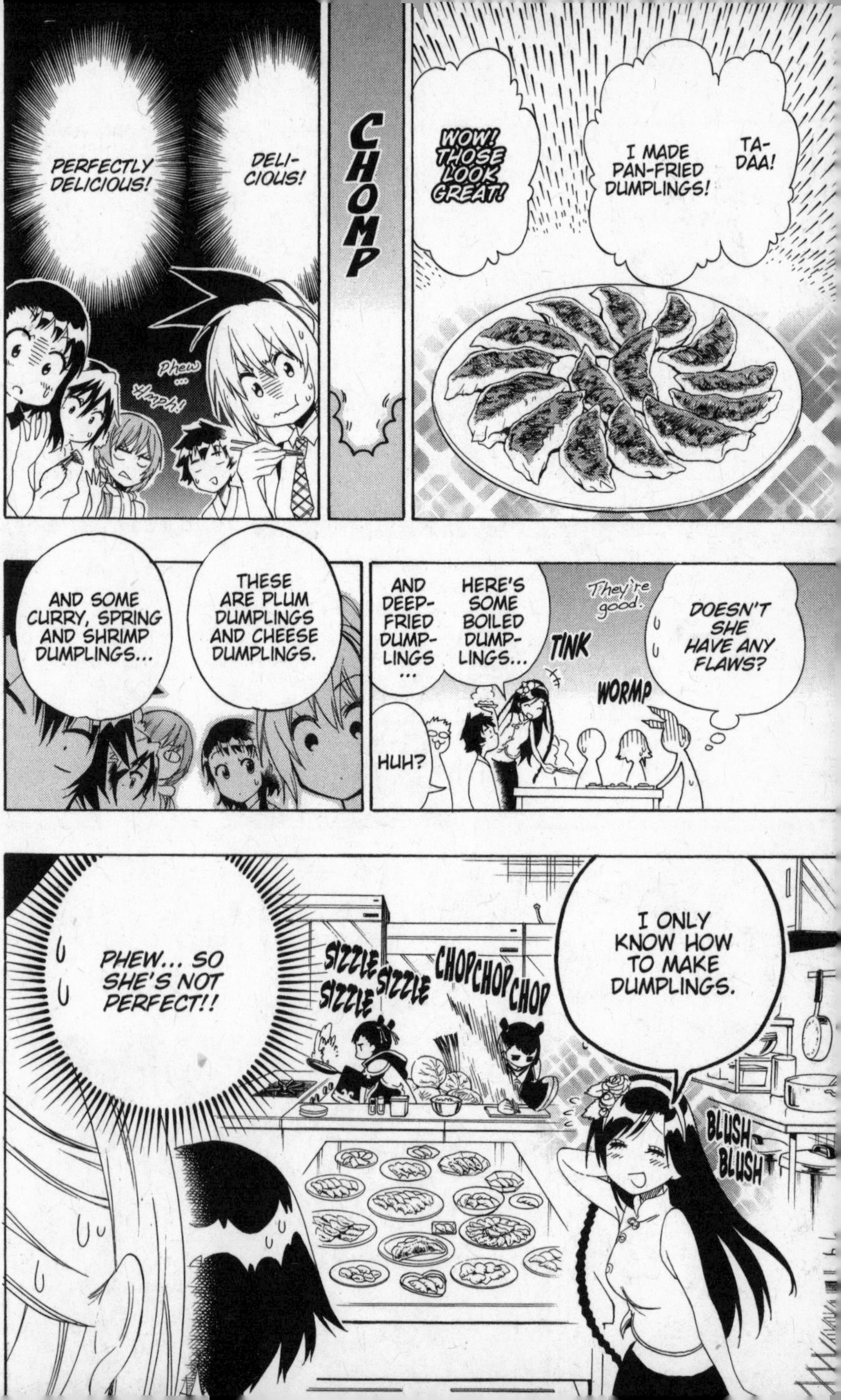
TA-DAA!
I MADE PAN-FRIED DUMPLINGS!
WOW! THOSE LOOK GREAT!
CHOMP
DELI-CIOUS!
PERFECTLY DELICIOUS!
Phew...
Hmph!
DOESN'T SHE HAVE ANY FLAWS?
They're good.
TINK
WORMP
HERE'S SOME BOILED DUMP-LINGS...
AND DEEP-FRIED DUMP-LINGS...
HUH?
THESE ARE PLUM DUMPLINGS AND CHEESE DUMPLINGS.
AND SOME CURRY, SPRING AND SHRIMP DUMPLINGS...
I ONLY KNOW HOW TO MAKE DUMPLINGS.
BLUSH BLUSH
CHOPCHOPCHOP
SIZZLE SIZZLE SIZZLE
PHEW... SO SHE'S NOT PERFECT!!

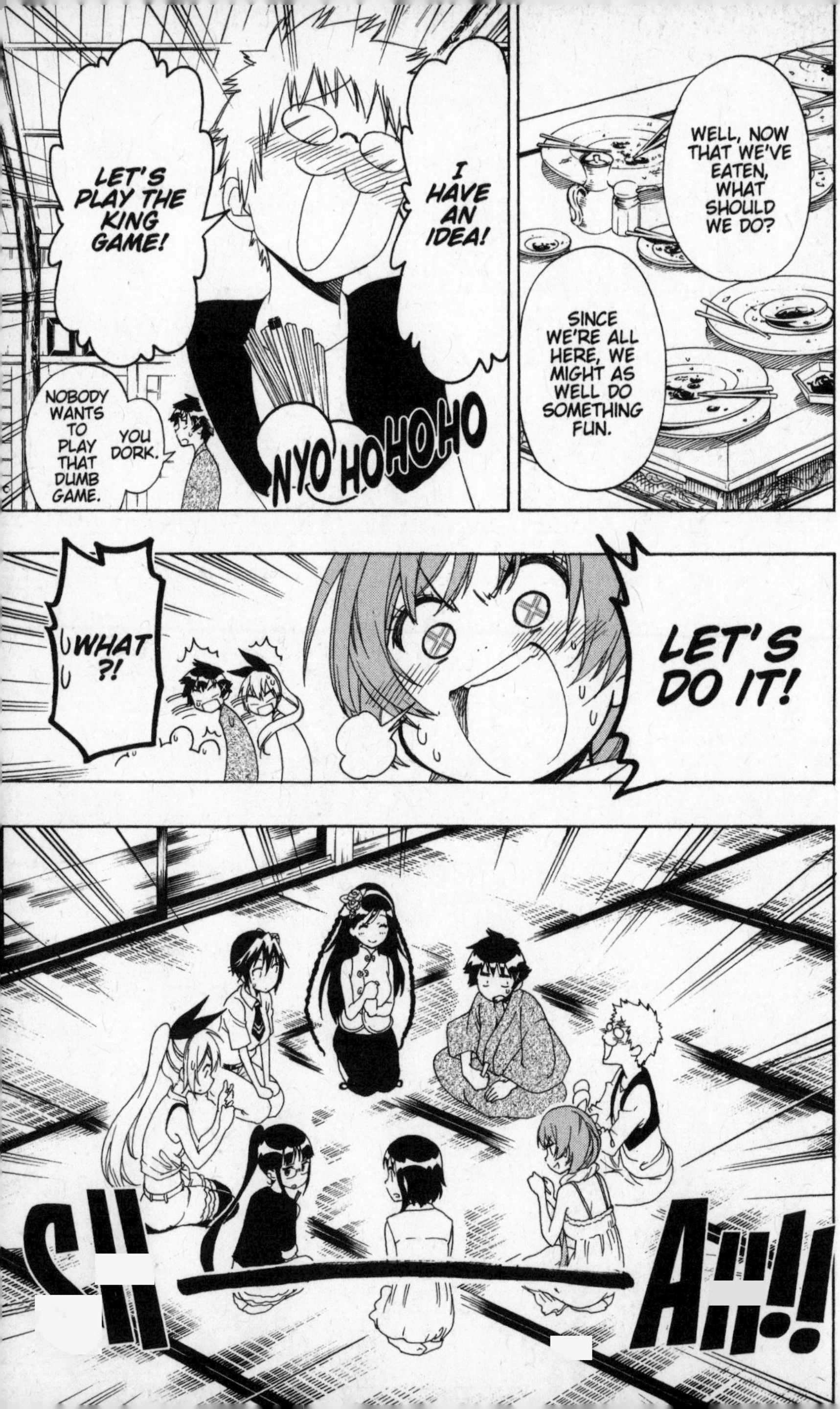
WELL, NOW THAT WE'VE EATEN, WHAT SHOULD WE DO?
SINCE WE'RE ALL HERE, WE MIGHT AS WELL DO SOMETHING FUN.
I HAVE AN IDEA!
LET'S PLAY THE KING GAME!
NYO HOHOHO
YOU DORK.
NOBODY WANTS TO PLAY THAT DUMB GAME.
LET'S DO IT!
WHAT ?!
SH
AH!!

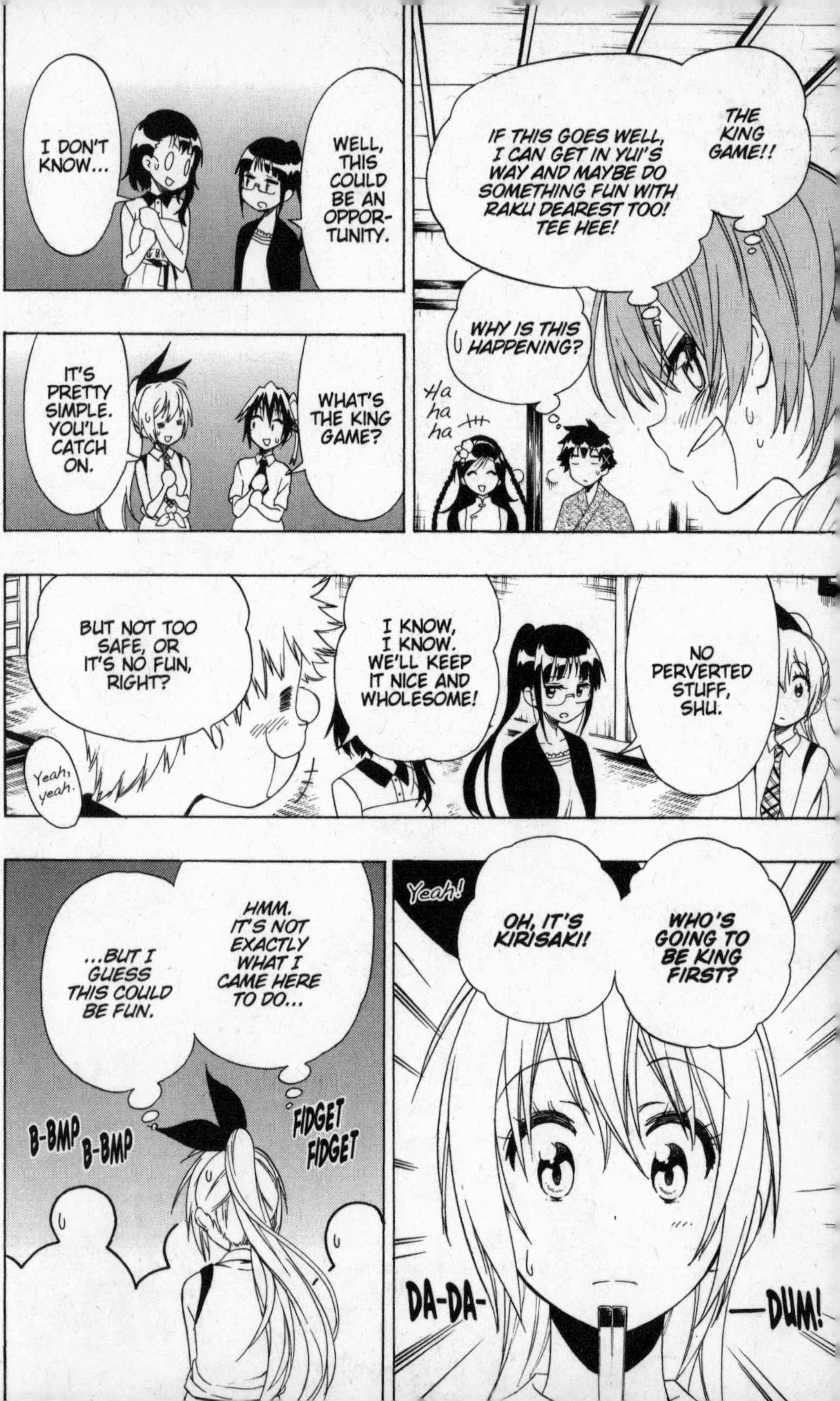
THE KING GAME!!
IF THIS GOES WELL, I CAN GET IN YUI'S WAY AND MAYBE DO SOMETHING FUN WITH RAKU DEAREST TOO! TEE HEE!
WHY IS THIS HAPPENING?
Ha ha ha
WELL, THIS COULD BE AN OPPOR-TUNITY.
I DON'T KNOW...
WHAT'S THE KING GAME?
IT'S PRETTY SIMPLE. YOU'LL CATCH ON.
NO PERVERTED STUFF, SHU.
I KNOW, I KNOW. WE'LL KEEP IT NICE AND WHOLESOME!
BUT NOT TOO SAFE, OR IT'S NO FUN, RIGHT?
Yeah, yeah.
Yeah!
WHO'S GOING TO BE KING FIRST?
OH, IT'S KIRISAKI!
DA-DA-
—DUM!
HMM. IT'S NOT EXACTLY WHAT I CAME HERE TO DO...
...BUT I GUESS THIS COULD BE FUN.
FIDGET FIDGET
B-BMP B-BMP

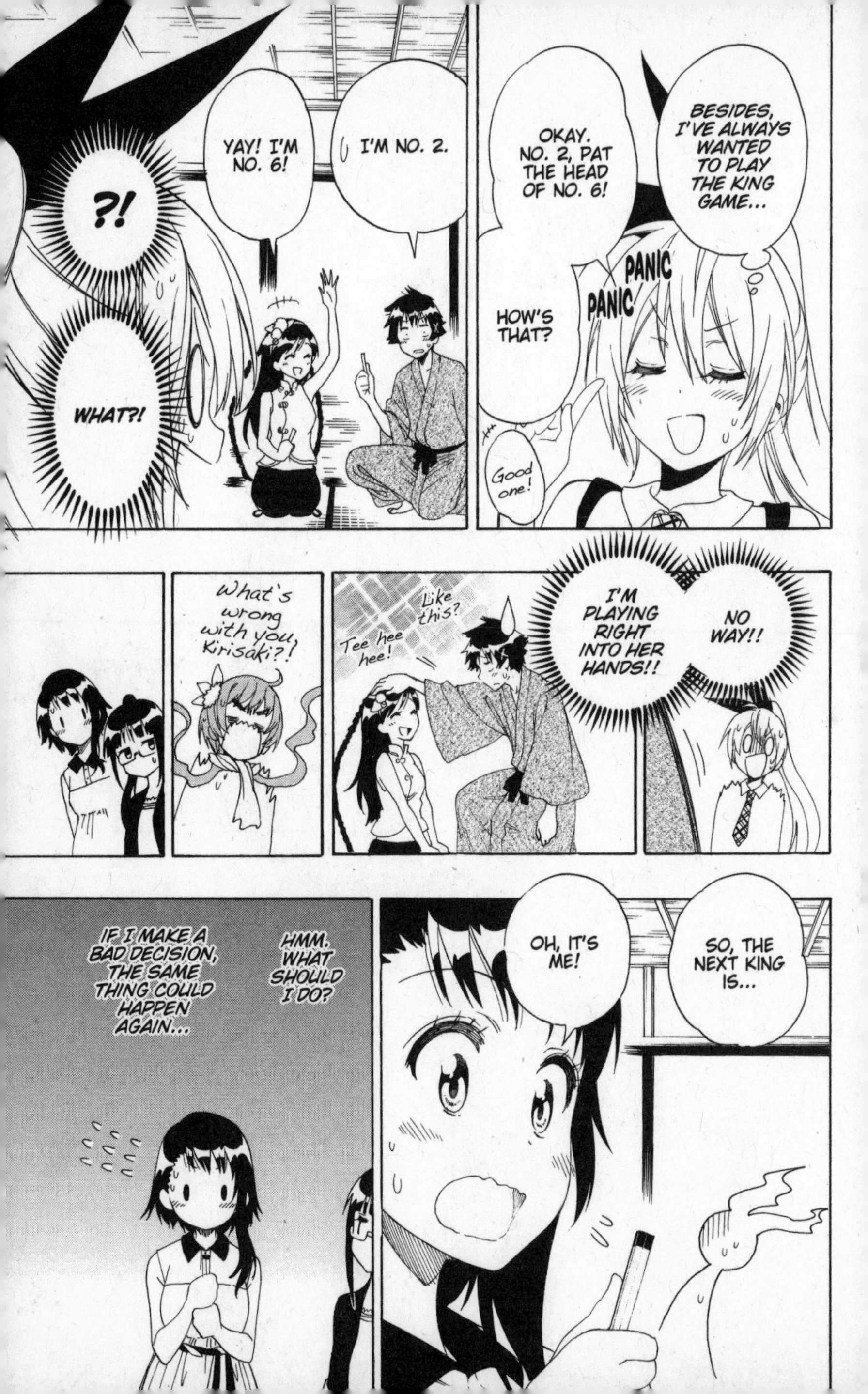
BESIDES, I'VE ALWAYS WANTED TO PLAY THE KING GAME...
OKAY. NO. 2, PAT THE HEAD OF NO. 6!
PANIC
PANIC
HOW'S THAT?
Good one!
I'M NO. 2.
YAY! I'M NO. 6!
?!
WHAT?!
NO WAY!!
I'M PLAYING RIGHT INTO HER HANDS!!
Like this?
Tee hee hee!
What's wrong with you, Kirisaki?!
SO, THE NEXT KING IS...
OH, IT'S ME!
HMM. WHAT SHOULD I DO?
IF I MAKE A BAD DECISION, THE SAME THING COULD HAPPEN AGAIN...

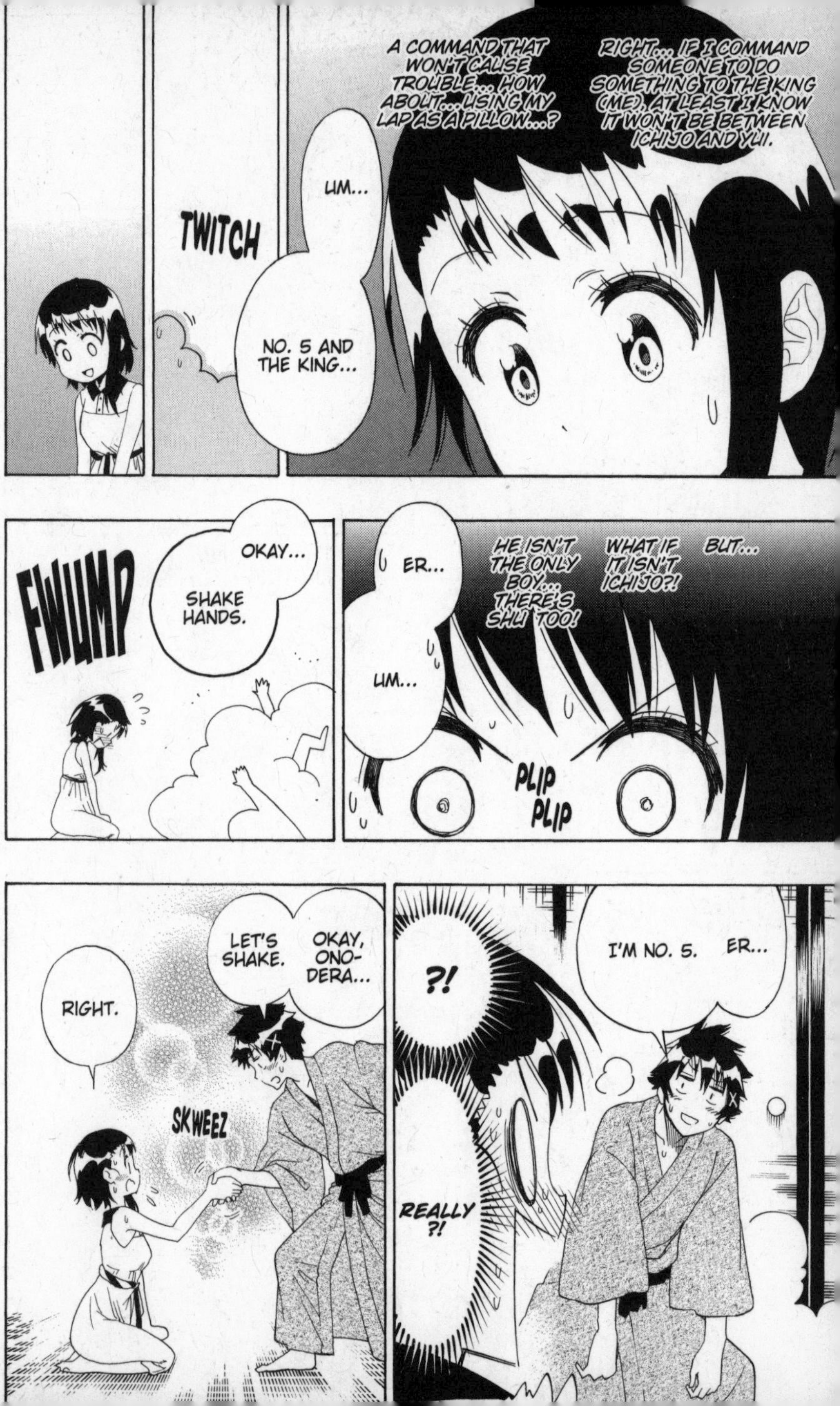
RIGHT... IF I COMMAND SOMEONE TO DO SOMETHING TO THE KING (ME), AT LEAST I KNOW IT WON'T BE BETWEEN ICHIJO AND YUI.
A COMMAND THAT WON'T CAUSE TROUBLE... HOW ABOUT... USING MY LAP AS A PILLOW...?
UM...
NO. 5 AND THE KING...
TWITCH
BUT...
WHAT IF IT ISN'T ICHIJO?!
HE ISN'T THE ONLY BOY... THERE'S SHU TOO!
ER...
UM...
PLIP PLIP
OKAY...
SHAKE HANDS.
FWUMP
ER...
I'M NO. 5.
?!
REALLY ?!
OKAY, ONO-DERA...
LET'S SHAKE.
RIGHT.
SKWEEZ

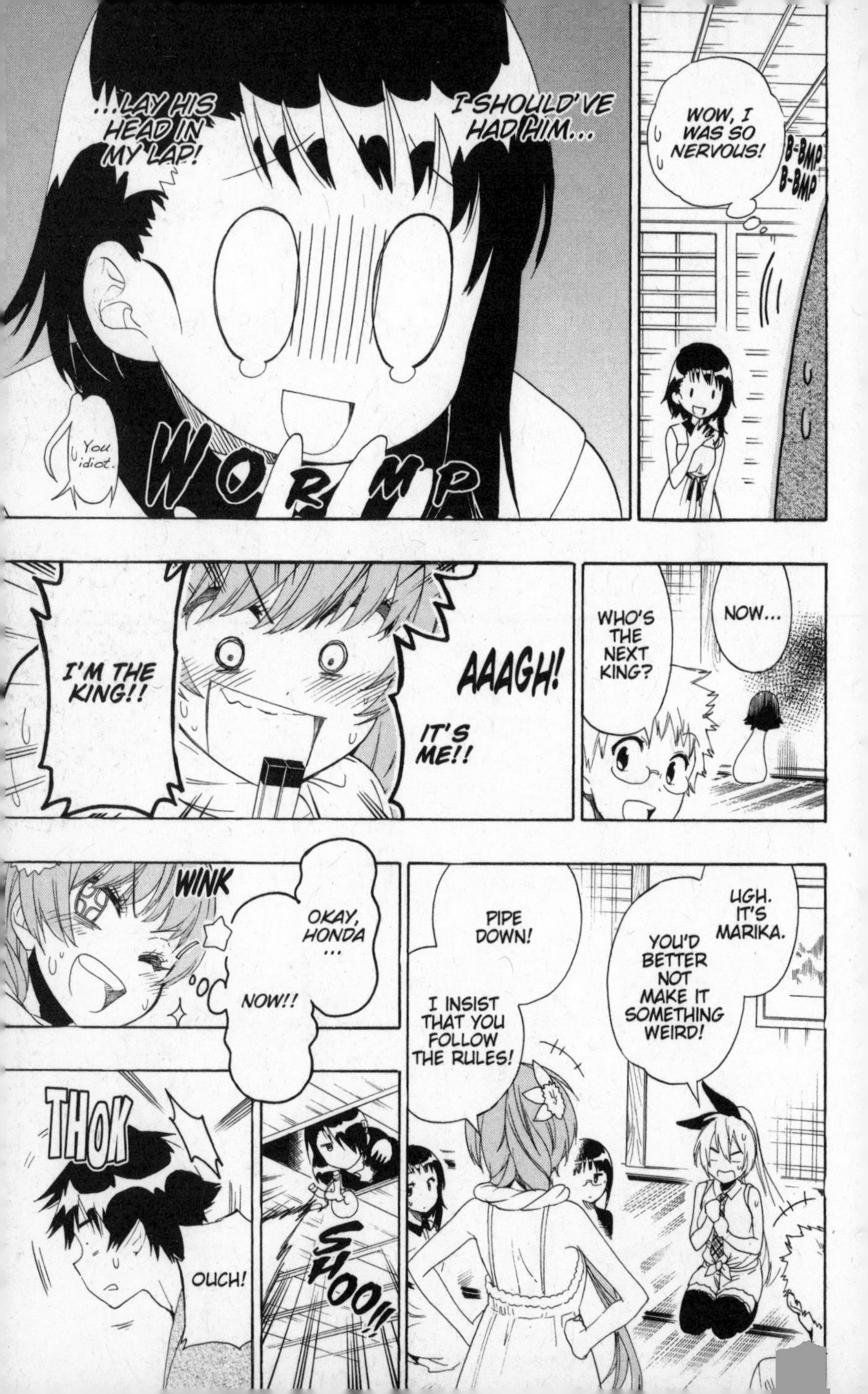
WOW, I WAS SO NERVOUS!
B-BMP B-BMP
I SHOULD'VE HAD HIM...
...LAY HIS HEAD IN MY LAP!
WORMP
You idiot.
NOW...
WHO'S THE NEXT KING?
AAAGH!
IT'S ME!!
I'M THE KING!!
UGH. IT'S MARIKA.
YOU'D BETTER NOT MAKE IT SOMETHING WEIRD!
PIPE DOWN!
I INSIST THAT YOU FOLLOW THE RULES!
WINK
OKAY, HONDA ...
NOW!!
SHOO!!
THOK
OUCH!

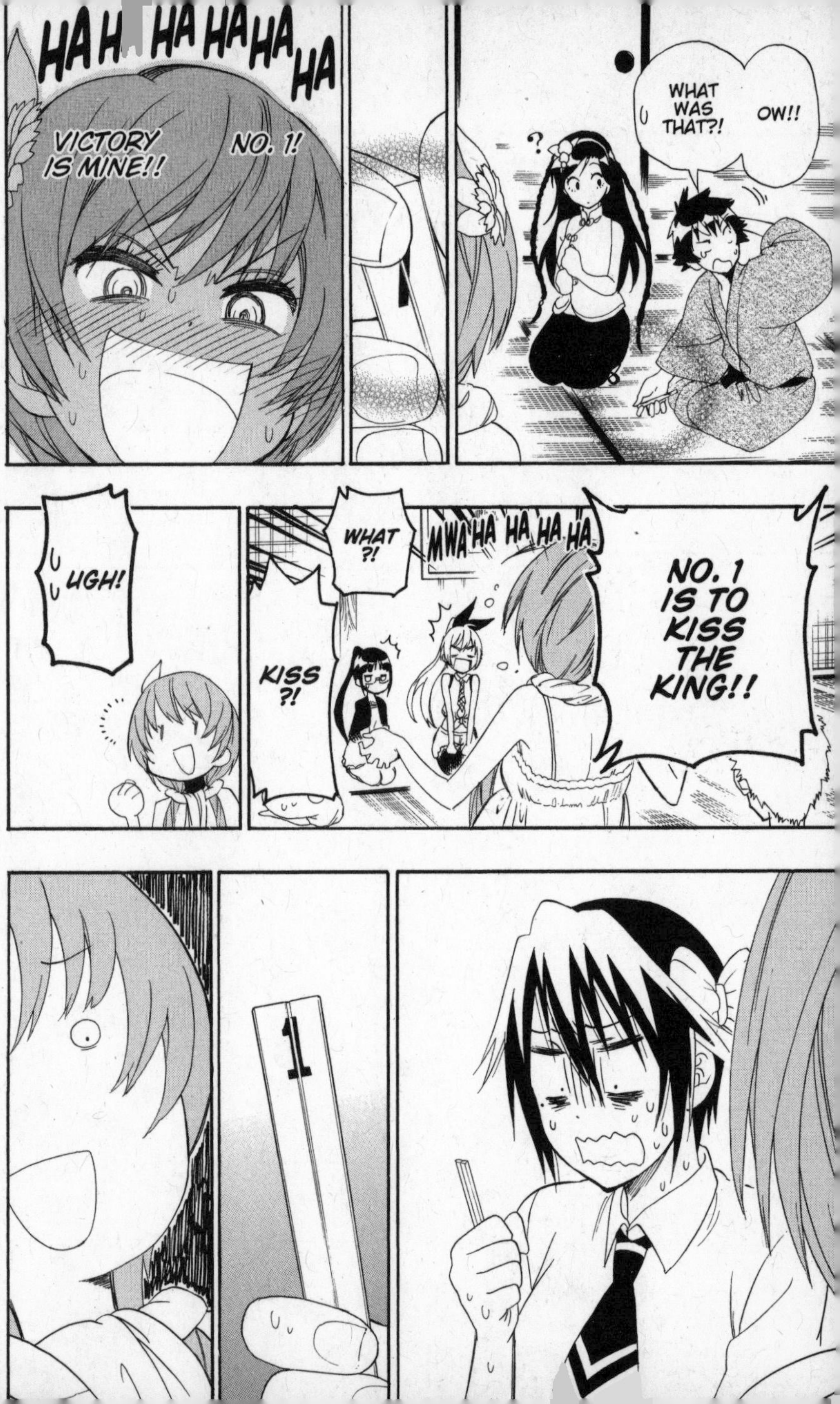
OW!!
WHAT WAS THAT?!
HA HA HA HA HA HA
NO. 1!
VICTORY IS MINE!!
NO. 1 IS TO KISS THE KING!!
MWA HA HA HA HA
WHAT ?!
KISS ?!
UGH!
1

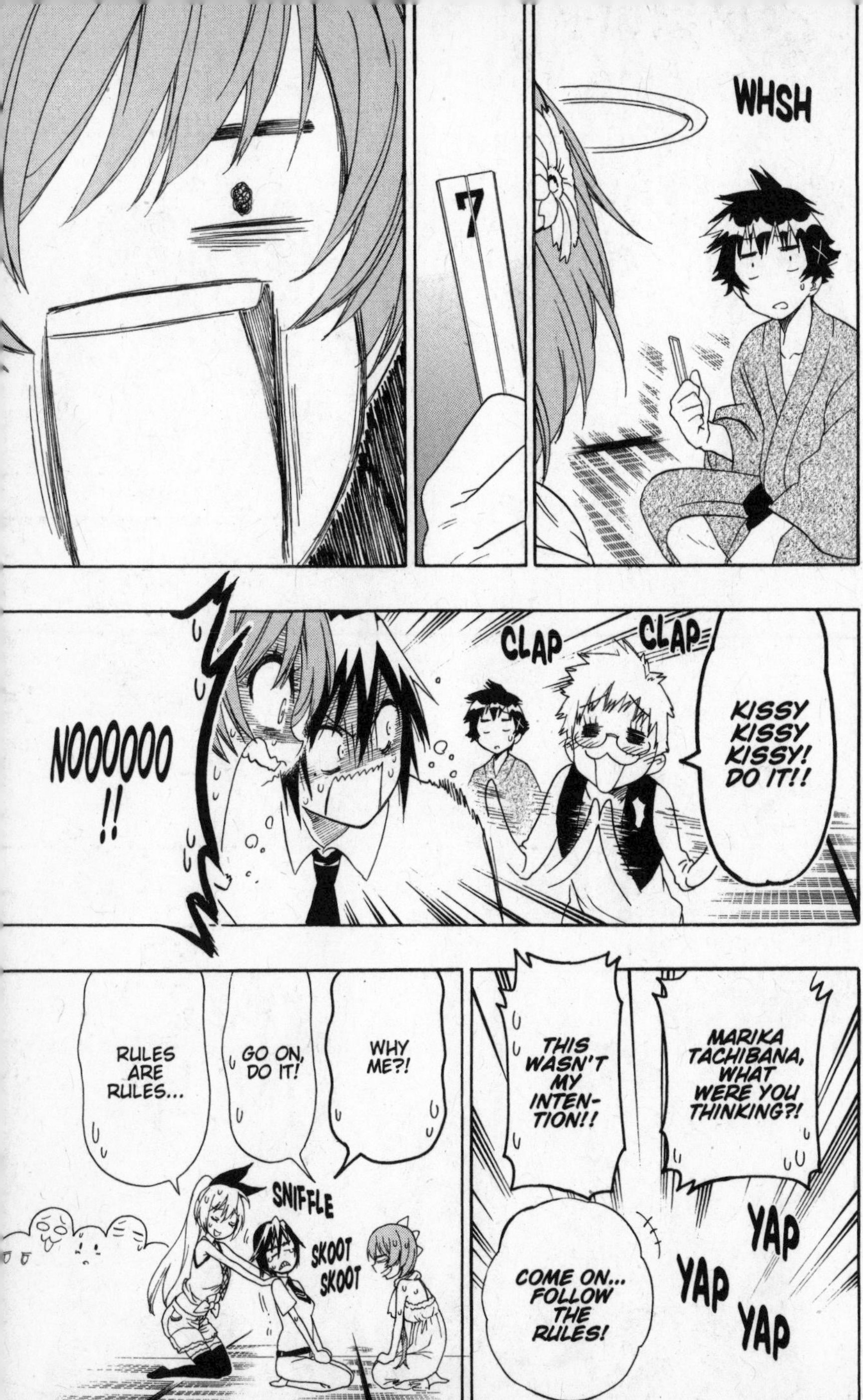
WHSH
KISSY KISSY KISSY! DO IT!!
CLAP
CLAP
NOOOOOO!!
MARIKA TACHIBANA, WHAT WERE YOU THINKING?!
THIS WASN'T MY INTEN-TION!!
YAP
YAP
YAP
COME ON... FOLLOW THE RULES!
WHY ME?!
GO ON, DO IT!
RULES ARE RULES...
SNIFFLE
SKOOT SKOOT

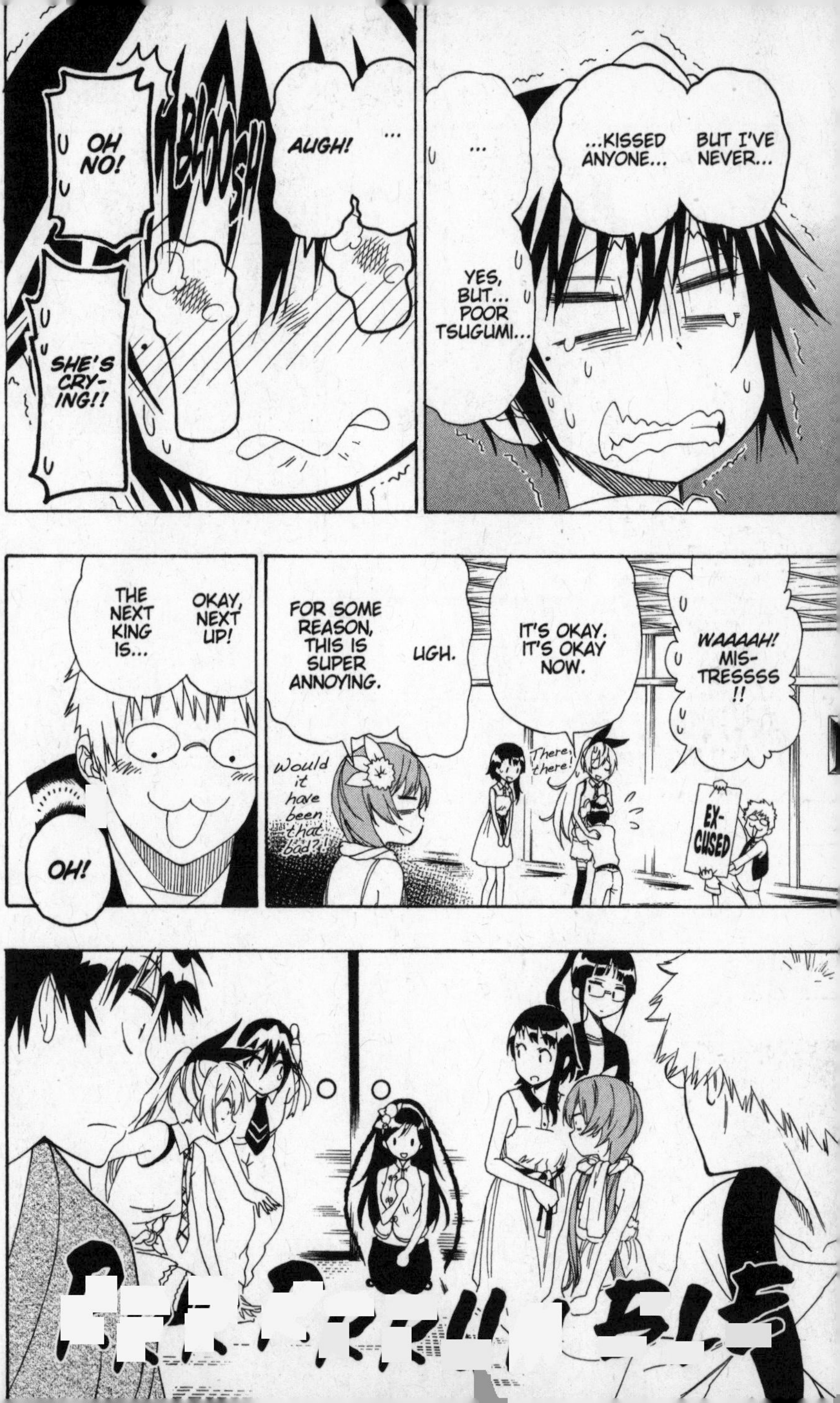
BUT I'VE NEVER...
...KISSED ANYONE...
...
YES, BUT... POOR TSUGUMI...
...
AUGH!
BLOOSH
OH NO!
SHE'S CRY-ING!!
WAAAAH! MIS-TRESSSS!!
IT'S OKAY. IT'S OKAY NOW.
There, there!
EX-CUSED
UGH.
FOR SOME REASON, THIS IS SUPER ANNOYING.
Would it have been that bad?!
OKAY, NEXT UP!
THE NEXT KING IS...
OH!

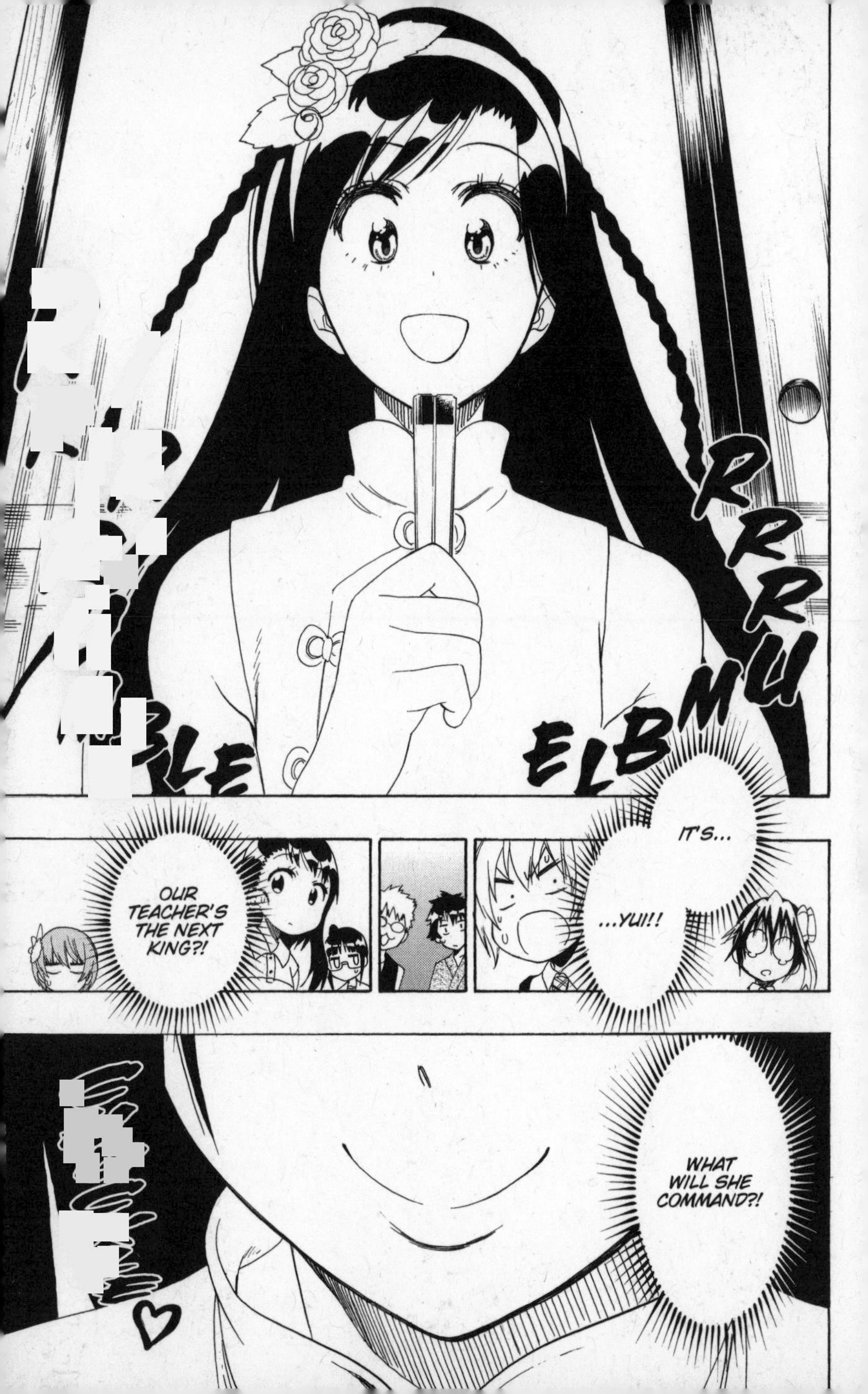
RRRUMBLE
BLE
IT'S...
...YUI!!
OUR TEACHER'S THE NEXT KING?!
WHAT WILL SHE COMMAND?!

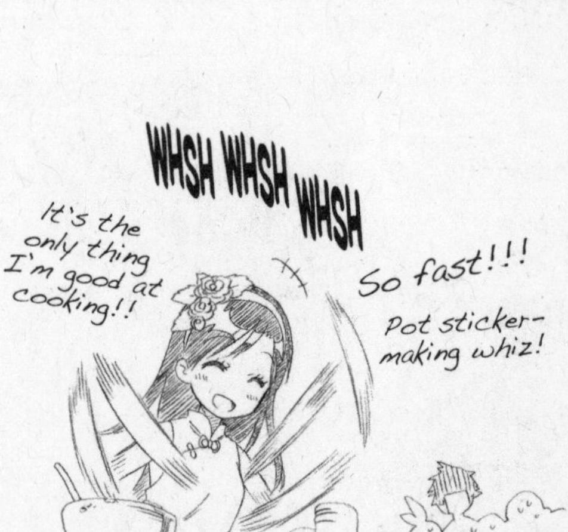
WHSH WHSH WHSH
It's the only thing I'm good at cooking!!
So fast!!!
Pot sticker-making whiz!

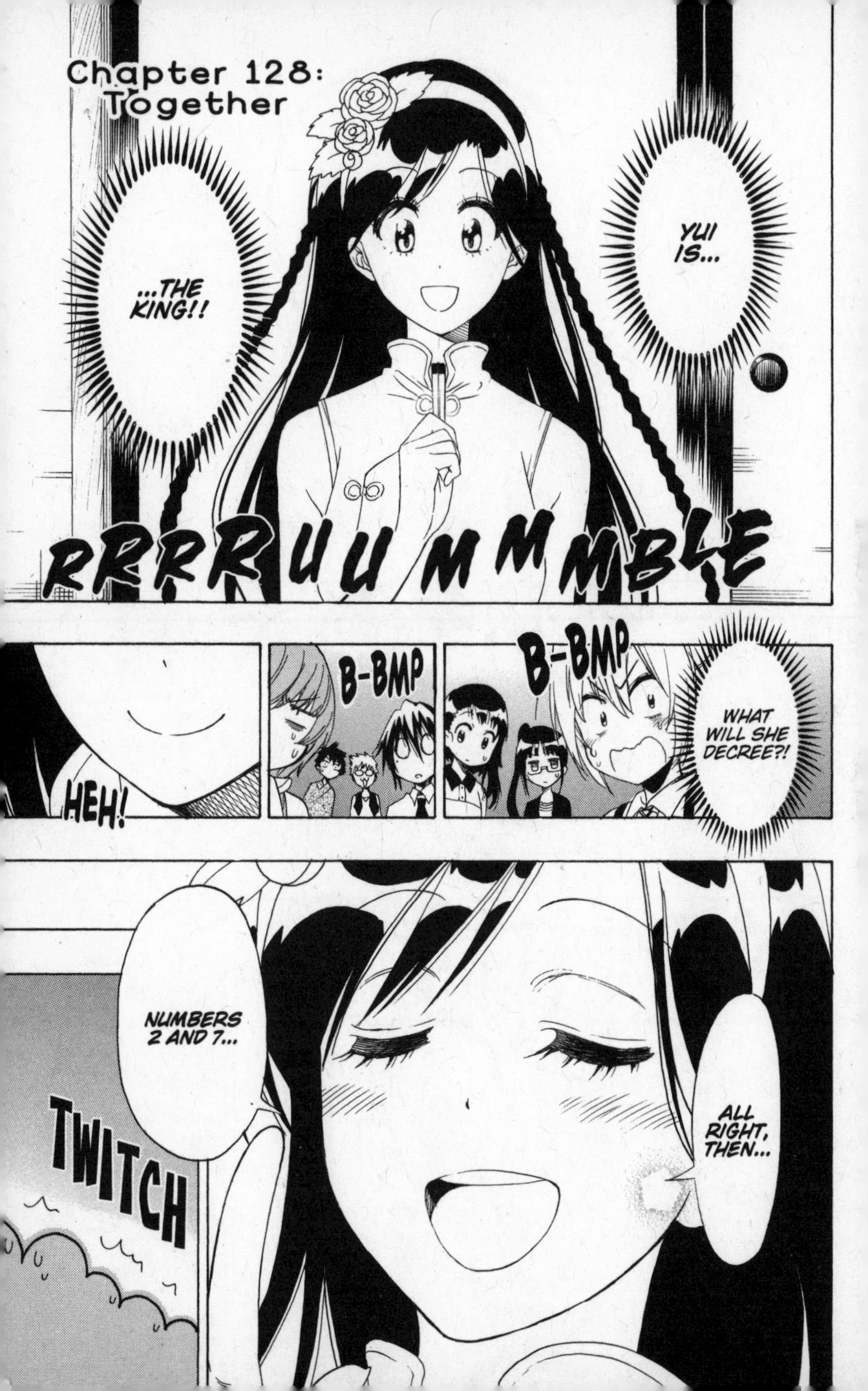
Chapter 128: Together
YUI IS...
...THE KING!!
RRRRUUMMMBLE
WHAT WILL SHE DECREE?!
B-BMP
B-BMP
HEH!
ALL RIGHT, THEN...
NUMBERS 2 AND 7...
TWITCH

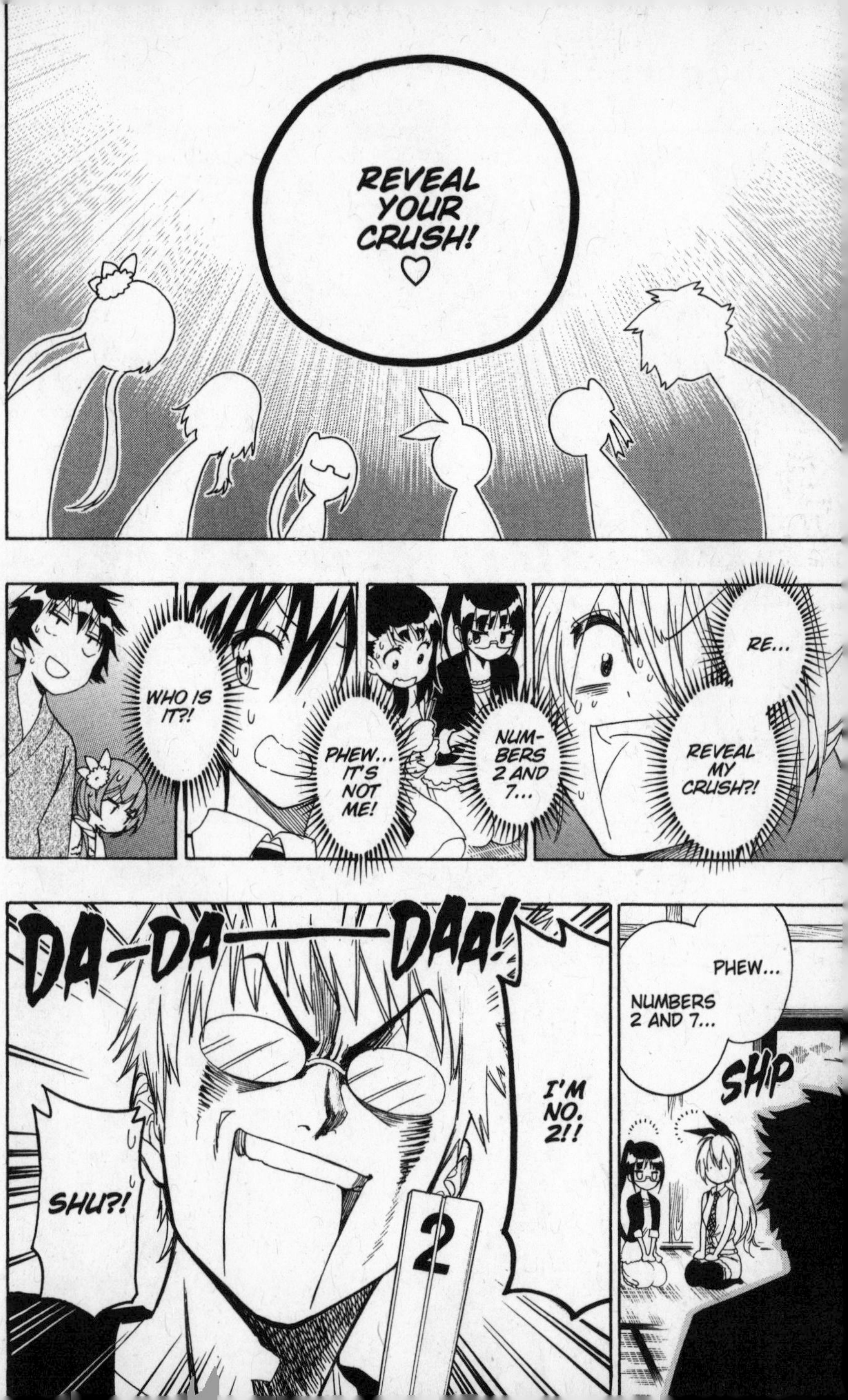
REVEAL YOUR CRUSH! ♡
RE...
REVEAL MY CRUSH?!
NUM-BERS 2 AND 7...
PHEW... IT'S NOT ME!
WHO IS IT?!
PHEW...
NUMBERS 2 AND 7...
SHIP
DA-DA——DAA!
I'M NO. 2!!
SHU?!
2

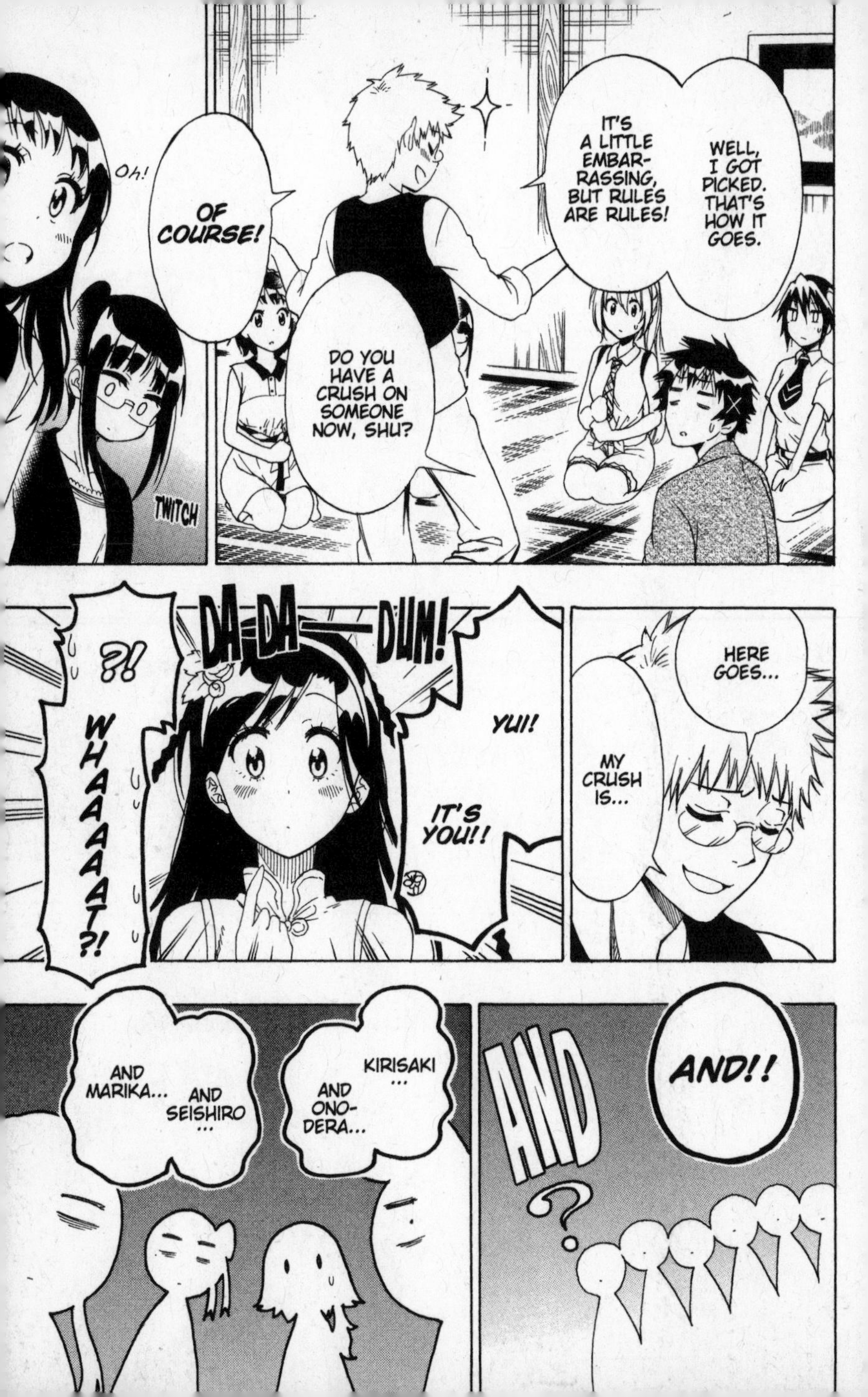
WELL, I GOT PICKED. THAT'S HOW IT GOES.
IT'S A LITTLE EMBARRASSING, BUT RULES ARE RULES!
OF COURSE!
DO YOU HAVE A CRUSH ON SOMEONE NOW, SHU?
Oh!
TWITCH
HERE GOES...
MY CRUSH IS...
YUI!
IT'S YOU!!
DA-DA—DUM!
?!
WHAAAAAAT?!
AND!!
AND
?
KIRISAKI...
AND ONODERA...
AND MARIKA...
AND SEISHIRO...

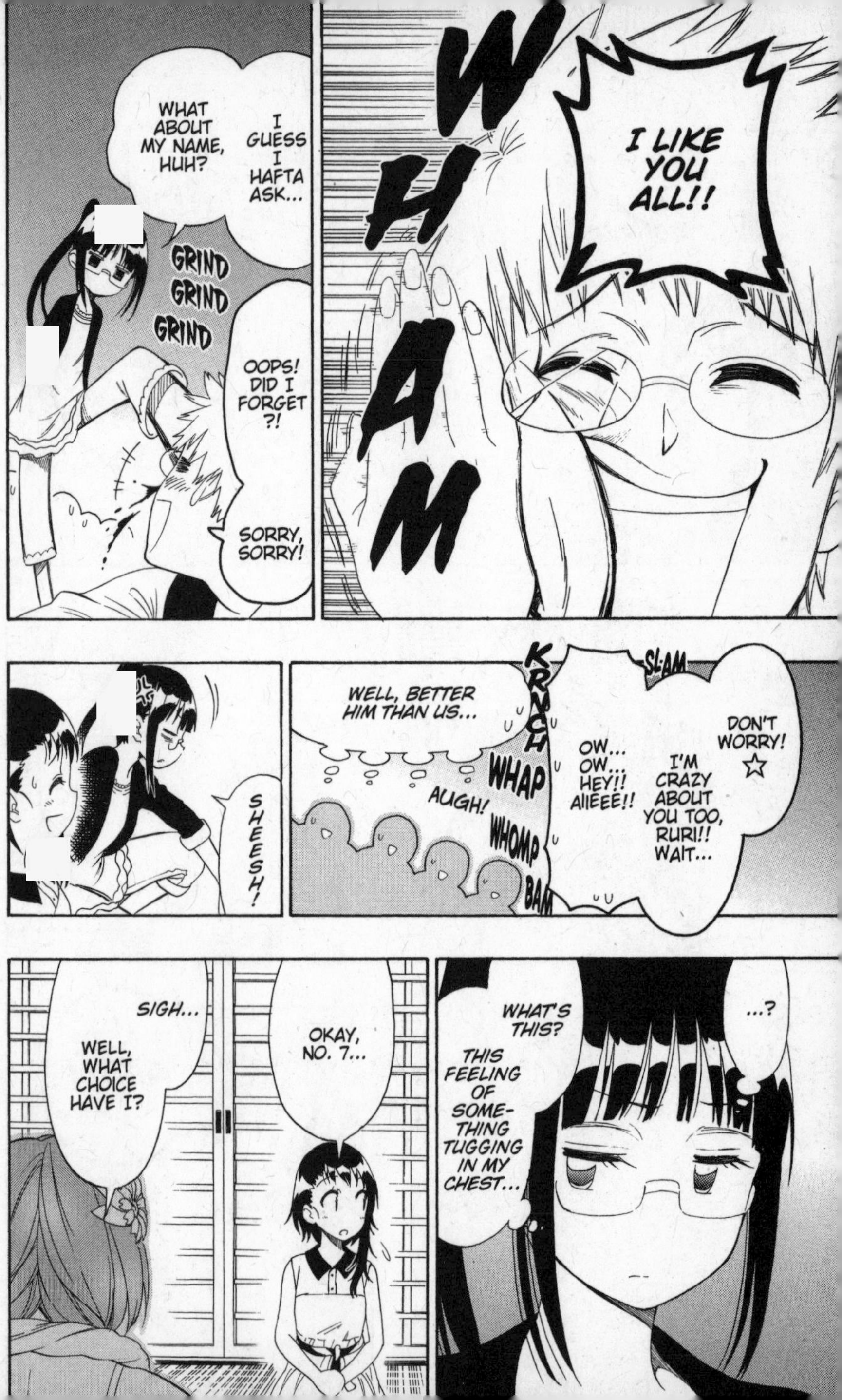
I LIKE YOU ALL!!
WHAM
I GUESS I HAFTA ASK...
WHAT ABOUT MY NAME, HUH?
GRIND GRIND GRIND
OOPS! DID I FORGET?!
SORRY, SORRY!
DON'T WORRY! ☆
I'M CRAZY ABOUT YOU TOO, RURI!! WAIT...
SLAM
OW... OW... HEY!! AIIEEE!!
KRNCH
WELL, BETTER HIM THAN US...
WHAP
AUGH!
WHOMP
BAM
SHEESH!
...?
WHAT'S THIS?
THIS FEELING OF SOMETHING TUGGING IN MY CHEST...
OKAY, NO. 7...
SIGH...
WELL, WHAT CHOICE HAVE I?

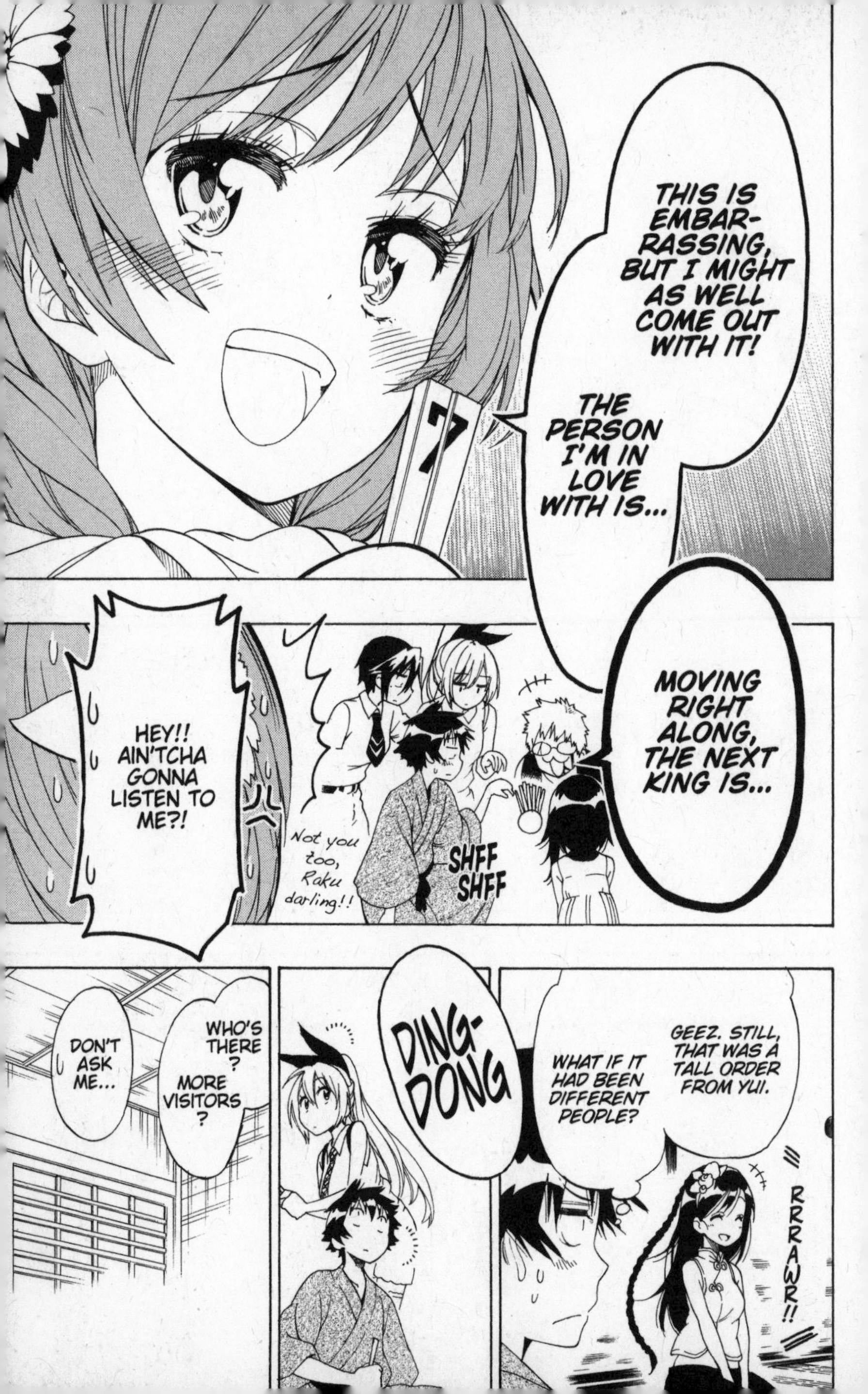
THIS IS EMBARRASSING, BUT I MIGHT AS WELL COME OUT WITH IT!
THE PERSON I'M IN LOVE WITH IS...
MOVING RIGHT ALONG, THE NEXT KING IS...
SHFF SHFF
Not you too, Raku darling!!
HEY!! AIN'TCHA GONNA LISTEN TO ME?!
GEEZ. STILL, THAT WAS A TALL ORDER FROM YUI.
WHAT IF IT HAD BEEN DIFFERENT PEOPLE?
RRRAWR!!
DING-DONG
WHO'S THERE?
MORE VISITORS?
DON'T ASK ME...

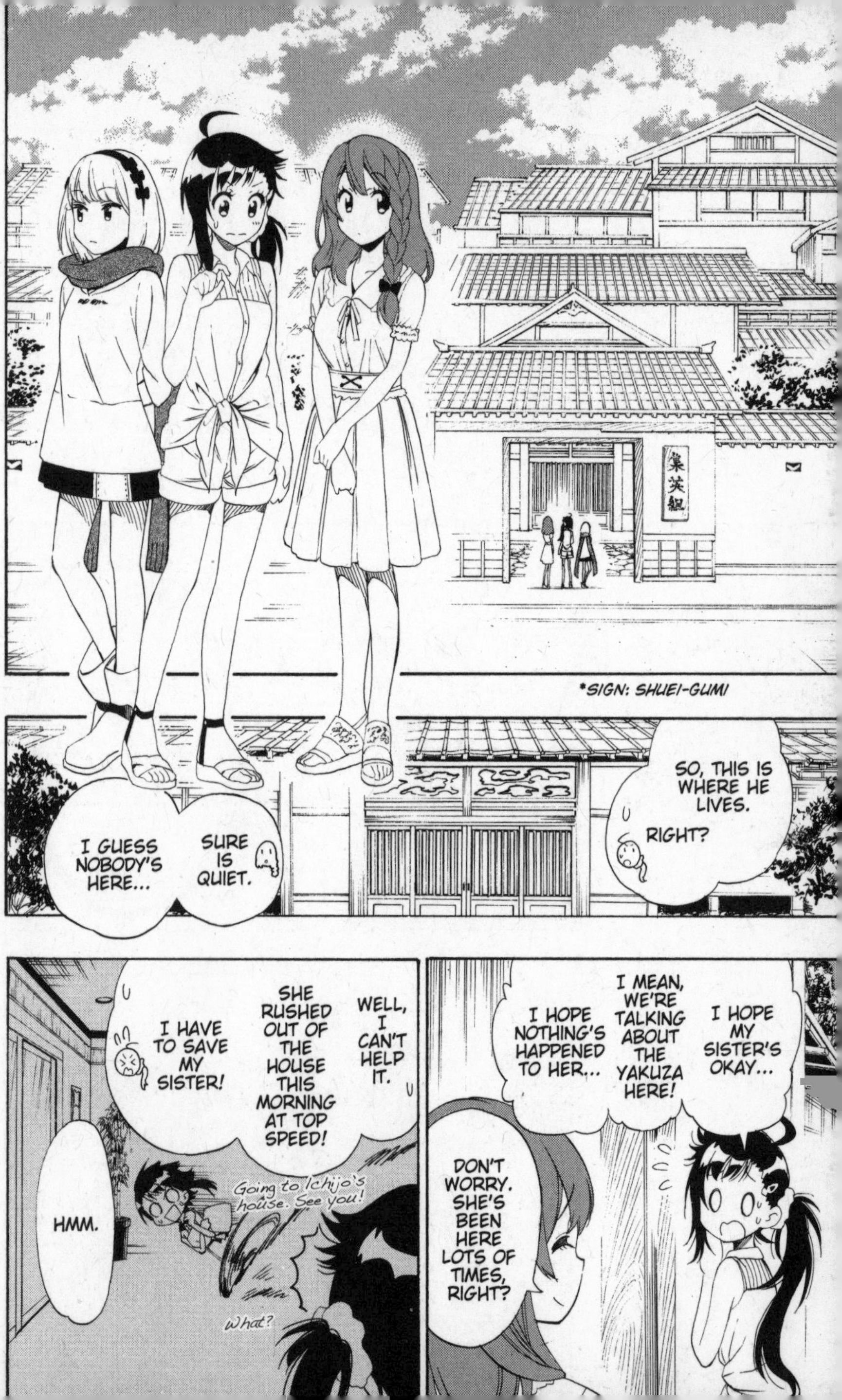
集英組
*SIGN: SHUEI-GUMI
SO, THIS IS WHERE HE LIVES.
RIGHT?
SURE IS QUIET.
I GUESS NOBODY'S HERE...
I HOPE MY SISTER'S OKAY...
I MEAN, WE'RE TALKING ABOUT THE YAKUZA HERE!
I HOPE NOTHING'S HAPPENED TO HER...
DON'T WORRY. SHE'S BEEN HERE LOTS OF TIMES, RIGHT?
WELL, I CAN'T HELP IT.
SHE RUSHED OUT OF THE HOUSE THIS MORNING AT TOP SPEED!
I HAVE TO SAVE MY SISTER!
Going to Ichijo's house. See you!
What?
HMM.

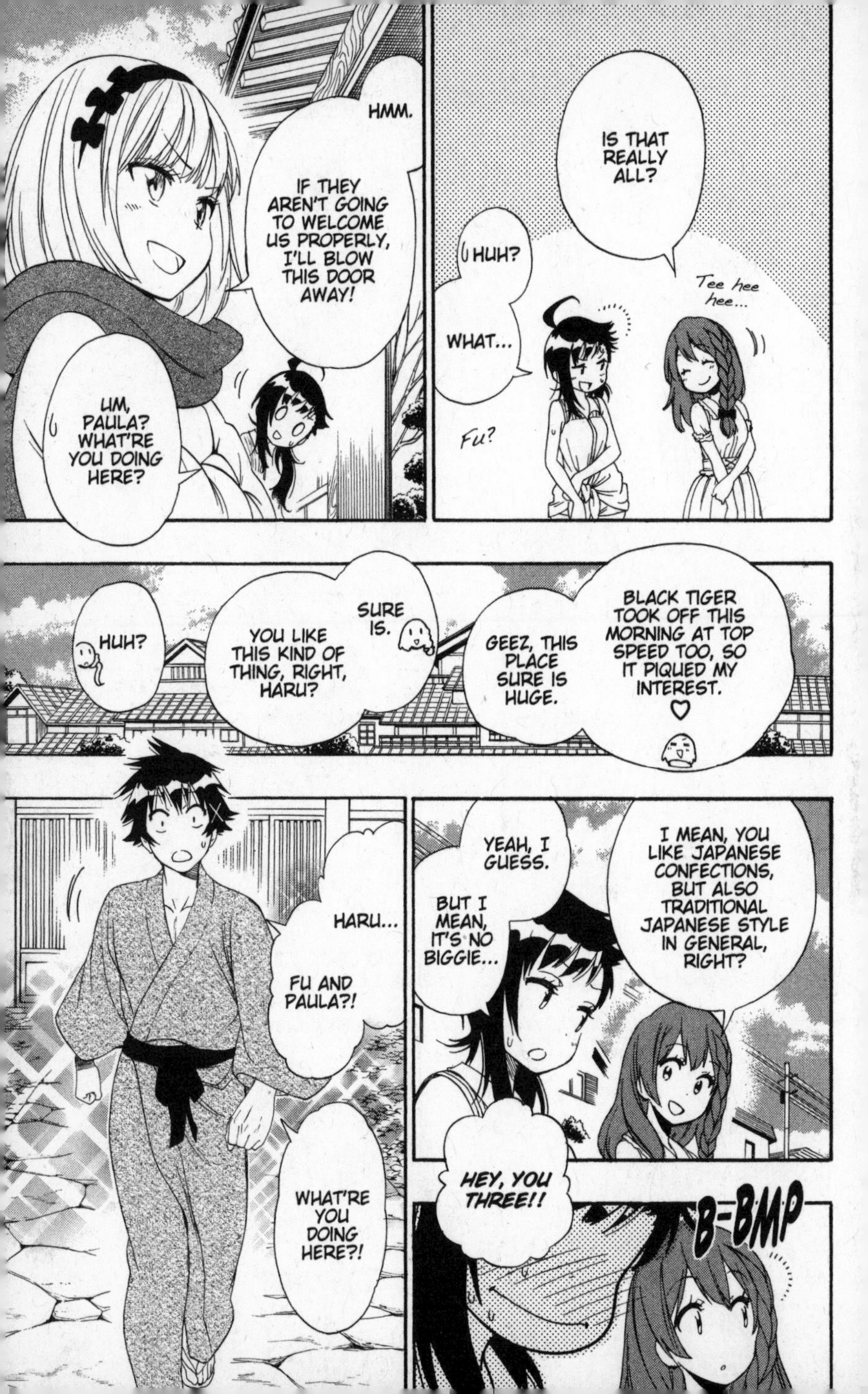
IS THAT REALLY ALL?
Tee hee hee...
HUH?
WHAT...
Fu?
HMM.
IF THEY AREN'T GOING TO WELCOME US PROPERLY, I'LL BLOW THIS DOOR AWAY!
UM, PAULA? WHAT'RE YOU DOING HERE?
BLACK TIGER TOOK OFF THIS MORNING AT TOP SPEED TOO, SO IT PIQUED MY INTEREST. ♡
GEEZ, THIS PLACE SURE IS HUGE.
SURE IS.
YOU LIKE THIS KIND OF THING, RIGHT, HARU?
HUH?
I MEAN, YOU LIKE JAPANESE CONFECTIONS, BUT ALSO TRADITIONAL JAPANESE STYLE IN GENERAL, RIGHT?
YEAH, I GUESS.
BUT I MEAN, IT'S NO BIGGIE...
HEY, YOU THREE!!
B-BMP
HARU...
FU AND PAULA?!
WHAT'RE YOU DOING HERE?!

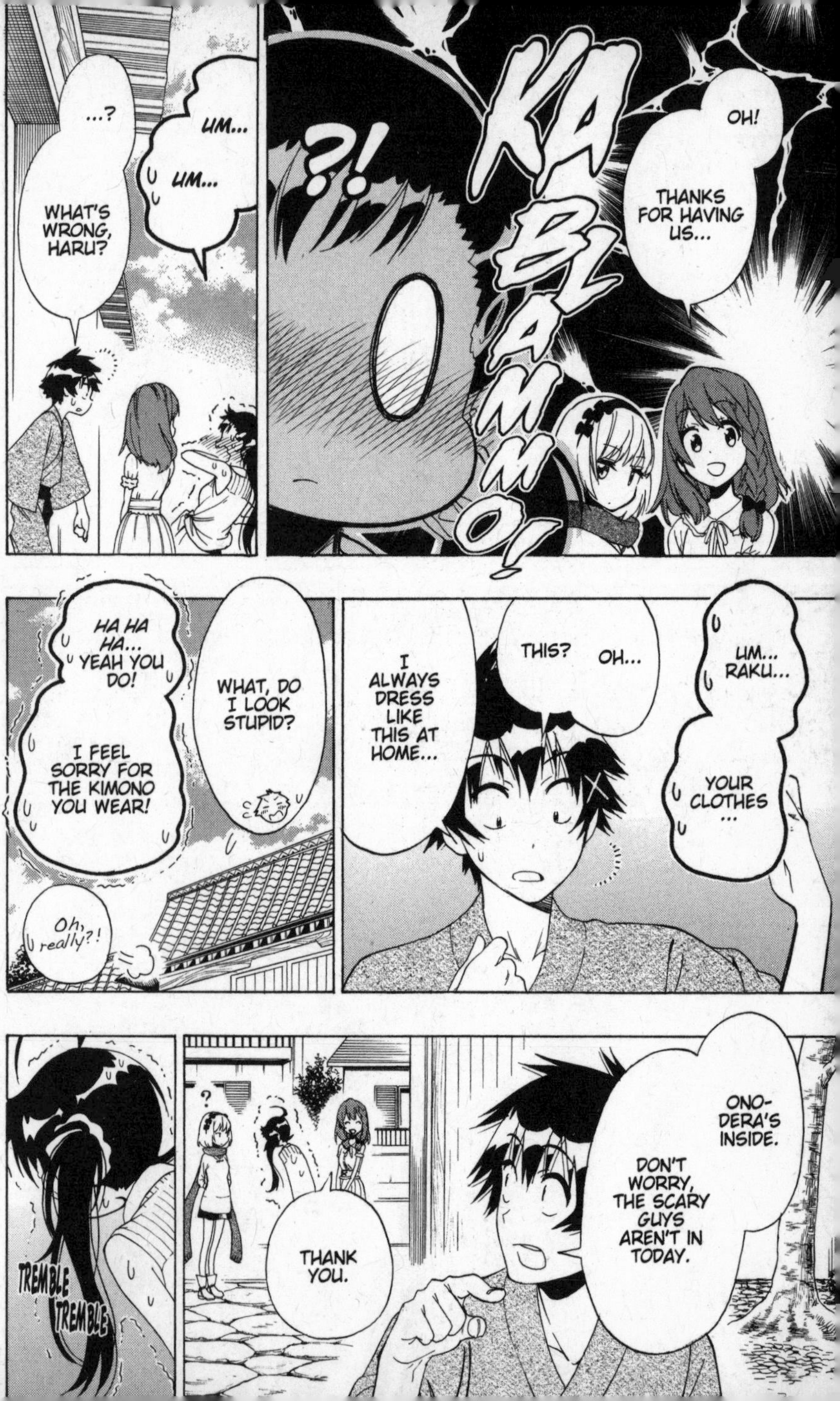
OH!
THANKS FOR HAVING US...
KA BLAMMO!
?!
UM... UM...
...?
WHAT'S WRONG, HARU?
UM... RAKU...
YOUR CLOTHES ...
THIS? OH...
I ALWAYS DRESS LIKE THIS AT HOME...
WHAT, DO I LOOK STUPID?
HA HA HA... YEAH YOU DO!
I FEEL SORRY FOR THE KIMONO YOU WEAR!
Oh, really?!
ONO-DERA'S INSIDE.
DON'T WORRY, THE SCARY GUYS AREN'T IN TODAY.
THANK YOU.
?
TREMBLE TREMBLE

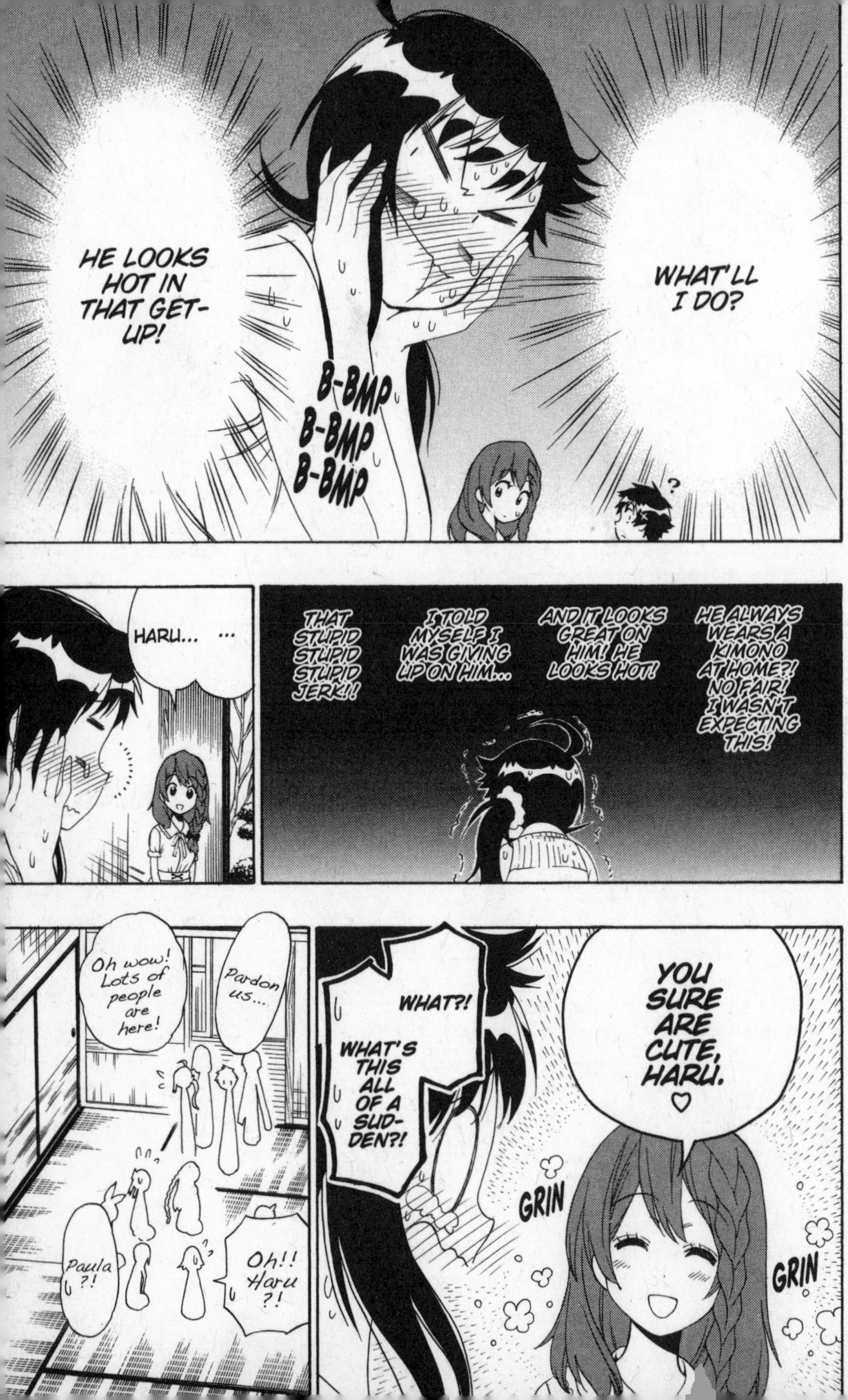
WHAT'LL I DO?
HE LOOKS HOT IN THAT GET-UP!
B-BMP B-BMP B-BMP
?
HE ALWAYS WEARS A KIMONO AT HOME?! NO FAIR! I WASN'T EXPECTING THIS!
AND IT LOOKS GREAT ON HIM! HE LOOKS HOT!
I TOLD MYSELF I WAS GIVING UP ON HIM...
THAT STUPID STUPID STUPID JERK!!
HARU... ...
YOU SURE ARE CUTE, HARU. ♡
GRIN
GRIN
WHAT?!
WHAT'S THIS ALL OF A SUD-DEN?!
Pardon us...
Oh wow! Lots of people are here!
Oh!! Haru?!
Paula?!

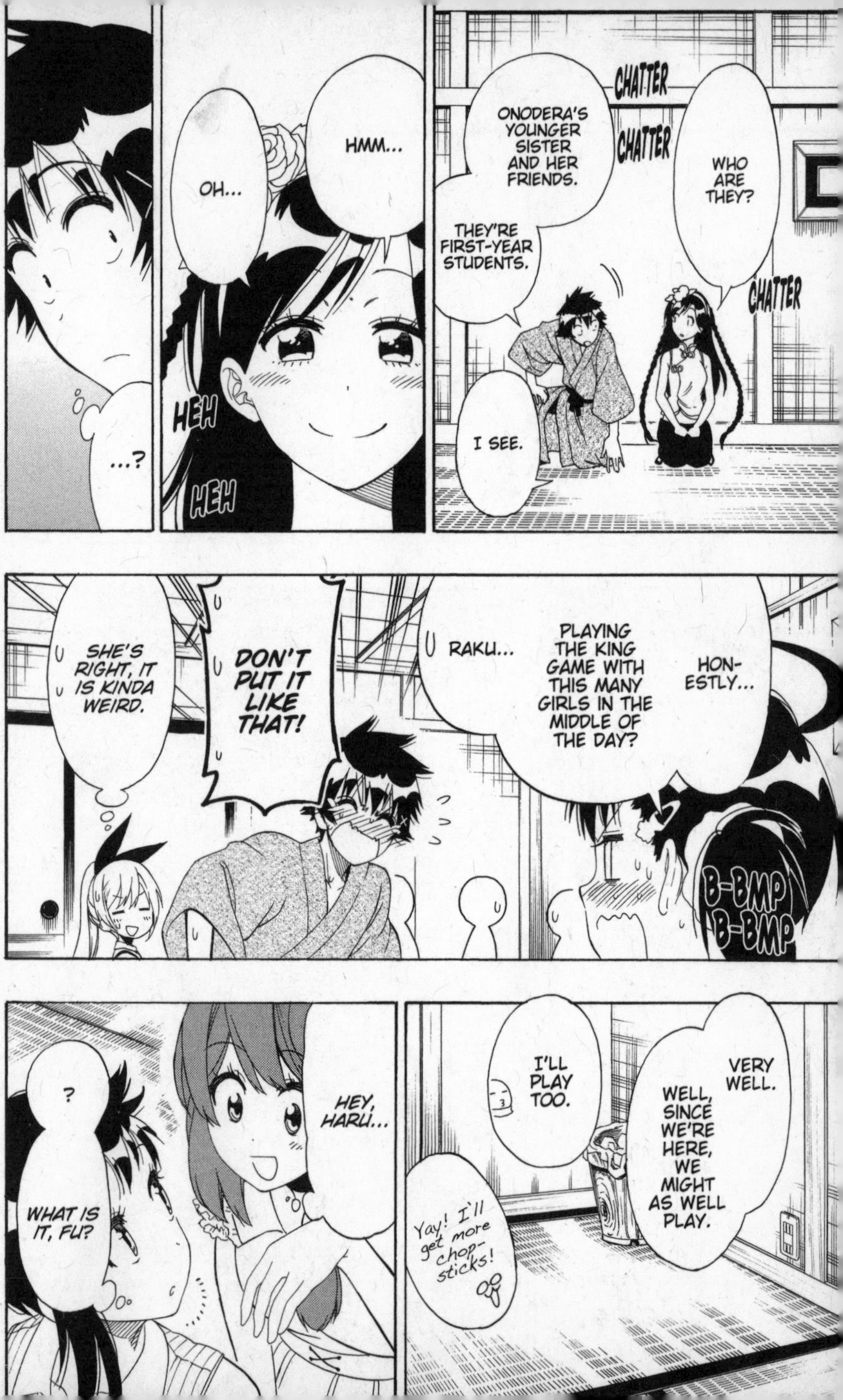
CHATTER
CHATTER
WHO ARE THEY?
ONODERA'S YOUNGER SISTER AND HER FRIENDS.
CHATTER
THEY'RE FIRST-YEAR STUDENTS.
I SEE.
HMM...
OH...
HEH
HEH
...?
HON-ESTLY...
PLAYING THE KING GAME WITH THIS MANY GIRLS IN THE MIDDLE OF THE DAY?
RAKU...
B-BMP
B-BMP
DON'T PUT IT LIKE THAT!
SHE'S RIGHT, IT IS KINDA WEIRD.
VERY WELL.
WELL, SINCE WE'RE HERE, WE MIGHT AS WELL PLAY.
I'LL PLAY TOO.
Yay! I'll get more chop-sticks!
HEY, HARU...
?
WHAT IS IT, FU?

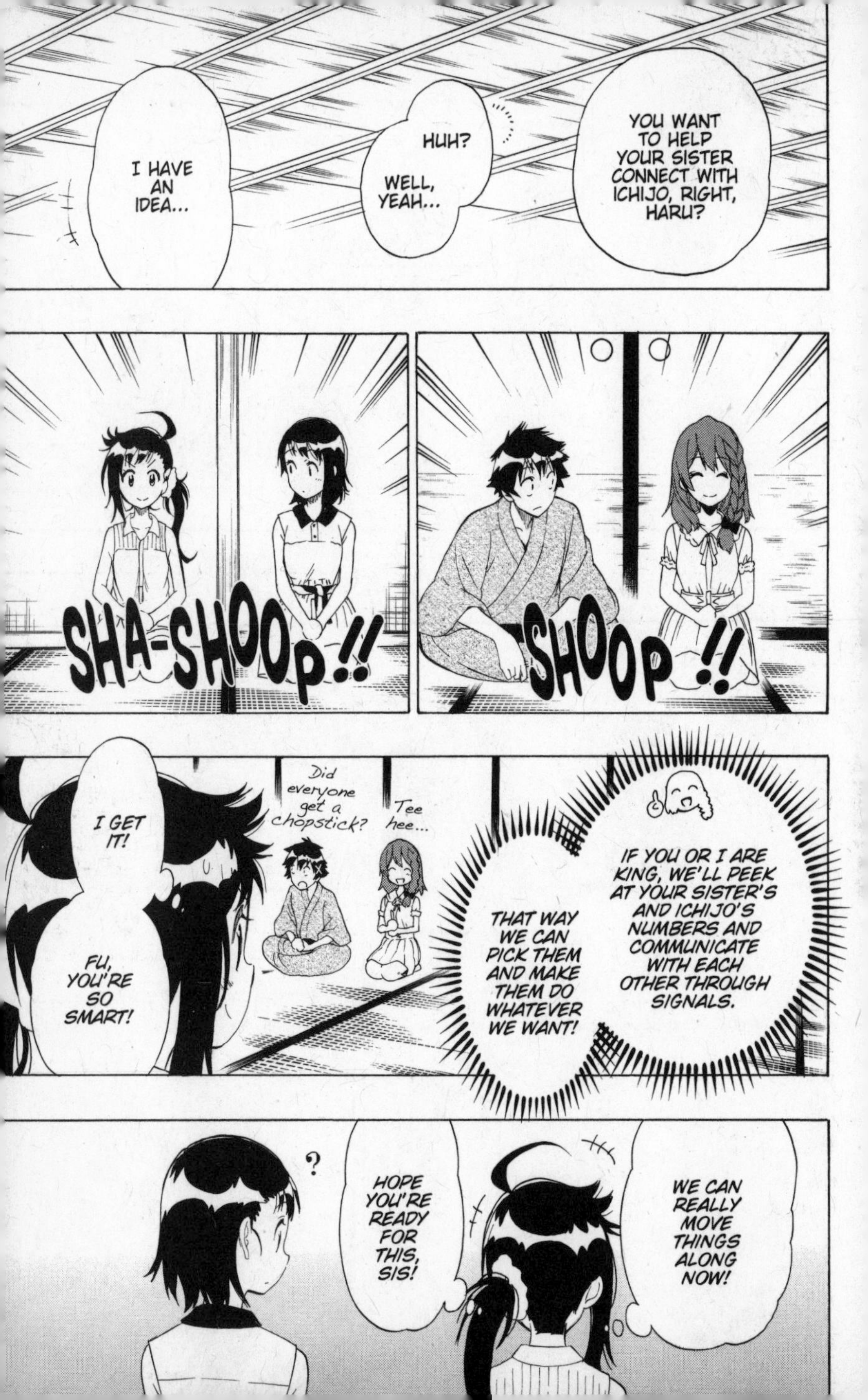
YOU WANT TO HELP YOUR SISTER CONNECT WITH ICHIJO, RIGHT, HARU?
HUH?
WELL, YEAH...
I HAVE AN IDEA...
SHOOP!!
SHA-SHOOP!!
IF YOU OR I ARE KING, WE'LL PEEK AT YOUR SISTER'S AND ICHIJO'S NUMBERS AND COMMUNICATE WITH EACH OTHER THROUGH SIGNALS.
THAT WAY WE CAN PICK THEM AND MAKE THEM DO WHATEVER WE WANT!
Tee hee...
Did everyone get a chopstick?
I GET IT!
FU, YOU'RE SO SMART!
WE CAN REALLY MOVE THINGS ALONG NOW!
HOPE YOU'RE READY FOR THIS, SIS!
?

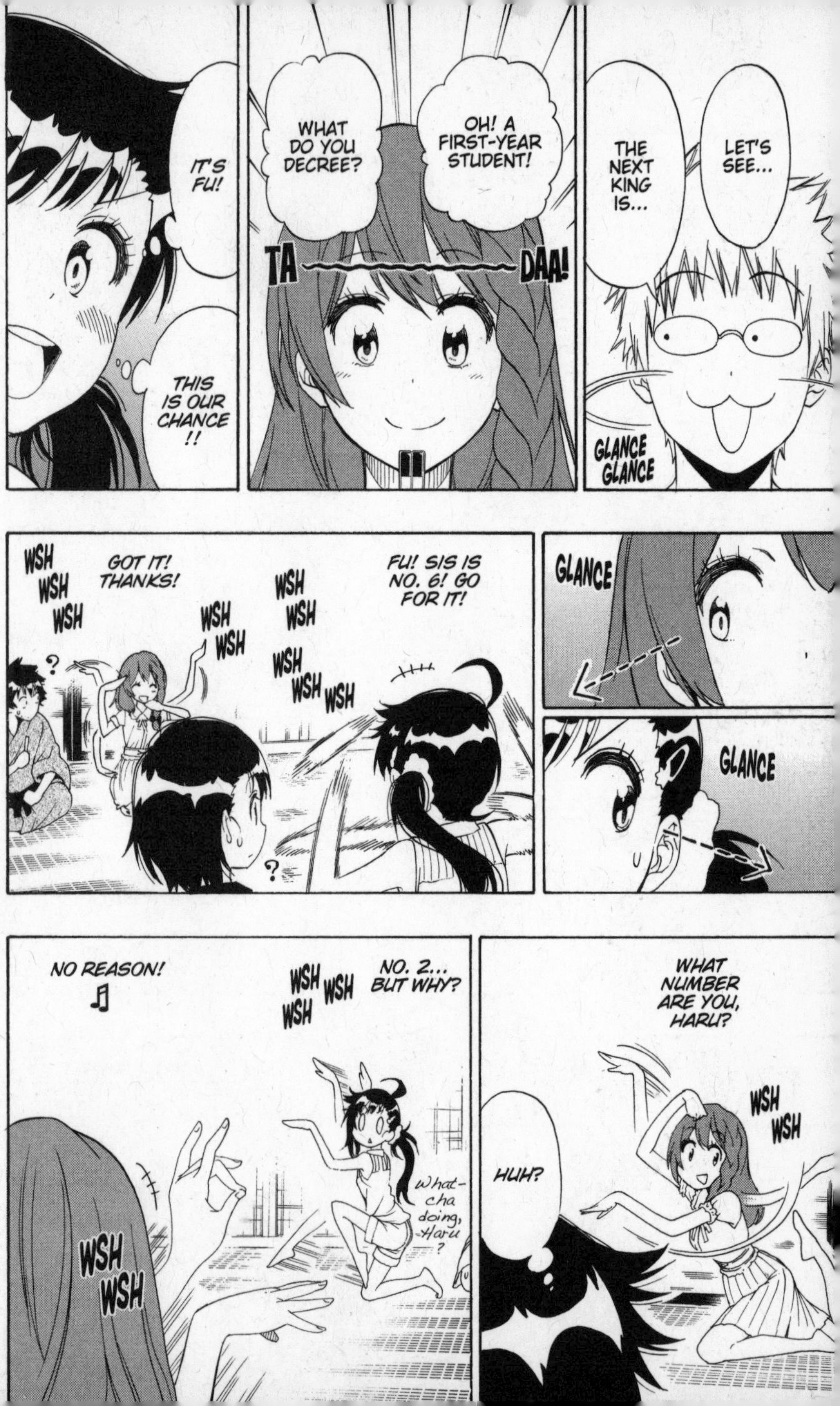
LET'S SEE...
THE NEXT KING IS...
GLANCE GLANCE
OH! A FIRST-YEAR STUDENT!
WHAT DO YOU DECREE?
TA—DAA!
IT'S FU!
THIS IS OUR CHANCE!!
GLANCE
GLANCE
FU! SIS IS NO. 6! GO FOR IT!
WSH WSH
WSH WSH WSH
WSH WSH
GOT IT! THANKS!
WSH WSH WSH
WHAT NUMBER ARE YOU, HARU?
WSH WSH
HUH?
NO. 2... BUT WHY?
WSH WSH WSH
What-cha doing, Haru?
NO REASON! ♫
WSH WSH

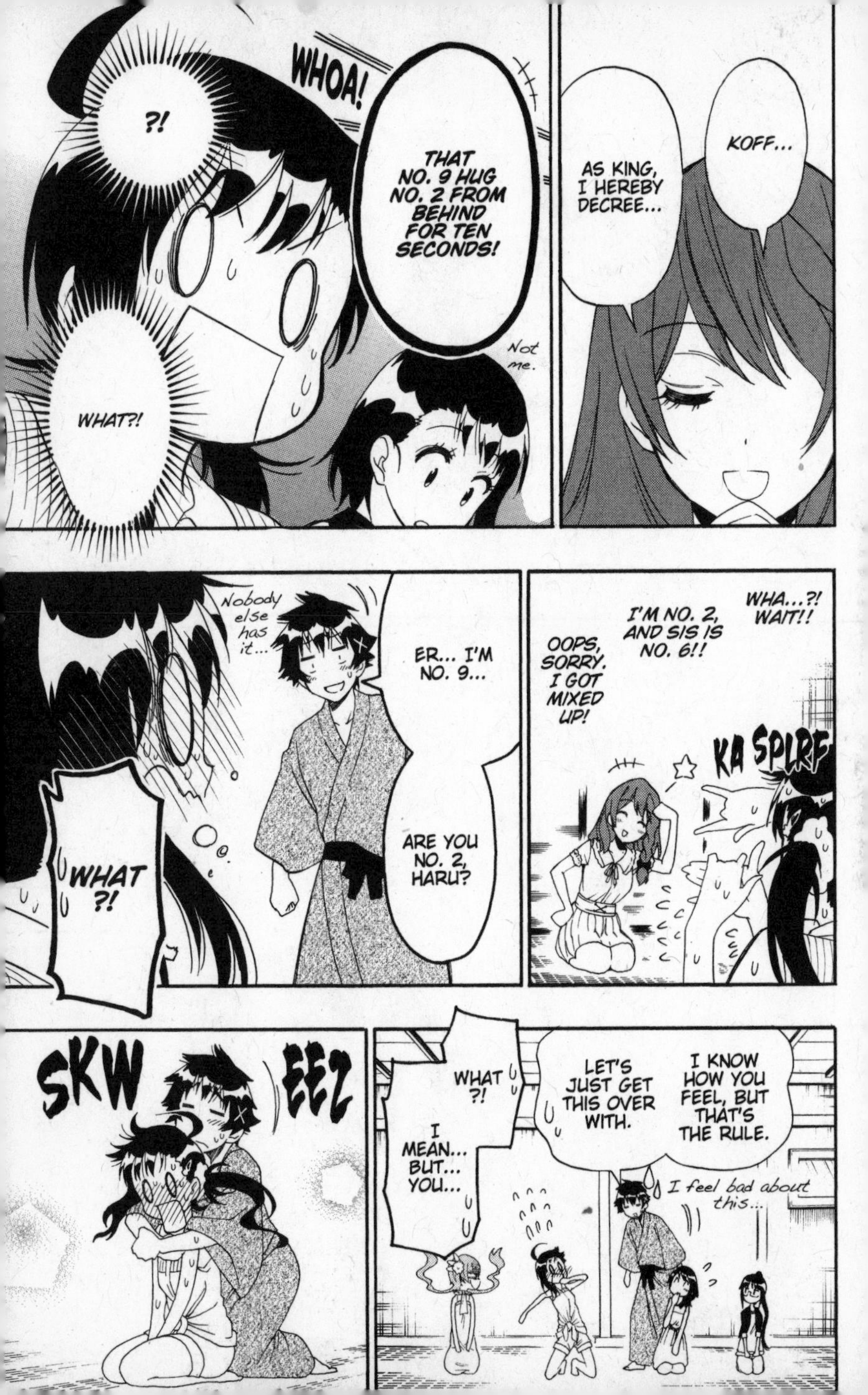
KOFF...
AS KING, I HEREBY DECREE...
THAT NO. 9 HUG NO. 2 FROM BEHIND FOR TEN SECONDS!
WHOA!
Not me.
?!
WHAT?!
WHA...?! WAIT!!
I'M NO. 2, AND SIS IS NO. 6!!
OOPS, SORRY. I GOT MIXED UP!
KA SPLRF
ER... I'M NO. 9...
ARE YOU NO. 2, HARU?
Nobody else has it...
WHAT?!
I KNOW HOW YOU FEEL, BUT THAT'S THE RULE.
LET'S JUST GET THIS OVER WITH.
I feel bad about this...
WHAT?!
I MEAN... BUT... YOU...
SKW EEZ

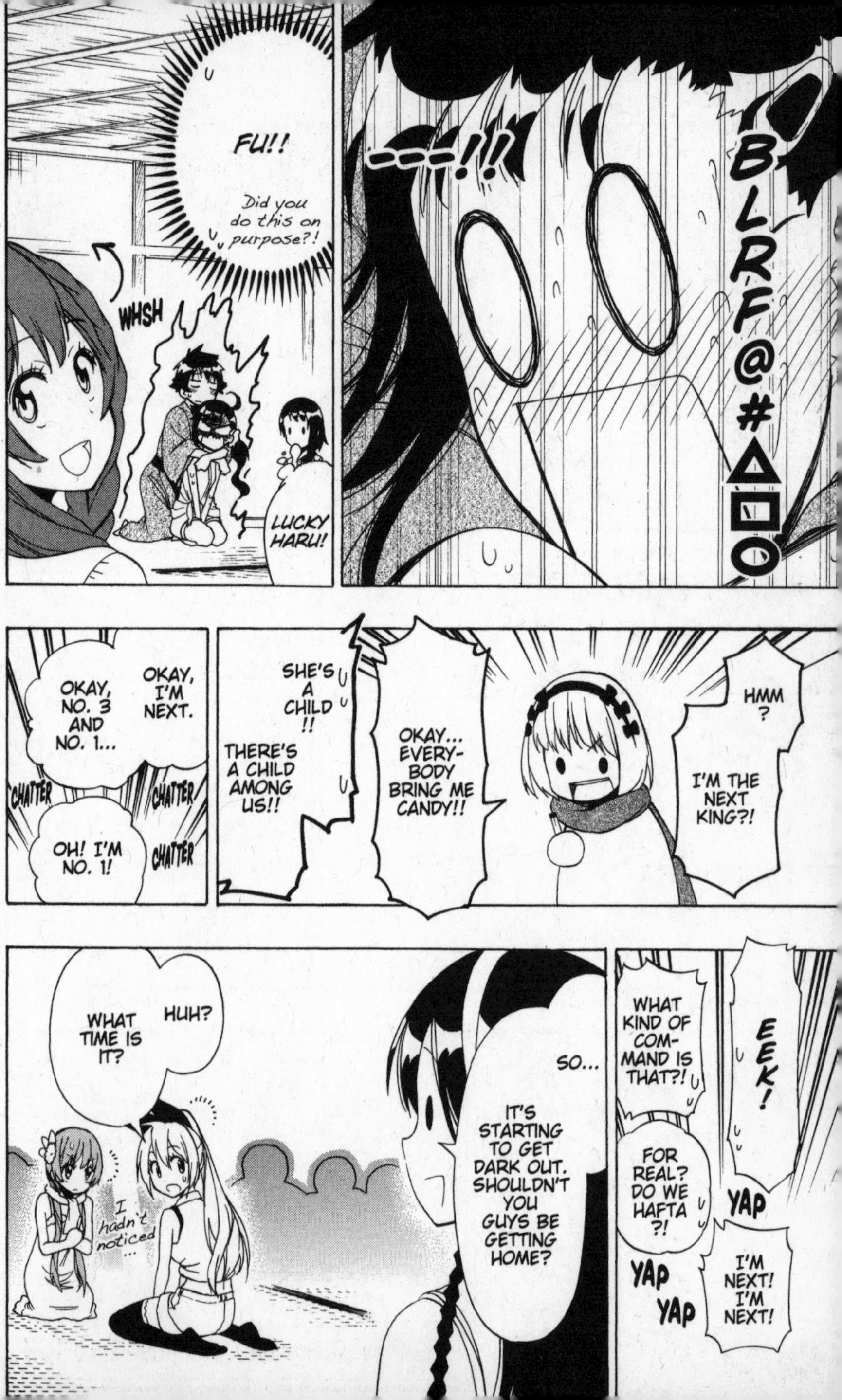
BLRF@#△□○
----!!!
FU!!
Did you do this on purpose?!
WHSH
LUCKY HARU!
HMM?
I'M THE NEXT KING?!
OKAY... EVERYBODY BRING ME CANDY!!
SHE'S A CHILD!!
THERE'S A CHILD AMONG US!!
OKAY, I'M NEXT.
OKAY, NO. 3 AND NO. 1...
CHATTER
CHATTER
CHATTER
OH! I'M NO. 1!
EEK!
WHAT KIND OF COMMAND IS THAT?!
FOR REAL? DO WE HAFTA?!
YAP
I'M NEXT! I'M NEXT!
YAP
YAP
SO...
IT'S STARTING TO GET DARK OUT. SHOULDN'T YOU GUYS BE GETTING HOME?
HUH?
WHAT TIME IS IT?
I hadn't noticed...

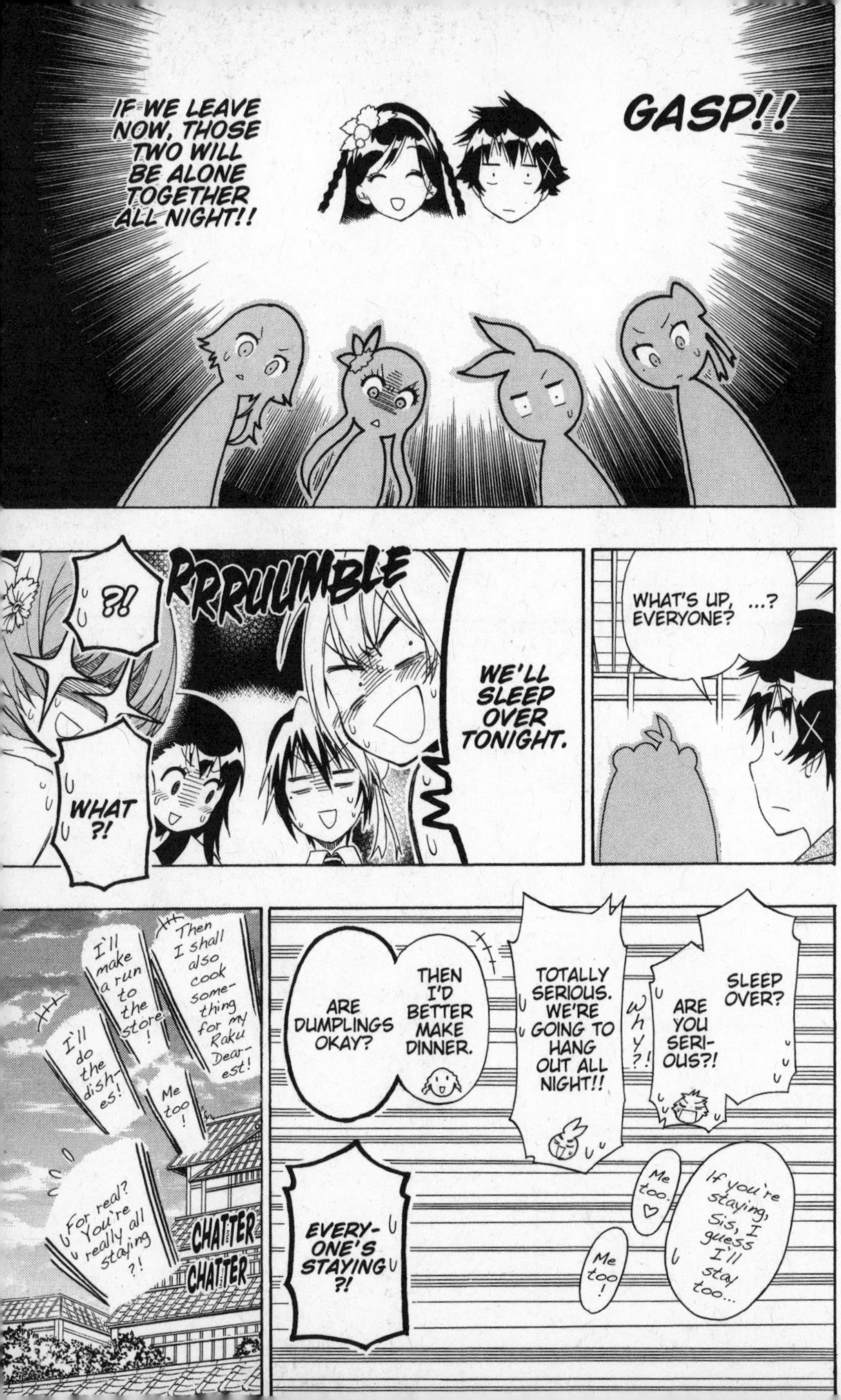
GASP!!
IF WE LEAVE NOW, THOSE TWO WILL BE ALONE TOGETHER ALL NIGHT!!
WHAT'S UP, EVERYONE?
...?
WE'LL SLEEP OVER TONIGHT.
RRRUUMBLE
?!
WHAT?!
SLEEP OVER?
ARE YOU SERI-OUS?!
why?!
TOTALLY SERIOUS. WE'RE GOING TO HANG OUT ALL NIGHT!!
THEN I'D BETTER MAKE DINNER.
ARE DUMPLINGS OKAY?
If you're staying, Sis, I guess I'll stay too...
Me too. ♥
Me too!
EVERY-ONE'S STAYING?!
Then I shall also cook some-thing for my Raku Dear-est!
I'll make a run to the store!
I'll do the dish-es!
Me too!
For real? You're really all staying?!
CHATTER CHATTER

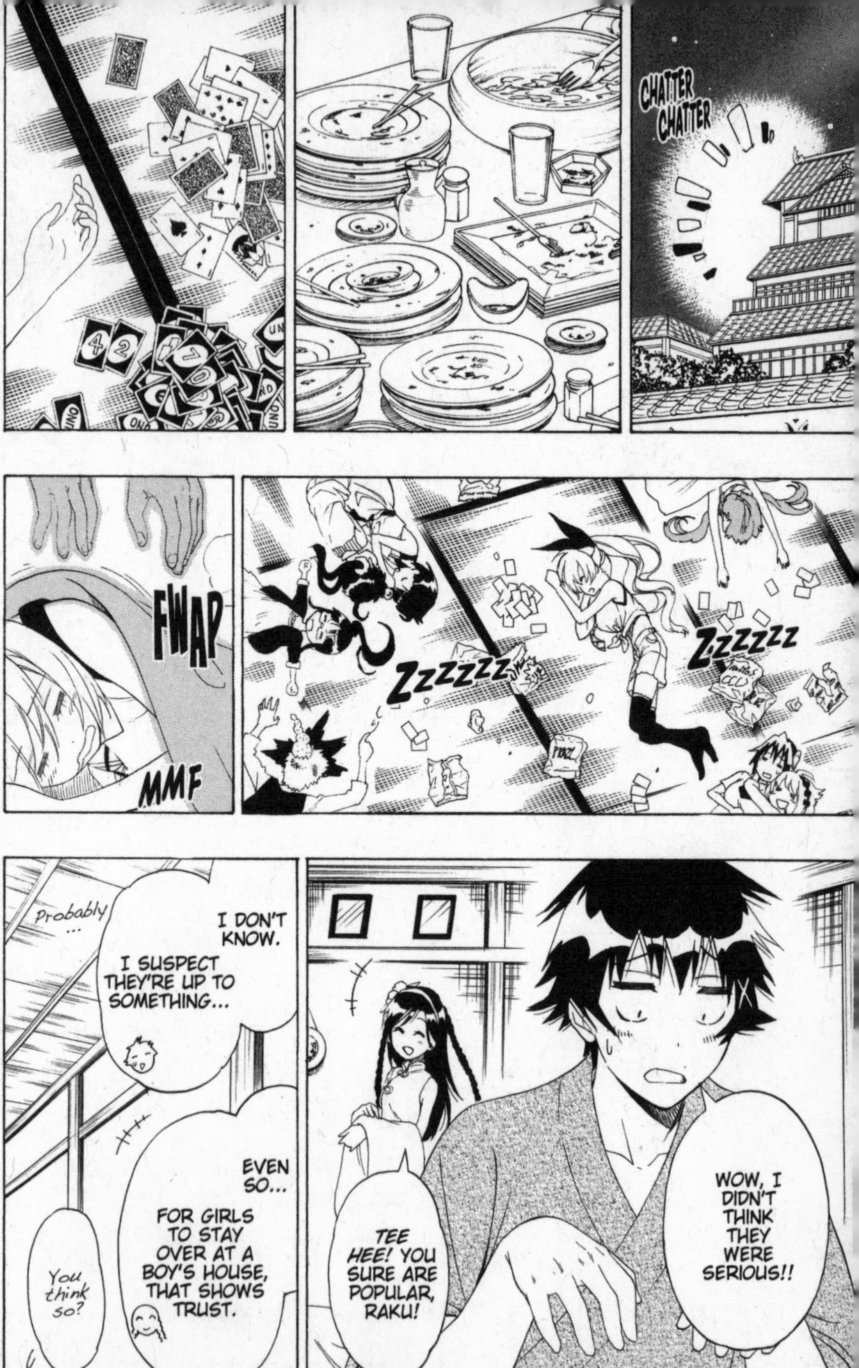
CHATTER CHATTER
ZZZZZZ
ZZZZZZ
FWAP
MMF
WOW, I DIDN'T THINK THEY WERE SERIOUS!!
TEE HEE! YOU SURE ARE POPULAR, RAKU!
I DON'T KNOW.
I SUSPECT THEY'RE UP TO SOMETHING...
Probably...
EVEN SO...
FOR GIRLS TO STAY OVER AT A BOY'S HOUSE, THAT SHOWS TRUST.
You think so?

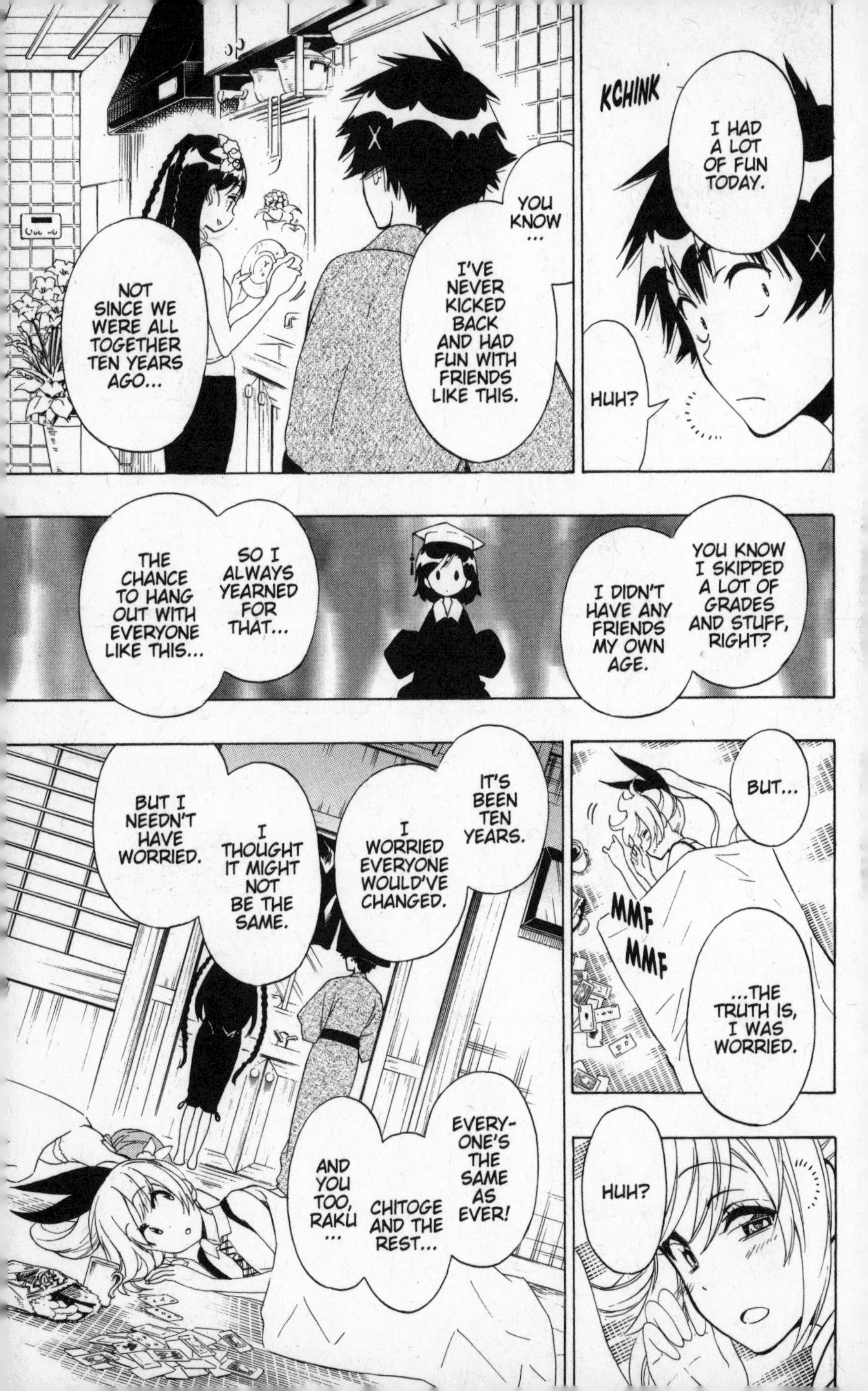
KCHINK
I HAD A LOT OF FUN TODAY.
HUH?
YOU KNOW...
I'VE NEVER KICKED BACK AND HAD FUN WITH FRIENDS LIKE THIS.
NOT SINCE WE WERE ALL TOGETHER TEN YEARS AGO...
YOU KNOW I SKIPPED A LOT OF GRADES AND STUFF, RIGHT?
I DIDN'T HAVE ANY FRIENDS MY OWN AGE.
SO I ALWAYS YEARNED FOR THAT...
THE CHANCE TO HANG OUT WITH EVERYONE LIKE THIS...
BUT...
MMF
MMF
...THE TRUTH IS, I WAS WORRIED.
HUH?
IT'S BEEN TEN YEARS.
I WORRIED EVERYONE WOULD'VE CHANGED.
I THOUGHT IT MIGHT NOT BE THE SAME.
BUT I NEEDN'T HAVE WORRIED.
EVERYONE'S THE SAME AS EVER!
CHITOGE AND THE REST...
AND YOU TOO, RAKU...

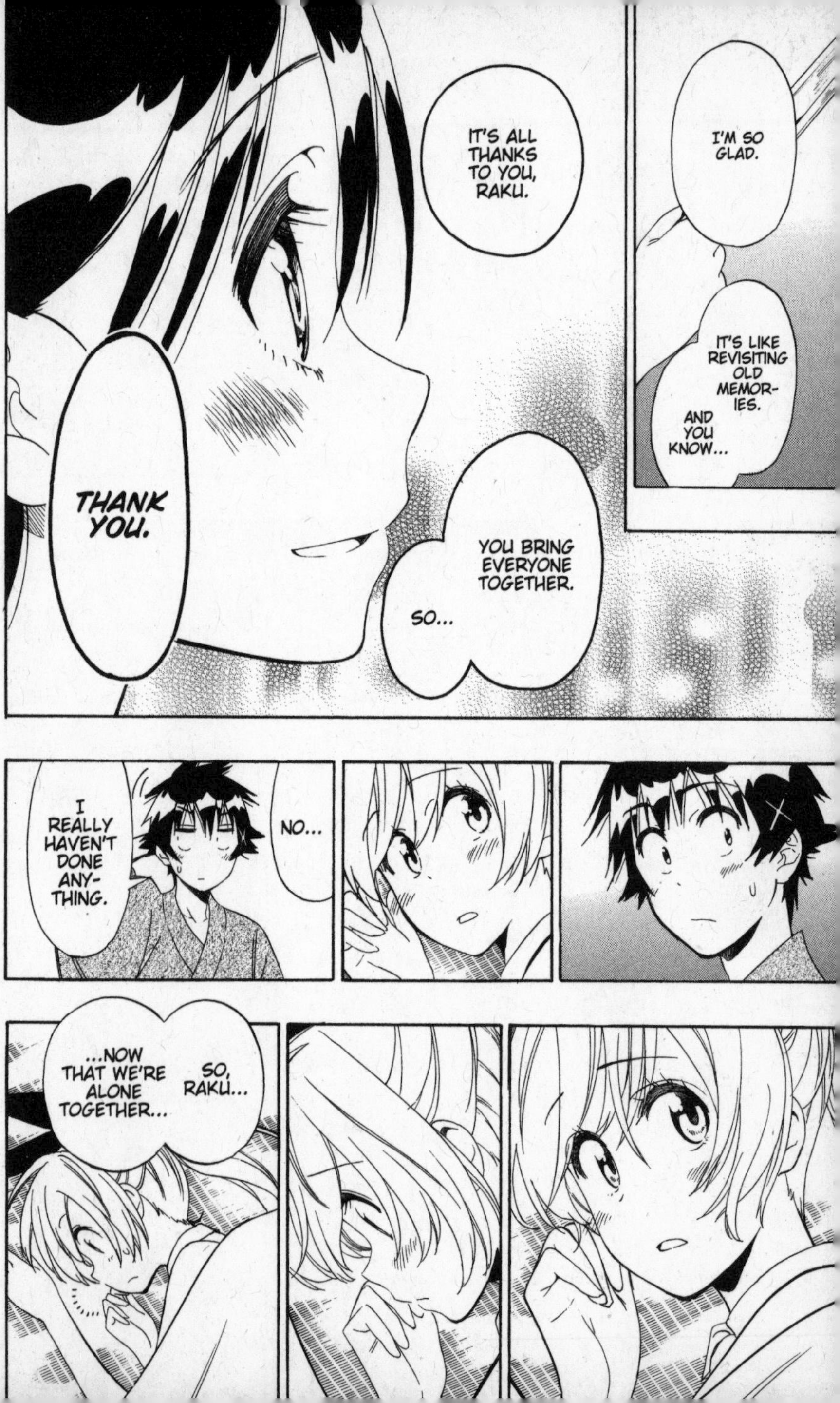
I'M SO GLAD.
IT'S LIKE REVISITING OLD MEMOR-IES.
AND YOU KNOW...
IT'S ALL THANKS TO YOU, RAKU.
YOU BRING EVERYONE TOGETHER.
SO...
THANK YOU.
NO...
I REALLY HAVEN'T DONE ANY-THING.
SO, RAKU...
...NOW THAT WE'RE ALONE TOGETHER...

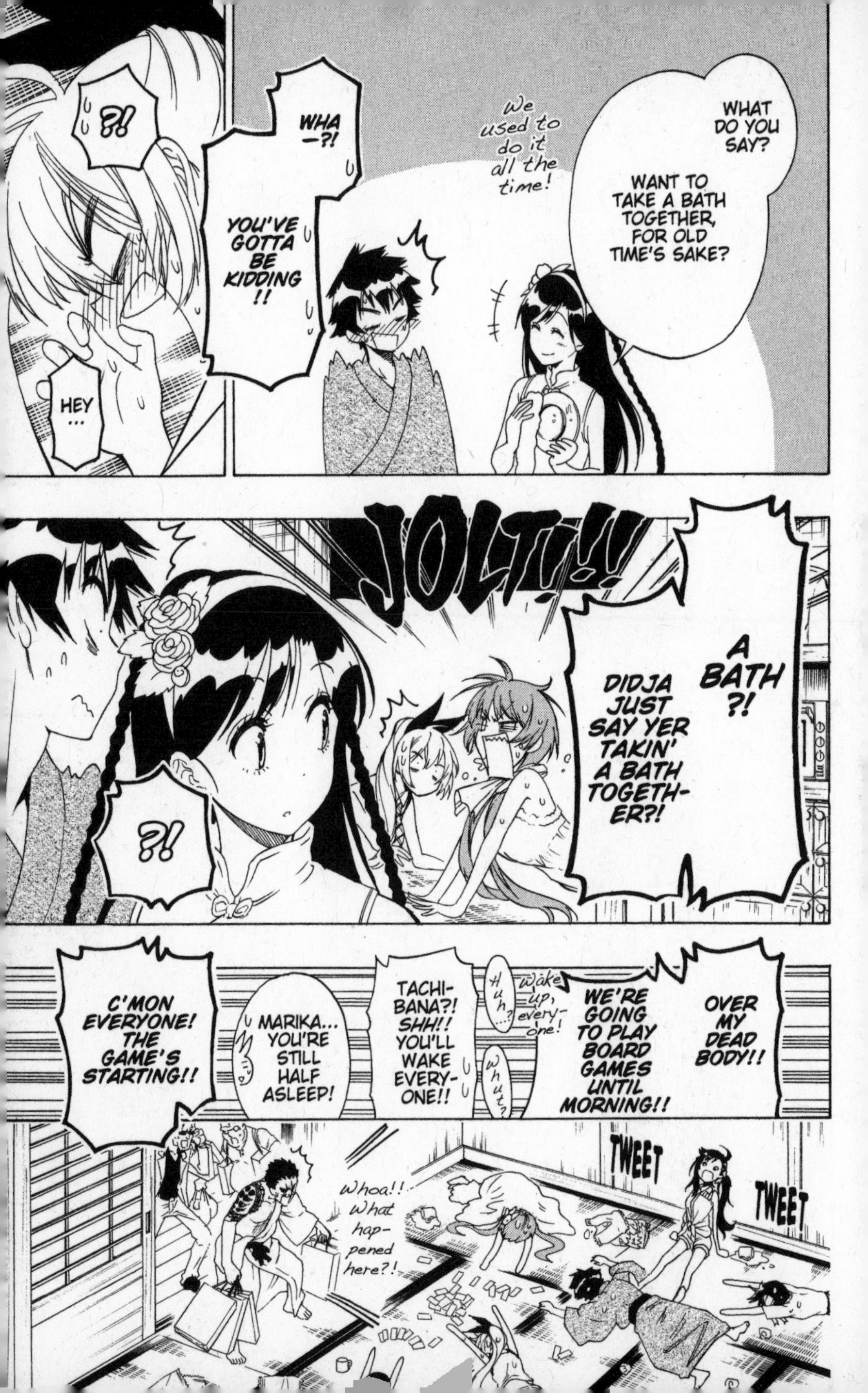
WHAT DO YOU SAY?
WANT TO TAKE A BATH TOGETHER, FOR OLD TIME'S SAKE?
We used to do it all the time!
WHA—?!
YOU'VE GOTTA BE KIDDING!!
?!
HEY...
JOLT!!
A BATH?!
DIDJA JUST SAY YER TAKIN' A BATH TOGETH-ER?!
?!
OVER MY DEAD BODY!!
WE'RE GOING TO PLAY BOARD GAMES UNTIL MORNING!!
Wake up, every-one!
Huh...?
Whut?
TACHI-BANA?! SHH!! YOU'LL WAKE EVERY-ONE!!
MARIKA... YOU'RE STILL HALF ASLEEP!
C'MON EVERYONE! THE GAME'S STARTING!!
TWEET
TWEET
Whoa!! What hap-pened here?!

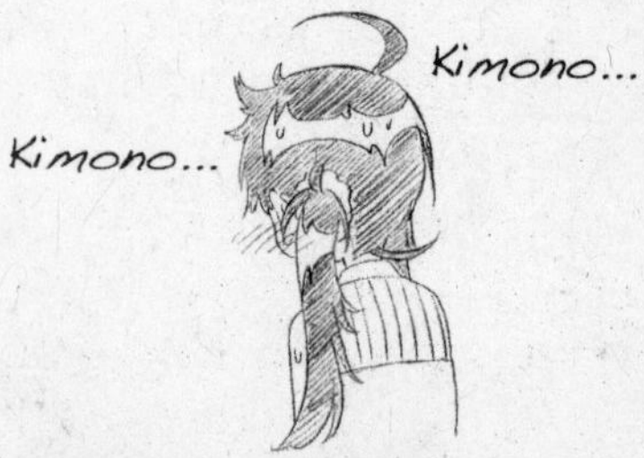
Kimono...
Kimono...

Chapter 129: Cold

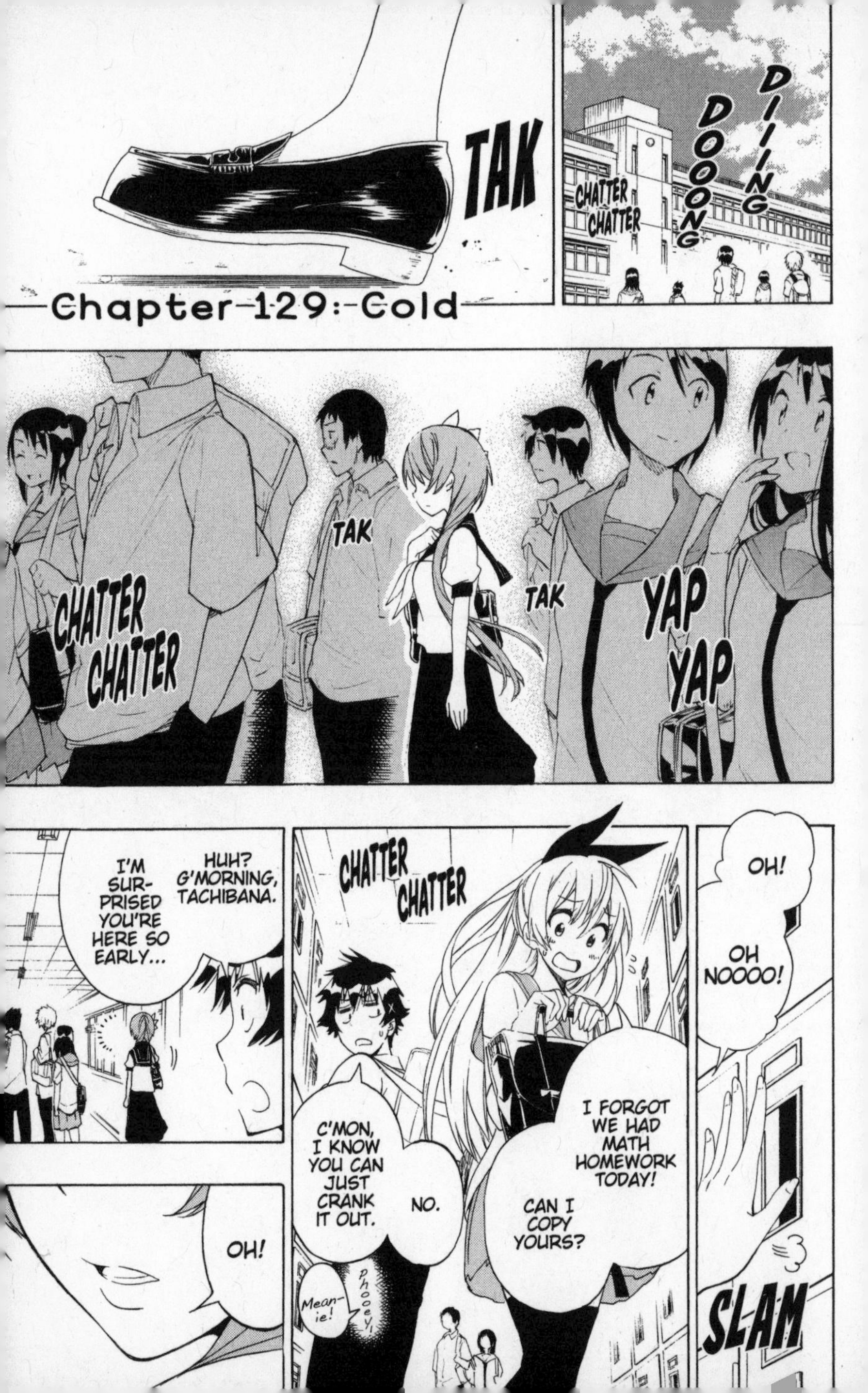
DIIING
DOOONG
CHATTER CHATTER
TAK
YAP YAP
TAK
TAK
CHATTER CHATTER
OH!
OH NOOOO!
SLAM
CHATTER CHATTER
I FORGOT WE HAD MATH HOMEWORK TODAY!
CAN I COPY YOURS?
NO.
C'MON, I KNOW YOU CAN JUST CRANK IT OUT.
Phooey!
Mean-ie!
HUH? G'MORNING, TACHIBANA.
I'M SUR-PRISED YOU'RE HERE SO EARLY...
OH!

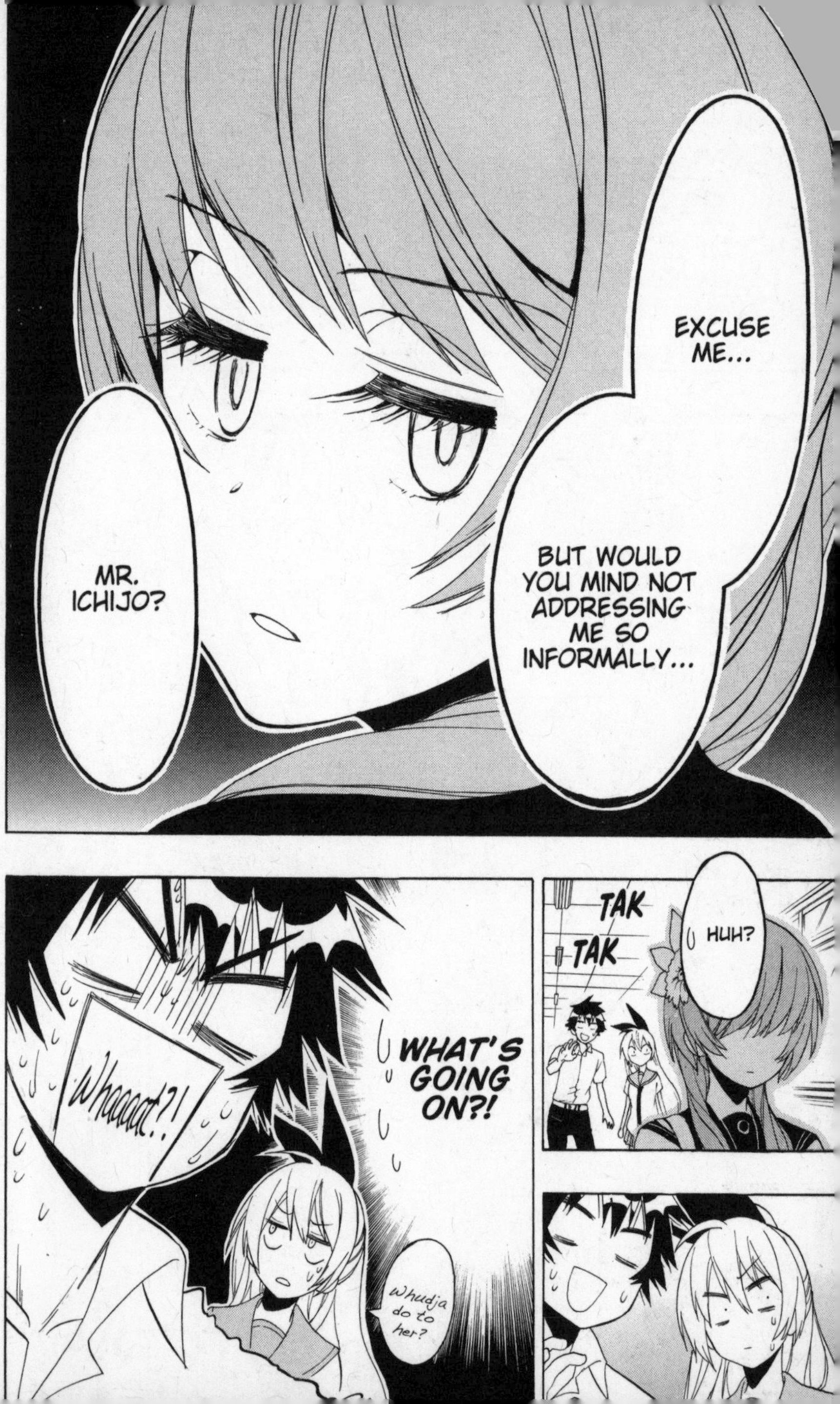
EXCUSE ME...
BUT WOULD YOU MIND NOT ADDRESSING ME SO INFORMALLY...
MR. ICHIJO?
TAK
TAK
HUH?
WHAT'S GOING ON?!
Whaaaat?!
Whudja do to her?

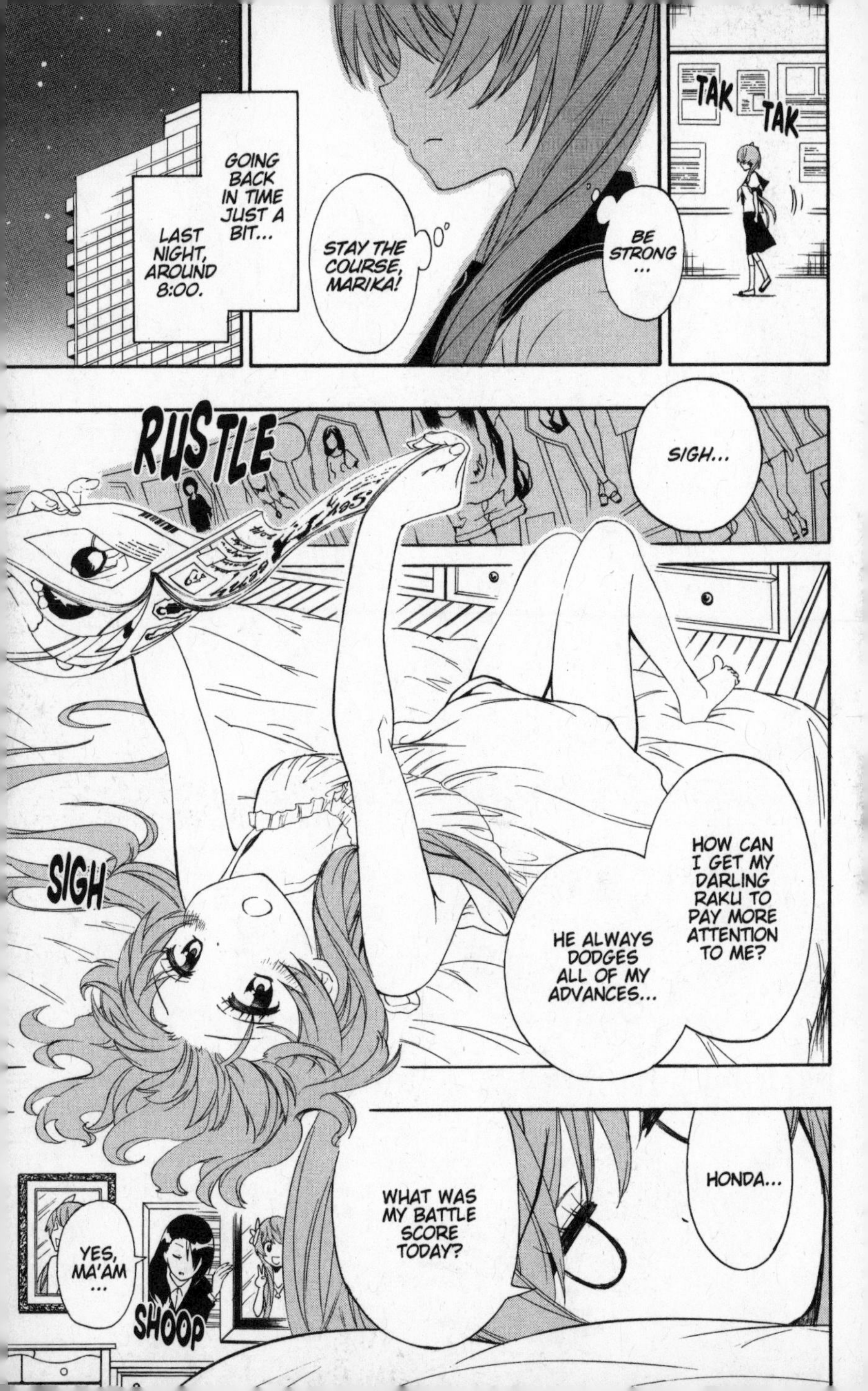
TAK
TAK
BE STRONG ...
STAY THE COURSE, MARIKA!
GOING BACK IN TIME JUST A BIT...
LAST NIGHT, AROUND 8:00.
SIGH...
RUSTLE
HOW CAN I GET MY DARLING RAKU TO PAY MORE ATTENTION TO ME?
HE ALWAYS DODGES ALL OF MY ADVANCES...
SIGH
HONDA...
WHAT WAS MY BATTLE SCORE TODAY?
YES, MA'AM ...
SHOOP

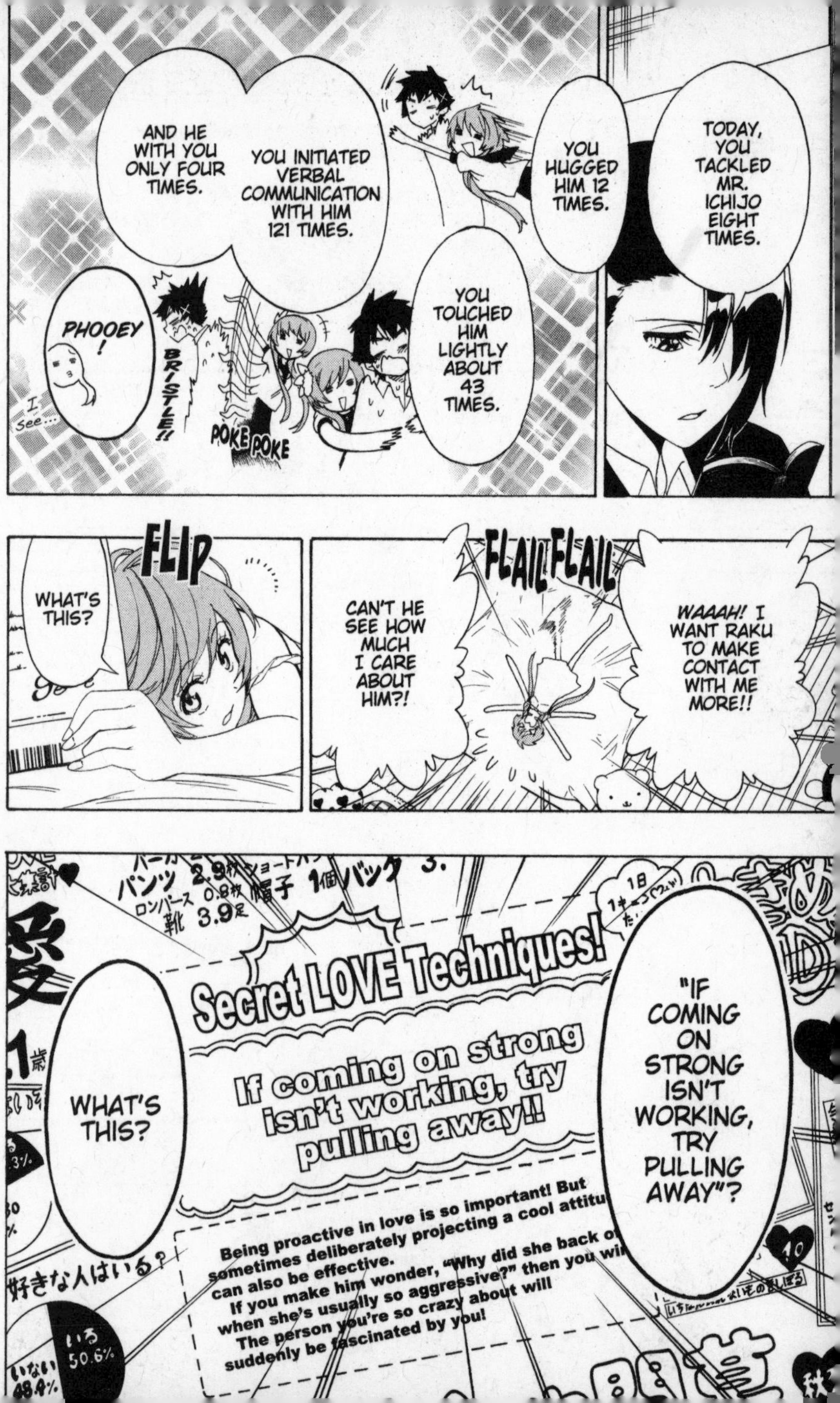
TODAY, YOU TACKLED MR. ICHIJO EIGHT TIMES.
YOU HUGGED HIM 12 TIMES.
YOU INITIATED VERBAL COMMUNICATION WITH HIM 121 TIMES.
AND HE WITH YOU ONLY FOUR TIMES.
YOU TOUCHED HIM LIGHTLY ABOUT 43 TIMES.
PHOOEY!
BRISTLE!!
POKE POKE
I see...
FLAIL FLAIL
WAAAH! I WANT RAKU TO MAKE CONTACT WITH ME MORE!!
CAN'T HE SEE HOW MUCH I CARE ABOUT HIM?!
FLIP
WHAT'S THIS?
"IF COMING ON STRONG ISN'T WORKING, TRY PULLING AWAY"?
パンツ 2.9枚
ロンパース 0.8枚 帽子 1個 バッグ 3.
靴 3.9足
Secret LOVE Techniques!
If coming on strong isn't working, try pulling away!!
Being proactive in love is so important! But sometimes deliberately projecting a cool attitu can also be effective.
If you make him wonder, "Why did she back o when she's usually so aggressive?" then you wi The person you're so crazy about will suddenly be fascinated by you!
好きな人はいる?
いる 50.6%
WHAT'S THIS?

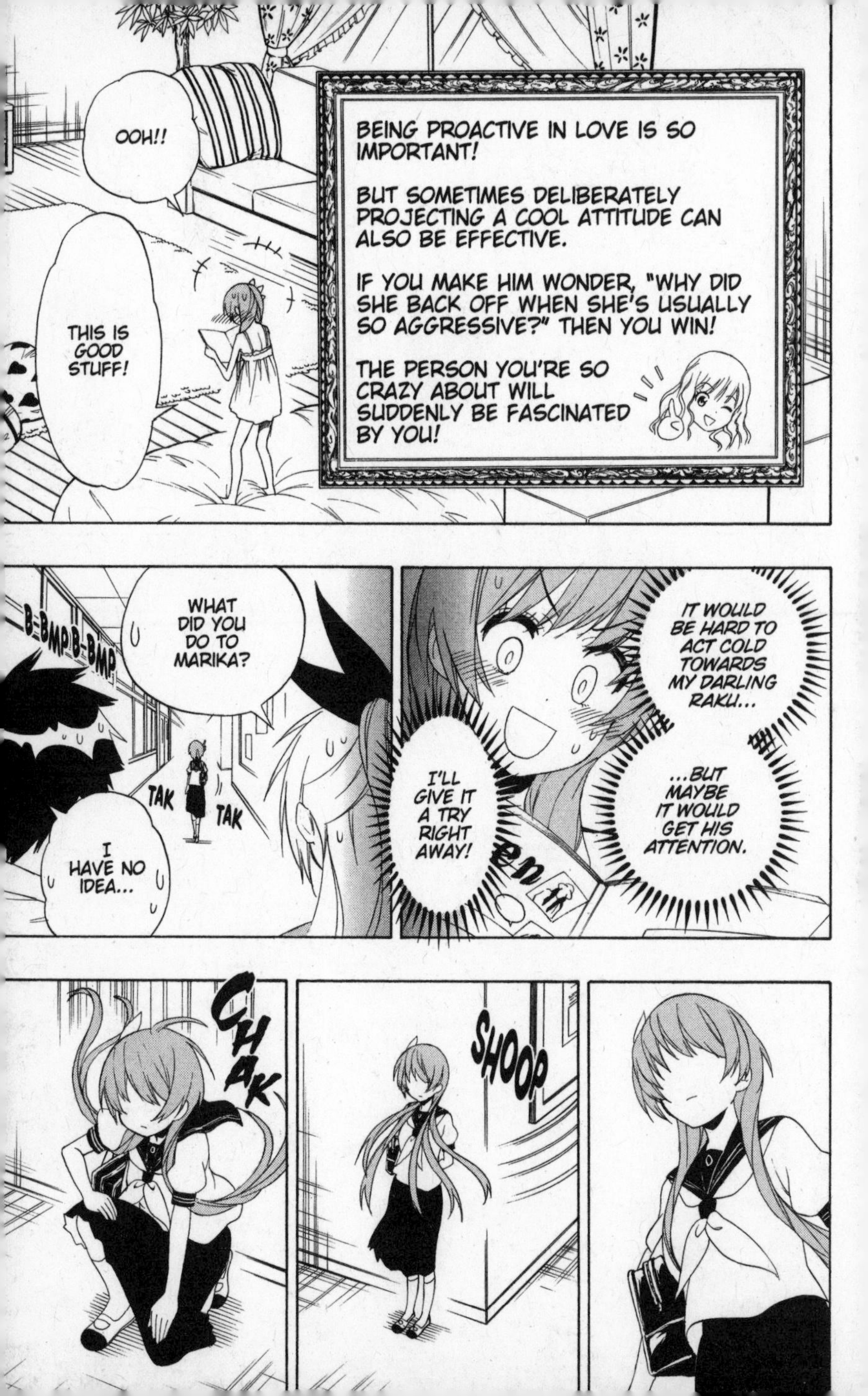
BEING PROACTIVE IN LOVE IS SO IMPORTANT!
BUT SOMETIMES DELIBERATELY PROJECTING A COOL ATTITUDE CAN ALSO BE EFFECTIVE.
IF YOU MAKE HIM WONDER, "WHY DID SHE BACK OFF WHEN SHE'S USUALLY SO AGGRESSIVE?" THEN YOU WIN!
THE PERSON YOU'RE SO CRAZY ABOUT WILL SUDDENLY BE FASCINATED BY YOU!
OOH!!
THIS IS GOOD STUFF!
IT WOULD BE HARD TO ACT COLD TOWARDS MY DARLING RAKU...
...BUT MAYBE IT WOULD GET HIS ATTENTION.
I'LL GIVE IT A TRY RIGHT AWAY!
B-BMP B-BMP
WHAT DID YOU DO TO MARIKA?
TAK
TAK
I HAVE NO IDEA...
SHOOP
CHAK

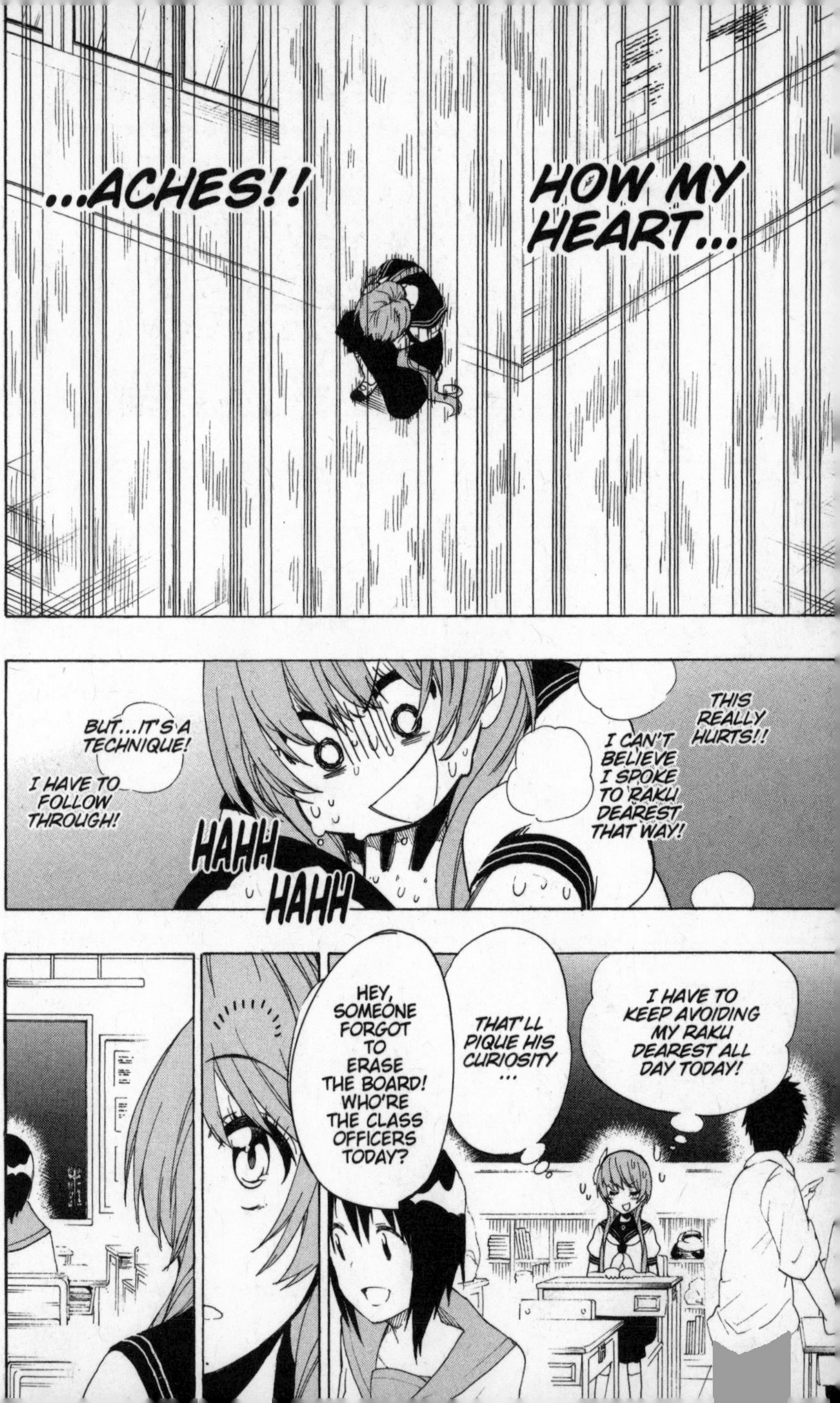
HOW MY HEART...
...ACHES!!
THIS REALLY HURTS!!
I CAN'T BELIEVE I SPOKE TO RAKU DEAREST THAT WAY!
BUT...IT'S A TECHNIQUE!
I HAVE TO FOLLOW THROUGH!
HAHH HAHH
I HAVE TO KEEP AVOIDING MY RAKU DEAREST ALL DAY TODAY!
THAT'LL PIQUE HIS CURIOSITY ...
HEY, SOMEONE FORGOT TO ERASE THE BOARD! WHO'RE THE CLASS OFFICERS TODAY?

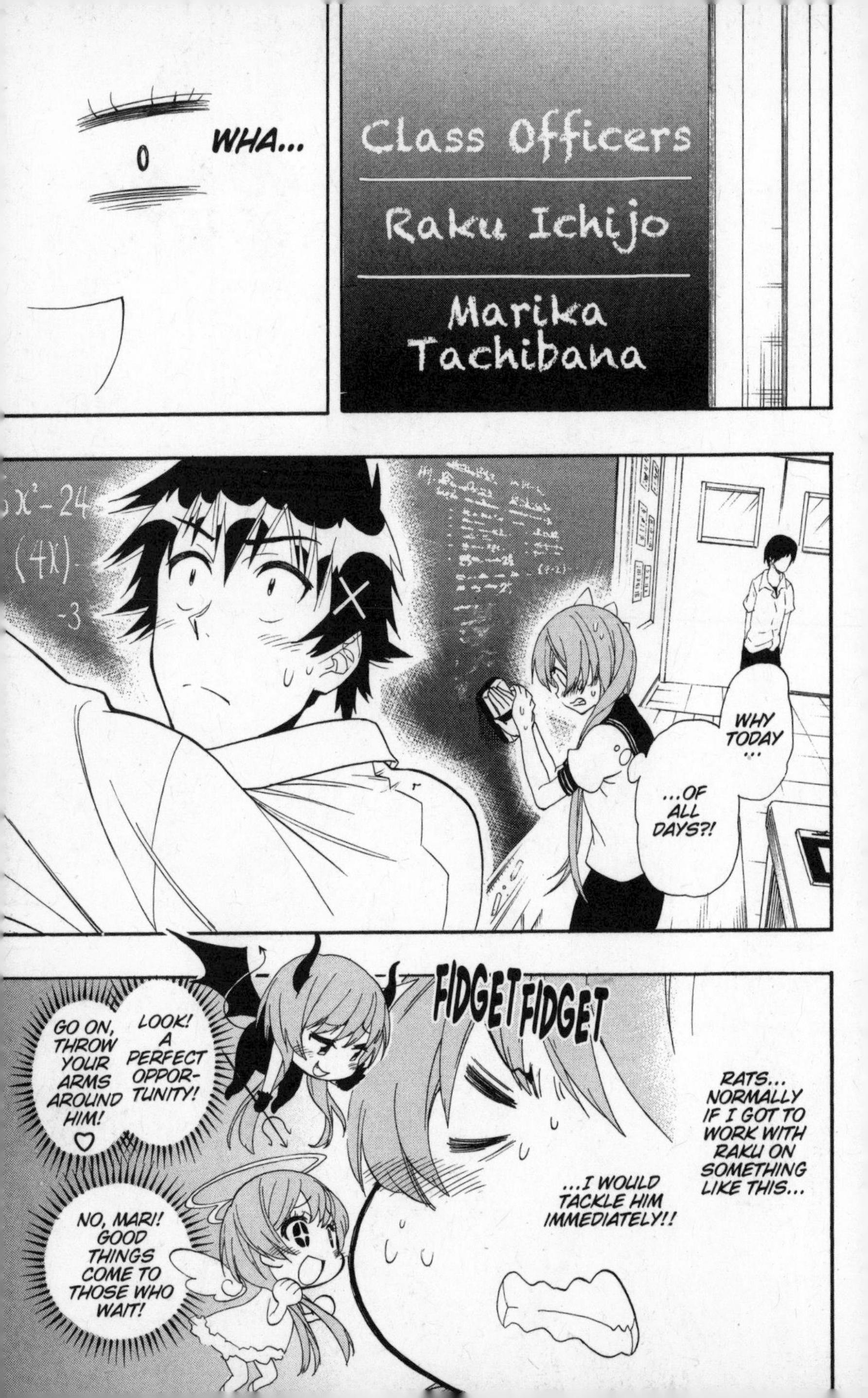
Class Officers
Raku Ichijo
Marika Tachibana
WHA...
WHY TODAY...
...OF ALL DAYS?!
FIDGET FIDGET
RATS... NORMALLY IF I GOT TO WORK WITH RAKU ON SOMETHING LIKE THIS...
...I WOULD TACKLE HIM IMMEDIATELY!!
LOOK! A PERFECT OPPOR-TUNITY!
GO ON, THROW YOUR ARMS AROUND HIM! ♡
NO, MARI! GOOD THINGS COME TO THOSE WHO WAIT!

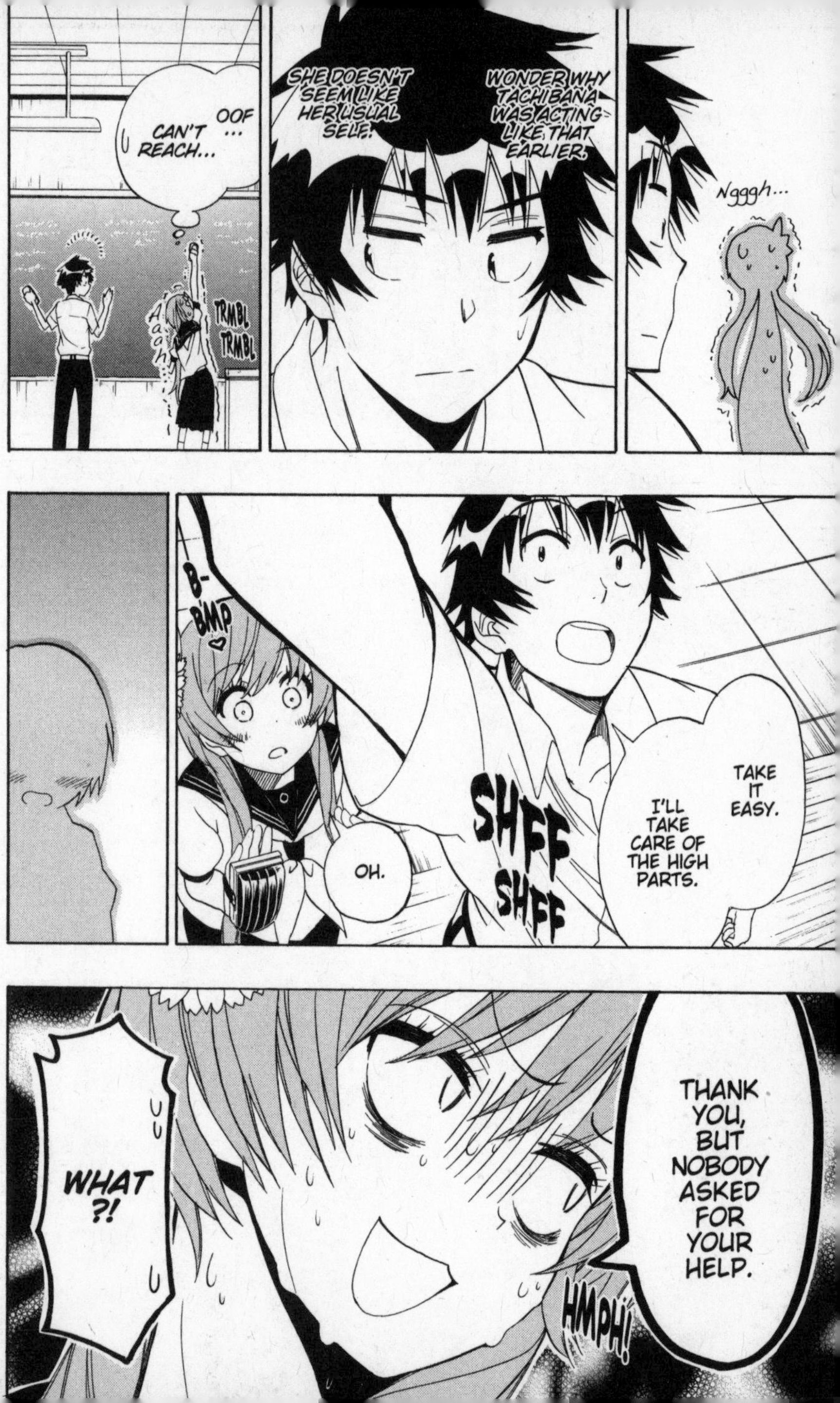
Ngggh...
WONDER WHY TACHIBANA WAS ACTING LIKE THAT EARLIER.
SHE DOESN'T SEEM LIKE HER USUAL SELF.
OOF ... CAN'T REACH...
Aaah
TRMBL TRMBL
TAKE IT EASY.
I'LL TAKE CARE OF THE HIGH PARTS.
SHFF SHFF
B-BMP ♡
OH.
THANK YOU, BUT NOBODY ASKED FOR YOUR HELP.
HMPH!
WHAT?!

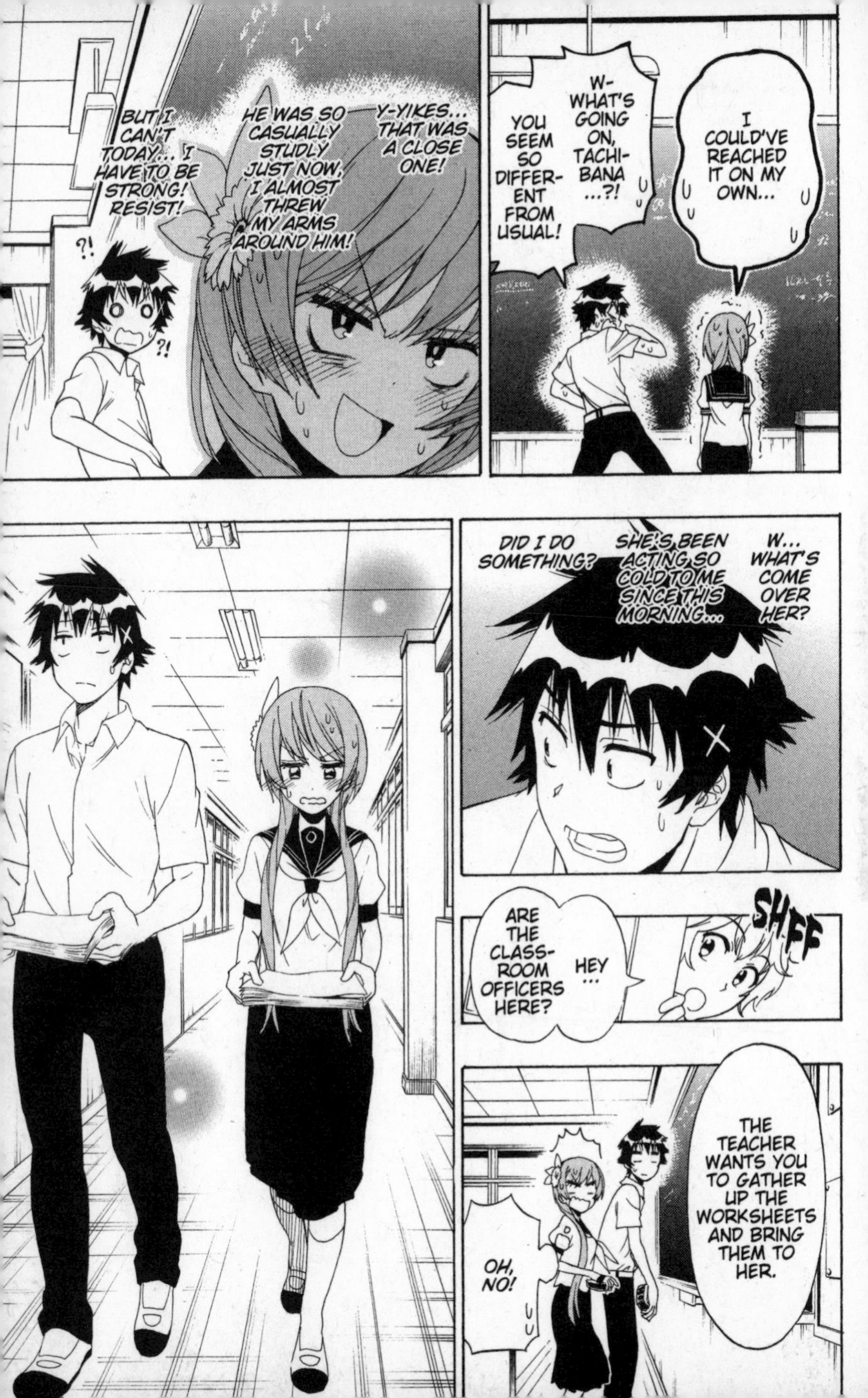
I COULD'VE REACHED IT ON MY OWN...
W-WHAT'S GOING ON, TACHIBANA...?!
YOU SEEM SO DIFFERENT FROM USUAL!
Y-YIKES... THAT WAS A CLOSE ONE!
HE WAS SO CASUALLY STUDLY JUST NOW, I ALMOST THREW MY ARMS AROUND HIM!
BUT I CAN'T TODAY... I HAVE TO BE STRONG! RESIST!
?!
?!
W... WHAT'S COME OVER HER?
SHE'S BEEN ACTING SO COLD TO ME SINCE THIS MORNING...
DID I DO SOMETHING?
SHFF
HEY...
ARE THE CLASSROOM OFFICERS HERE?
THE TEACHER WANTS YOU TO GATHER UP THE WORKSHEETS AND BRING THEM TO HER.
OH, NO!

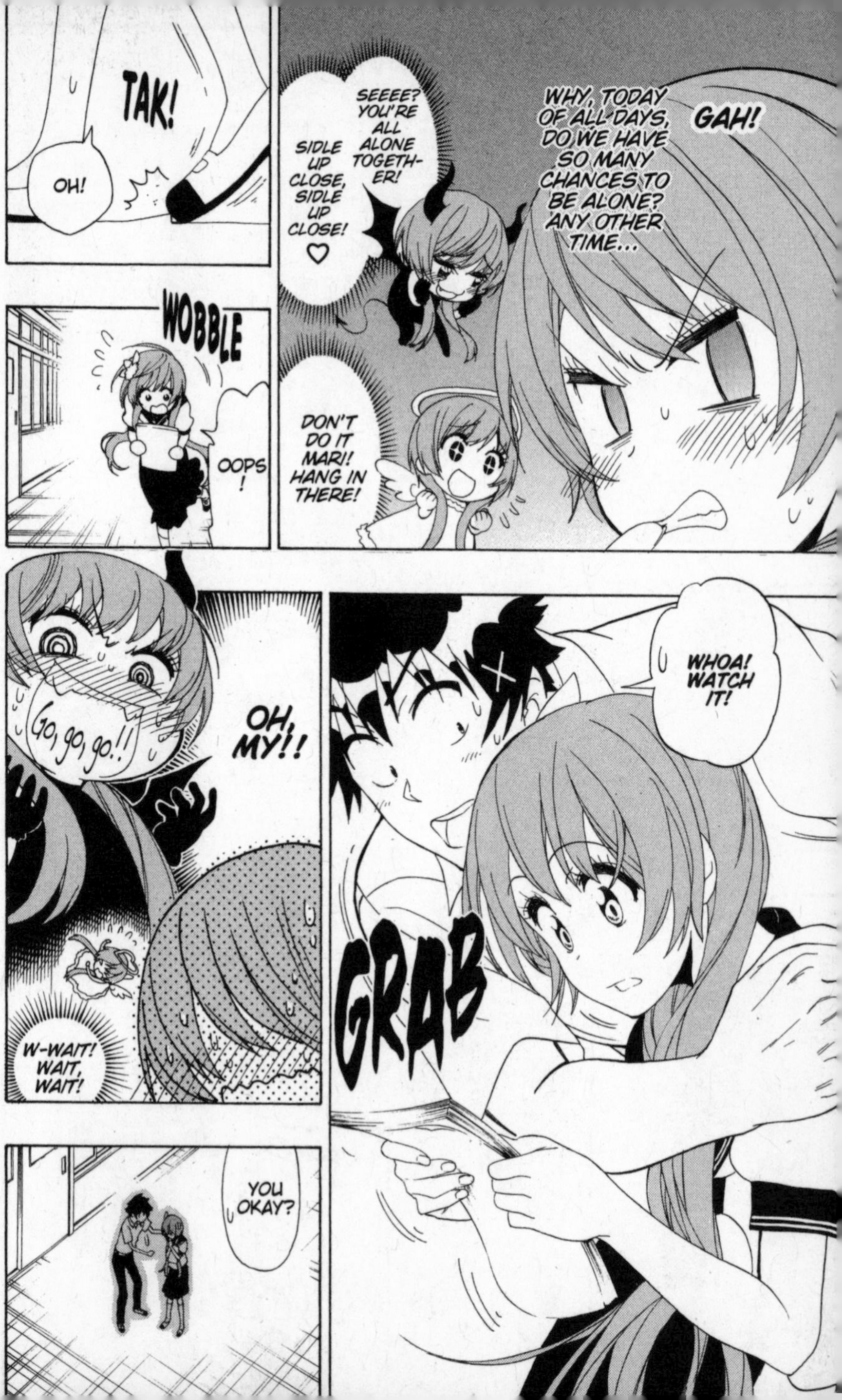
GAH!
WHY, TODAY OF ALL DAYS, DO WE HAVE SO MANY CHANCES TO BE ALONE? ANY OTHER TIME...
SEEEE? YOU'RE ALL ALONE TOGETHER!
SIDLE UP CLOSE, SIDLE UP CLOSE! ♡
DON'T DO IT MARI! HANG IN THERE!
TAK!
OH!
WOBBLE
OOPS!
WHOA! WATCH IT!
GRAB
OH, MY!!
Go, go, go!!
W-WAIT! WAIT, WAIT!
YOU OKAY?

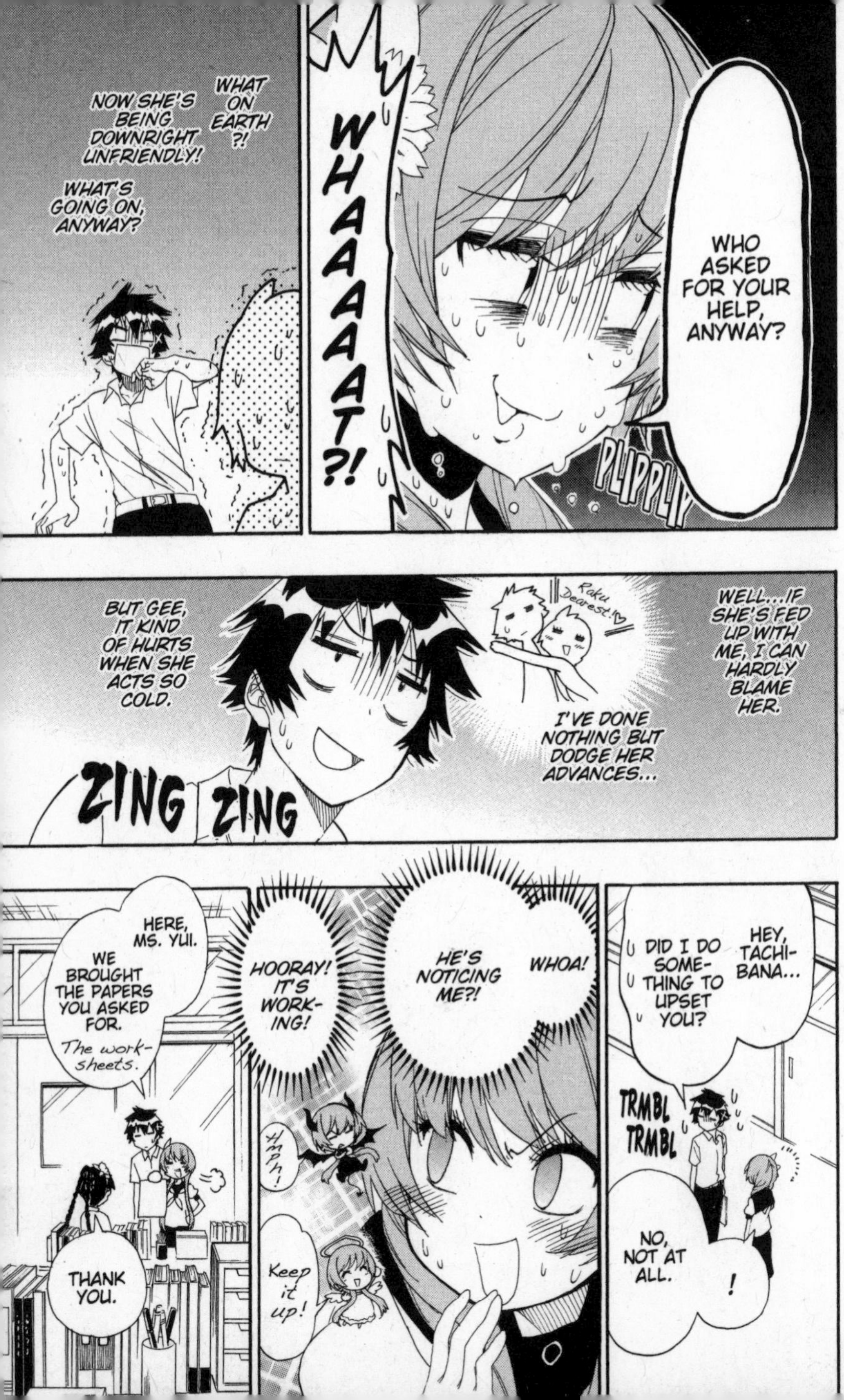
WHO ASKED FOR YOUR HELP, ANYWAY?
PLIPPLIP
WHAAAAAAT?!
WHAT ON EARTH?!
NOW SHE'S BEING DOWNRIGHT UNFRIENDLY!
WHAT'S GOING ON, ANYWAY?
WELL... IF SHE'S FED UP WITH ME, I CAN HARDLY BLAME HER.
Raku Dearest! ♥
I'VE DONE NOTHING BUT DODGE HER ADVANCES...
BUT GEE, IT KIND OF HURTS WHEN SHE ACTS SO COLD.
ZING ZING
HEY, TACHIBANA...
DID I DO SOME-THING TO UPSET YOU?
TRMBL TRMBL
NO, NOT AT ALL.
!
WHOA!
HE'S NOTICING ME?!
HOORAY! IT'S WORK-ING!
Hmph!
Keep it up!
HERE, MS. YUI.
WE BROUGHT THE PAPERS YOU ASKED FOR.
The work-sheets.
THANK YOU.

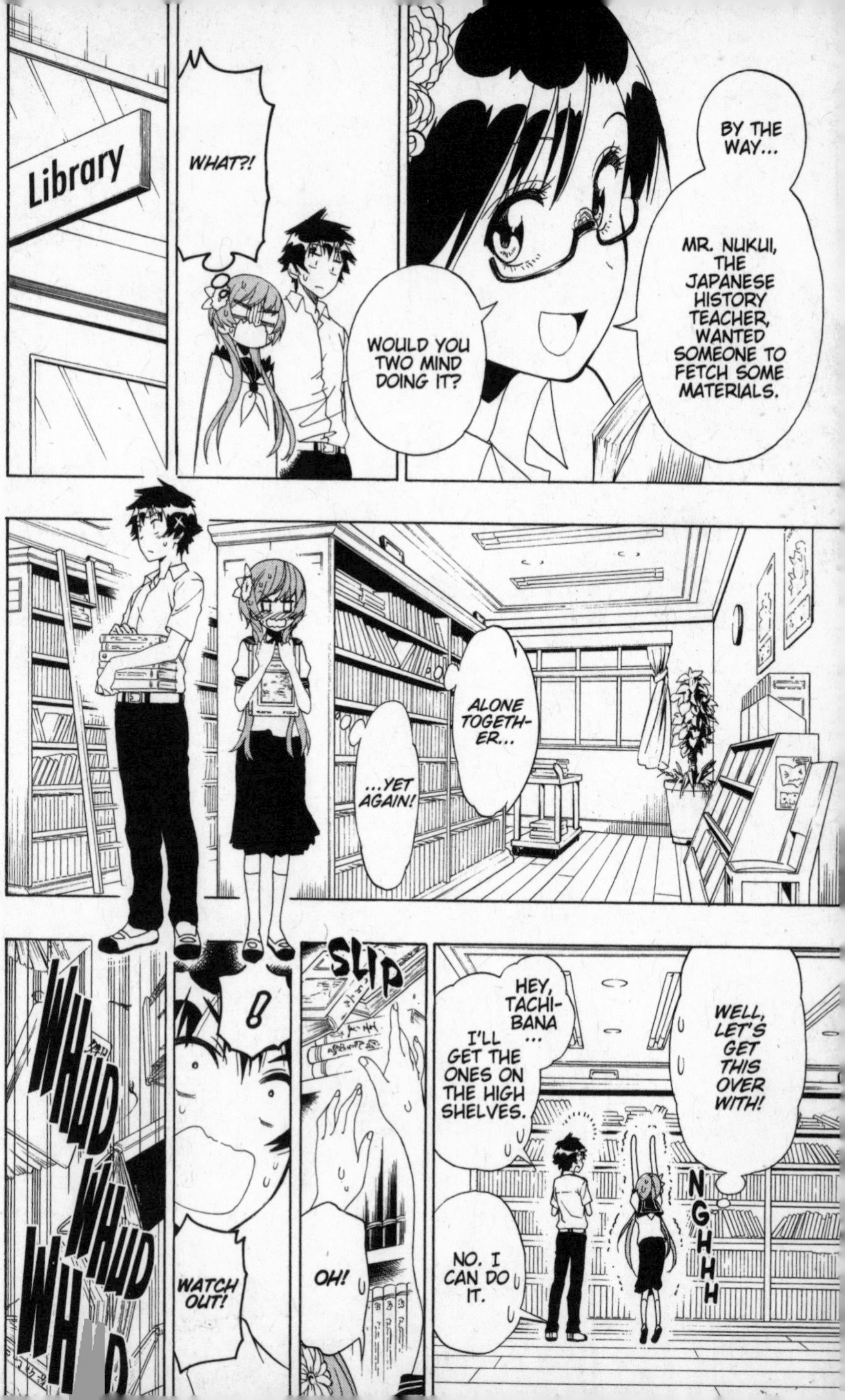
BY THE WAY...
MR. NUKUI, THE JAPANESE HISTORY TEACHER, WANTED SOMEONE TO FETCH SOME MATERIALS.
WOULD YOU TWO MIND DOING IT?
WHAT?!
Library
ALONE TOGETHER...
...YET AGAIN!
WELL, LET'S GET THIS OVER WITH!
HEY, TACHIBANA...
I'LL GET THE ONES ON THE HIGH SHELVES.
NO. I CAN DO IT.
NGHHH
SLIP
OH!
!
WATCH OUT!
WHUD
WHUD

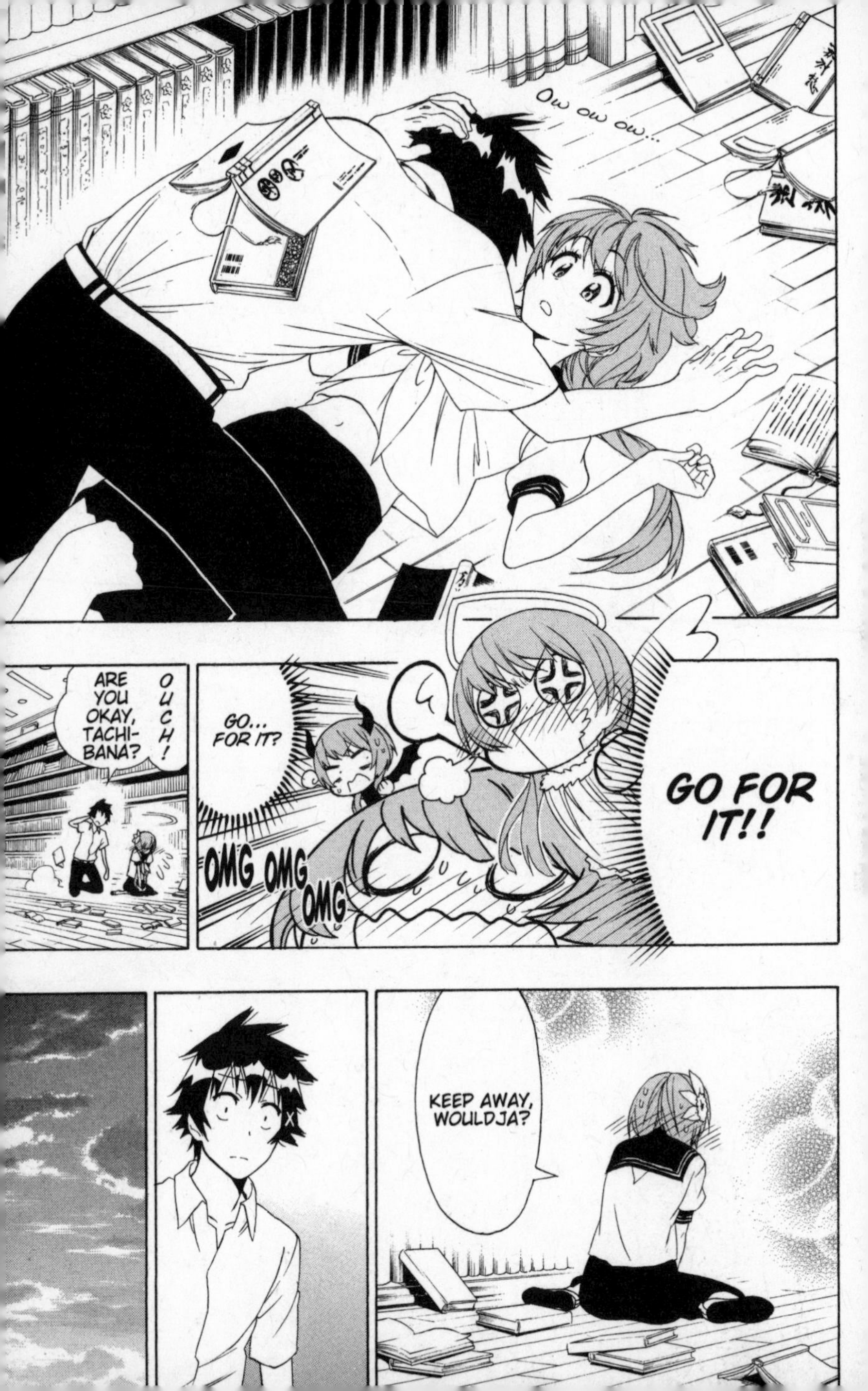
Ow ow ow...
GO FOR IT!!
GO... FOR IT?
OMG OMG OMG
OUCH!
ARE YOU OKAY, TACHIBANA?
KEEP AWAY, WOULDJA?

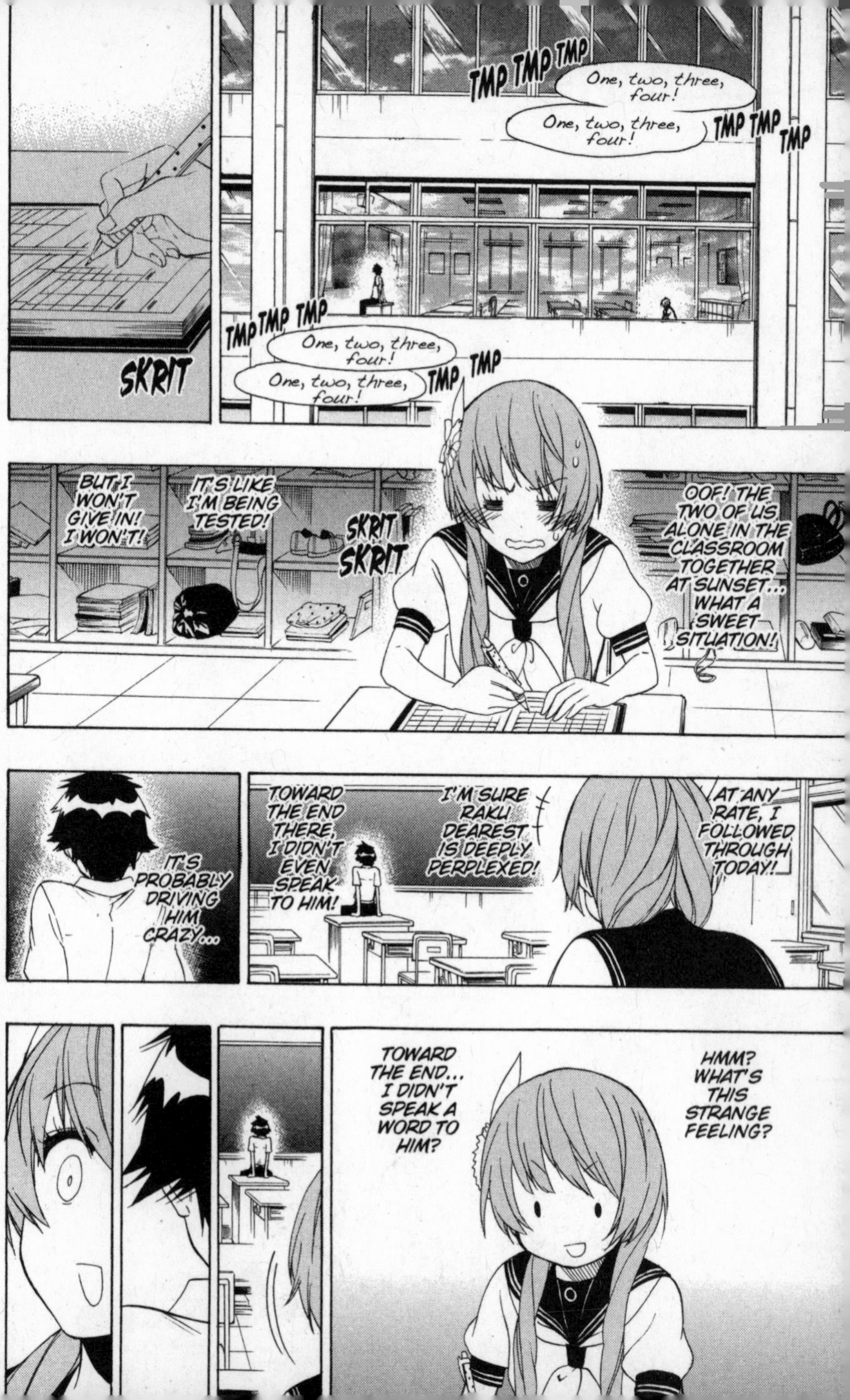
TMP TMP TMP
One, two, three, four!
One, two, three, four!
TMP TMP TMP
TMP TMP TMP
One, two, three, four!
One, two, three, four!
TMP TMP
SKRIT
OOF! THE TWO OF US ALONE IN THE CLASSROOM TOGETHER AT SUNSET... WHAT A SWEET SITUATION!
SKRIT SKRIT
IT'S LIKE I'M BEING TESTED!
BUT I WON'T GIVE IN! I WON'T!
AT ANY RATE, I FOLLOWED THROUGH TODAY!
I'M SURE RAKU DEAREST IS DEEPLY PERPLEXED!
TOWARD THE END THERE, I DIDN'T EVEN SPEAK TO HIM!
IT'S PROBABLY DRIVING HIM CRAZY...
HMM? WHAT'S THIS STRANGE FEELING?
TOWARD THE END... I DIDN'T SPEAK A WORD TO HIM?

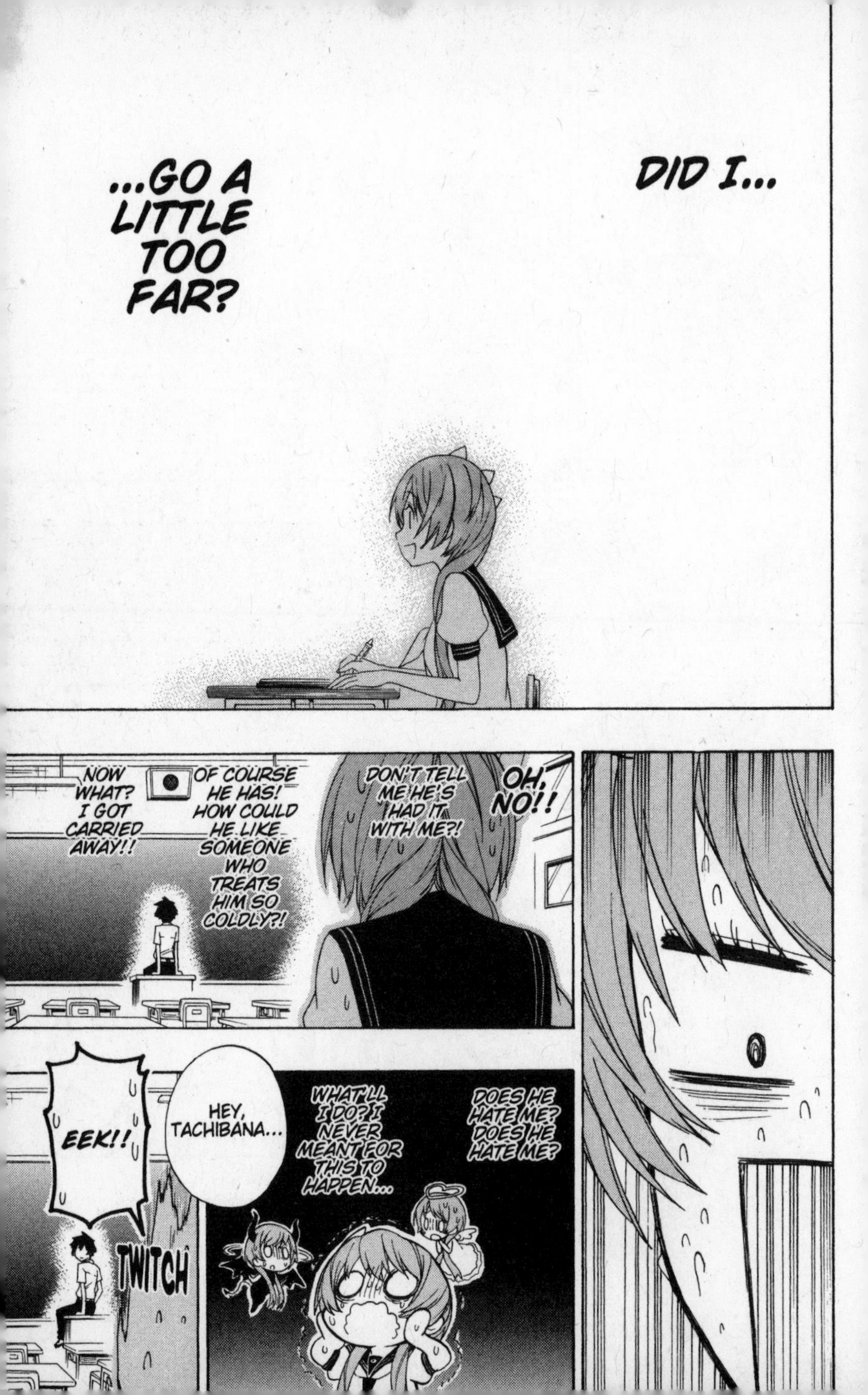
DID I...
...GO A LITTLE TOO FAR?
OH, NO!!
DON'T TELL ME HE'S HAD IT WITH ME?!
OF COURSE HE HAS! HOW COULD HE LIKE SOMEONE WHO TREATS HIM SO COLDLY?!
NOW WHAT? I GOT CARRIED AWAY!!
DOES HE HATE ME? DOES HE HATE ME?
WHAT'LL I DO? I NEVER MEANT FOR THIS TO HAPPEN...
HEY, TACHIBANA...
EEK!!
TWITCH

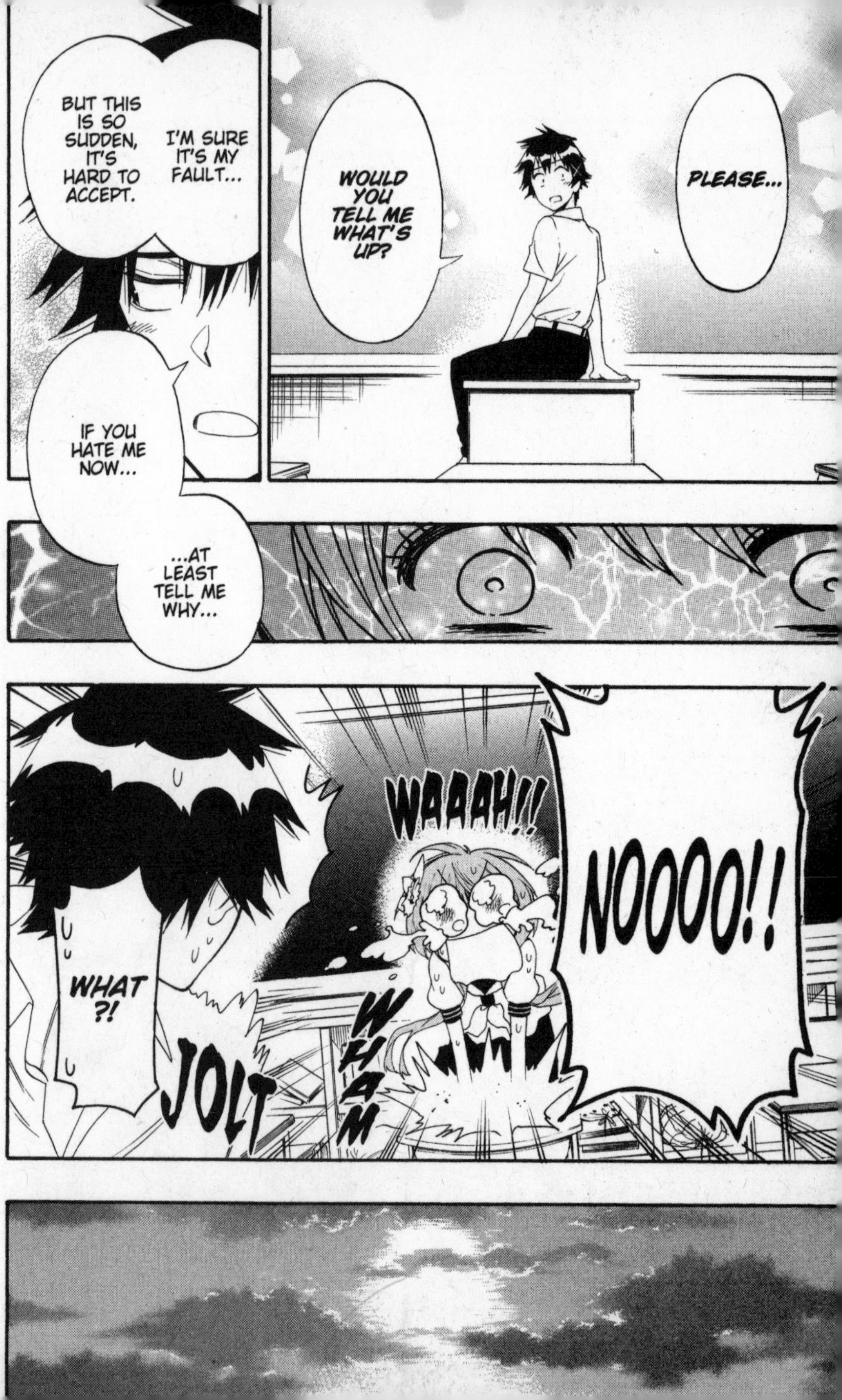
PLEASE...
WOULD YOU TELL ME WHAT'S UP?
I'M SURE IT'S MY FAULT...
BUT THIS IS SO SUDDEN, IT'S HARD TO ACCEPT.
IF YOU HATE ME NOW...
...AT LEAST TELL ME WHY...
NOOOO!!
WAAAH!!
WHAM
WHAT?!
JOLT

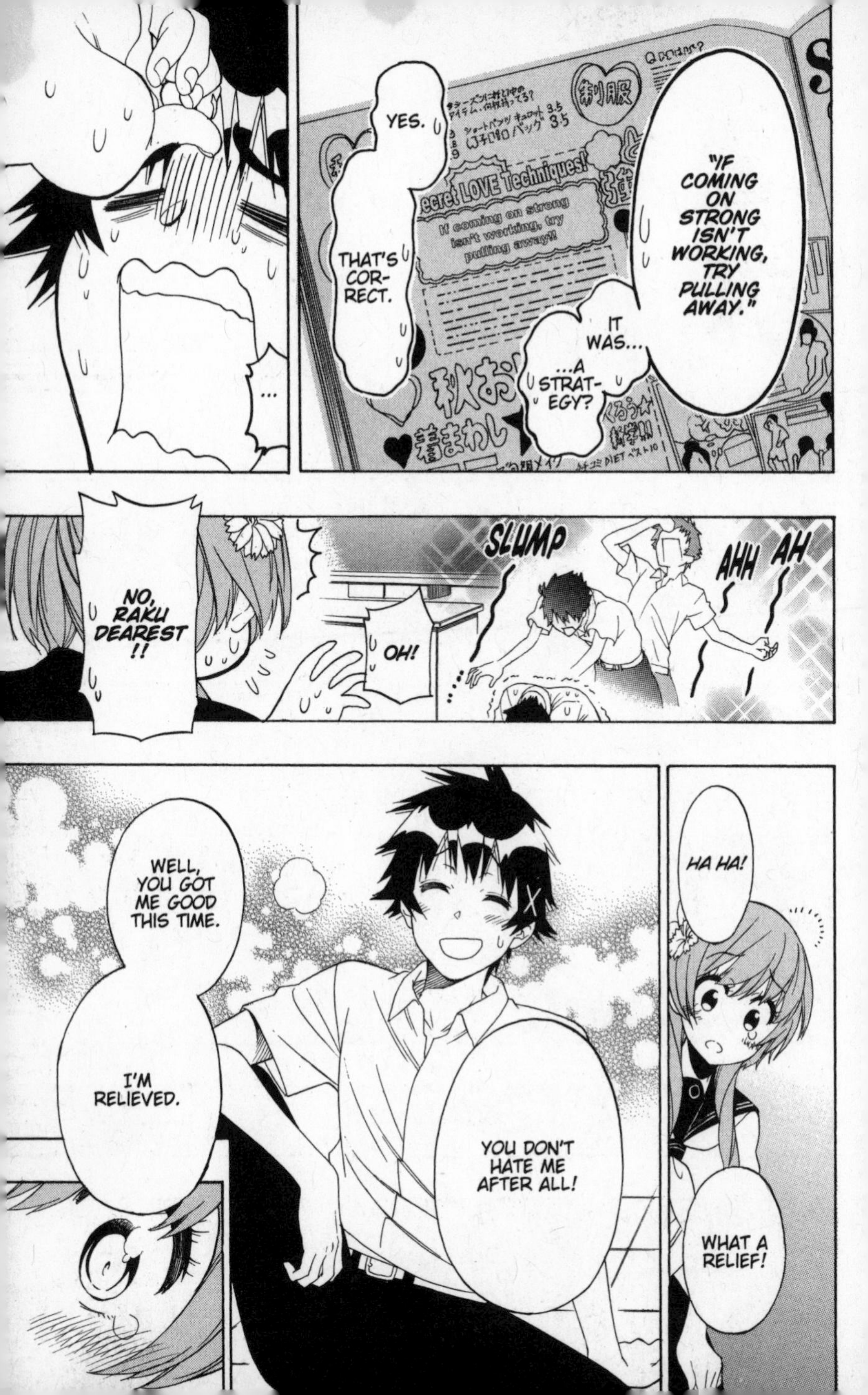
"IF COMING ON STRONG ISN'T WORKING, TRY PULLING AWAY."
制服
ecret LOVE Techniques!
If coming on strong isn't working, try pulling away!!
IT WAS...
...A STRATEGY?
YES.
THAT'S COR-RECT.
...
AH
AHH
SLUMP
OH!
NO, RAKU DEAREST!!
HA HA!
WHAT A RELIEF!
WELL, YOU GOT ME GOOD THIS TIME.
I'M RELIEVED.
YOU DON'T HATE ME AFTER ALL!

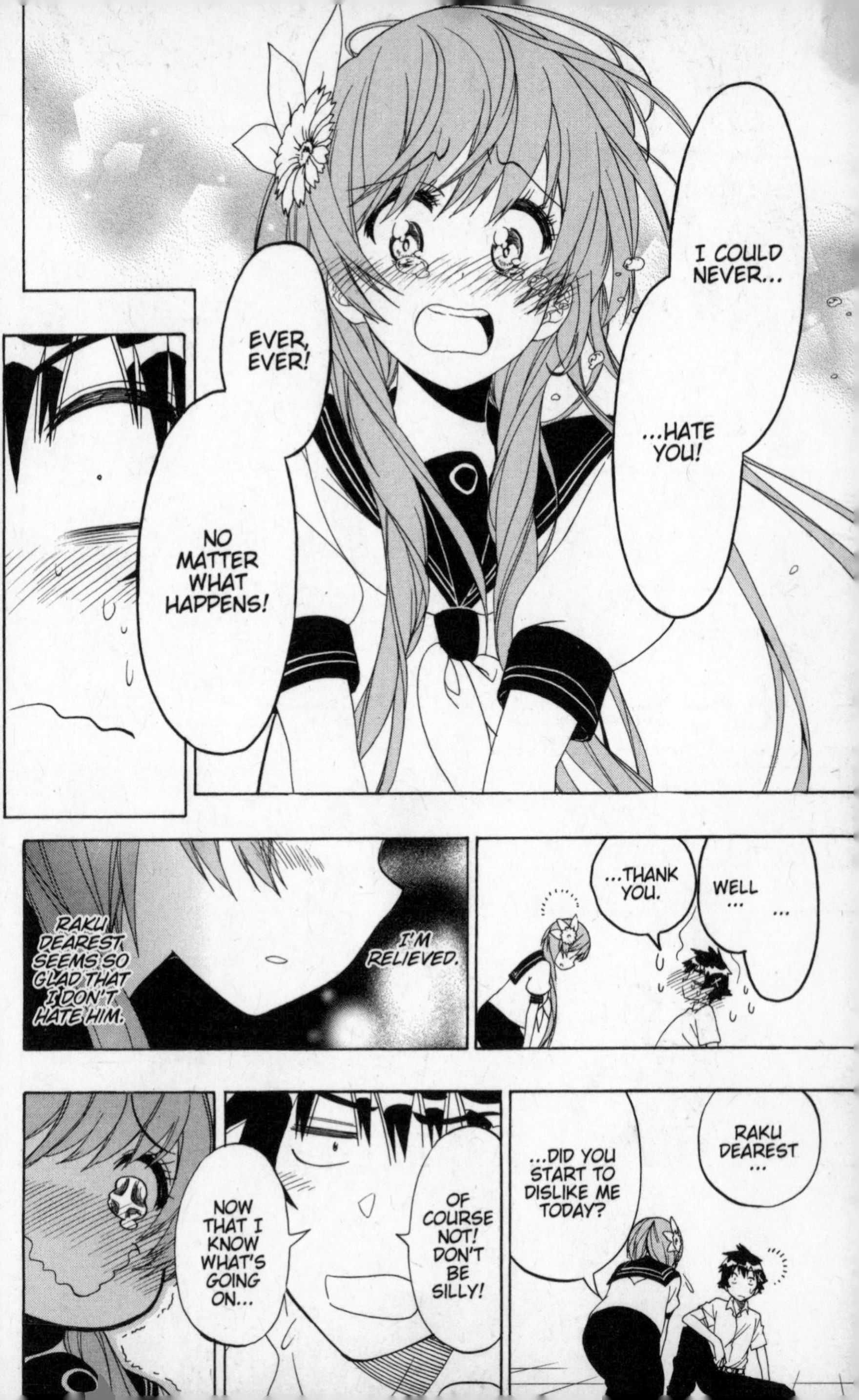
I COULD NEVER...
...HATE YOU!
EVER, EVER!
NO MATTER WHAT HAPPENS!
WELL ... ...
...THANK YOU.
I'M RELIEVED.
RAKU DEAREST SEEMS SO GLAD THAT I DON'T HATE HIM.
RAKU DEAREST ...
...DID YOU START TO DISLIKE ME TODAY?
OF COURSE NOT! DON'T BE SILLY!
NOW THAT I KNOW WHAT'S GOING ON...

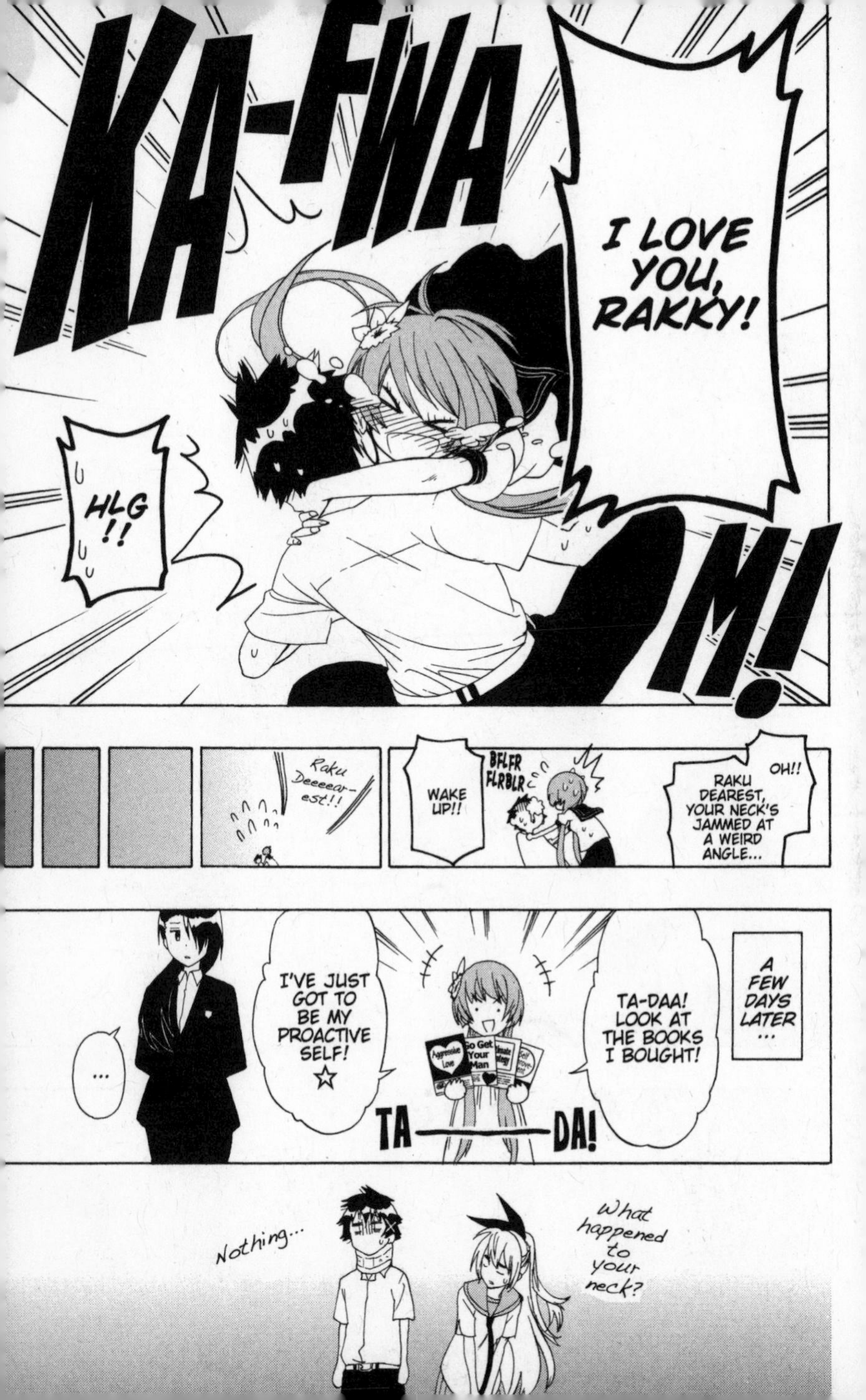
I LOVE YOU, RAKKY!
KA-FWA
M!
HLG!!
OH!!
RAKU DEAREST, YOUR NECK'S JAMMED AT A WEIRD ANGLE...
BFLFR FLRBLR
WAKE UP!!
Raku Deeeearest!!
A FEW DAYS LATER...
TA-DAA! LOOK AT THE BOOKS I BOUGHT!
TA—DA!
Aggressive Love
So Get Your Man
I'VE JUST GOT TO BE MY PROACTIVE SELF! ☆
...
What happened to your neck?
Nothing...

Angel Marika & Demon Marika

The avatar of love who rules Marika's conscience. When Marika's id starts to get the better of her, Angel Marika whispers admonitions and keeps Marika in check. But at a certain point, certain stimuli overcome her, and she joins forces with Demon Marika. Not highly dependable.

Favorite thing:
　Raku Dearest
Least Favorite Thing:
　Unrequited love
Special Move:
　Angel Pretty Impact
　(Move where she
　hugs Raku)

The evil entity who rules Marika's id. Eggs Marika on from the inside and drives her to acts of sexual harassment. But even when she takes a break, Marika continues to commit sexual harassment, leading her to wonder, "Why am I here?"

Favorite Thing:
　Raku Dearest
Least Favorite Thing:
　Unfulfillment
Special Move:
　Evil Diver Go to Hell
　(Move where she
　hugs Raku)

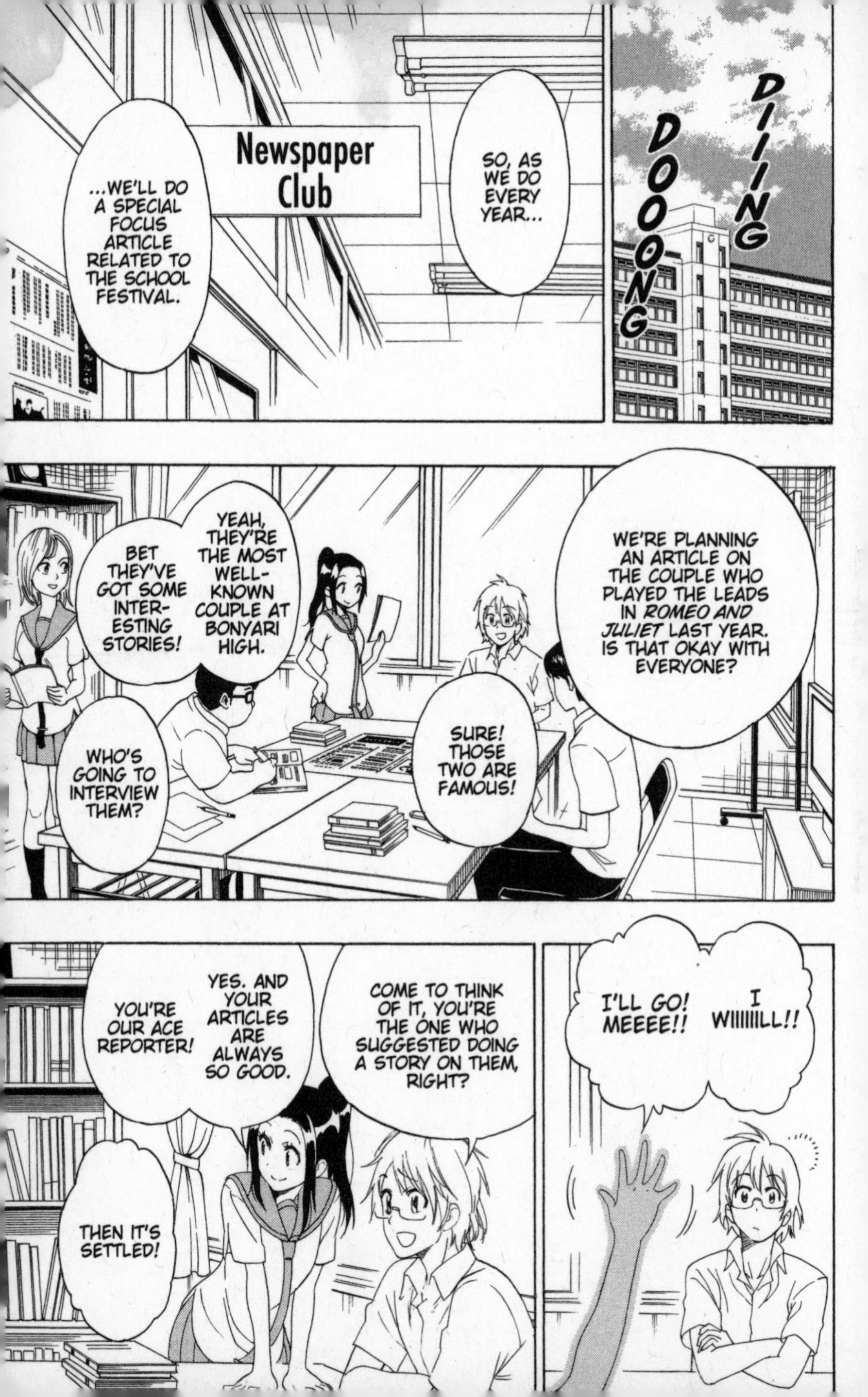
DIIING
DOOONG
SO, AS WE DO EVERY YEAR...
Newspaper Club
...WE'LL DO A SPECIAL FOCUS ARTICLE RELATED TO THE SCHOOL FESTIVAL.
WE'RE PLANNING AN ARTICLE ON THE COUPLE WHO PLAYED THE LEADS IN *ROMEO AND JULIET* LAST YEAR. IS THAT OKAY WITH EVERYONE?
SURE! THOSE TWO ARE FAMOUS!
YEAH, THEY'RE THE MOST WELL-KNOWN COUPLE AT BONYARI HIGH.
BET THEY'VE GOT SOME INTER-ESTING STORIES!
WHO'S GOING TO INTERVIEW THEM?
I WIIIIIILL!!
I'LL GO! MEEEE!!
COME TO THINK OF IT, YOU'RE THE ONE WHO SUGGESTED DOING A STORY ON THEM, RIGHT?
YES. AND YOUR ARTICLES ARE ALWAYS SO GOOD.
YOU'RE OUR ACE REPORTER!
THEN IT'S SETTLED!

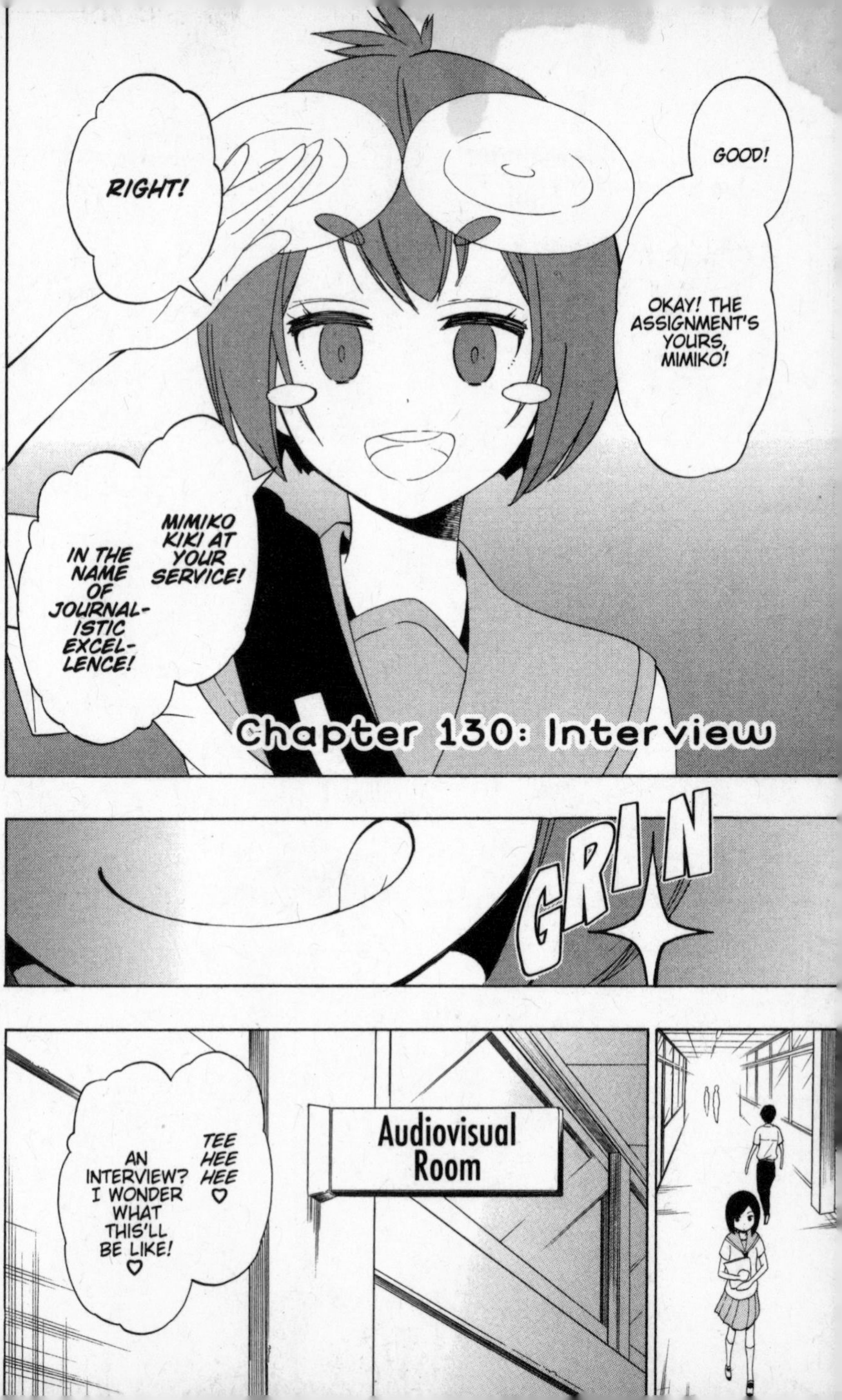
GOOD!
OKAY! THE ASSIGNMENT'S YOURS, MIMIKO!
RIGHT!
MIMIKO KIKI AT YOUR SERVICE!
IN THE NAME OF JOURNALISTIC EXCELLENCE!
Chapter 130: Interview
GRIN
Audiovisual Room
TEE HEE HEE ♡
AN INTERVIEW? I WONDER WHAT THIS'LL BE LIKE! ♡

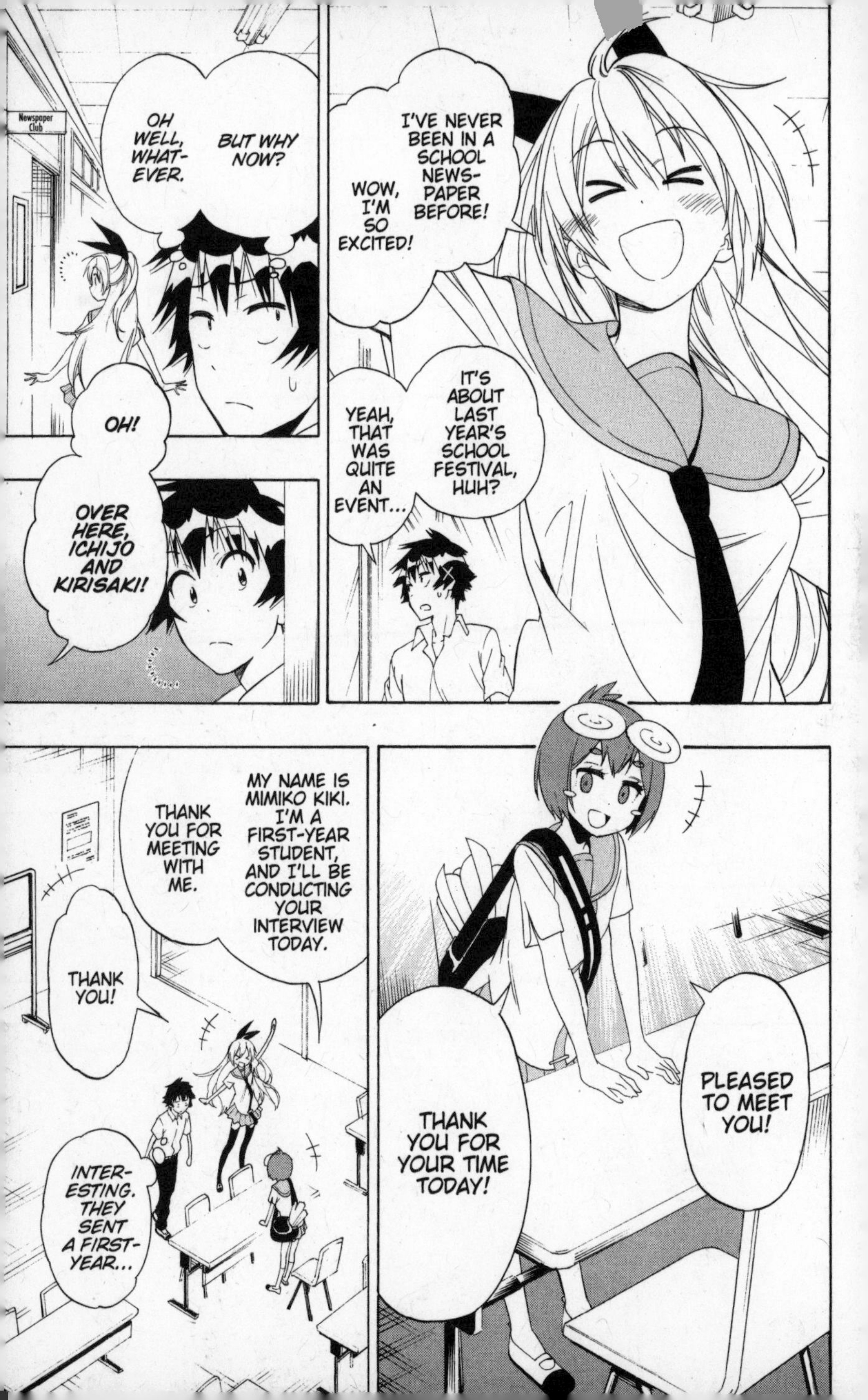
I'VE NEVER BEEN IN A SCHOOL NEWSPAPER BEFORE!
WOW, I'M SO EXCITED!
IT'S ABOUT LAST YEAR'S SCHOOL FESTIVAL, HUH?
YEAH, THAT WAS QUITE AN EVENT...
Newspaper Club
BUT WHY NOW?
OH WELL, WHATEVER.
OH!
OVER HERE, ICHIJO AND KIRISAKI!
PLEASED TO MEET YOU!
THANK YOU FOR YOUR TIME TODAY!
MY NAME IS MIMIKO KIKI. I'M A FIRST-YEAR STUDENT, AND I'LL BE CONDUCTING YOUR INTERVIEW TODAY.
THANK YOU FOR MEETING WITH ME.
THANK YOU!
INTERESTING. THEY SENT A FIRST-YEAR...

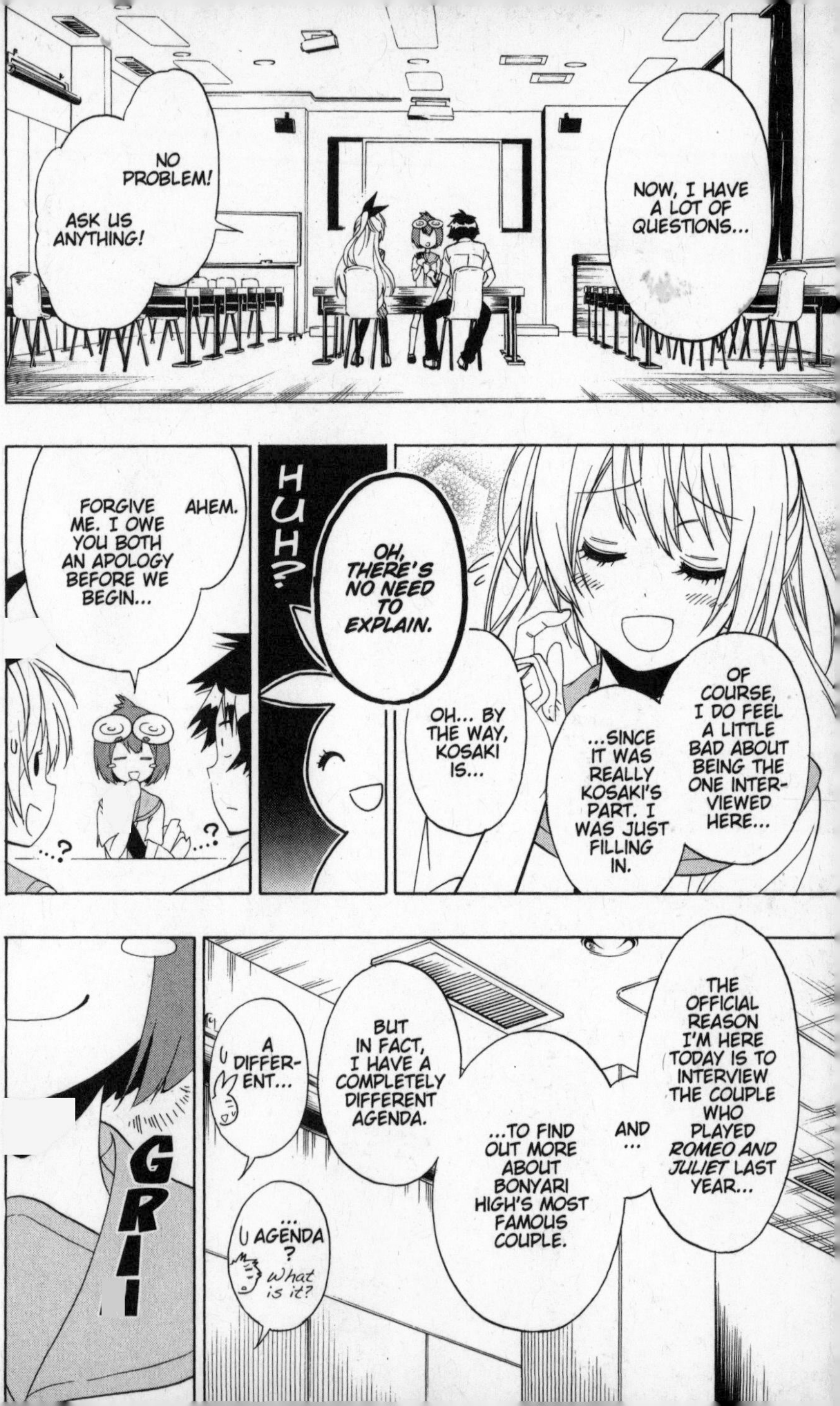
NOW, I HAVE A LOT OF QUESTIONS...
NO PROBLEM! ASK US ANYTHING!
OF COURSE, I DO FEEL A LITTLE BAD ABOUT BEING THE ONE INTERVIEWED HERE...
...SINCE IT WAS REALLY KOSAKI'S PART. I WAS JUST FILLING IN.
OH... BY THE WAY, KOSAKI IS...
OH, THERE'S NO NEED TO EXPLAIN.
HUH?
AHEM.
FORGIVE ME. I OWE YOU BOTH AN APOLOGY BEFORE WE BEGIN...
...?
...?
THE OFFICIAL REASON I'M HERE TODAY IS TO INTERVIEW THE COUPLE WHO PLAYED *ROMEO AND JULIET* LAST YEAR...
AND...
...TO FIND OUT MORE ABOUT BONYARI HIGH'S MOST FAMOUS COUPLE.
BUT IN FACT, I HAVE A COMPLETELY DIFFERENT AGENDA.
A DIFFERENT...
...AGENDA?
What is it?
GRII

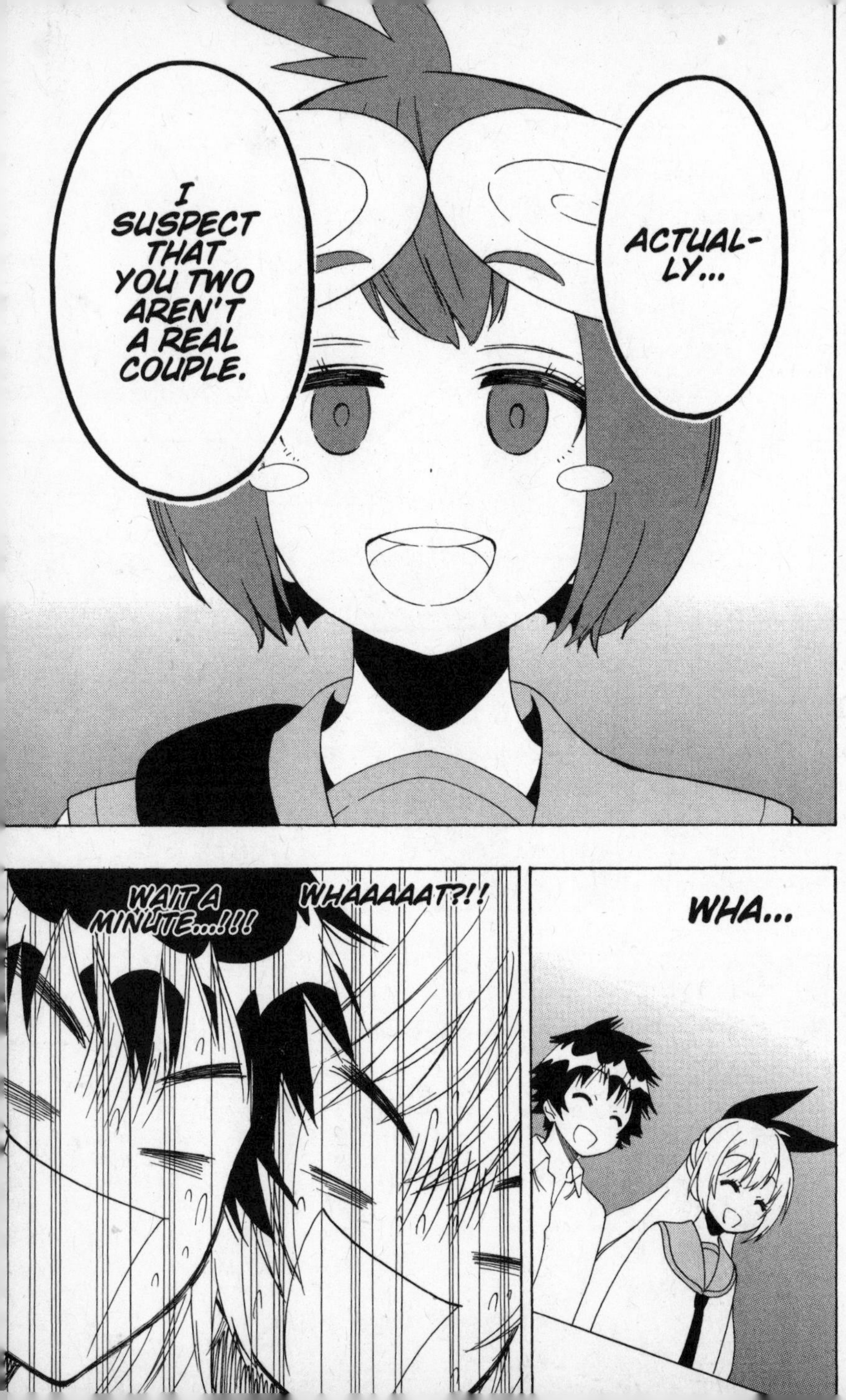
ACTUAL-LY...
I SUSPECT THAT YOU TWO AREN'T A REAL COUPLE.
WHA...
WHAAAAAT?!!
WAIT A MINUTE...!!!

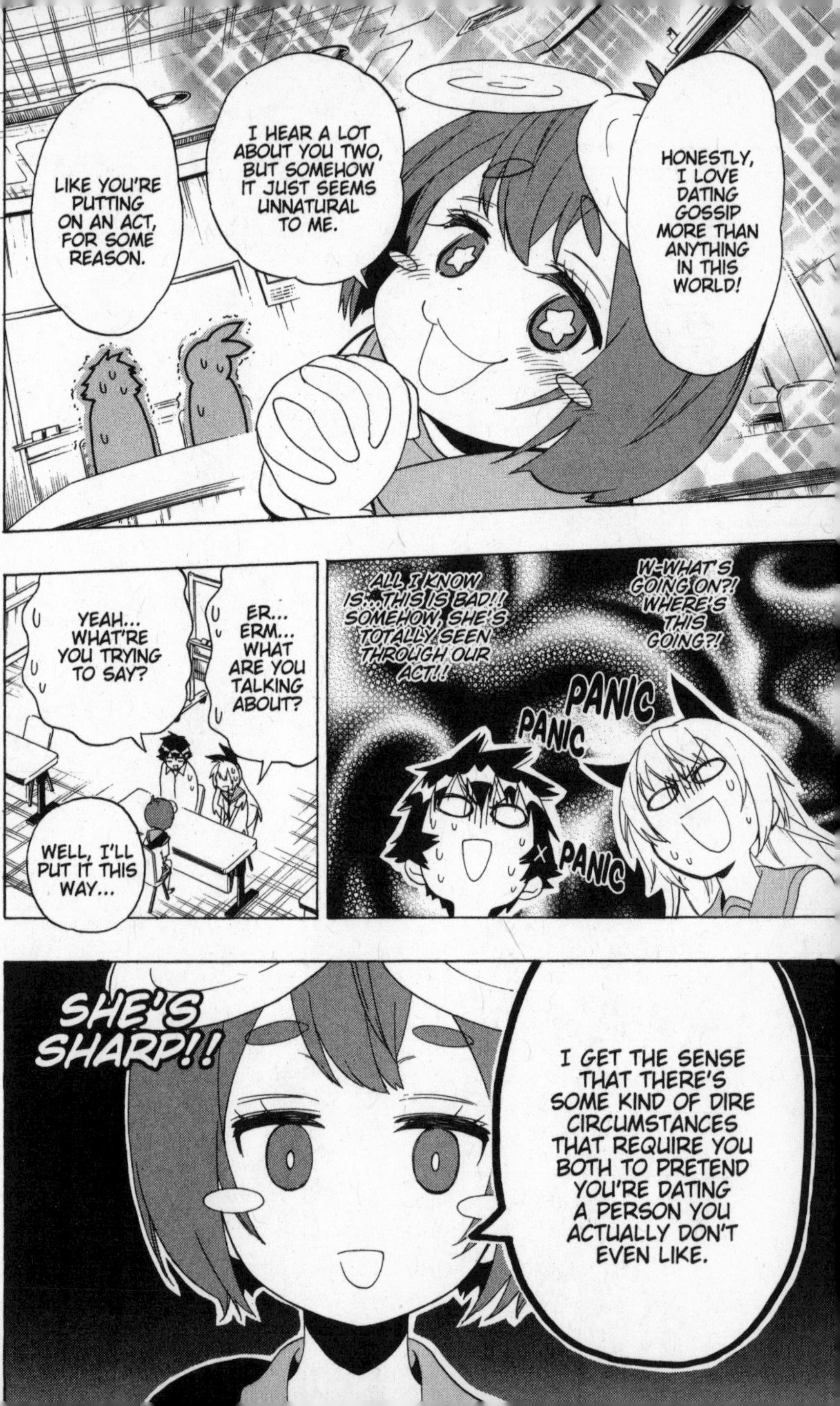
HONESTLY, I LOVE DATING GOSSIP MORE THAN ANYTHING IN THIS WORLD!
I HEAR A LOT ABOUT YOU TWO, BUT SOMEHOW IT JUST SEEMS UNNATURAL TO ME.
LIKE YOU'RE PUTTING ON AN ACT, FOR SOME REASON.
W-WHAT'S GOING ON?! WHERE'S THIS GOING?!
ALL I KNOW IS... THIS IS BAD!! SOMEHOW, SHE'S TOTALLY SEEN THROUGH OUR ACT!!
PANIC
PANIC
PANIC
ER... ERM... WHAT ARE YOU TALKING ABOUT?
YEAH... WHAT'RE YOU TRYING TO SAY?
WELL, I'LL PUT IT THIS WAY...
I GET THE SENSE THAT THERE'S SOME KIND OF DIRE CIRCUMSTANCES THAT REQUIRE YOU BOTH TO PRETEND YOU'RE DATING A PERSON YOU ACTUALLY DON'T EVEN LIKE.
SHE'S SHARP!!

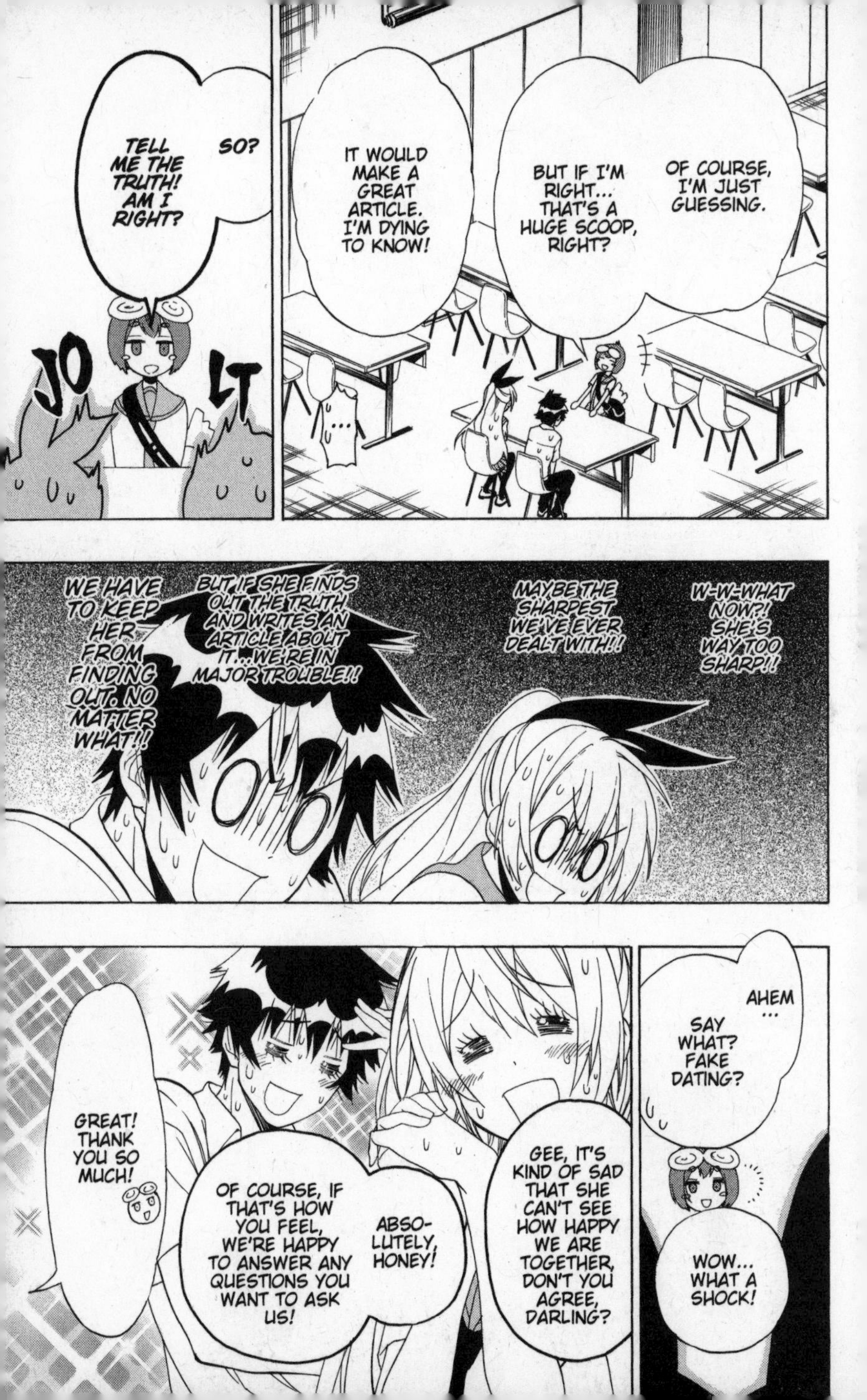
OF COURSE, I'M JUST GUESSING.
BUT IF I'M RIGHT... THAT'S A HUGE SCOOP, RIGHT?
IT WOULD MAKE A GREAT ARTICLE. I'M DYING TO KNOW!
...
SO?
TELL ME THE TRUTH! AM I RIGHT?
JOLT
W-W-WHAT NOW?! SHE'S WAY TOO SHARP!!
MAYBE THE SHARPEST WE'VE EVER DEALT WITH!!
BUT IF SHE FINDS OUT THE TRUTH AND WRITES AN ARTICLE ABOUT IT... WE'RE IN MAJOR TROUBLE!!
WE HAVE TO KEEP HER FROM FINDING OUT, NO MATTER WHAT!!
AHEM...
SAY WHAT? FAKE DATING?
WOW... WHAT A SHOCK!
GEE, IT'S KIND OF SAD THAT SHE CAN'T SEE HOW HAPPY WE ARE TOGETHER, DON'T YOU AGREE, DARLING?
ABSOLUTELY, HONEY!
OF COURSE, IF THAT'S HOW YOU FEEL, WE'RE HAPPY TO ANSWER ANY QUESTIONS YOU WANT TO ASK US!
GREAT! THANK YOU SO MUCH!

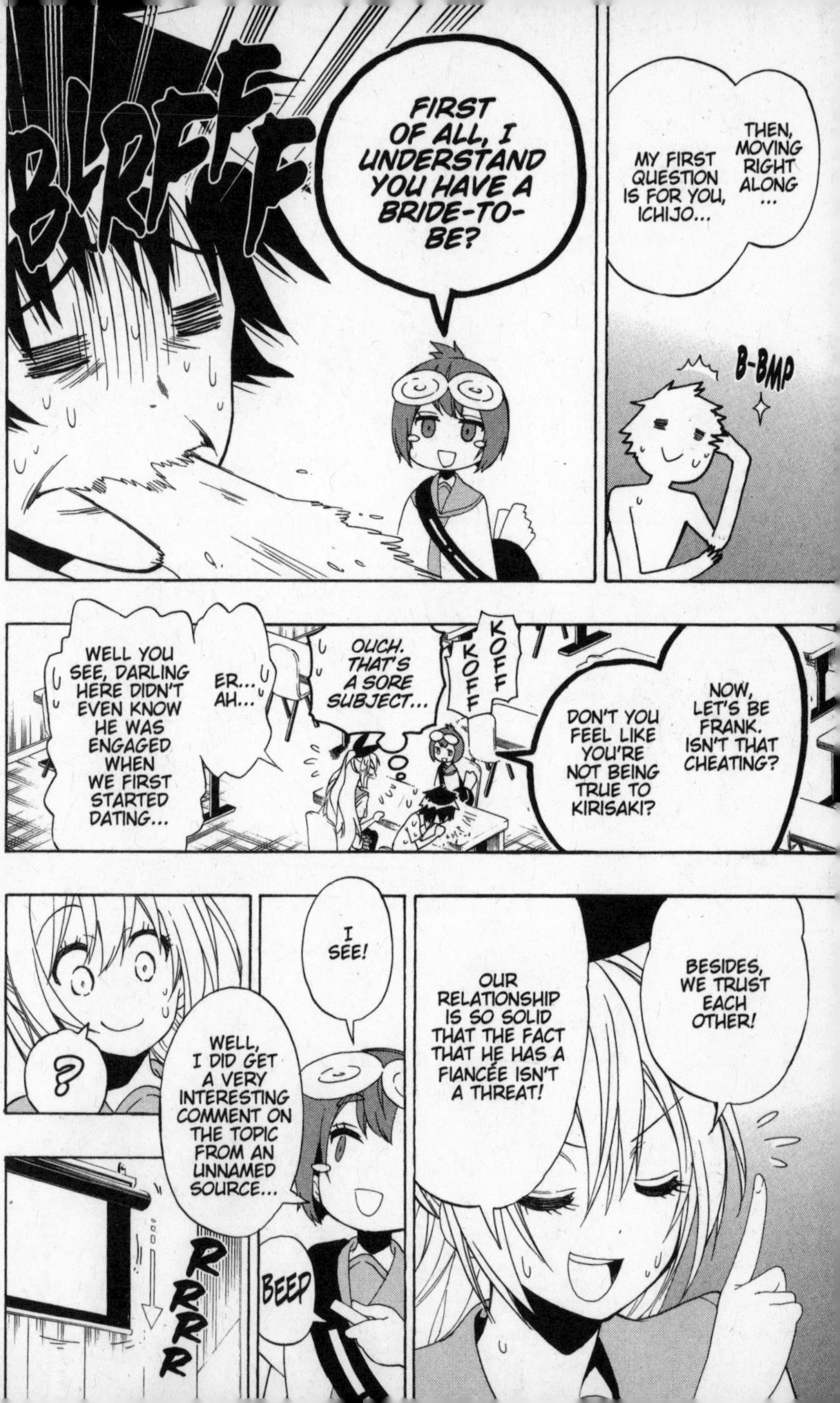
THEN, MOVING RIGHT ALONG...
MY FIRST QUESTION IS FOR YOU, ICHIJO...
B-BMP
FIRST OF ALL, I UNDERSTAND YOU HAVE A BRIDE-TO-BE?
NOW, LET'S BE FRANK. ISN'T THAT CHEATING?
DON'T YOU FEEL LIKE YOU'RE NOT BEING TRUE TO KIRISAKI?
KOFF KOFF
OUCH. THAT'S A SORE SUBJECT...
ER... AH...
WELL YOU SEE, DARLING HERE DIDN'T EVEN KNOW HE WAS ENGAGED WHEN WE FIRST STARTED DATING...
BESIDES, WE TRUST EACH OTHER!
OUR RELATIONSHIP IS SO SOLID THAT THE FACT THAT HE HAS A FIANCÉE ISN'T A THREAT!
I SEE!
WELL, I DID GET A VERY INTERESTING COMMENT ON THE TOPIC FROM AN UNNAMED SOURCE...
BEEP
RRRRR
?

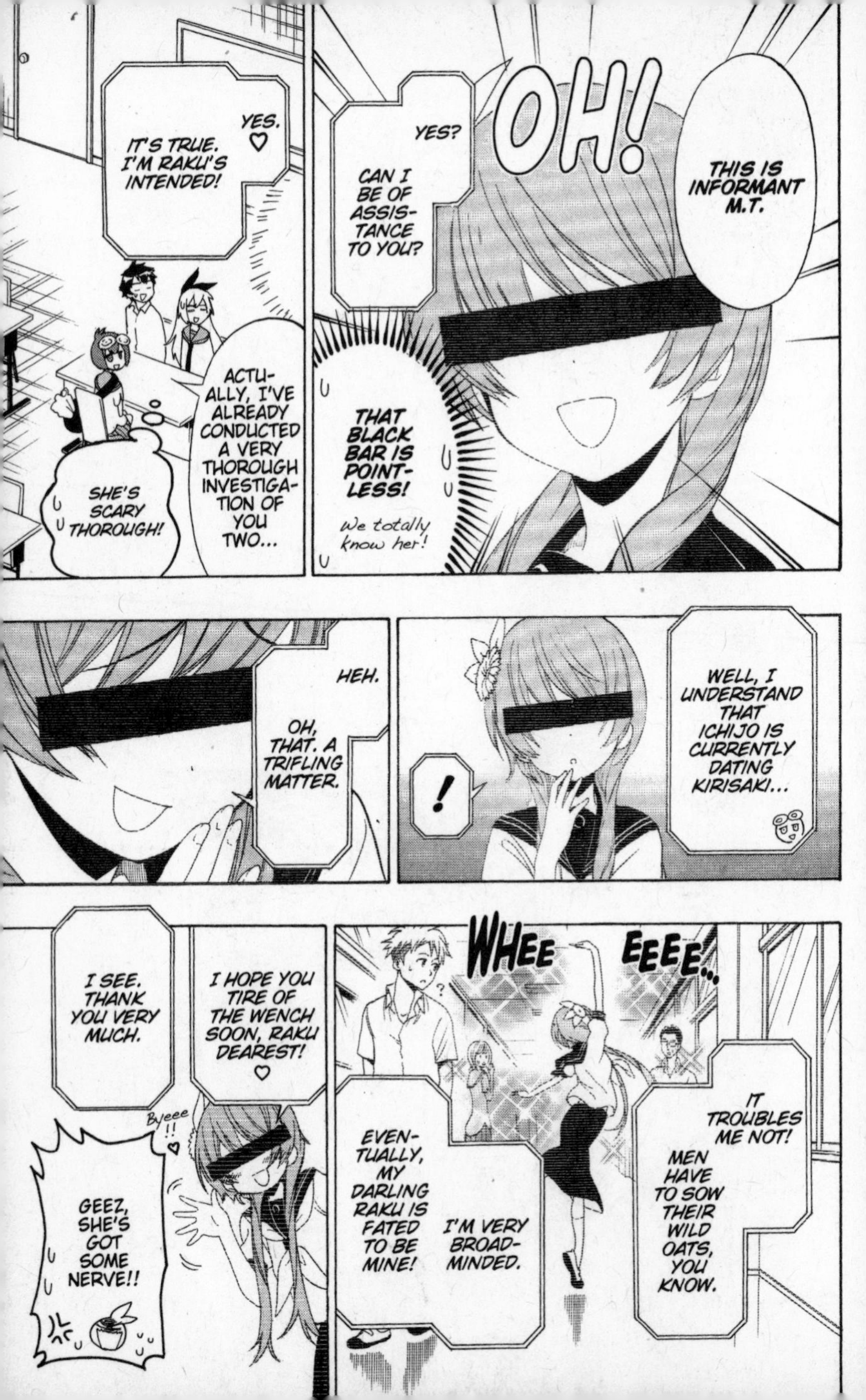
THIS IS INFORMANT M.T.
OH!
YES? CAN I BE OF ASSISTANCE TO YOU?
THAT BLACK BAR IS POINTLESS!
We totally know her!
YES. ♡ IT'S TRUE. I'M RAKU'S INTENDED!
ACTUALLY, I'VE ALREADY CONDUCTED A VERY THOROUGH INVESTIGATION OF YOU TWO...
SHE'S SCARY THOROUGH!
WELL, I UNDERSTAND THAT ICHIJO IS CURRENTLY DATING KIRISAKI...
!
HEH.
OH, THAT. A TRIFLING MATTER.
WHEE EEEE...
IT TROUBLES ME NOT! MEN HAVE TO SOW THEIR WILD OATS, YOU KNOW.
I'M VERY BROAD-MINDED.
EVENTUALLY, MY DARLING RAKU IS FATED TO BE MINE!
I HOPE YOU TIRE OF THE WENCH SOON, RAKU DEAREST! ♡
I SEE. THANK YOU VERY MUCH.
Byeee!! ♡
GEEZ, SHE'S GOT SOME NERVE!!

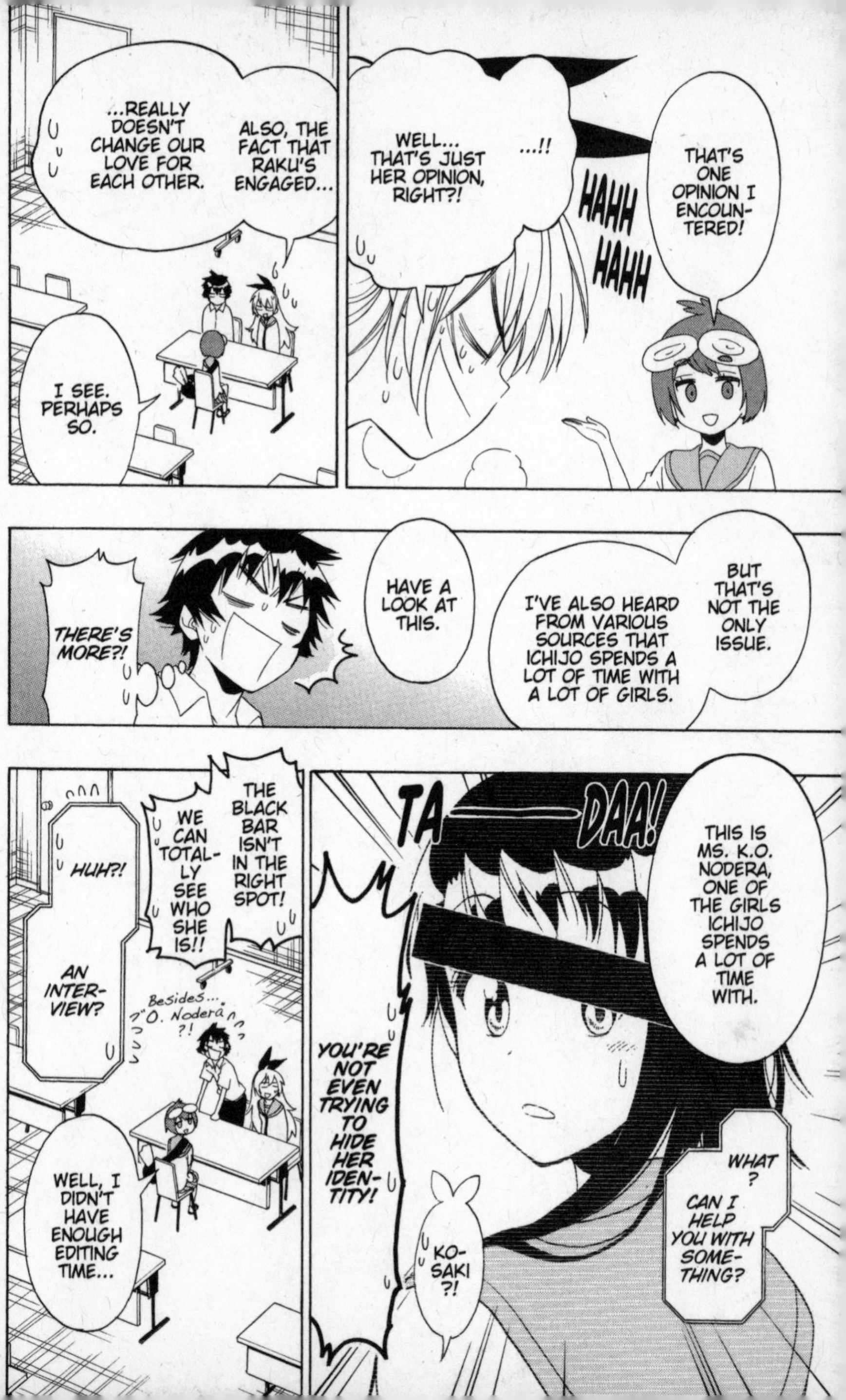
THAT'S ONE OPINION I ENCOUNTERED!
HAHH HAHH
...!!
WELL... THAT'S JUST HER OPINION, RIGHT?!
ALSO, THE FACT THAT RAKU'S ENGAGED...
...REALLY DOESN'T CHANGE OUR LOVE FOR EACH OTHER.
I SEE. PERHAPS SO.
BUT THAT'S NOT THE ONLY ISSUE.
I'VE ALSO HEARD FROM VARIOUS SOURCES THAT ICHIJO SPENDS A LOT OF TIME WITH A LOT OF GIRLS.
HAVE A LOOK AT THIS.
THERE'S MORE?!
TA—DAA!
THIS IS MS. K.O. NODERA, ONE OF THE GIRLS ICHIJO SPENDS A LOT OF TIME WITH.
YOU'RE NOT EVEN TRYING TO HIDE HER IDENTITY!
WHAT? CAN I HELP YOU WITH SOMETHING?
KO-SAKI?!
THE BLACK BAR ISN'T IN THE RIGHT SPOT!
WE CAN TOTALLY SEE WHO SHE IS!!
HUH?!
AN INTERVIEW?
Besides... O. Nodera ?!
WELL, I DIDN'T HAVE ENOUGH EDITING TIME...

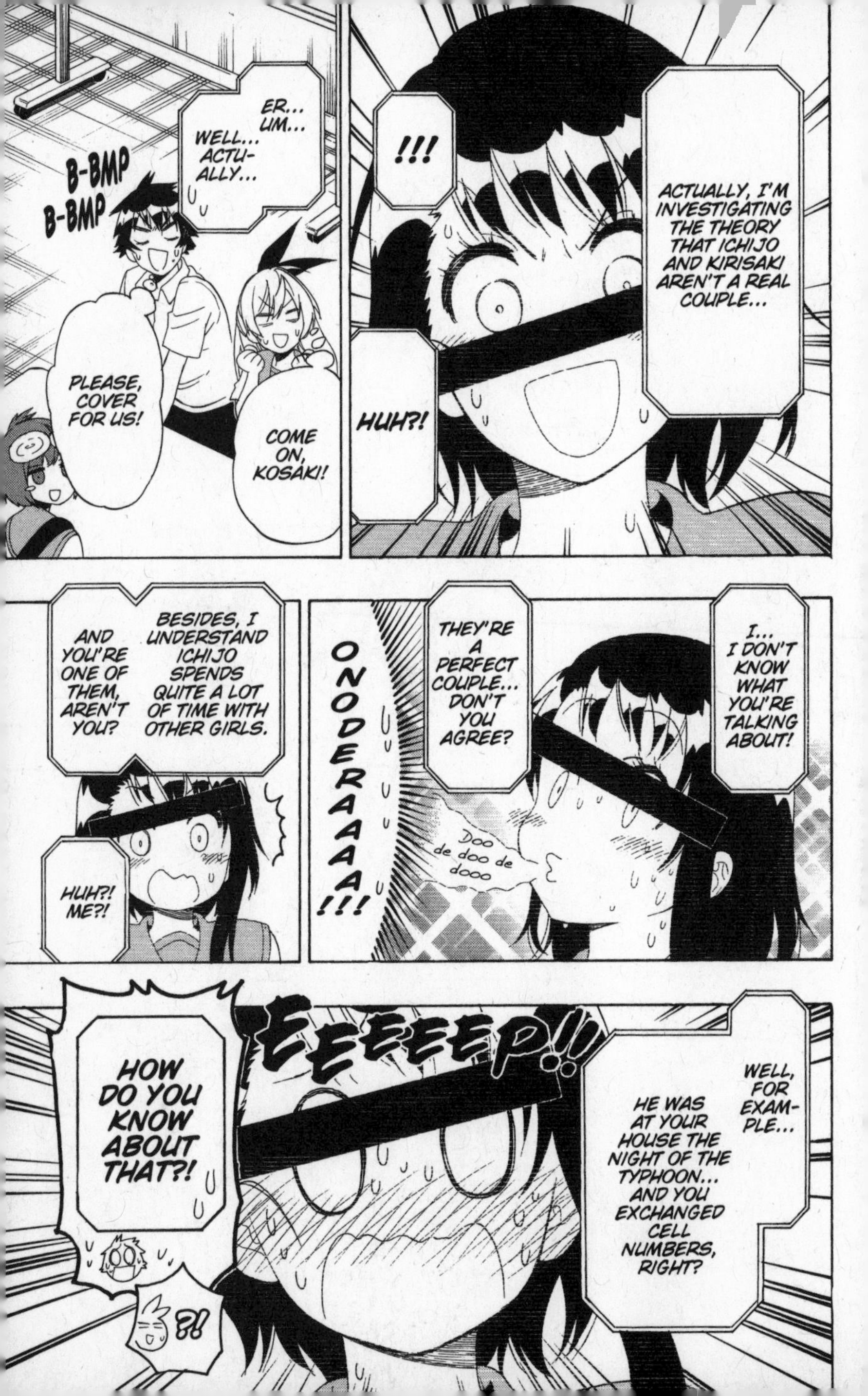
ACTUALLY, I'M INVESTIGATING THE THEORY THAT ICHIJO AND KIRISAKI AREN'T A REAL COUPLE...
!!!
HUH?!
ER... UM...
WELL... ACTUALLY...
B-BMP B-BMP
COME ON, KOSAKI!
PLEASE, COVER FOR US!
I... I DON'T KNOW WHAT YOU'RE TALKING ABOUT!
THEY'RE A PERFECT COUPLE... DON'T YOU AGREE?
ONODERAAAA!!!
Doo de doo de dooo
BESIDES, I UNDERSTAND ICHIJO SPENDS QUITE A LOT OF TIME WITH OTHER GIRLS.
AND YOU'RE ONE OF THEM, AREN'T YOU?
HUH?! ME?!
WELL, FOR EXAMPLE...
HE WAS AT YOUR HOUSE THE NIGHT OF THE TYPHOON... AND YOU EXCHANGED CELL NUMBERS, RIGHT?
EEEEEEP!!
HOW DO YOU KNOW ABOUT THAT?!
?!

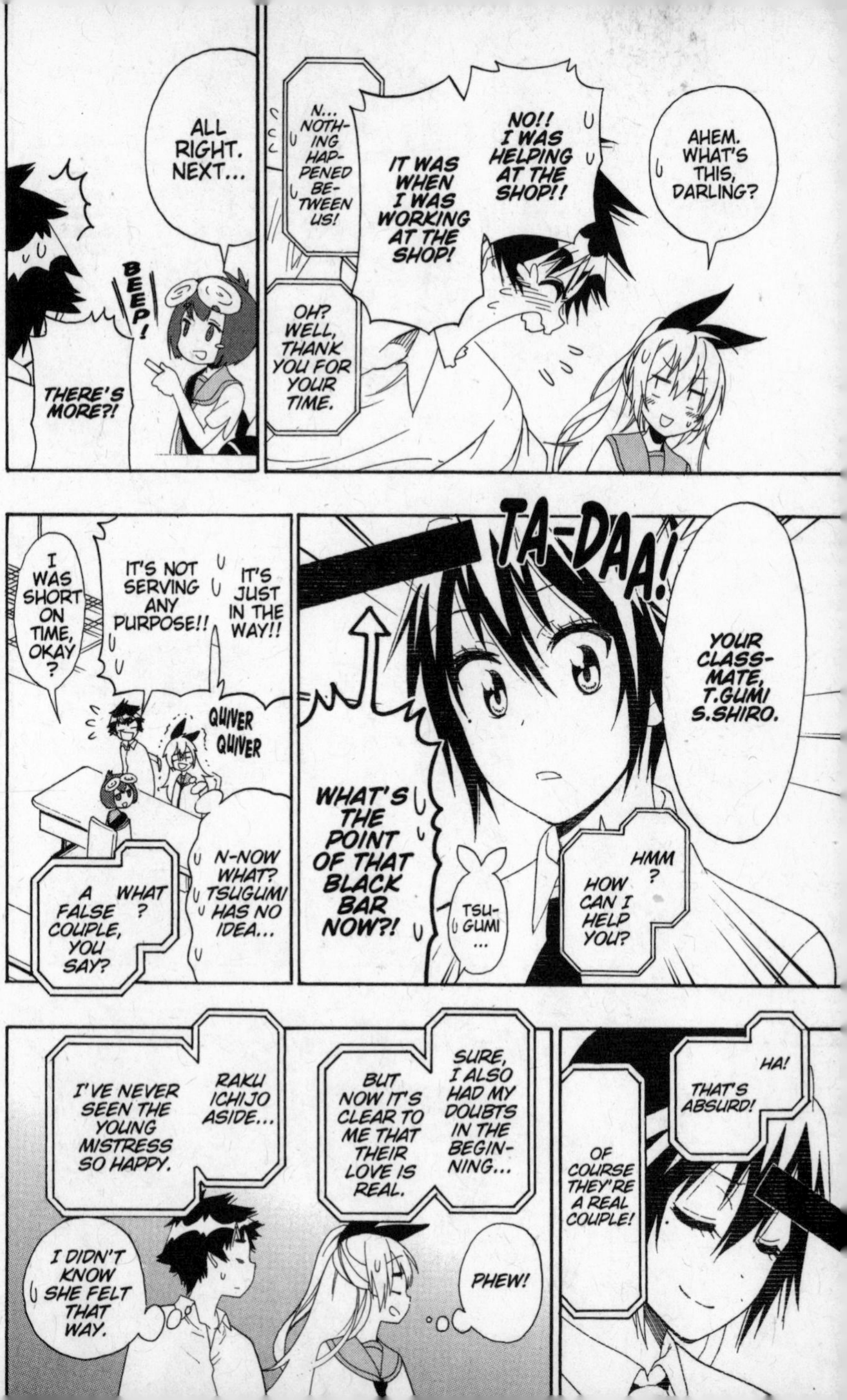
AHEM. WHAT'S THIS, DARLING?
NO!! I WAS HELPING AT THE SHOP!!
IT WAS WHEN I WAS WORKING AT THE SHOP!
N... NOTHING HAPPENED BETWEEN US!
OH? WELL, THANK YOU FOR YOUR TIME.
ALL RIGHT. NEXT...
BEEP!
THERE'S MORE?!
TA-DAA!
YOUR CLASSMATE, T.GUMI S.SHIRO.
HMM? HOW CAN I HELP YOU?
TSUGUMI...
WHAT'S THE POINT OF THAT BLACK BAR NOW?!
IT'S JUST IN THE WAY!!
IT'S NOT SERVING ANY PURPOSE!!
I WAS SHORT ON TIME, OKAY?
QUIVER QUIVER
N-NOW WHAT? TSUGUMI HAS NO IDEA...
WHAT? A FALSE COUPLE, YOU SAY?
HA! THAT'S ABSURD!
OF COURSE THEY'RE A REAL COUPLE!
SURE, I ALSO HAD MY DOUBTS IN THE BEGINNING...
BUT NOW IT'S CLEAR TO ME THAT THEIR LOVE IS REAL.
RAKU ICHIJO ASIDE...
I'VE NEVER SEEN THE YOUNG MISTRESS SO HAPPY.
PHEW!
I DIDN'T KNOW SHE FELT THAT WAY.

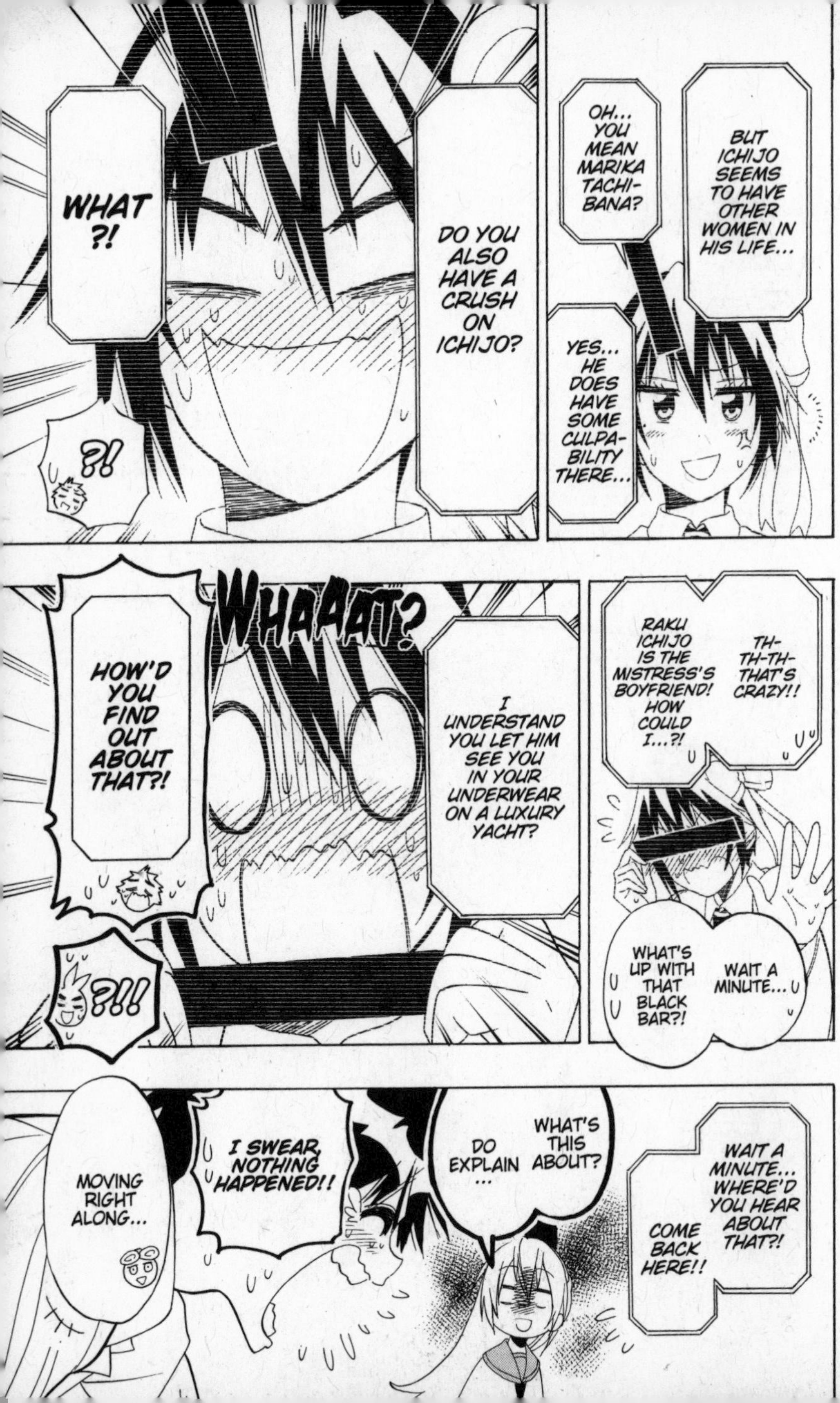
BUT ICHIJO SEEMS TO HAVE OTHER WOMEN IN HIS LIFE...
OH... YOU MEAN MARIKA TACHIBANA?
YES... HE DOES HAVE SOME CULPABILITY THERE...
DO YOU ALSO HAVE A CRUSH ON ICHIJO?
WHAT?!
?!
TH-TH-TH-THAT'S CRAZY!!
RAKU ICHIJO IS THE MISTRESS'S BOYFRIEND! HOW COULD I...?!
WAIT A MINUTE...
WHAT'S UP WITH THAT BLACK BAR?!
I UNDERSTAND YOU LET HIM SEE YOU IN YOUR UNDERWEAR ON A LUXURY YACHT?
WHAAAT?
HOW'D YOU FIND OUT ABOUT THAT?!
?!!
WAIT A MINUTE... WHERE'D YOU HEAR ABOUT THAT?!
COME BACK HERE!!
WHAT'S THIS ABOUT?
DO EXPLAIN...
I SWEAR, NOTHING HAPPENED!!
MOVING RIGHT ALONG...

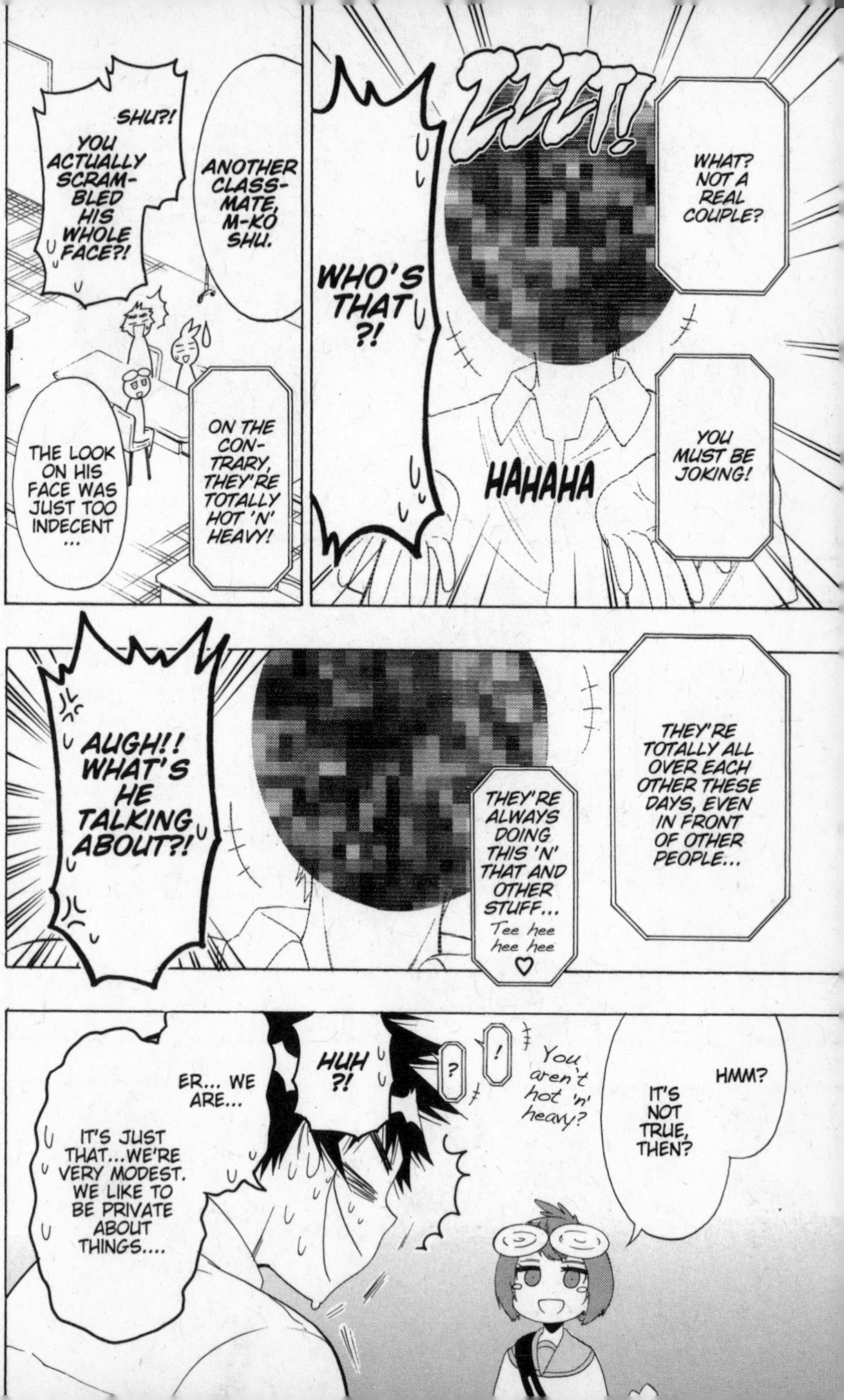
ZZZT!
WHAT? NOT A REAL COUPLE?
YOU MUST BE JOKING!
HAHAHA
WHO'S THAT ?!
ANOTHER CLASSMATE, M-KO SHU.
SHU?! YOU ACTUALLY SCRAMBLED HIS WHOLE FACE?!
ON THE CONTRARY, THEY'RE TOTALLY HOT 'N' HEAVY!
THE LOOK ON HIS FACE WAS JUST TOO INDECENT ...
THEY'RE TOTALLY ALL OVER EACH OTHER THESE DAYS, EVEN IN FRONT OF OTHER PEOPLE...
THEY'RE ALWAYS DOING THIS 'N' THAT AND OTHER STUFF... Tee hee hee hee ♡
AUGH!! WHAT'S HE TALKING ABOUT?!
HMM?
IT'S NOT TRUE, THEN?
You aren't hot 'n' heavy?
!
?
HUH ?!
ER... WE ARE...
IT'S JUST THAT...WE'RE VERY MODEST. WE LIKE TO BE PRIVATE ABOUT THINGS....

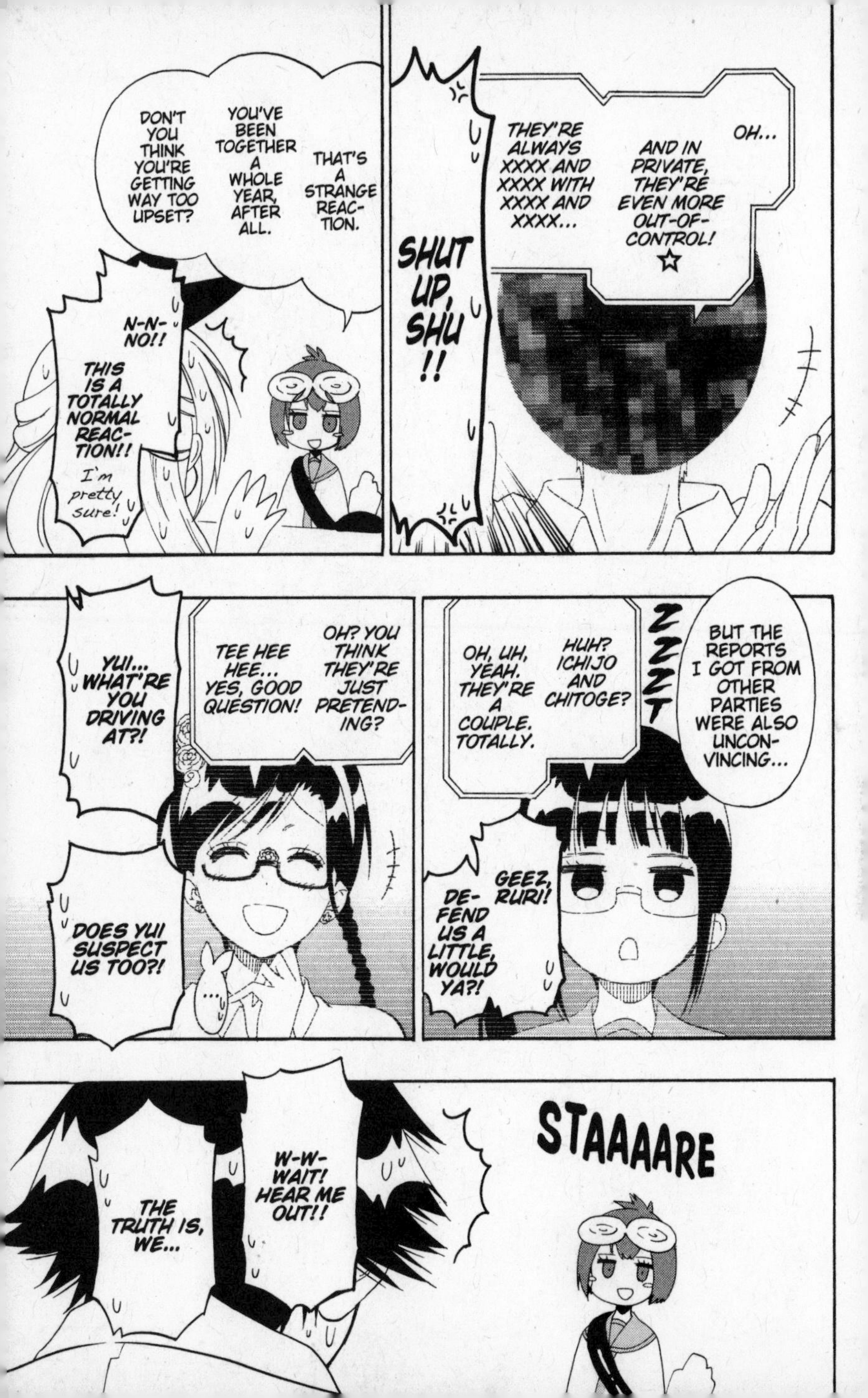
OH...
AND IN PRIVATE, THEY'RE EVEN MORE OUT-OF-CONTROL! ☆
THEY'RE ALWAYS XXXX AND XXXX WITH XXXX AND XXXX...
SHUT UP, SHU!!
THAT'S A STRANGE REACTION.
YOU'VE BEEN TOGETHER A WHOLE YEAR, AFTER ALL.
DON'T YOU THINK YOU'RE GETTING WAY TOO UPSET?
N-N-NO!! THIS IS A TOTALLY NORMAL REACTION!! I'm pretty sure!
BUT THE REPORTS I GOT FROM OTHER PARTIES WERE ALSO UNCONVINCING...
ZZZT
HUH? ICHIJO AND CHITOGE?
OH, UH, YEAH. THEY'RE A COUPLE. TOTALLY.
GEEZ, RURI! DEFEND US A LITTLE, WOULD YA?!
OH? YOU THINK THEY'RE JUST PRETENDING?
TEE HEE HEE... YES, GOOD QUESTION!
YUI... WHAT'RE YOU DRIVING AT?!
DOES YUI SUSPECT US TOO?!
...
STAAAARE
W-W-WAIT! HEAR ME OUT!!
THE TRUTH IS, WE...

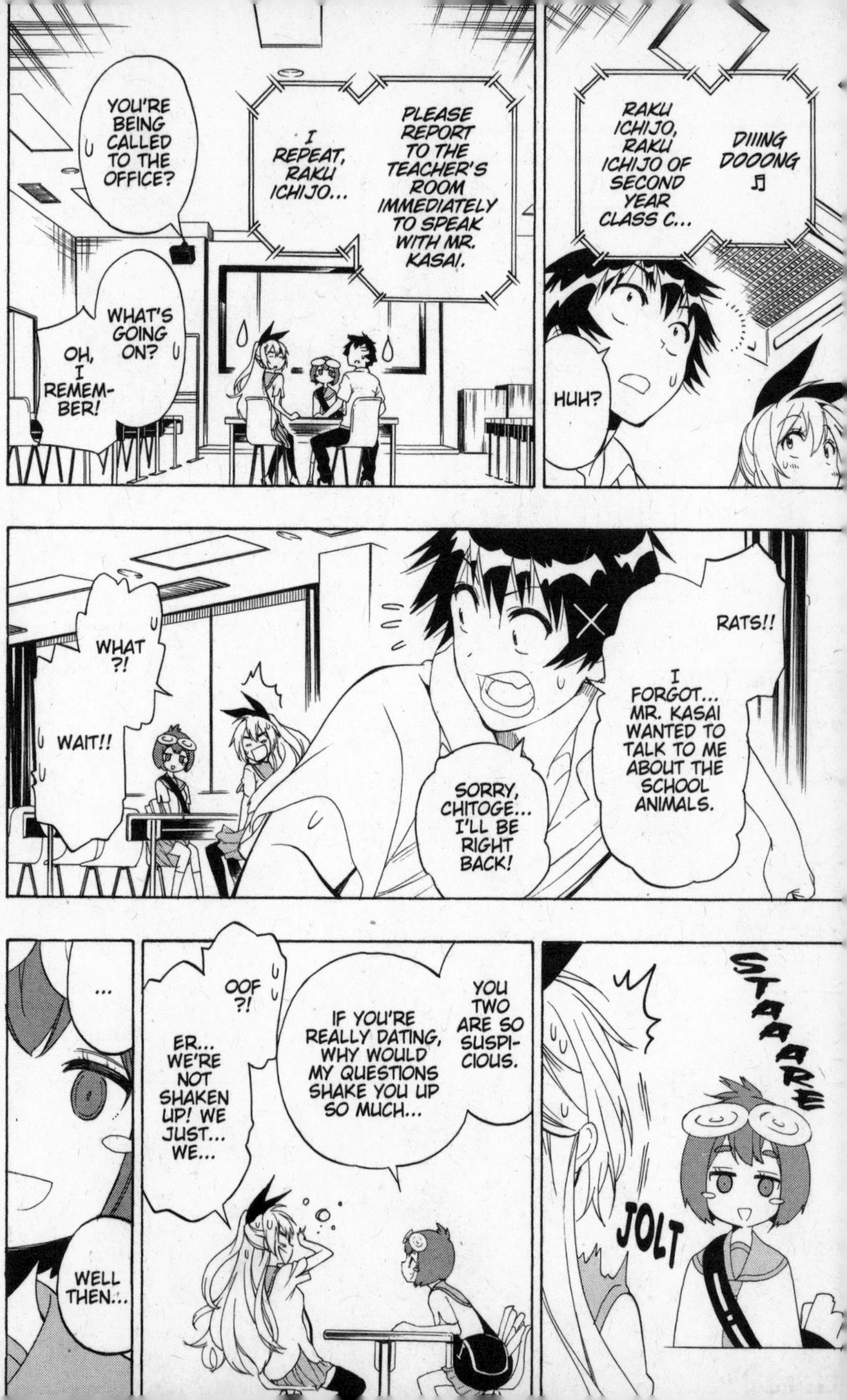
DIIING DOOONG ♫
RAKU ICHIJO, RAKU ICHIJO OF SECOND YEAR CLASS C...
HUH?
I REPEAT, RAKU ICHIJO... PLEASE REPORT TO THE TEACHER'S ROOM IMMEDIATELY TO SPEAK WITH MR. KASAI.
YOU'RE BEING CALLED TO THE OFFICE?
WHAT'S GOING ON?
OH, I REMEMBER!
RATS!!
I FORGOT... MR. KASAI WANTED TO TALK TO ME ABOUT THE SCHOOL ANIMALS.
SORRY, CHITOGE... I'LL BE RIGHT BACK!
WHAT?!
WAIT!!
STAAARE
JOLT
YOU TWO ARE SO SUSPICIOUS.
IF YOU'RE REALLY DATING, WHY WOULD MY QUESTIONS SHAKE YOU UP SO MUCH...
OOF?!
ER... WE'RE NOT SHAKEN UP! WE JUST... WE...
...
WELL THEN...

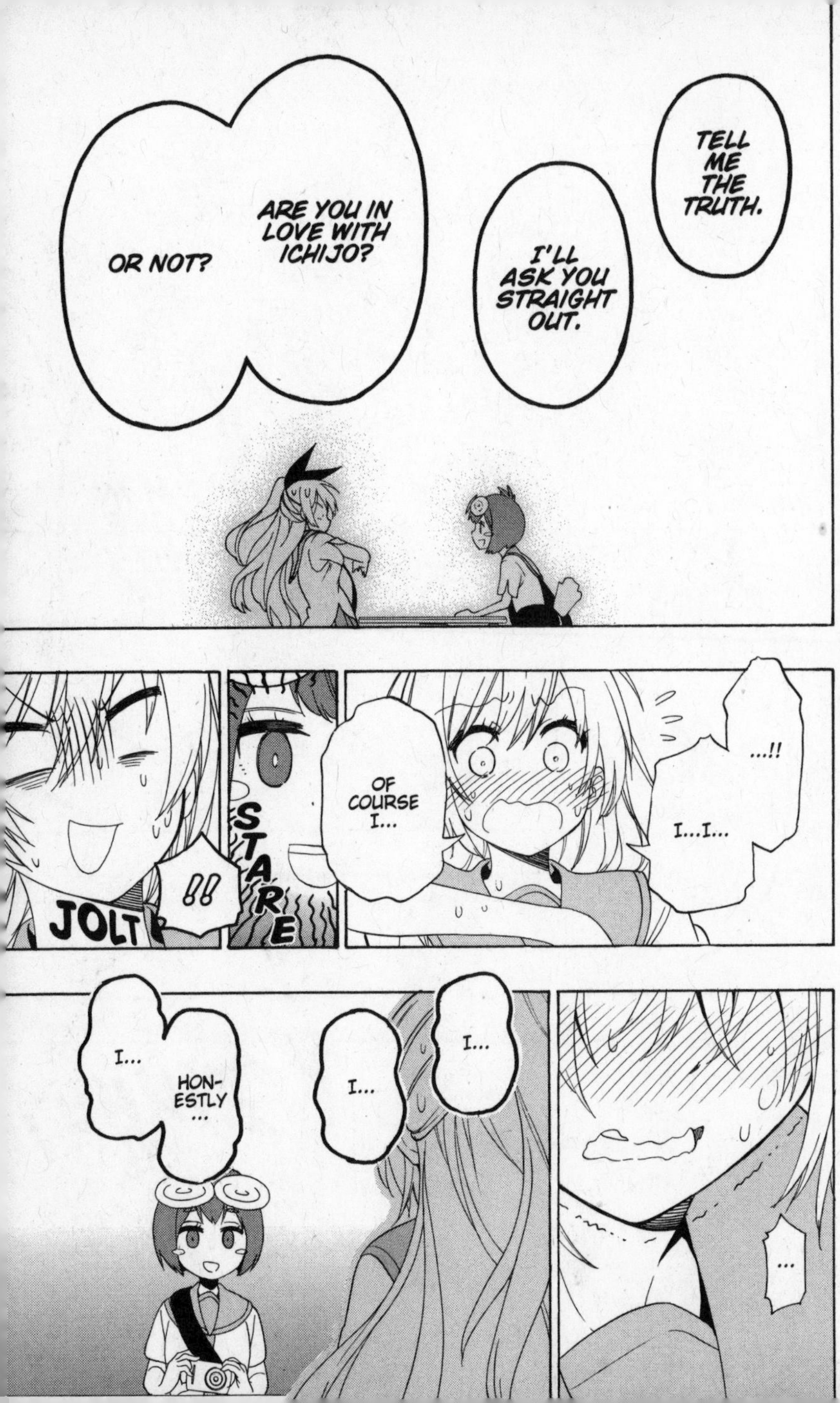
TELL ME THE TRUTH.
I'LL ASK YOU STRAIGHT OUT.
ARE YOU IN LOVE WITH ICHIJO?
OR NOT?
...!!
I...I...
OF COURSE I...
STARE
!!
JOLT
...
I...
I...
I...
HON-ESTLY ...

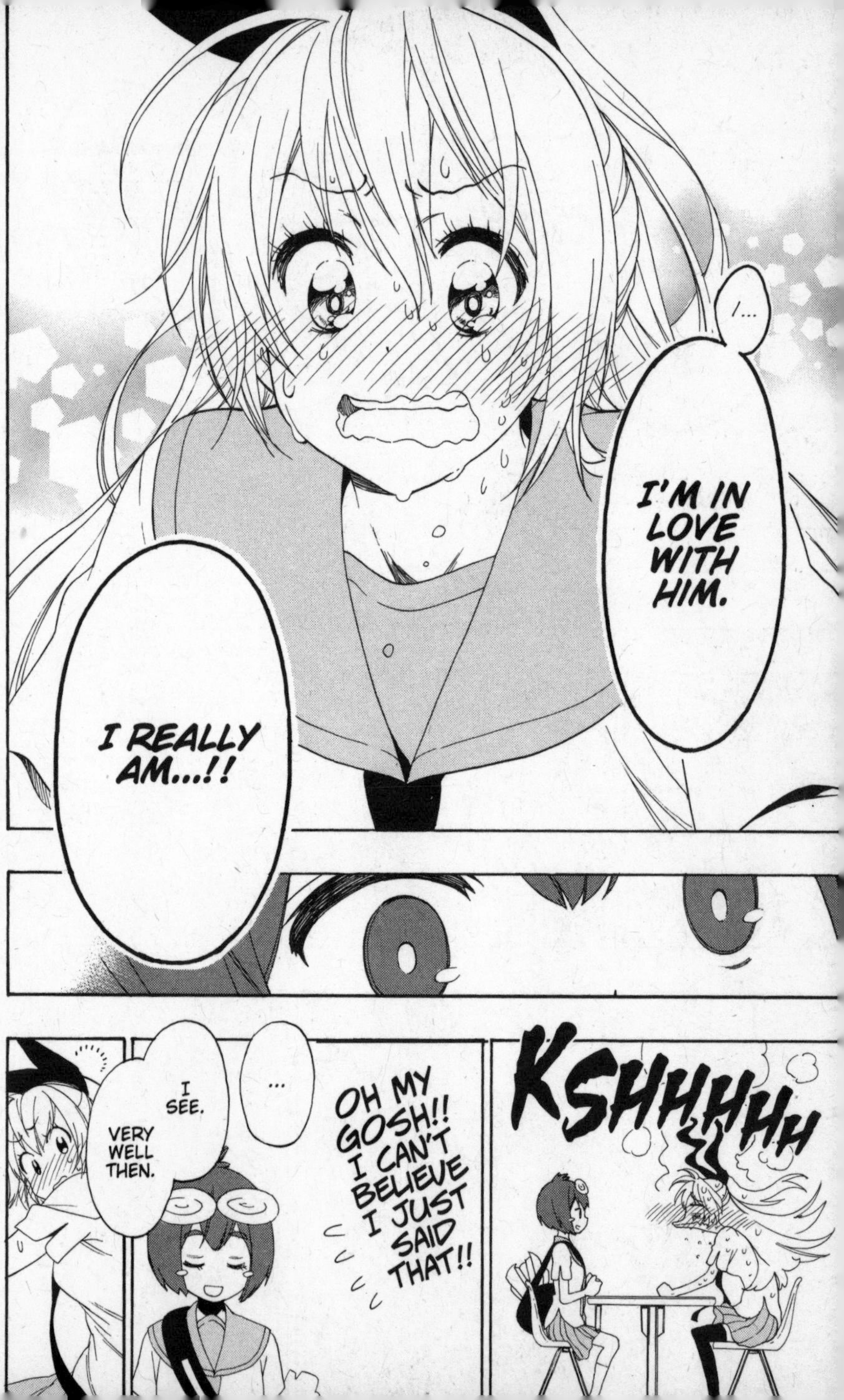
I...
I'M IN LOVE WITH HIM.
I REALLY AM...!!
KSHHHHH
OH MY GOSH!! I CAN'T BELIEVE I JUST SAID THAT!!
...
I SEE.
VERY WELL THEN.

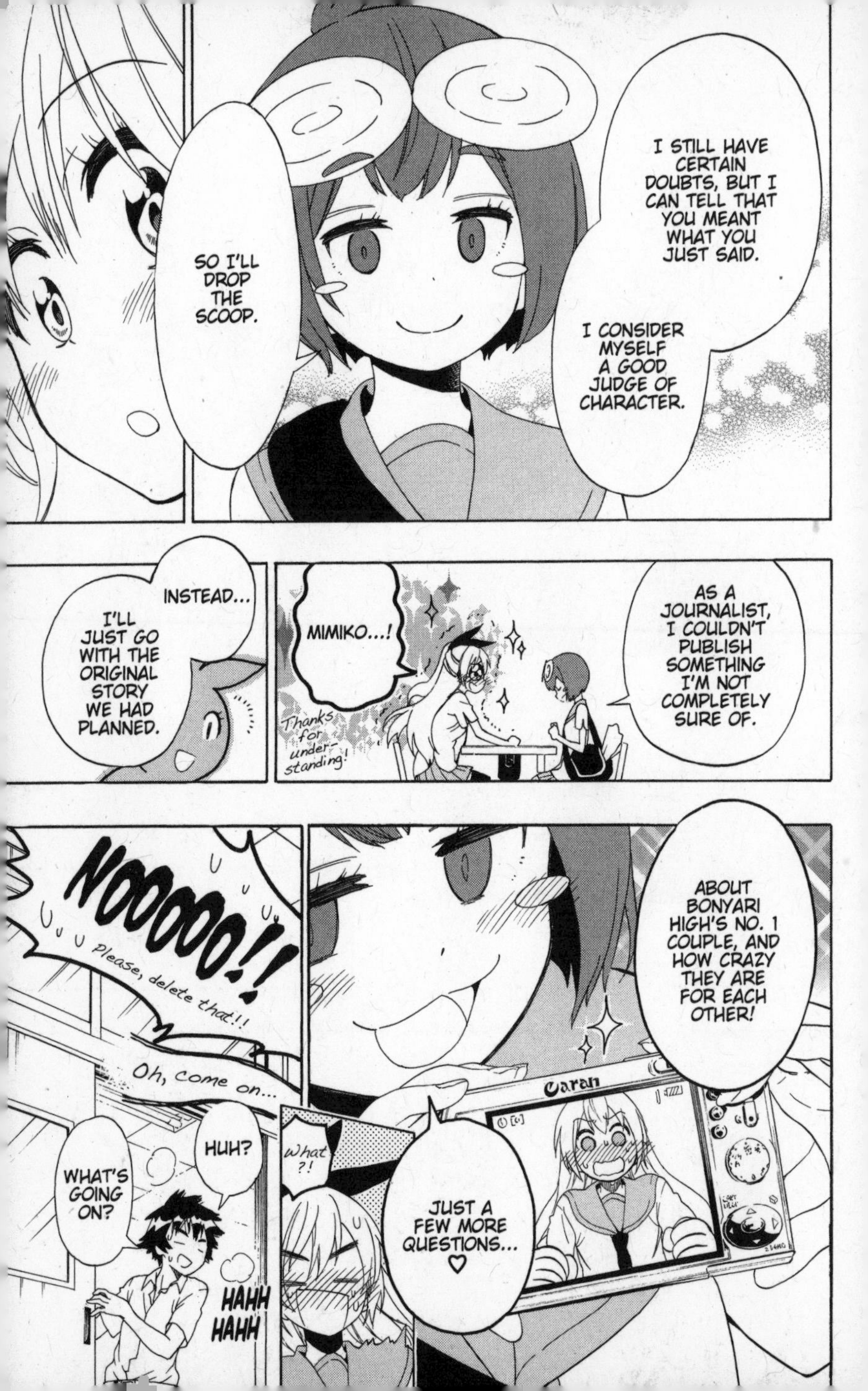
I STILL HAVE CERTAIN DOUBTS, BUT I CAN TELL THAT YOU MEANT WHAT YOU JUST SAID.
I CONSIDER MYSELF A GOOD JUDGE OF CHARACTER.
SO I'LL DROP THE SCOOP.
AS A JOURNALIST, I COULDN'T PUBLISH SOMETHING I'M NOT COMPLETELY SURE OF.
MIMIKO...!
Thanks for understanding!
INSTEAD...
I'LL JUST GO WITH THE ORIGINAL STORY WE HAD PLANNED.
ABOUT BONYARI HIGH'S NO. 1 COUPLE, AND HOW CRAZY THEY ARE FOR EACH OTHER!
Caran
JUST A FEW MORE QUESTIONS... ♡
What?!
NOOOOO!!
Please, delete that!!
Oh, come on...
HUH?
WHAT'S GOING ON?
HAHH HAHH

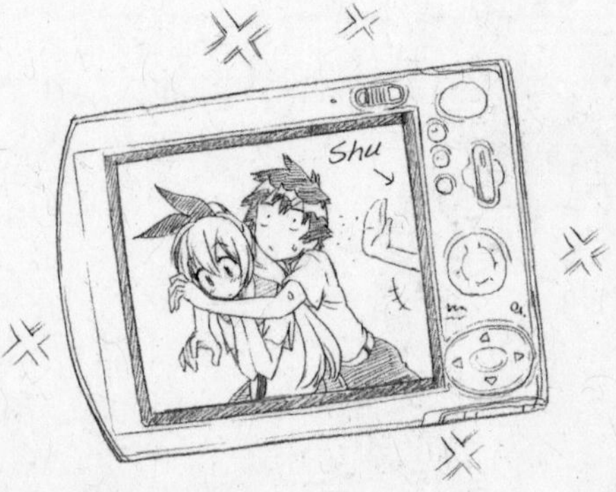
Shu

Chitoge: "Hey! Whendja take this?!"

Mimiko: "Shall I print it for you?"

Chitoge: "Yes!!!"

Chitoge: "I mean, no! Delete it!!"

Mimiko: "Aww..."

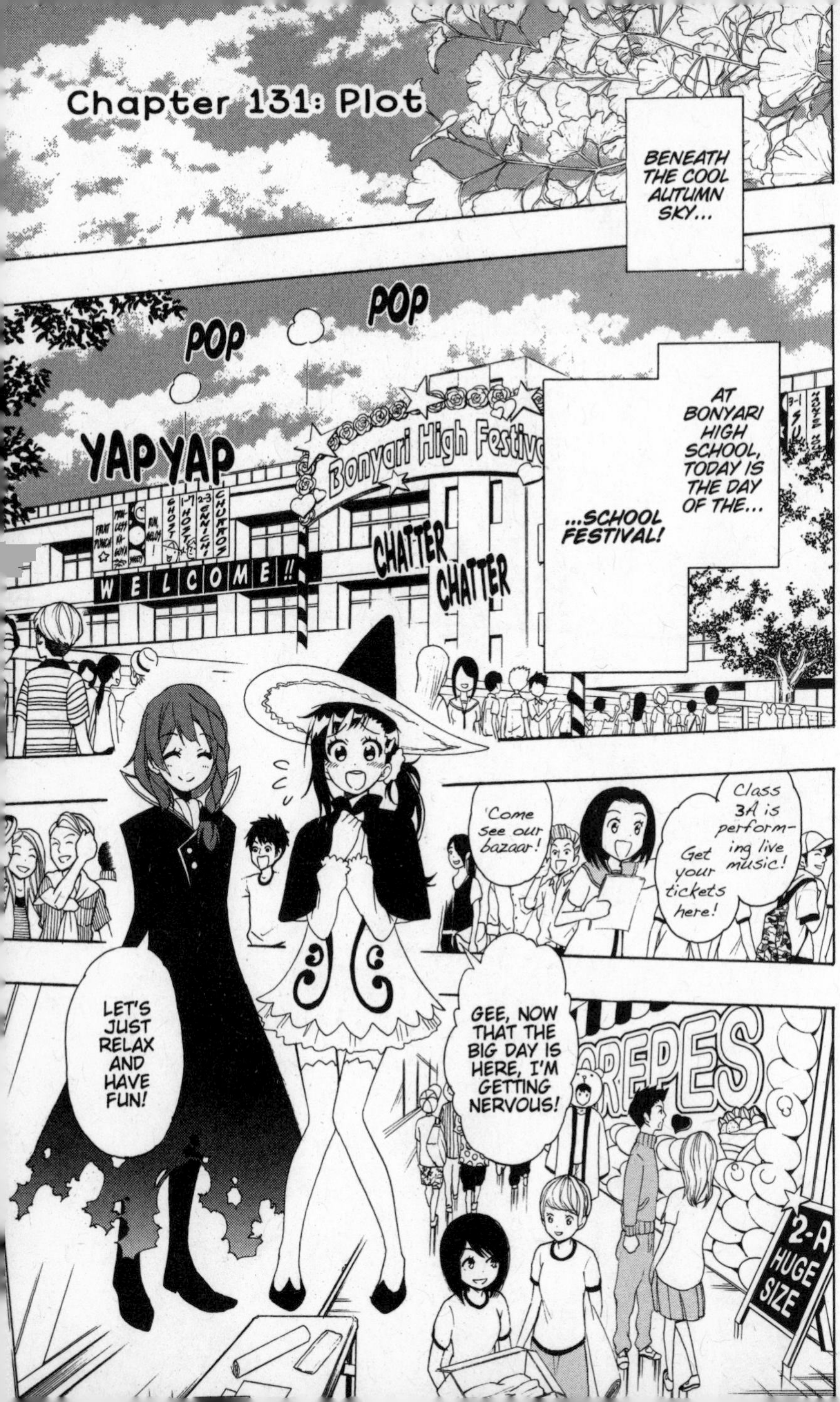
Chapter 131: Plot
BENEATH THE COOL AUTUMN SKY...
POP
POP
AT BONYARI HIGH SCHOOL, TODAY IS THE DAY OF THE...
...SCHOOL FESTIVAL!
Bonyari High Festiv
YAP YAP
CHATTER CHATTER
WELCOME!!
Class 3A is performing live music!
Get your tickets here!
'Come see our bazaar!
GEE, NOW THAT THE BIG DAY IS HERE, I'M GETTING NERVOUS!
LET'S JUST RELAX AND HAVE FUN!
CREPES
2-A HUGE SIZE

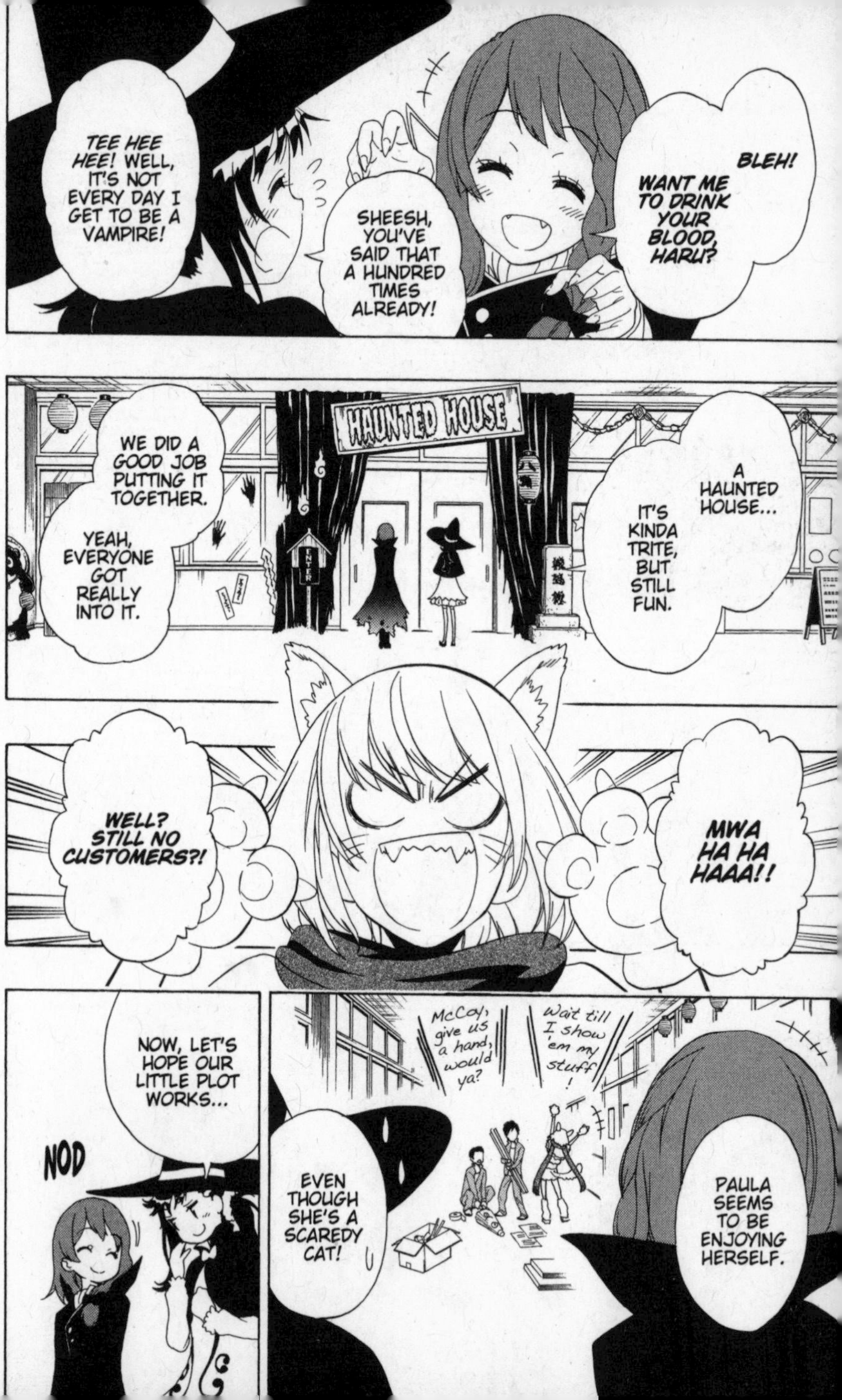
BLEH!
WANT ME TO DRINK YOUR BLOOD, HARU?
SHEESH, YOU'VE SAID THAT A HUNDRED TIMES ALREADY!
TEE HEE HEE! WELL, IT'S NOT EVERY DAY I GET TO BE A VAMPIRE!
HAUNTED HOUSE
A HAUNTED HOUSE...
IT'S KINDA TRITE, BUT STILL FUN.
ENTER
WE DID A GOOD JOB PUTTING IT TOGETHER.
YEAH, EVERYONE GOT REALLY INTO IT.
MWA HA HA HAAA!!
WELL? STILL NO CUSTOMERS?!
PAULA SEEMS TO BE ENJOYING HERSELF.
Wait till I show 'em my stuff!
McCoy, give us a hand, would ya?
EVEN THOUGH SHE'S A SCAREDY CAT!
NOW, LET'S HOPE OUR LITTLE PLOT WORKS...
NOD

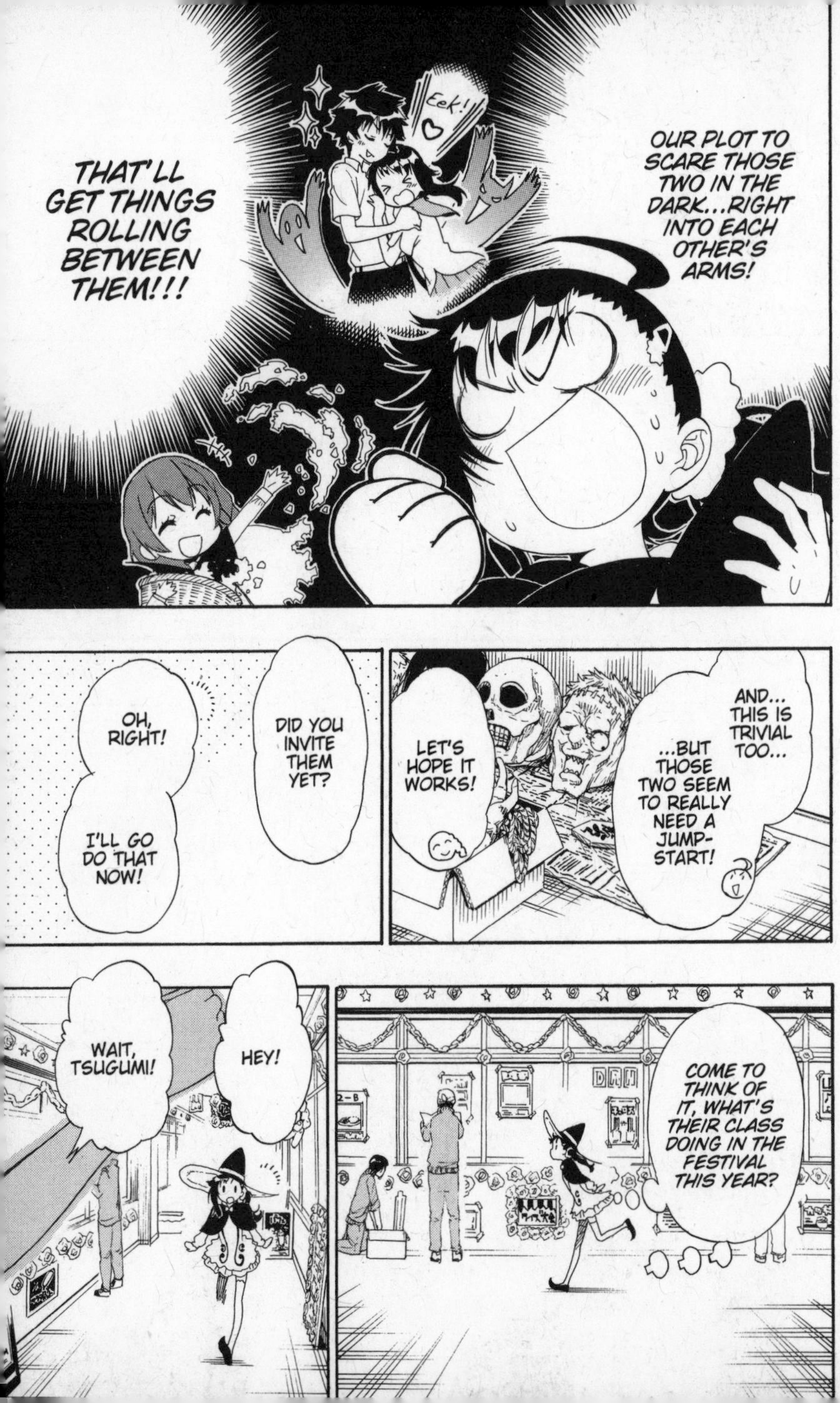
OUR PLOT TO SCARE THOSE TWO IN THE DARK...RIGHT INTO EACH OTHER'S ARMS!
Eek!
THAT'LL GET THINGS ROLLING BETWEEN THEM!!!
AND... THIS IS TRIVIAL TOO...
...BUT THOSE TWO SEEM TO REALLY NEED A JUMP-START!
LET'S HOPE IT WORKS!
DID YOU INVITE THEM YET?
OH, RIGHT!
I'LL GO DO THAT NOW!
COME TO THINK OF IT, WHAT'S THEIR CLASS DOING IN THE FESTIVAL THIS YEAR?
HEY!
WAIT, TSUGUMI!

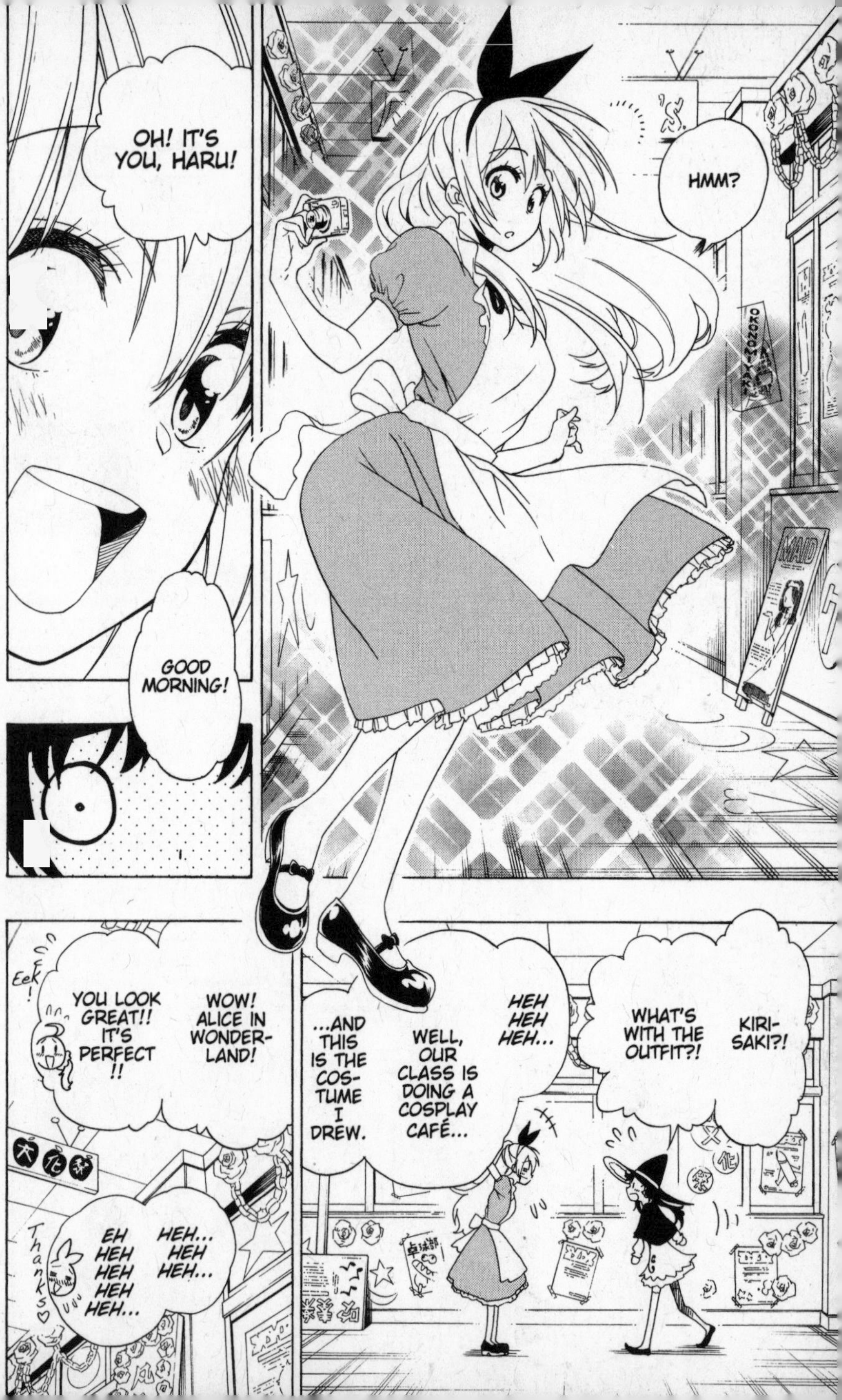
HMM?
OKONOMIYAKI
MAID
OH! IT'S YOU, HARU!
GOOD MORNING!
KIRI-SAKI?!
WHAT'S WITH THE OUTFIT?!
HEH HEH HEH...
WELL, OUR CLASS IS DOING A COSPLAY CAFÉ...
...AND THIS IS THE COS-TUME I DREW.
WOW! ALICE IN WONDER-LAND!
YOU LOOK GREAT!! IT'S PERFECT!!
Eek!
HEH... HEH HEH...
EH HEH HEH HEH HEH...
Thanks♡

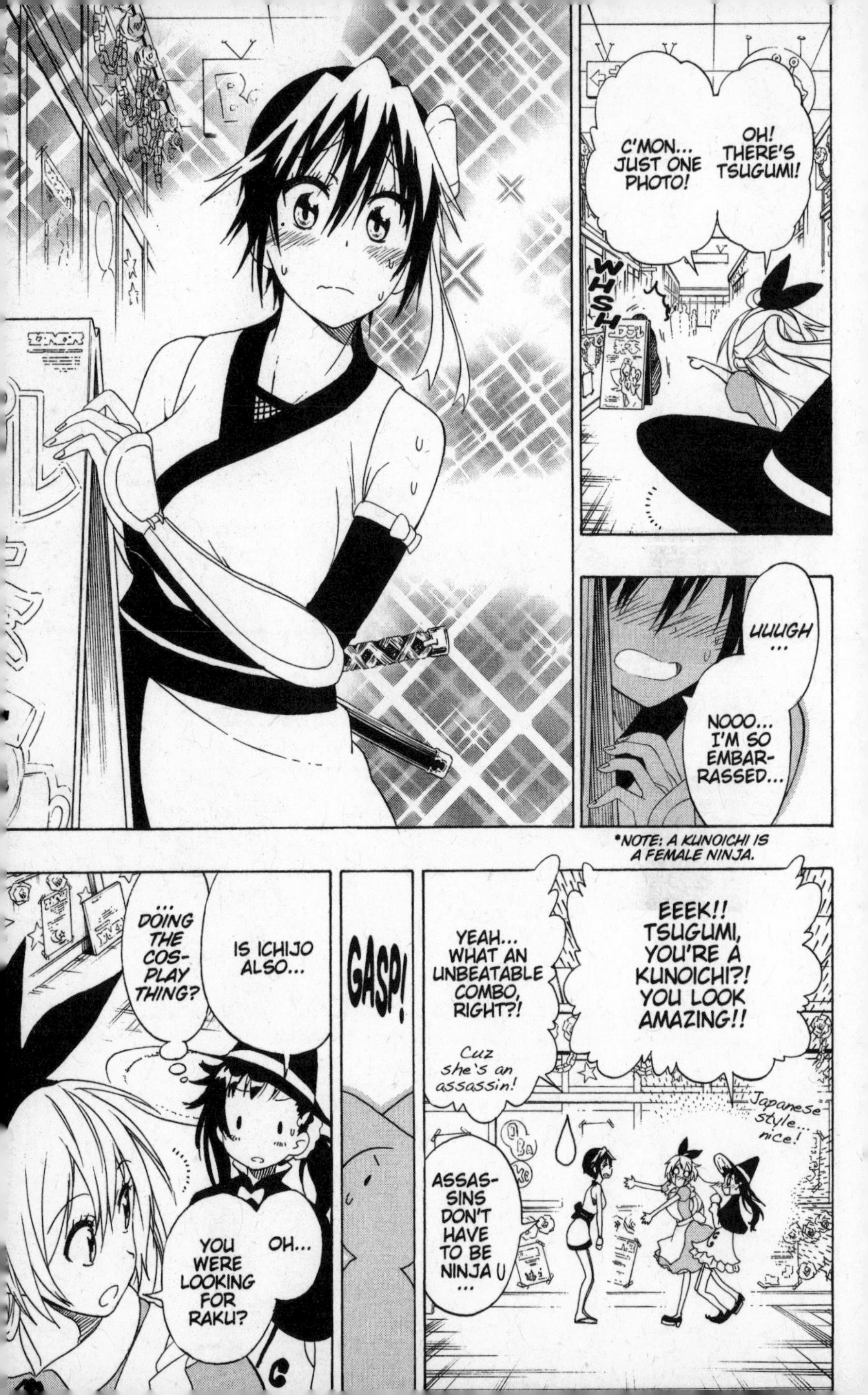
OH! THERE'S TSUGUMI!
C'MON... JUST ONE PHOTO!
WHSH
UUUGH...
NOOO... I'M SO EMBARRASSED...
*NOTE: A KUNOICHI IS A FEMALE NINJA.
EEEK!! TSUGUMI, YOU'RE A KUNOICHI?! YOU LOOK AMAZING!!
Japanese style... nice!
YEAH... WHAT AN UNBEATABLE COMBO, RIGHT?!
Cuz she's an assassin!
ASSAS-SINS DON'T HAVE TO BE NINJA...
GASP!
IS ICHIJO ALSO...
...DOING THE COS-PLAY THING?
OH...
YOU WERE LOOKING FOR RAKU?

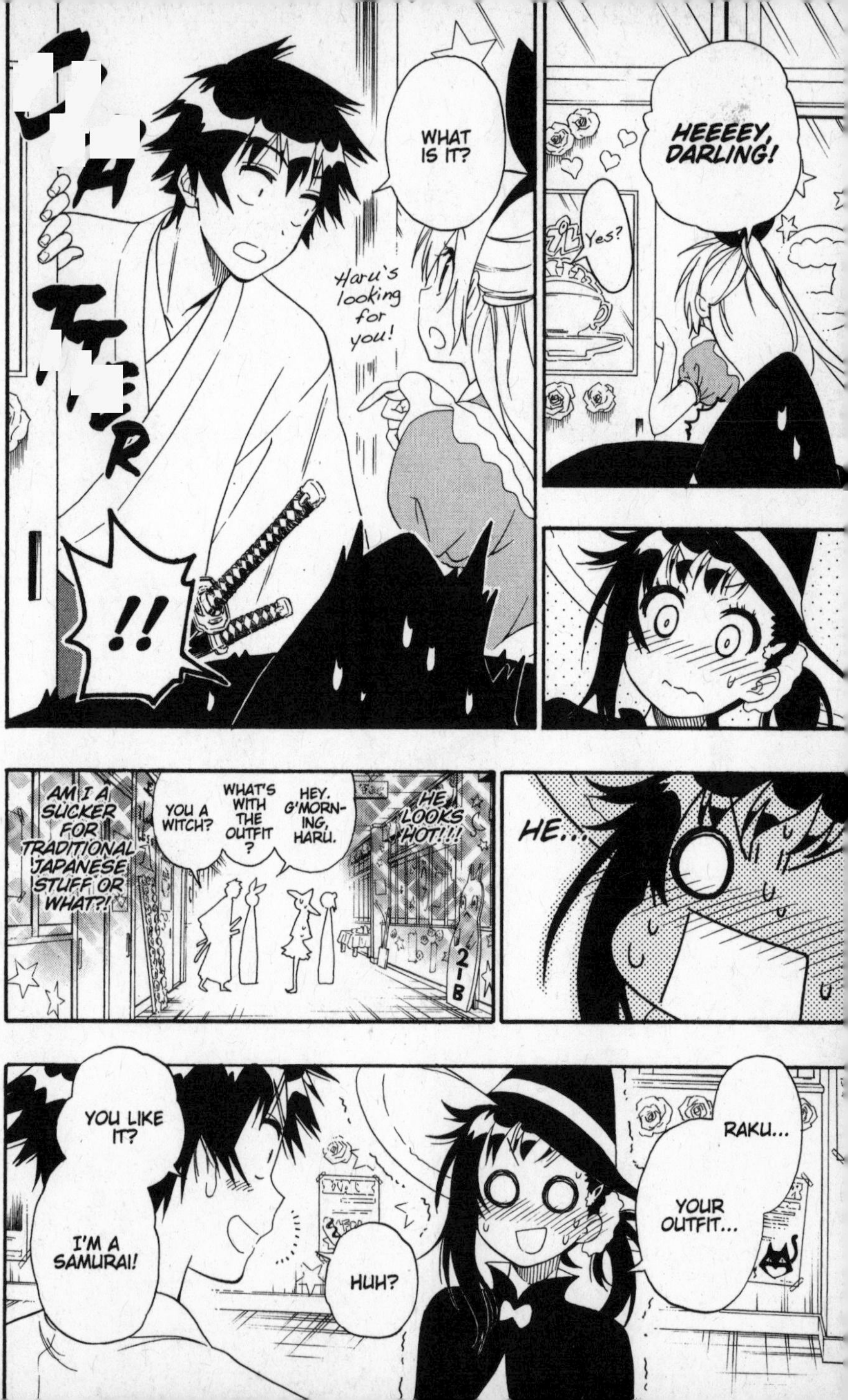
HEEEEY, DARLING!
Yes?
WHAT IS IT?
Haru's looking for you!
!!
HE...
HE LOOKS HOT!!!
HEY. G'MORNING, HARU.
WHAT'S WITH THE OUTFIT?
YOU A WITCH?
AM I A SUCKER FOR TRADITIONAL JAPANESE STUFF OR WHAT?!
RAKU...
YOUR OUTFIT...
HUH?
YOU LIKE IT?
I'M A SAMURAI!

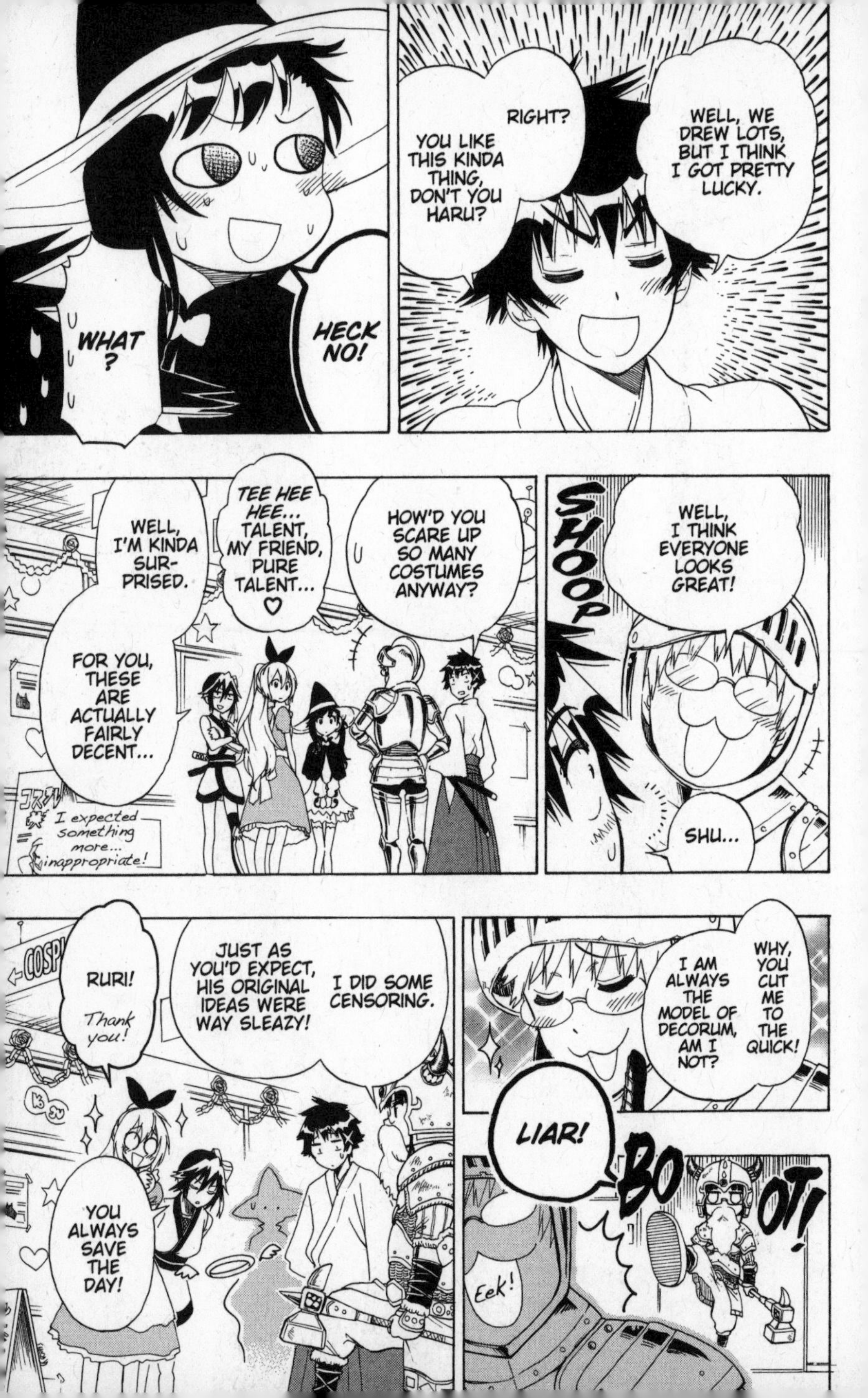
WELL, WE DREW LOTS, BUT I THINK I GOT PRETTY LUCKY.
RIGHT?
YOU LIKE THIS KINDA THING, DON'T YOU HARU?
HECK NO!
WHAT?
SHOOOP
WELL, I THINK EVERYONE LOOKS GREAT!
SHU...
HOW'D YOU SCARE UP SO MANY COSTUMES ANYWAY?
TEE HEE HEE... TALENT, MY FRIEND, PURE TALENT... ♡
WELL, I'M KINDA SUR-PRISED.
FOR YOU, THESE ARE ACTUALLY FAIRLY DECENT...
I expected something more... inappropriate!
WHY, YOU CUT ME TO THE QUICK!
I AM ALWAYS THE MODEL OF DECORUM, AM I NOT?
LIAR!
BOOOT!
Eek!
I DID SOME CENSORING.
JUST AS YOU'D EXPECT, HIS ORIGINAL IDEAS WERE WAY SLEAZY!
RURI!
Thank you!
YOU ALWAYS SAVE THE DAY!

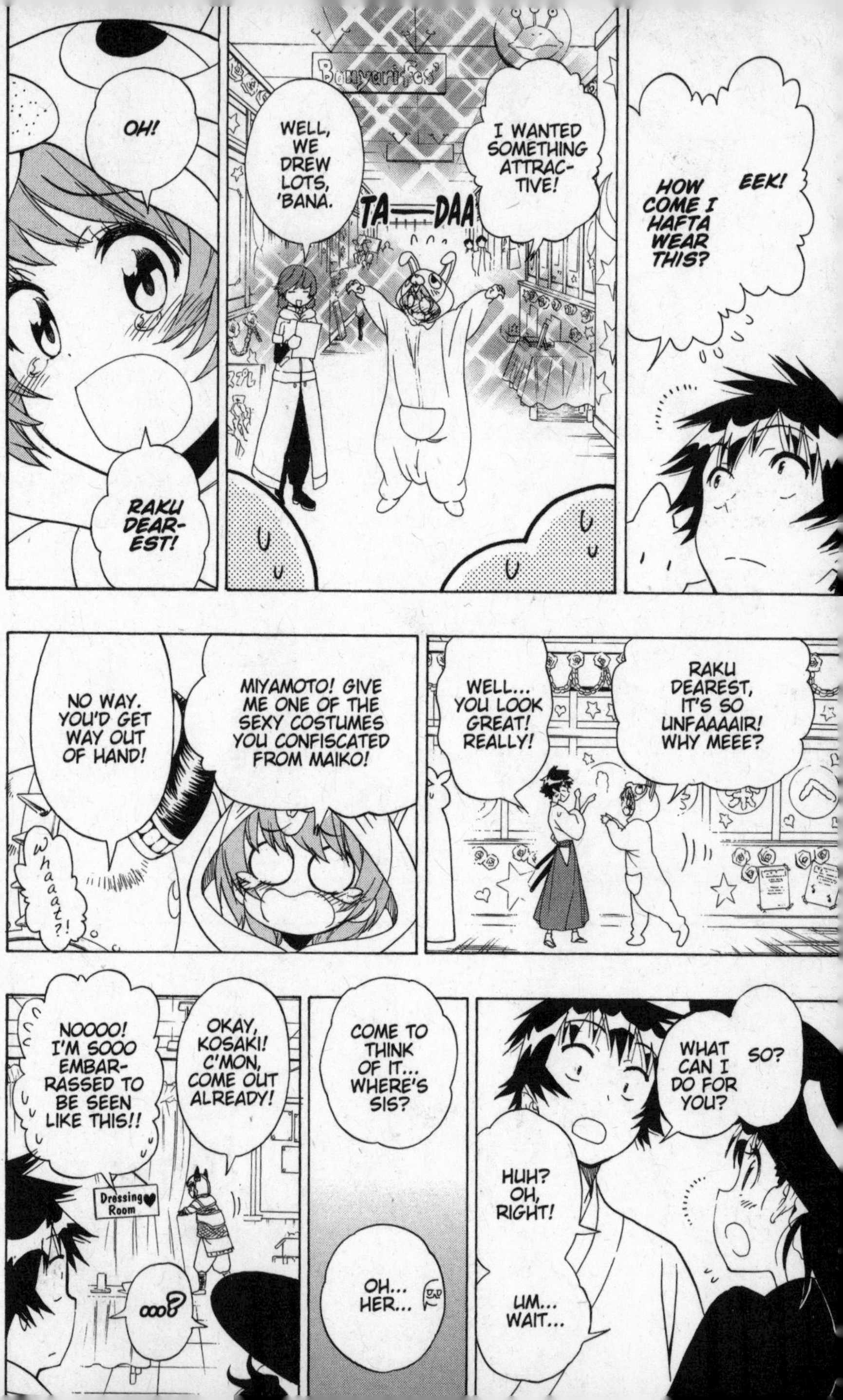
EEK!
HOW COME I HAFTA WEAR THIS?
I WANTED SOMETHING ATTRAC- TIVE!
TA—DAA
WELL, WE DREW LOTS, 'BANA.
OH!
RAKU DEAR- EST!
RAKU DEAREST, IT'S SO UNFAAAAIR! WHY MEEE?
WELL... YOU LOOK GREAT! REALLY!
MIYAMOTO! GIVE ME ONE OF THE SEXY COSTUMES YOU CONFISCATED FROM MAIKO!
NO WAY. YOU'D GET WAY OUT OF HAND!
Whaaat?!
SO?
WHAT CAN I DO FOR YOU?
HUH? OH, RIGHT!
UM... WAIT...
COME TO THINK OF IT... WHERE'S SIS?
OH... HER...
OKAY, KOSAKI! C'MON, COME OUT ALREADY!
NOOOO! I'M SOOO EMBAR- RASSED TO BE SEEN LIKE THIS!!
Dressing Room
ooo?

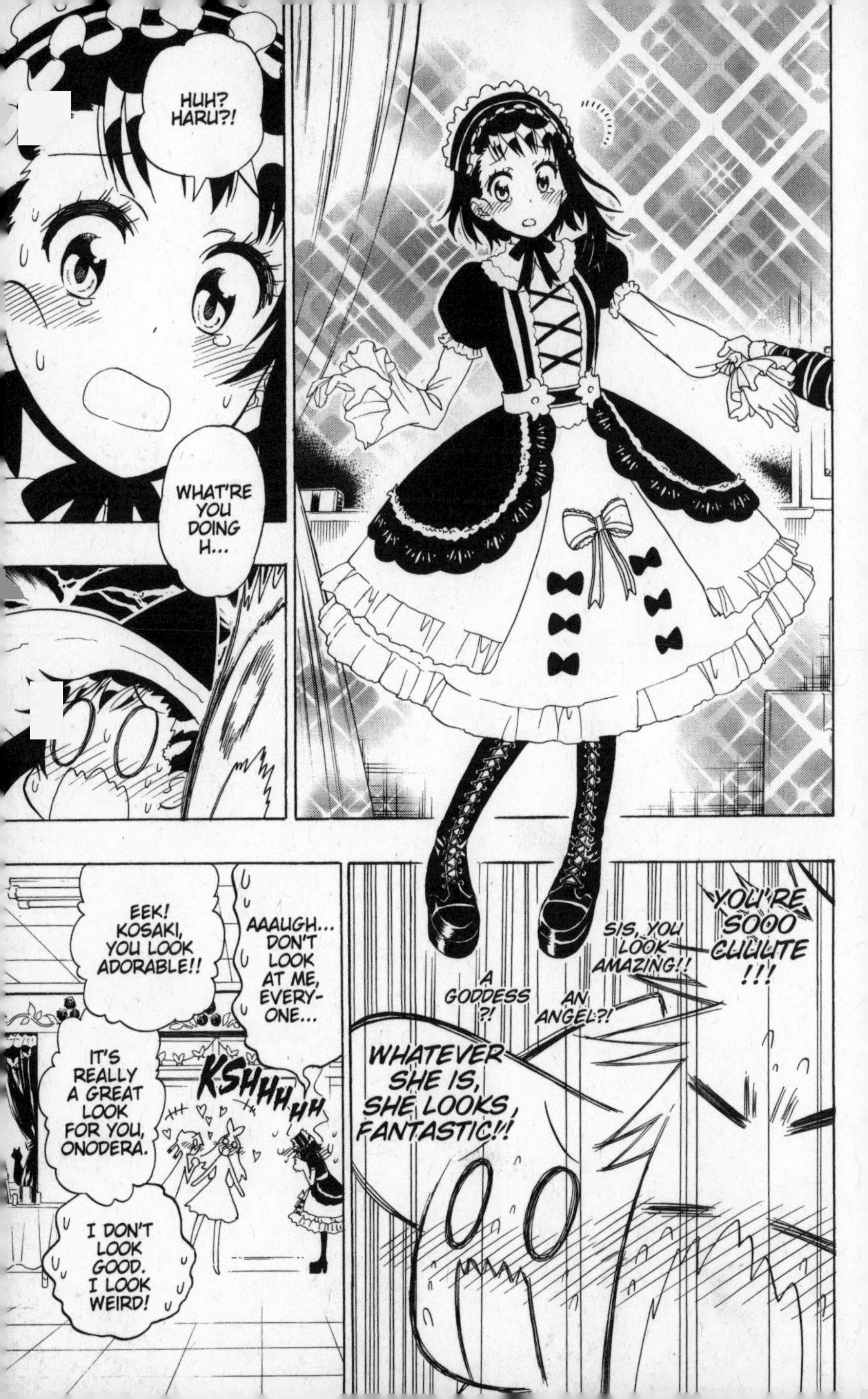
HUH? HARU?!
WHAT'RE YOU DOING H...
YOU'RE SOOO CUUUUTE!!!
SIS, YOU LOOK AMAZING!!
AN ANGEL?!
A GODDESS?!
WHATEVER SHE IS, SHE LOOKS FANTASTIC!!
AAAUGH... DON'T LOOK AT ME, EVERYONE...
EEK! KOSAKI, YOU LOOK ADORABLE!!
KSHHHHH
IT'S REALLY A GREAT LOOK FOR YOU, ONODERA.
I DON'T LOOK GOOD. I LOOK WEIRD!

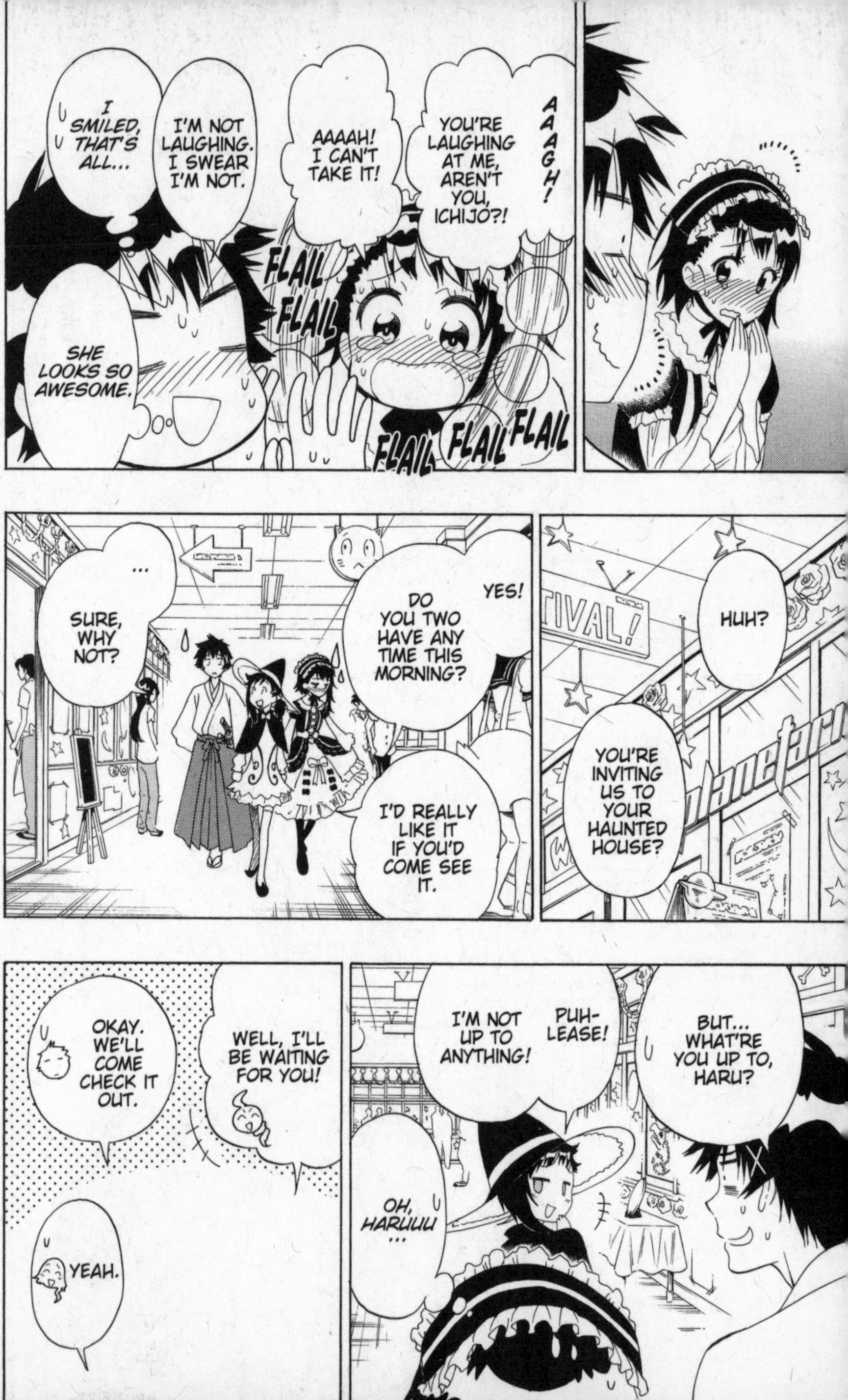
AAAGH!
YOU'RE LAUGHING AT ME, AREN'T YOU, ICHIJO?!
AAAAH! I CAN'T TAKE IT!
FLAIL FLAIL
FLAIL FLAIL FLAIL
I'M NOT LAUGHING. I SWEAR I'M NOT.
I SMILED, THAT'S ALL...
SHE LOOKS SO AWESOME.
HUH?
YOU'RE INVITING US TO YOUR HAUNTED HOUSE?
YES!
DO YOU TWO HAVE ANY TIME THIS MORNING?
I'D REALLY LIKE IT IF YOU'D COME SEE IT.
...
SURE, WHY NOT?
BUT... WHAT'RE YOU UP TO, HARU?
PUH-LEASE!
I'M NOT UP TO ANYTHING!
OH, HARUUU...
WELL, I'LL BE WAITING FOR YOU!
OKAY. WE'LL COME CHECK IT OUT.
YEAH.

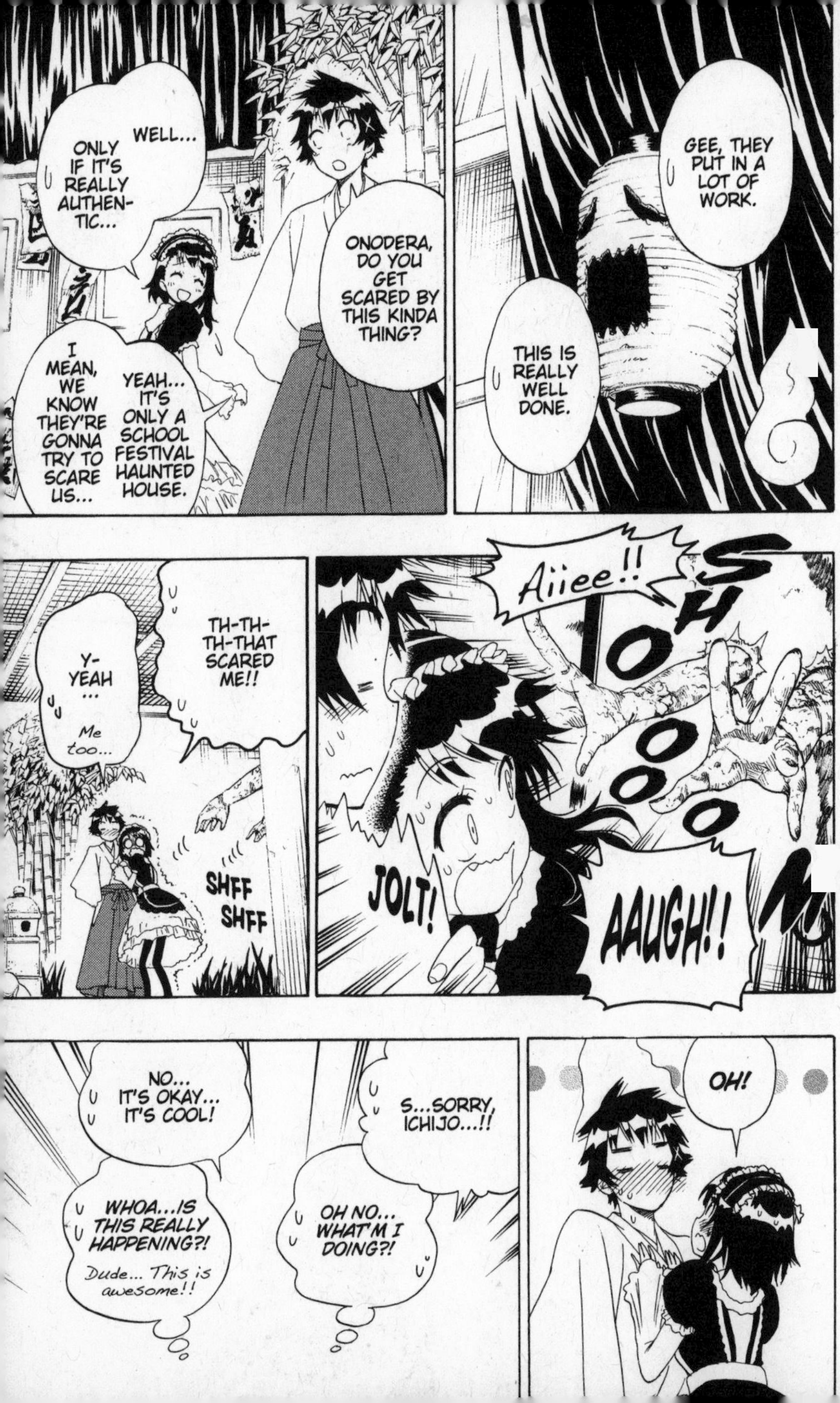
GEE, THEY PUT IN A LOT OF WORK.
THIS IS REALLY WELL DONE.
ONODERA, DO YOU GET SCARED BY THIS KINDA THING?
WELL... ONLY IF IT'S REALLY AUTHENTIC...
YEAH... IT'S ONLY A SCHOOL FESTIVAL HAUNTED HOUSE.
I MEAN, WE KNOW THEY'RE GONNA TRY TO SCARE US...
Aiiee!!
SHOOOOOM
AAUGH!!
JOLT!
TH-TH-TH-THAT SCARED ME!!
Y-YEAH...
Me too...
SHFF SHFF
OH!
S...SORRY, ICHIJO...!!
OH NO... WHAT'M I DOING?!
NO... IT'S OKAY... IT'S COOL!
WHOA...IS THIS REALLY HAPPENING?!
Dude... This is awesome!!

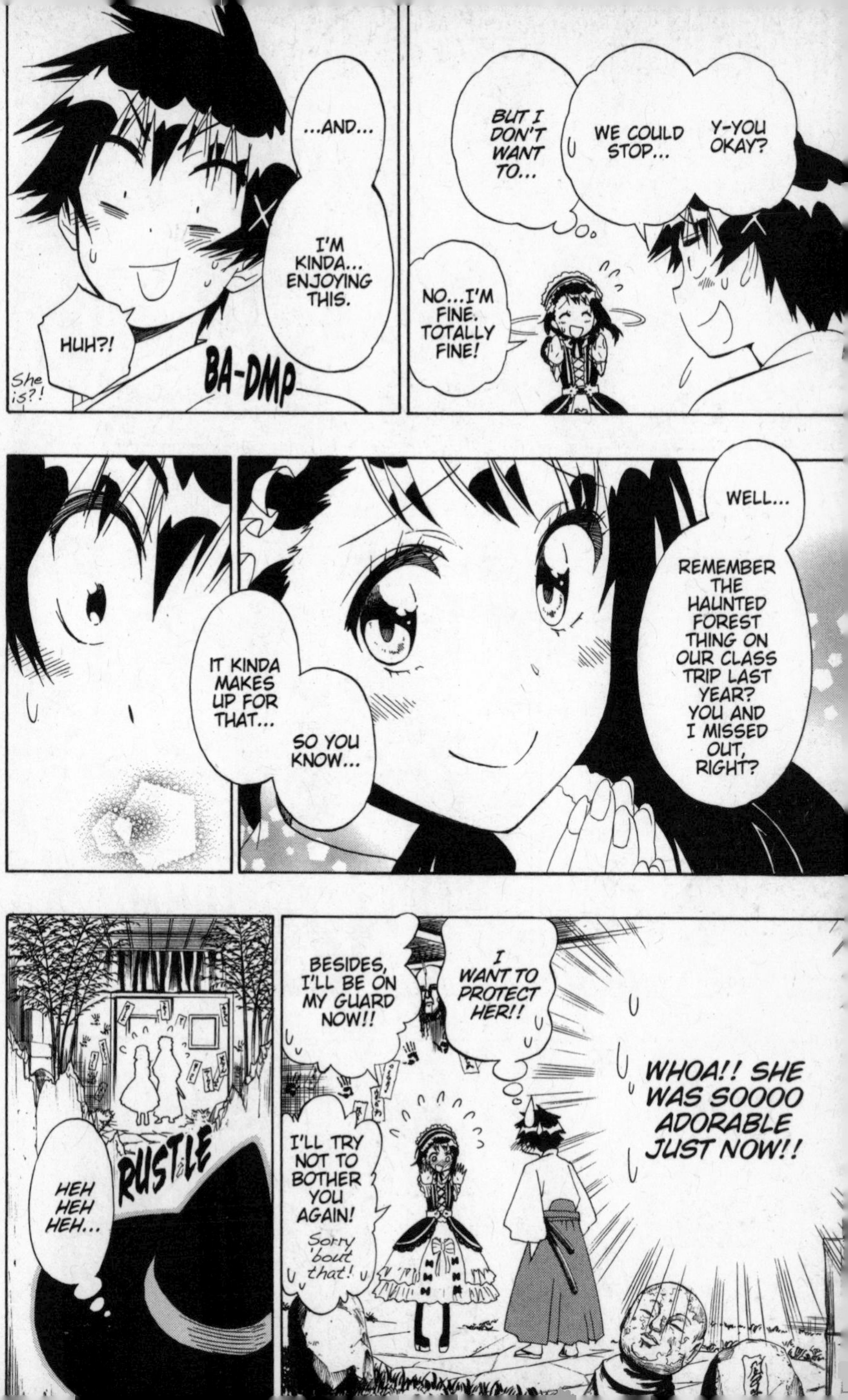
Y-YOU OKAY?
WE COULD STOP...
BUT I DON'T WANT TO...
NO...I'M FINE. TOTALLY FINE!
...AND...
I'M KINDA... ENJOYING THIS.
HUH?!
BA-DMP
She is?!
WELL...
REMEMBER THE HAUNTED FOREST THING ON OUR CLASS TRIP LAST YEAR? YOU AND I MISSED OUT, RIGHT?
IT KINDA MAKES UP FOR THAT...
SO YOU KNOW...
WHOA!! SHE WAS SOOOO ADORABLE JUST NOW!!
I WANT TO PROTECT HER!!
BESIDES, I'LL BE ON MY GUARD NOW!!
I'LL TRY NOT TO BOTHER YOU AGAIN!
Sorry 'bout that!
RUSTLE
HEH HEH HEH...

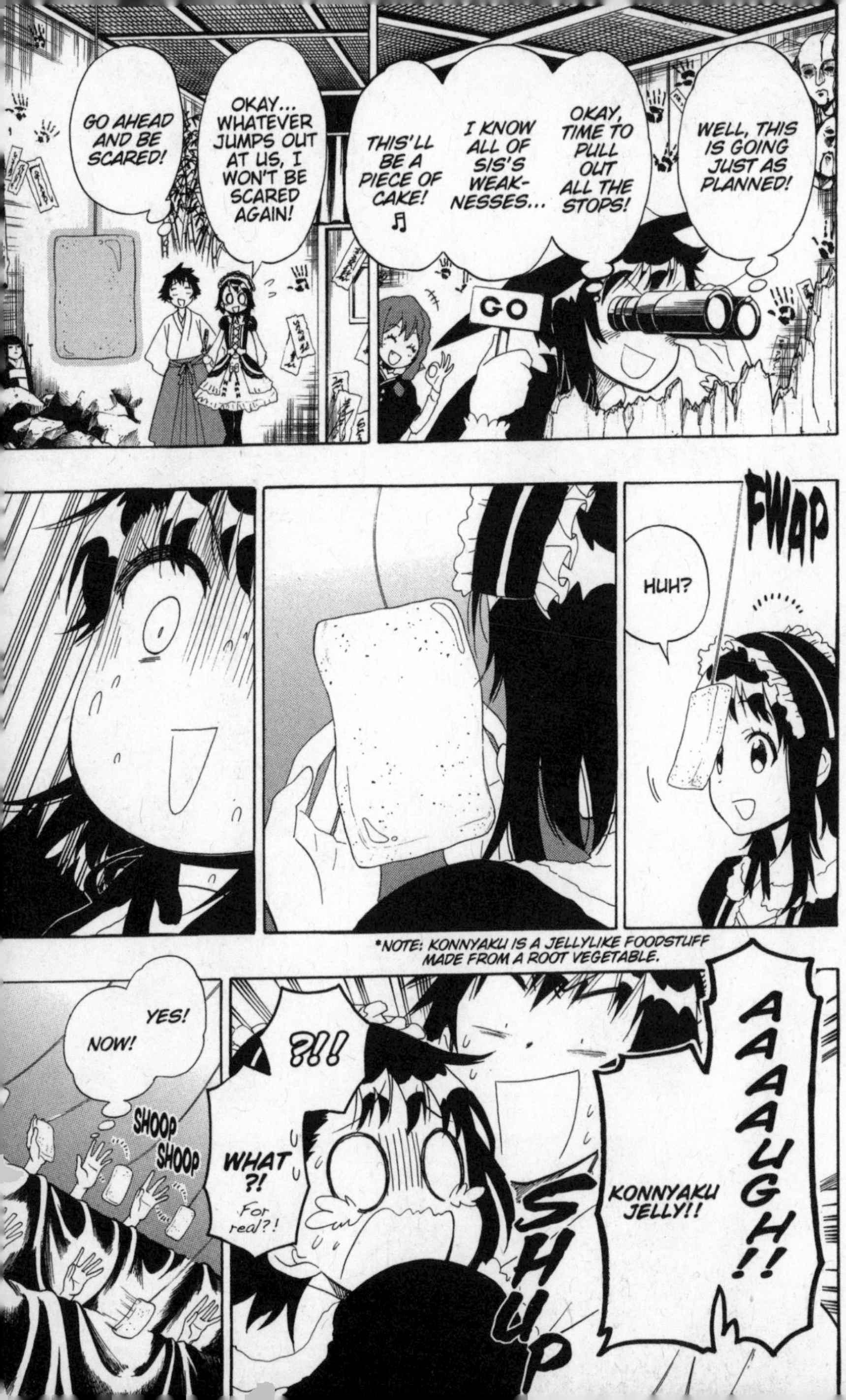
WELL, THIS IS GOING JUST AS PLANNED!
OKAY, TIME TO PULL OUT ALL THE STOPS!
I KNOW ALL OF SIS'S WEAKNESSES...
THIS'LL BE A PIECE OF CAKE! ♫
GO
OKAY... WHATEVER JUMPS OUT AT US, I WON'T BE SCARED AGAIN!
GO AHEAD AND BE SCARED!
FWAP
HUH?
*NOTE: KONNYAKU IS A JELLYLIKE FOODSTUFF MADE FROM A ROOT VEGETABLE.
AAAAUGH!!
KONNYAKU JELLY!!
SHUP
?!!
WHAT?!
For real?!
YES!
NOW!
SHOOP SHOOP

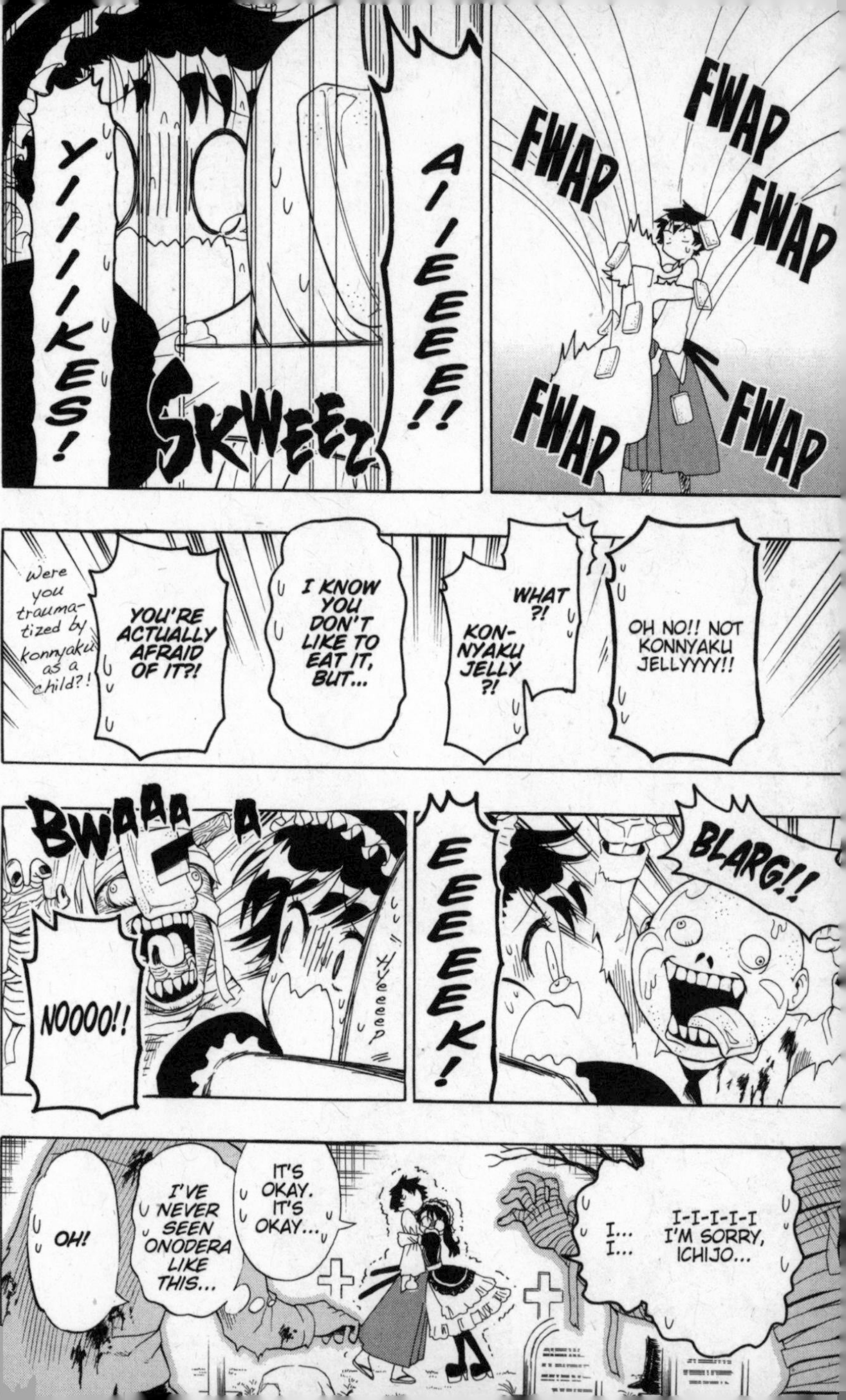
FWAP
FWAP
FWAP
FWAP
AIIEEEE!!
SKWEEZ
YIIIIIKES!
OH NO!! NOT KONNYAKU JELLYYYY!!
WHAT ?!
KON-NYAKU JELLY ?!
I KNOW YOU DON'T LIKE TO EAT IT, BUT...
YOU'RE ACTUALLY AFRAID OF IT?!
Were you traumatized by konnyaku as a child?!
BLARG!!
EEEEEEK!
BWAAAA
HYEEEEP
NOOOO!!
I-I-I-I-I I'M SORRY, ICHIJO...
I... I...
IT'S OKAY. IT'S OKAY...
I'VE NEVER SEEN ONODERA LIKE THIS...
OH!

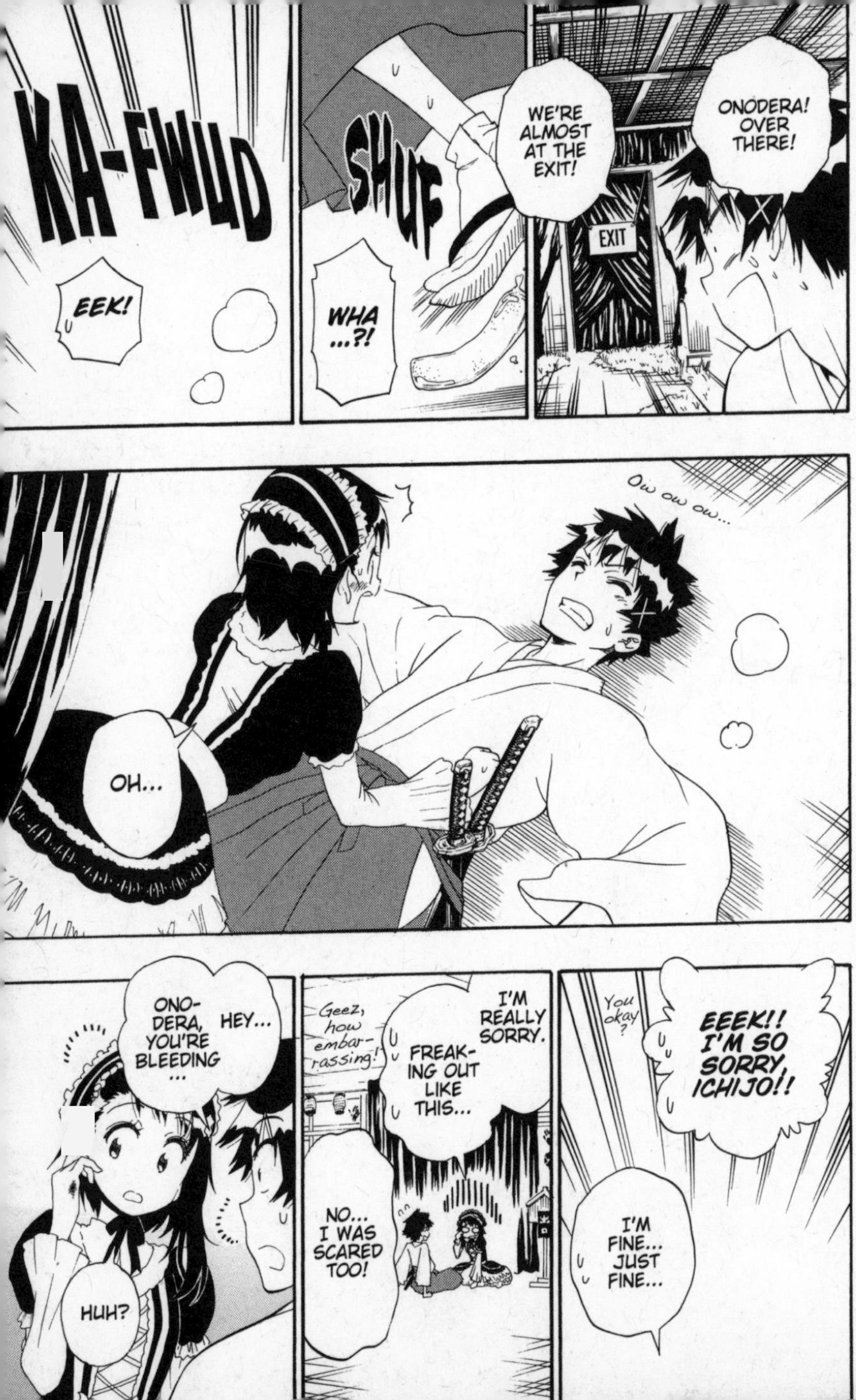
ONODERA! OVER THERE!
WE'RE ALMOST AT THE EXIT!
EXIT
SHUF
WHA...?!
KA-FWUD
EEK!
Ow ow ow...
OH...
EEEK!! I'M SO SORRY, ICHIJO!!
You okay?
I'M FINE... JUST FINE...
I'M REALLY SORRY.
FREAKING OUT LIKE THIS...
Geez, how embarrassing!
NO... I WAS SCARED TOO!
HEY...
ONODERA, YOU'RE BLEEDING...
HUH?

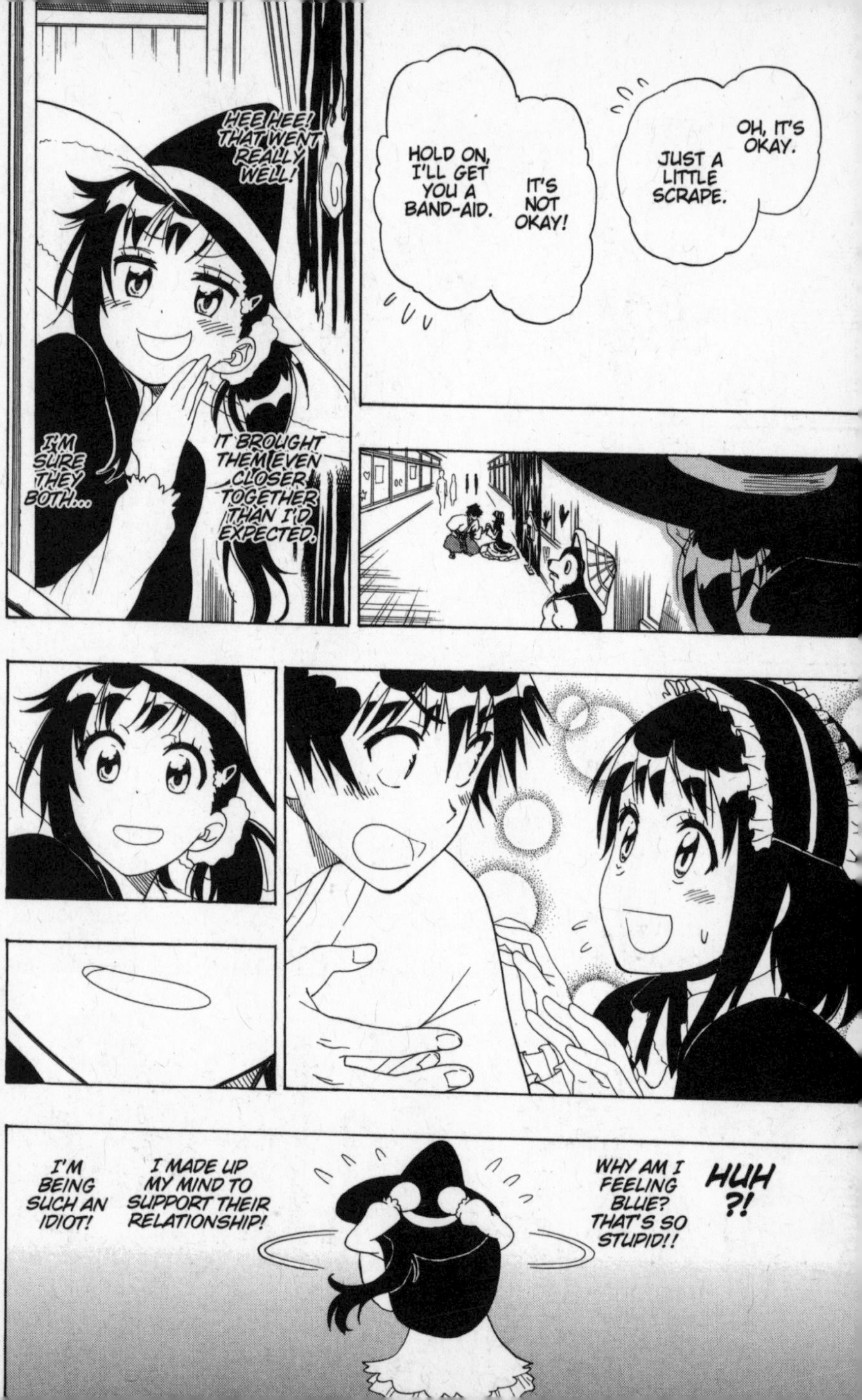
OH, IT'S OKAY. JUST A LITTLE SCRAPE.
IT'S NOT OKAY! HOLD ON, I'LL GET YOU A BAND-AID.
HEE HEE! THAT WENT REALLY WELL!
IT BROUGHT THEM EVEN CLOSER TOGETHER THAN I'D EXPECTED.
I'M SURE THEY BOTH...
HUH ?!
WHY AM I FEELING BLUE? THAT'S SO STUPID!!
I MADE UP MY MIND TO SUPPORT THEIR RELATIONSHIP!
I'M BEING SUCH AN IDIOT!

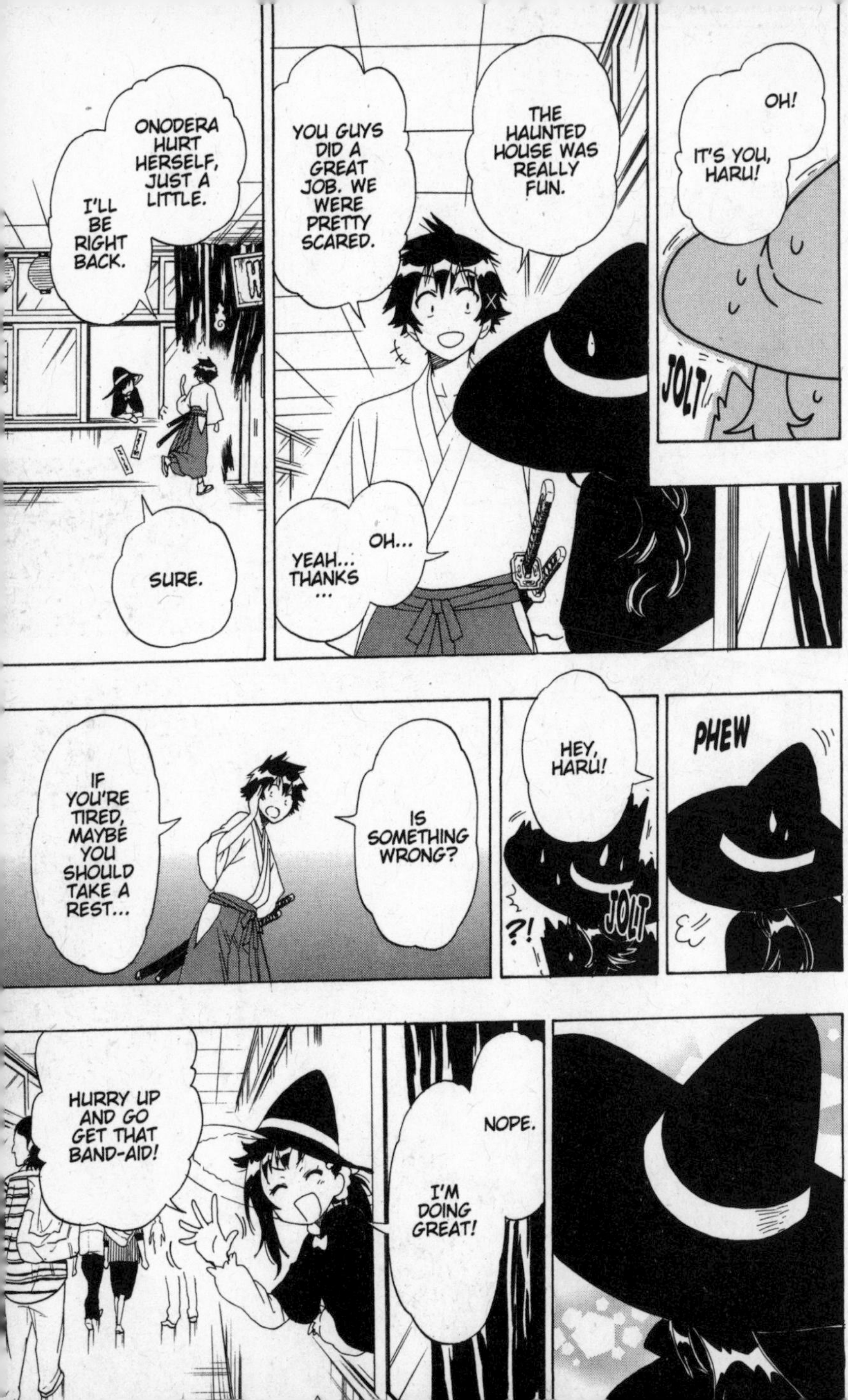
OH!
IT'S YOU, HARU!
JOLT
THE HAUNTED HOUSE WAS REALLY FUN.
YOU GUYS DID A GREAT JOB. WE WERE PRETTY SCARED.
OH...
YEAH... THANKS...
ONODERA HURT HERSELF, JUST A LITTLE.
I'LL BE RIGHT BACK.
SURE.
PHEW
HEY, HARU!
?!
JOLT
IS SOMETHING WRONG?
IF YOU'RE TIRED, MAYBE YOU SHOULD TAKE A REST...
NOPE.
I'M DOING GREAT!
HURRY UP AND GO GET THAT BAND-AID!

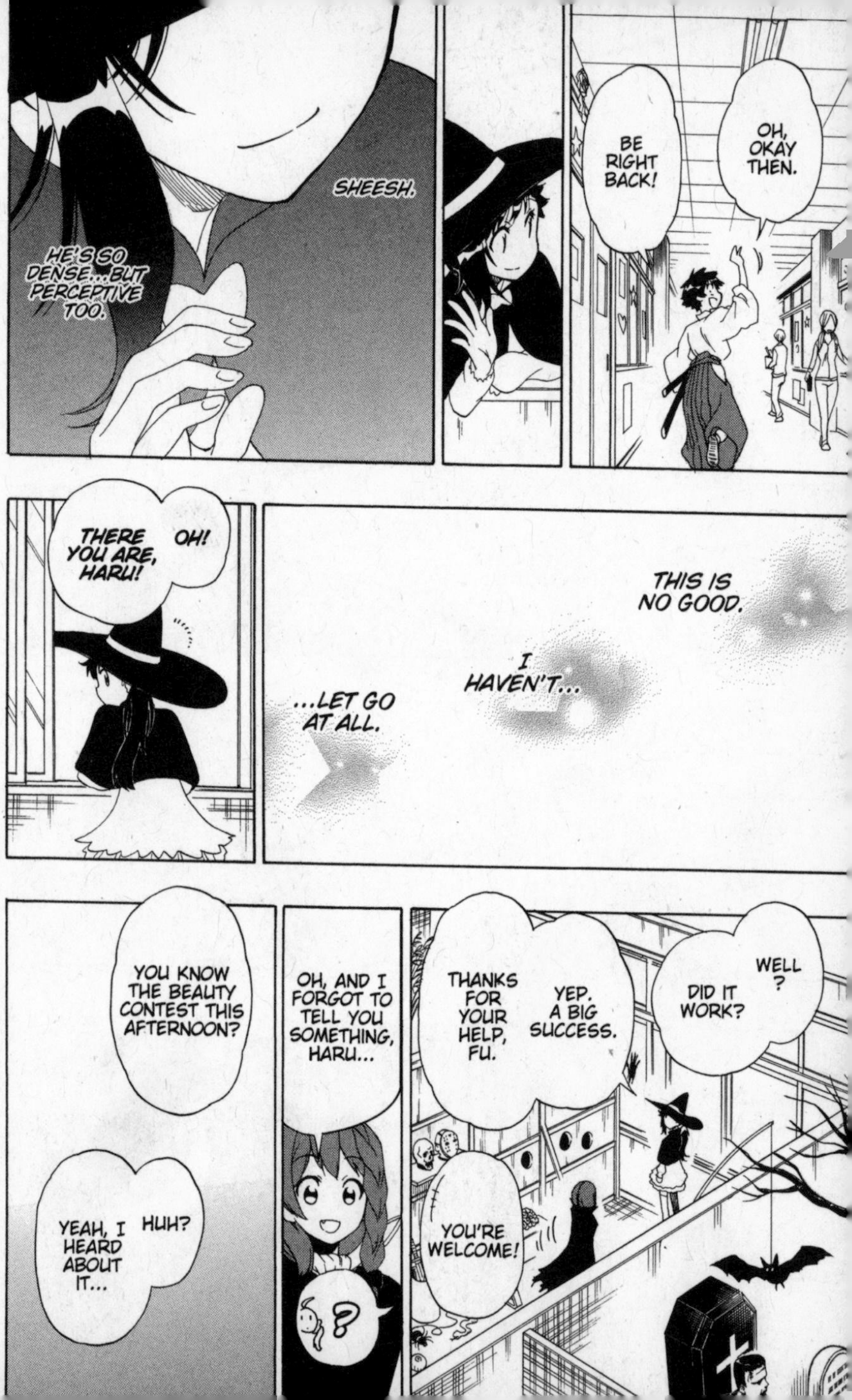
OH, OKAY THEN.
BE RIGHT BACK!
SHEESH.
HE'S SO DENSE...BUT PERCEPTIVE TOO.
THIS IS NO GOOD.
I HAVEN'T...
...LET GO AT ALL.
OH!
THERE YOU ARE, HARU!
WELL?
DID IT WORK?
YEP. A BIG SUCCESS.
THANKS FOR YOUR HELP, FU.
YOU'RE WELCOME!
OH, AND I FORGOT TO TELL YOU SOMETHING, HARU...
?
YOU KNOW THE BEAUTY CONTEST THIS AFTERNOON?
HUH?
YEAH, I HEARD ABOUT IT...

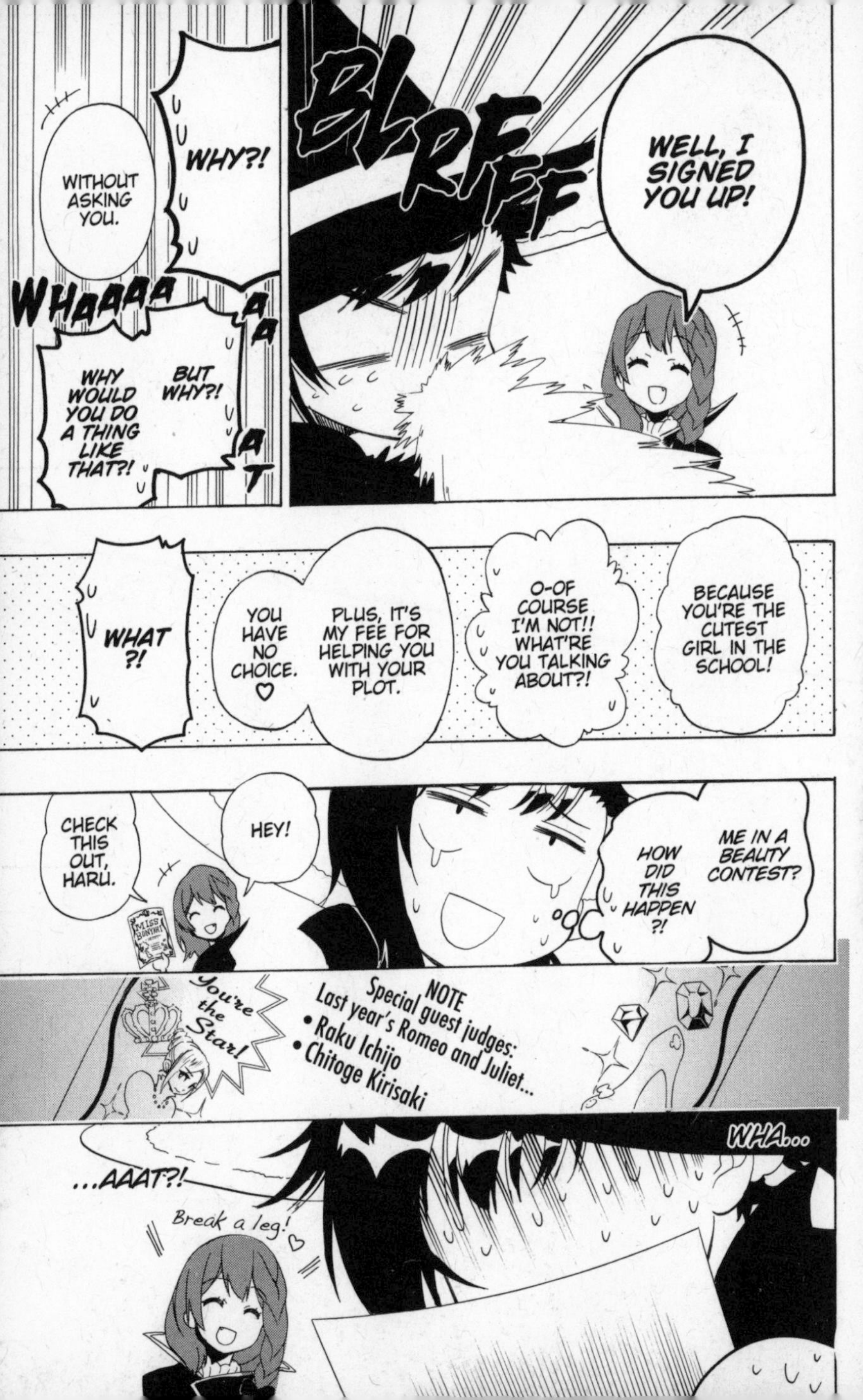
BLRIFF
WELL, I SIGNED YOU UP!
WHY?!
WITHOUT ASKING YOU.
WHAAAAAAAT
BUT WHY?!
WHY WOULD YOU DO A THING LIKE THAT?!
BECAUSE YOU'RE THE CUTEST GIRL IN THE SCHOOL!
O-OF COURSE I'M NOT!! WHAT'RE YOU TALKING ABOUT?!
PLUS, IT'S MY FEE FOR HELPING YOU WITH YOUR PLOT.
YOU HAVE NO CHOICE. ♡
WHAT ?!
ME IN A BEAUTY CONTEST?
HOW DID THIS HAPPEN ?!
HEY!
CHECK THIS OUT, HARU.
NOTE
Special guest judges:
Last year's Romeo and Juliet...
• Raku Ichijo
• Chitoge Kirisaki
You're the Star!
WHA...
...AAAT?!
Break a leg! ♡

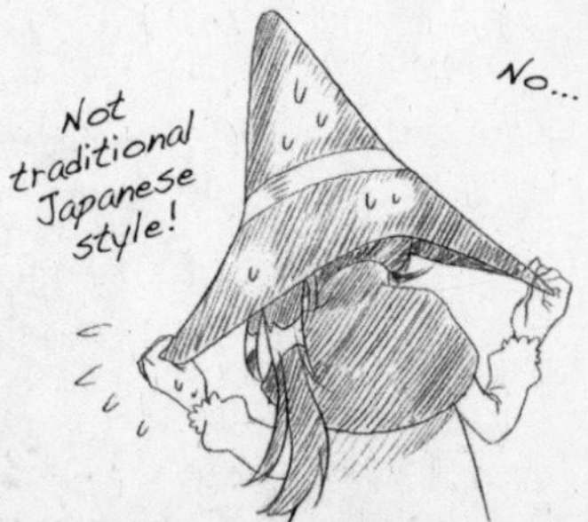
No...
Not traditional Japanese style!

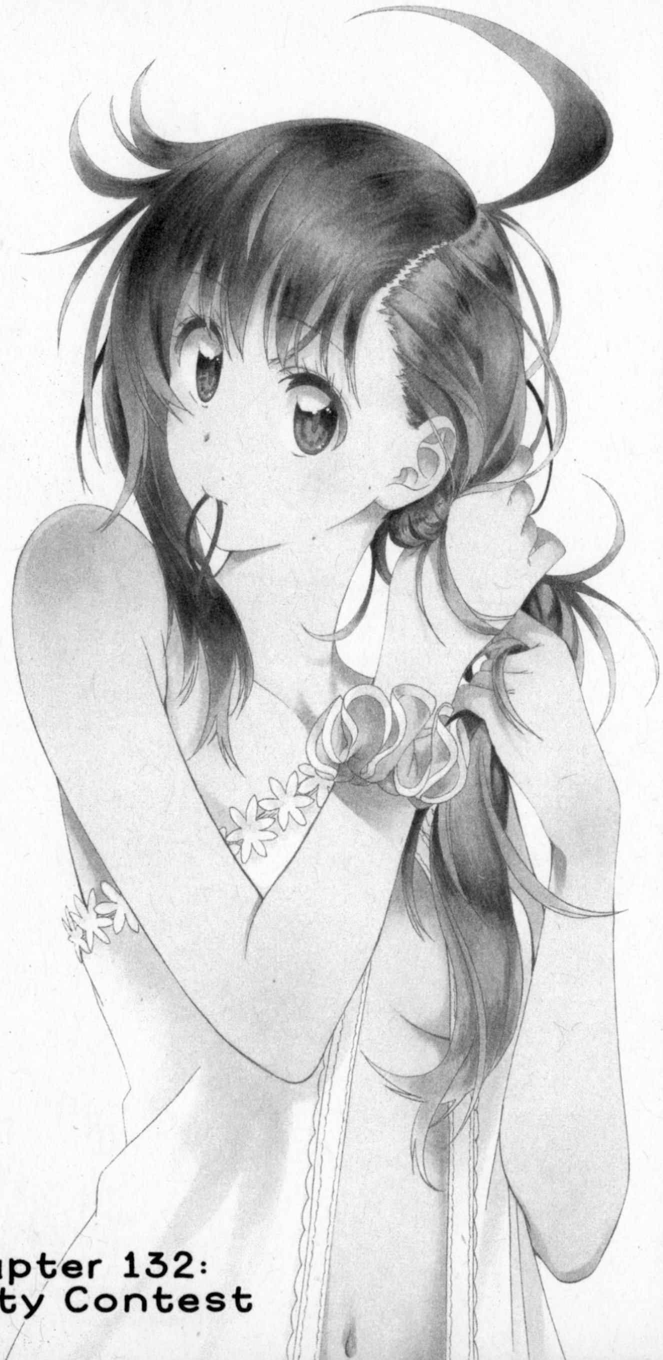

Chapter 132: Beauty Contest

NISEKOI
False Love

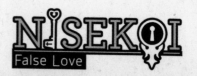

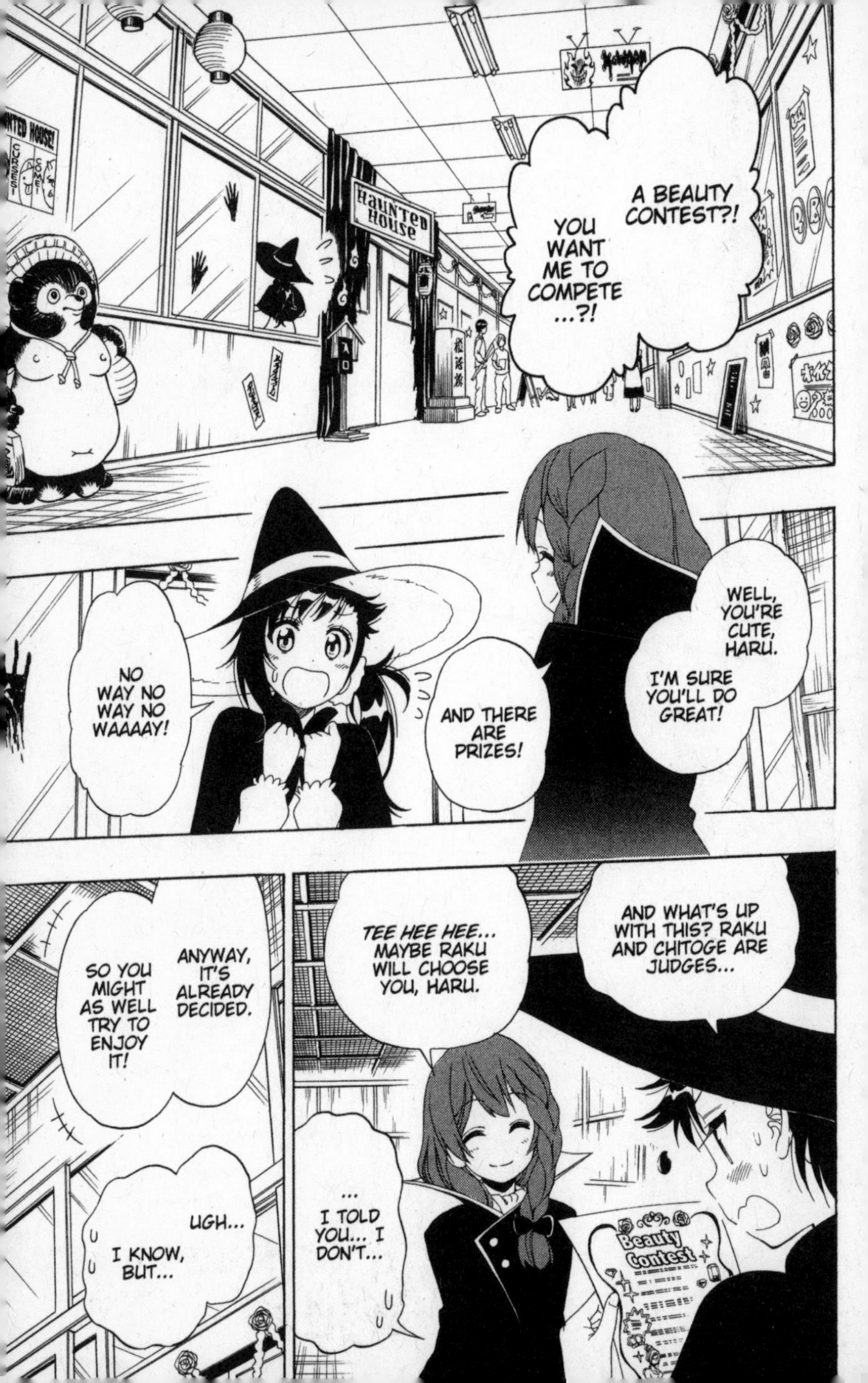
HAUNTED HOUSE
A BEAUTY CONTEST?!
YOU WANT ME TO COMPETE ...?!
WELL, YOU'RE CUTE, HARU.
I'M SURE YOU'LL DO GREAT!
AND THERE ARE PRIZES!
NO WAY NO WAY NO WAAAAY!
AND WHAT'S UP WITH THIS? RAKU AND CHITOGE ARE JUDGES...
TEE HEE HEE... MAYBE RAKU WILL CHOOSE YOU, HARU.
... I TOLD YOU... I DON'T...
Beauty Contest
ANYWAY, IT'S ALREADY DECIDED.
SO YOU MIGHT AS WELL TRY TO ENJOY IT!
UGH...
I KNOW, BUT...

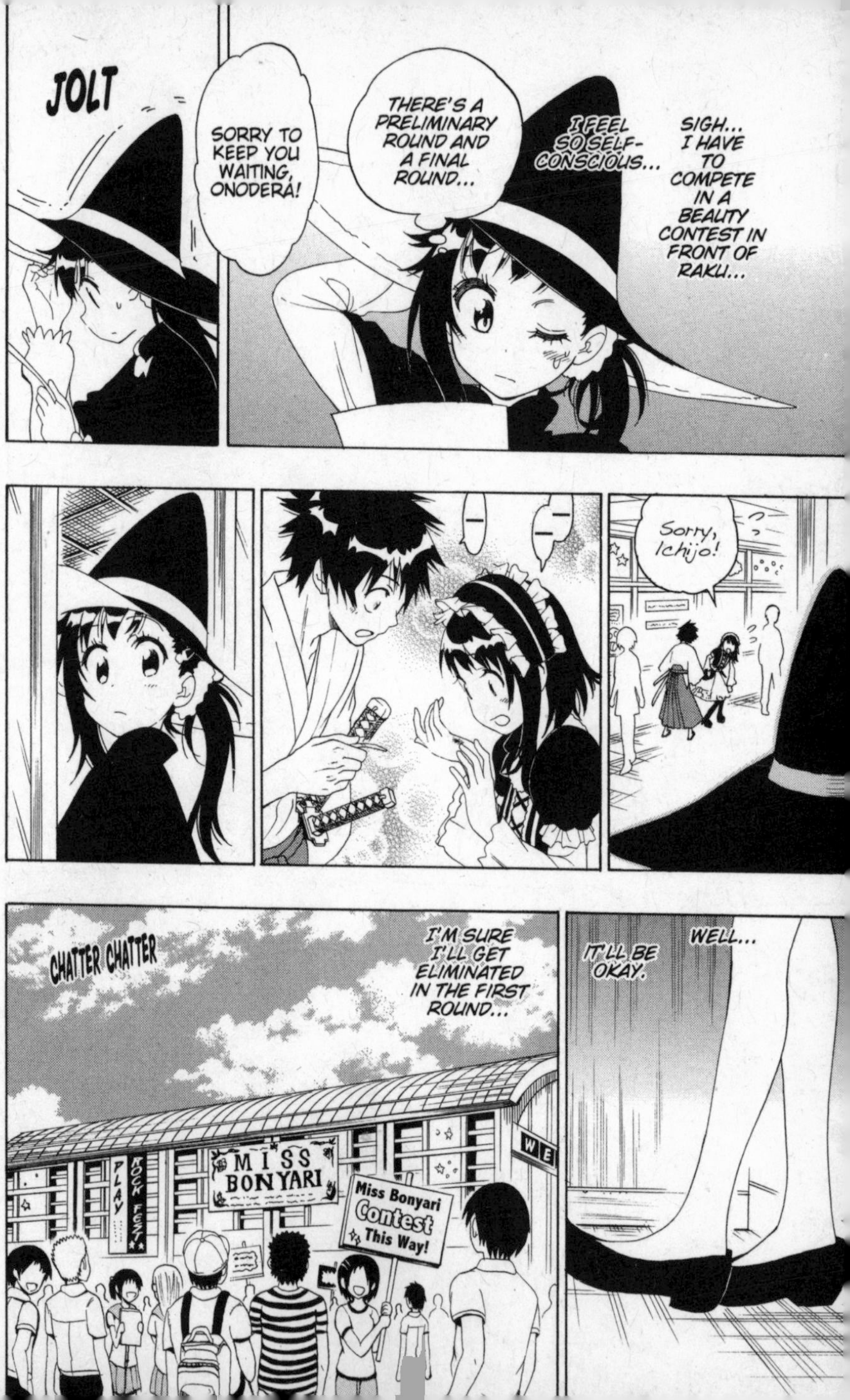
SIGH... I HAVE TO COMPETE IN A BEAUTY CONTEST IN FRONT OF RAKU...
I FEEL SO SELF-CONSCIOUS...
THERE'S A PRELIMINARY ROUND AND A FINAL ROUND...
SORRY TO KEEP YOU WAITING, ONODERA!
JOLT
Sorry, Ichijo!
WELL...
IT'LL BE OKAY.
I'M SURE I'LL GET ELIMINATED IN THE FIRST ROUND...
CHATTER CHATTER
WE
MISS BONYARI
Miss Bonyari Contest This Way!
ROCK FEST
PLAY

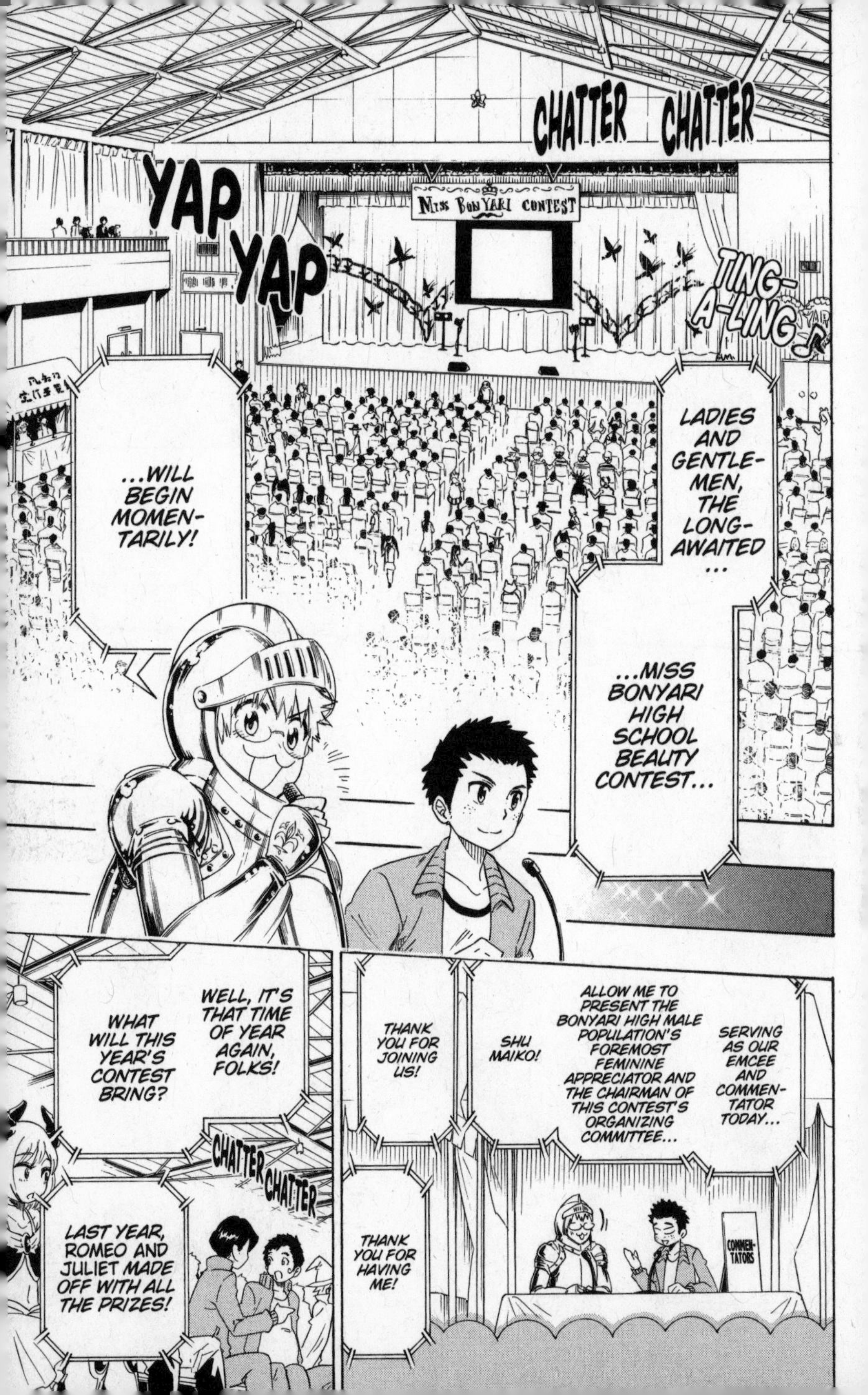
MISS BONYARI CONTEST
CHATTER CHATTER
TING-A-LING
YAP YAP
LADIES AND GENTLEMEN, THE LONG-AWAITED…
…MISS BONYARI HIGH SCHOOL BEAUTY CONTEST…
…WILL BEGIN MOMENTARILY!
SERVING AS OUR EMCEE AND COMMENTATOR TODAY…
ALLOW ME TO PRESENT THE BONYARI HIGH MALE POPULATION'S FOREMOST FEMININE APPRECIATOR AND THE CHAIRMAN OF THIS CONTEST'S ORGANIZING COMMITTEE…
SHU MAIKO!
THANK YOU FOR JOINING US!
THANK YOU FOR HAVING ME!
COMMENTATORS
WELL, IT'S THAT TIME OF YEAR AGAIN, FOLKS!
WHAT WILL THIS YEAR'S CONTEST BRING?
CHATTER CHATTER
LAST YEAR, ROMEO AND JULIET MADE OFF WITH ALL THE PRIZES!

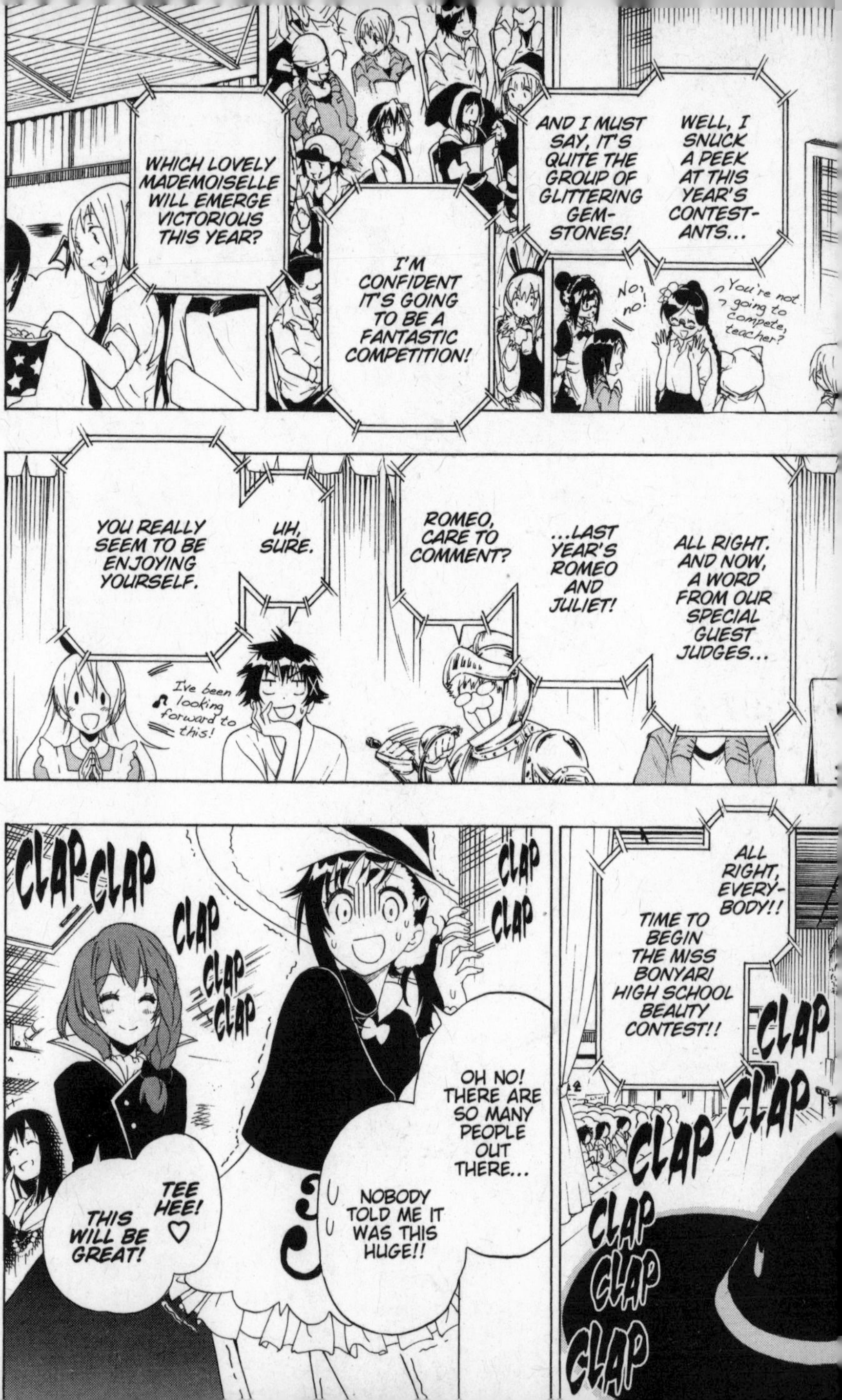
WELL, I SNUCK A PEEK AT THIS YEAR'S CONTESTANTS...
AND I MUST SAY, IT'S QUITE THE GROUP OF GLITTERING GEMSTONES!
You're not going to compete, teacher?
No, no!
I'M CONFIDENT IT'S GOING TO BE A FANTASTIC COMPETITION!
WHICH LOVELY MADEMOISELLE WILL EMERGE VICTORIOUS THIS YEAR?
ALL RIGHT. AND NOW, A WORD FROM OUR SPECIAL GUEST JUDGES...
...LAST YEAR'S ROMEO AND JULIET!
ROMEO, CARE TO COMMENT?
UH, SURE.
YOU REALLY SEEM TO BE ENJOYING YOURSELF.
I've been looking forward to this!
ALL RIGHT, EVERYBODY!!
TIME TO BEGIN THE MISS BONYARI HIGH SCHOOL BEAUTY CONTEST!!
CLAP CLAP
CLAP CLAP
CLAP CLAP CLAP
CLAP CLAP
OH NO! THERE ARE SO MANY PEOPLE OUT THERE...
NOBODY TOLD ME IT WAS THIS HUGE!!
CLAP CLAP CLAP
CLAP CLAP
CLAP
TEE HEE! ♡
THIS WILL BE GREAT!

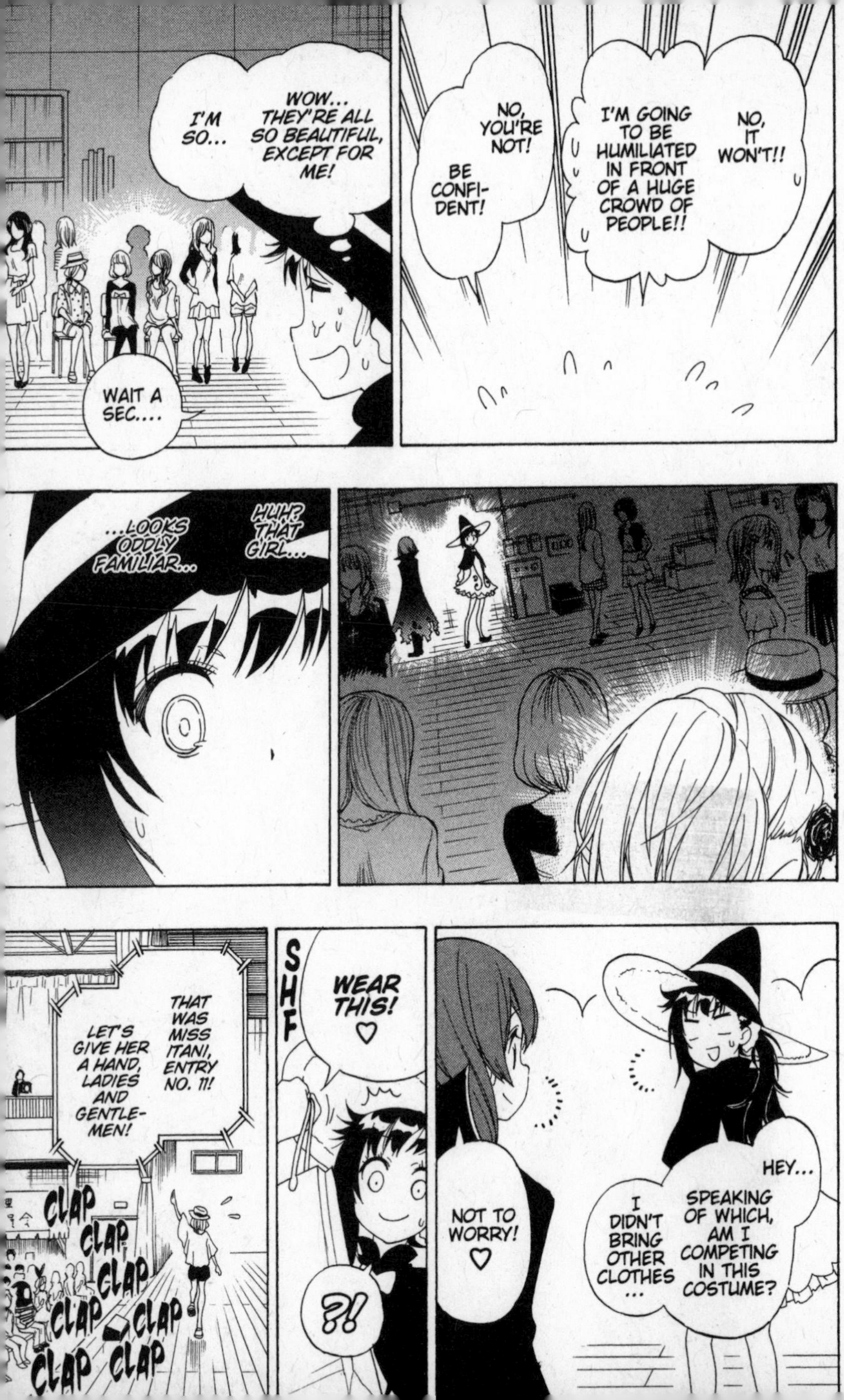
NO, IT WON'T!!
I'M GOING TO BE HUMILIATED IN FRONT OF A HUGE CROWD OF PEOPLE!!
NO, YOU'RE NOT!
BE CONFIDENT!
WOW... THEY'RE ALL SO BEAUTIFUL, EXCEPT FOR ME!
I'M SO...
WAIT A SEC....
HUH? THAT GIRL...
...LOOKS ODDLY FAMILIAR...
HEY...
SPEAKING OF WHICH, AM I COMPETING IN THIS COSTUME?
I DIDN'T BRING OTHER CLOTHES...
NOT TO WORRY! ♡
SHF
WEAR THIS! ♡
?!
THAT WAS MISS ITANI, ENTRY NO. 11!
LET'S GIVE HER A HAND, LADIES AND GENTLEMEN!
CLAP CLAP CLAP CLAP CLAP CLAP CLAP CLAP

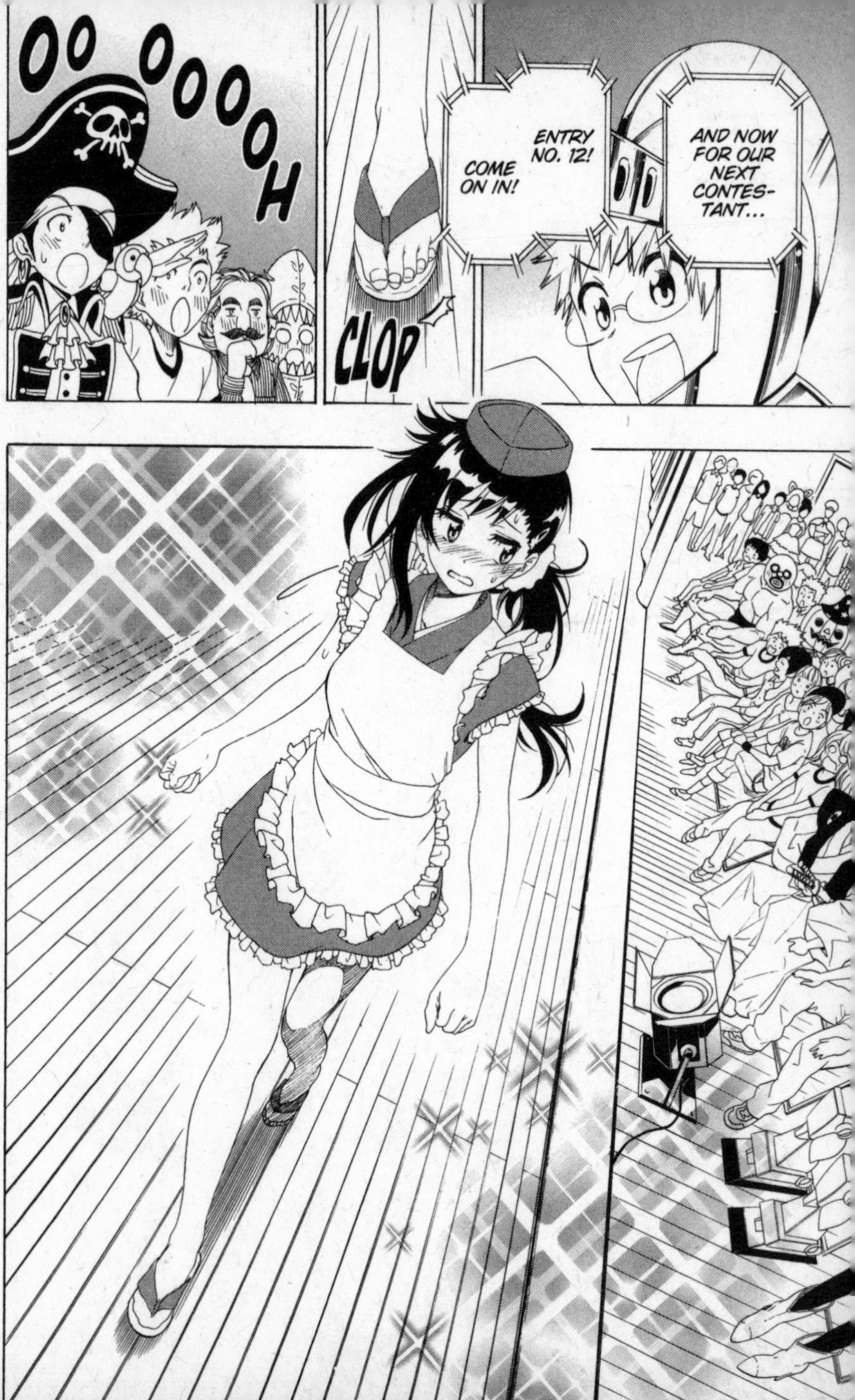
AND NOW FOR OUR NEXT CONTESTANT...
ENTRY NO. 12! COME ON IN!
CLOP
OO OOOOOH

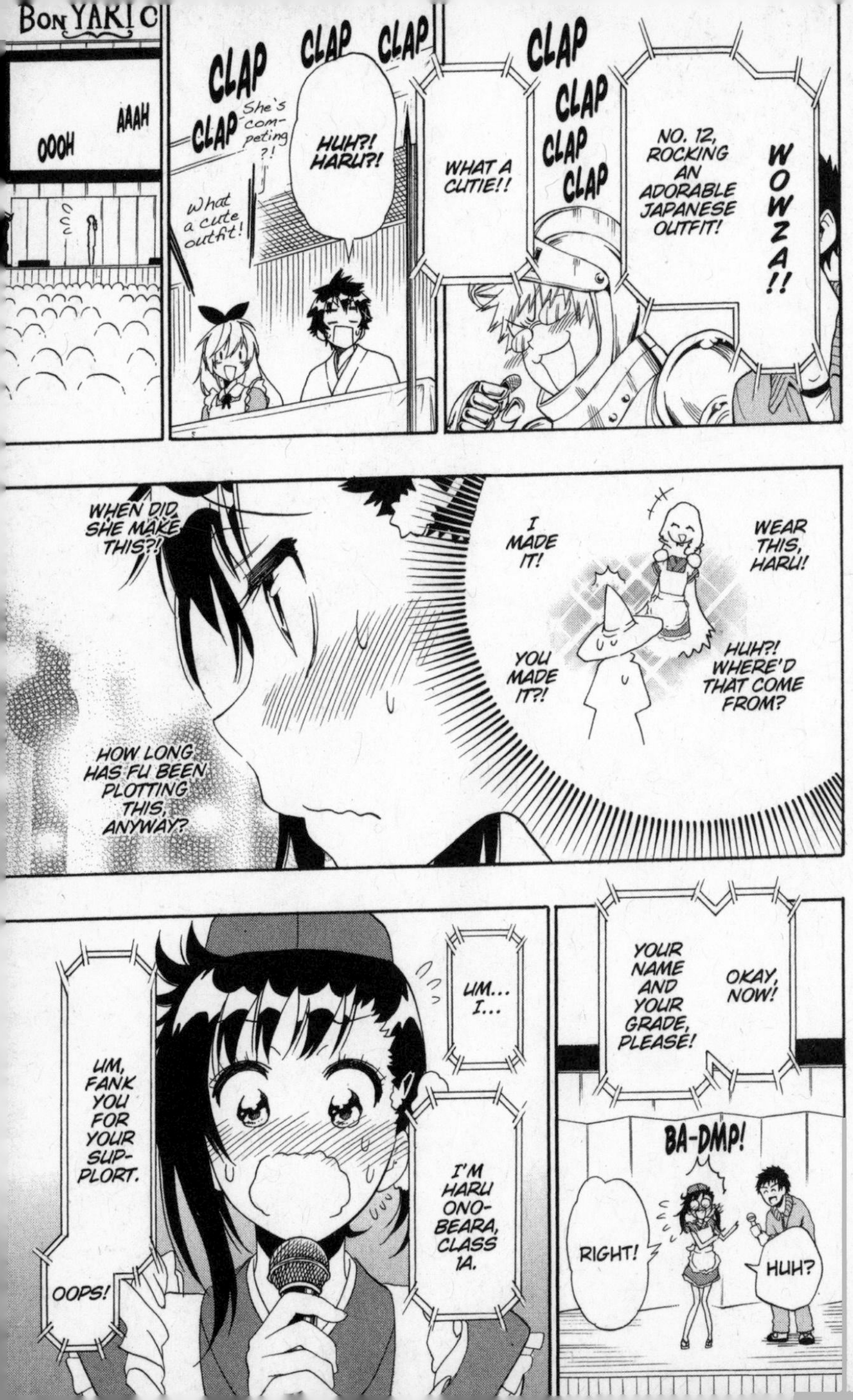
WOWZA!!
NO. 12, ROCKING AN ADORABLE JAPANESE OUTFIT!
CLAP CLAP CLAP CLAP
WHAT A CUTIE!!
CLAP CLAP CLAP CLAP
HUH?! HARU?!
She's competing?!
What a cute outfit!
BON YAKI C
AAAH
OOOH
WEAR THIS, HARU!
I MADE IT!
HUH?! WHERE'D THAT COME FROM?
YOU MADE IT?!
WHEN DID SHE MAKE THIS?!
HOW LONG HAS FU BEEN PLOTTING THIS, ANYWAY?
OKAY, NOW!
YOUR NAME AND YOUR GRADE, PLEASE!
BA-DMP!
HUH?
RIGHT!
UM... I...
I'M HARU ONO-BEARA, CLASS 1A.
UM, FANK YOU FOR YOUR SUP-PLORT.
OOPS!

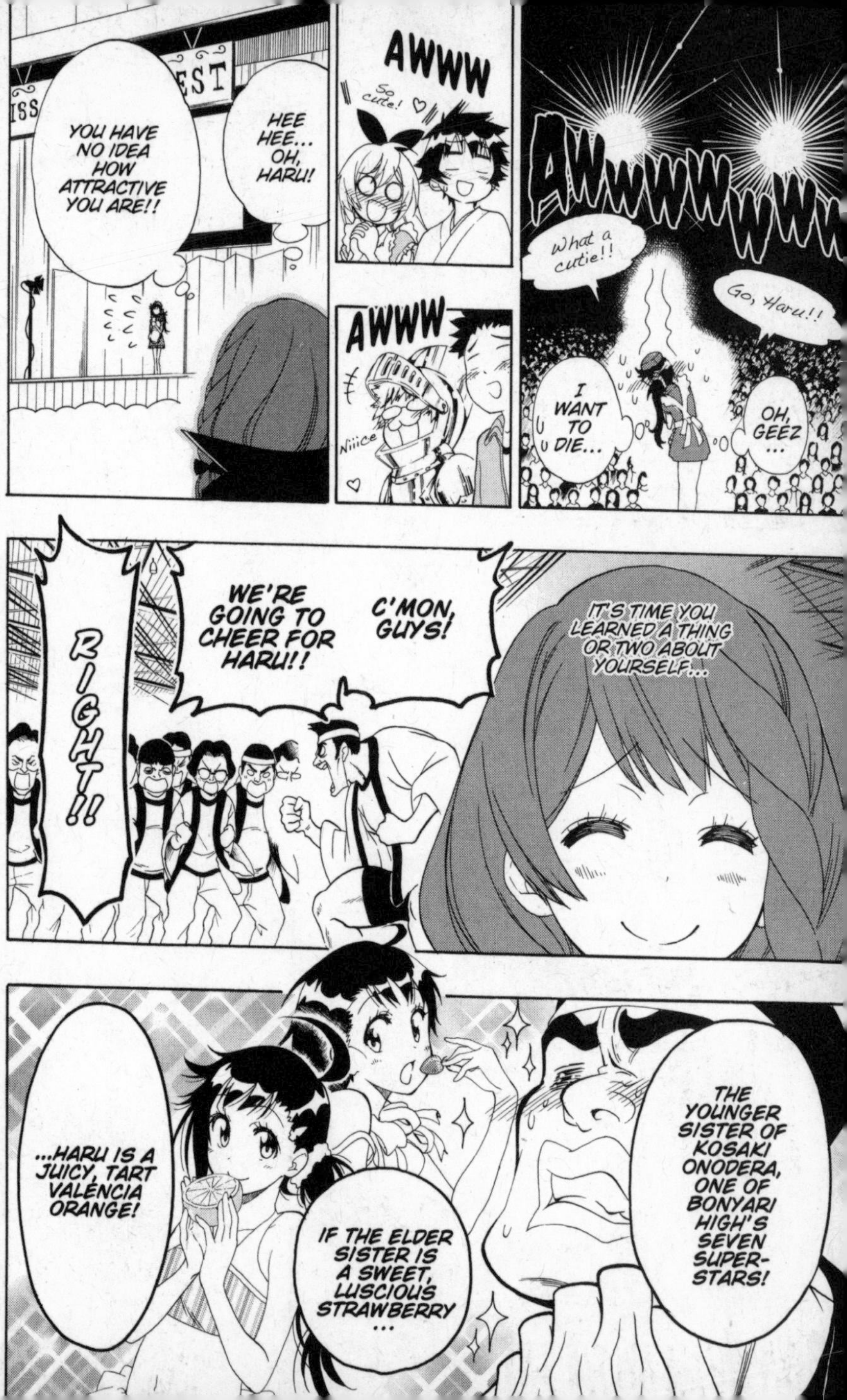
AWWWWWWWW
What a cutie!!
Go, Haru!!
OH, GEEZ...
I WANT TO DIE...
AWWW
So cute!
AWWW
Niiice
HEE HEE... OH, HARU!
YOU HAVE NO IDEA HOW ATTRACTIVE YOU ARE!!
IT'S TIME YOU LEARNED A THING OR TWO ABOUT YOURSELF...
C'MON, GUYS!
WE'RE GOING TO CHEER FOR HARU!!
RIGHT!!
THE YOUNGER SISTER OF KOSAKI ONODERA, ONE OF BONYARI HIGH'S SEVEN SUPER-STARS!
IF THE ELDER SISTER IS A SWEET, LUSCIOUS STRAWBERRY...
...HARU IS A JUICY, TART VALÉNCIA ORANGE!

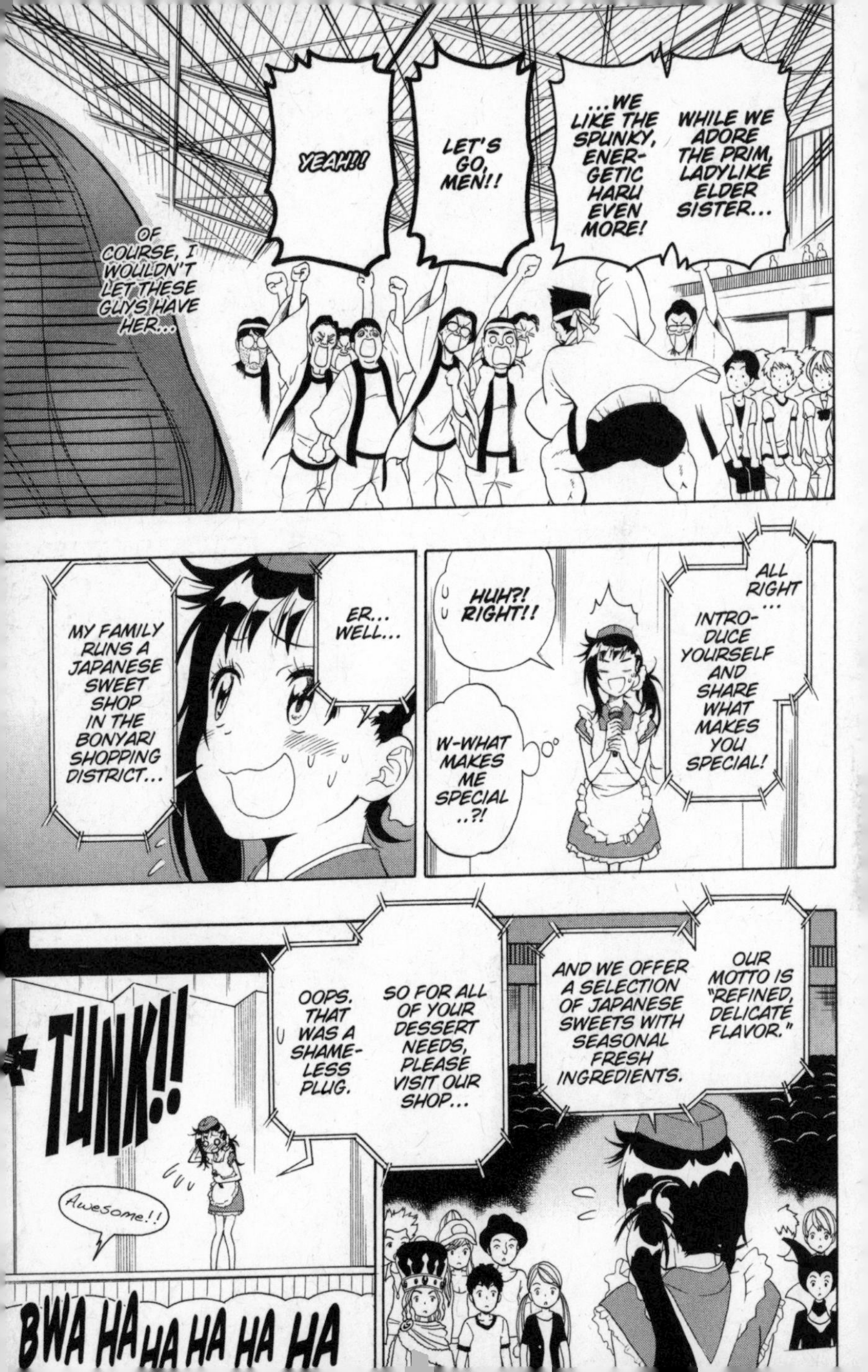
WHILE WE ADORE THE PRIM, LADYLIKE ELDER SISTER...
...WE LIKE THE SPUNKY, ENERGETIC HARU EVEN MORE!
LET'S GO, MEN!!
YEAH!!
OF COURSE, I WOULDN'T LET THESE GUYS HAVE HER...
ALL RIGHT... INTRODUCE YOURSELF AND SHARE WHAT MAKES YOU SPECIAL!
HUH?! RIGHT!!
W-WHAT MAKES ME SPECIAL..?!
ER... WELL...
MY FAMILY RUNS A JAPANESE SWEET SHOP IN THE BONYARI SHOPPING DISTRICT...
OUR MOTTO IS "REFINED, DELICATE FLAVOR."
AND WE OFFER A SELECTION OF JAPANESE SWEETS WITH SEASONAL FRESH INGREDIENTS.
SO FOR ALL OF YOUR DESSERT NEEDS, PLEASE VISIT OUR SHOP...
OOPS. THAT WAS A SHAMELESS PLUG.
TUNK!!
Awesome!!
BWA HA HA HA HA HA HA

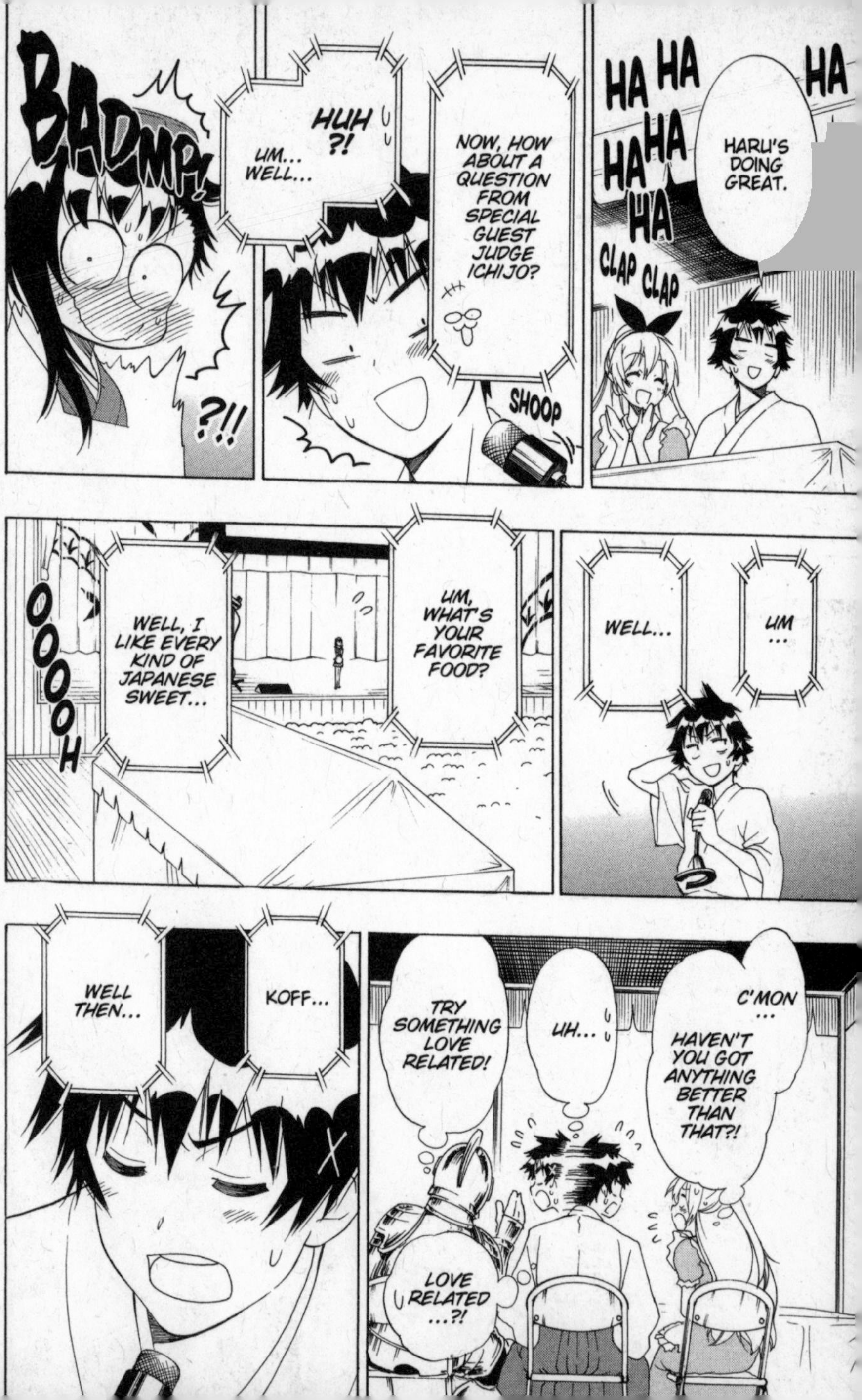
HA HA HA HA HA HA
CLAP CLAP
HARU'S DOING GREAT.
NOW, HOW ABOUT A QUESTION FROM SPECIAL GUEST JUDGE ICHIJO?
SHOOP
HUH ?!
UM... WELL...
BADMP!
?!!
UM ...
WELL...
UM, WHAT'S YOUR FAVORITE FOOD?
WELL, I LIKE EVERY KIND OF JAPANESE SWEET...
OOOOOH
C'MON ...
HAVEN'T YOU GOT ANYTHING BETTER THAN THAT?!
UH...
TRY SOMETHING LOVE RELATED!
LOVE RELATED ...?!
KOFF...
WELL THEN...

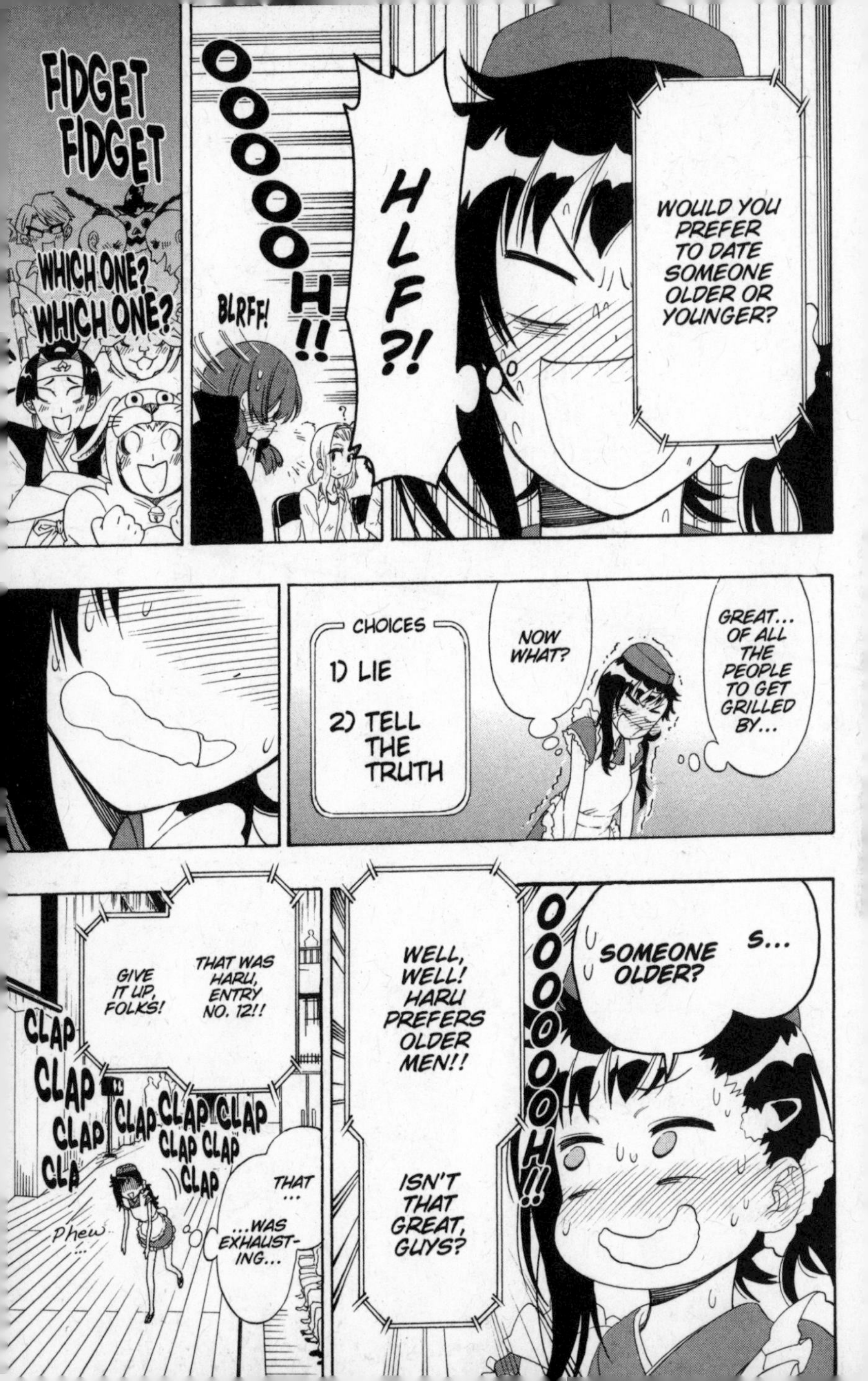
WOULD YOU PREFER TO DATE SOMEONE OLDER OR YOUNGER?
HLF?!
OOOOOH!!
BLRFF!
FIDGET FIDGET
WHICH ONE? WHICH ONE?
GREAT... OF ALL THE PEOPLE TO GET GRILLED BY...
NOW WHAT?
CHOICES
1) LIE
2) TELL THE TRUTH
S...
SOMEONE OLDER?
OOOOOOOOOH!!
WELL, WELL! HARU PREFERS OLDER MEN!!
ISN'T THAT GREAT, GUYS?
THAT WAS HARU, ENTRY NO. 12!!
GIVE IT UP, FOLKS!
CLAP CLAP CLAP CLA
CLAP CLAP CLAP
CLAP CLAP CLAP
THAT ...
...WAS EXHAUST-ING...
Phew...

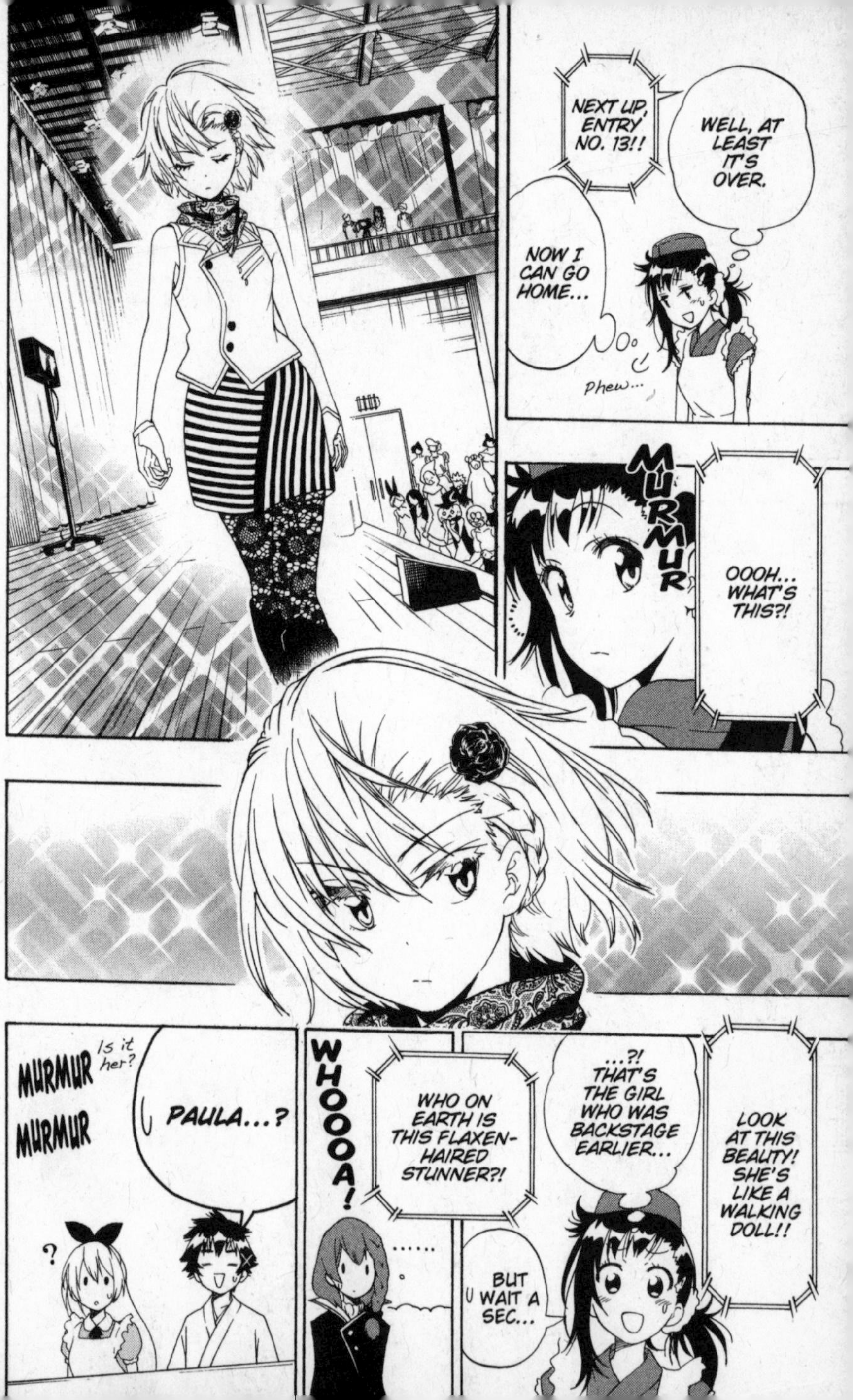
NEXT UP, ENTRY NO. 13!!
WELL, AT LEAST IT'S OVER.
NOW I CAN GO HOME...
Phew...
MURMUR
OOOH... WHAT'S THIS?!
LOOK AT THIS BEAUTY! SHE'S LIKE A WALKING DOLL!!
...?! THAT'S THE GIRL WHO WAS BACKSTAGE EARLIER...
BUT WAIT A SEC...
WHO ON EARTH IS THIS FLAXEN-HAIRED STUNNER?!
......
WHOOOA!
PAULA...?
Is it her?
MURMUR
MURMUR
?

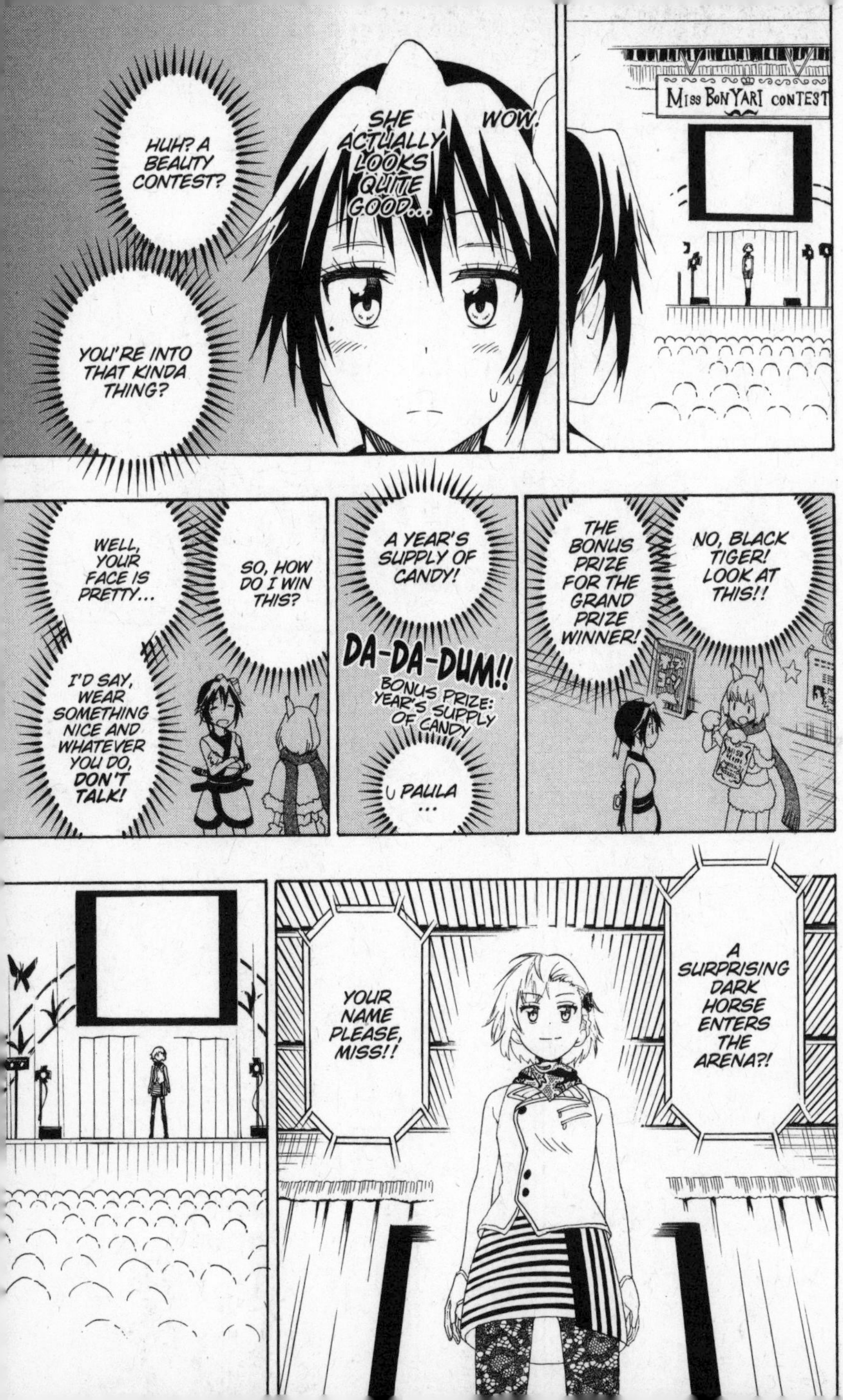
MISS BONYARI CONTEST
WOW.
SHE ACTUALLY LOOKS QUITE GOOD...
HUH? A BEAUTY CONTEST?
YOU'RE INTO THAT KINDA THING?
NO, BLACK TIGER! LOOK AT THIS!!
THE BONUS PRIZE FOR THE GRAND PRIZE WINNER!
A YEAR'S SUPPLY OF CANDY!
DA-DA-DUM!!
BONUS PRIZE: YEAR'S SUPPLY OF CANDY
PAULA ...
SO, HOW DO I WIN THIS?
WELL, YOUR FACE IS PRETTY...
I'D SAY, WEAR SOMETHING NICE AND WHATEVER YOU DO, DON'T TALK!
A SURPRISING DARK HORSE ENTERS THE ARENA?!
YOUR NAME PLEASE, MISS!!

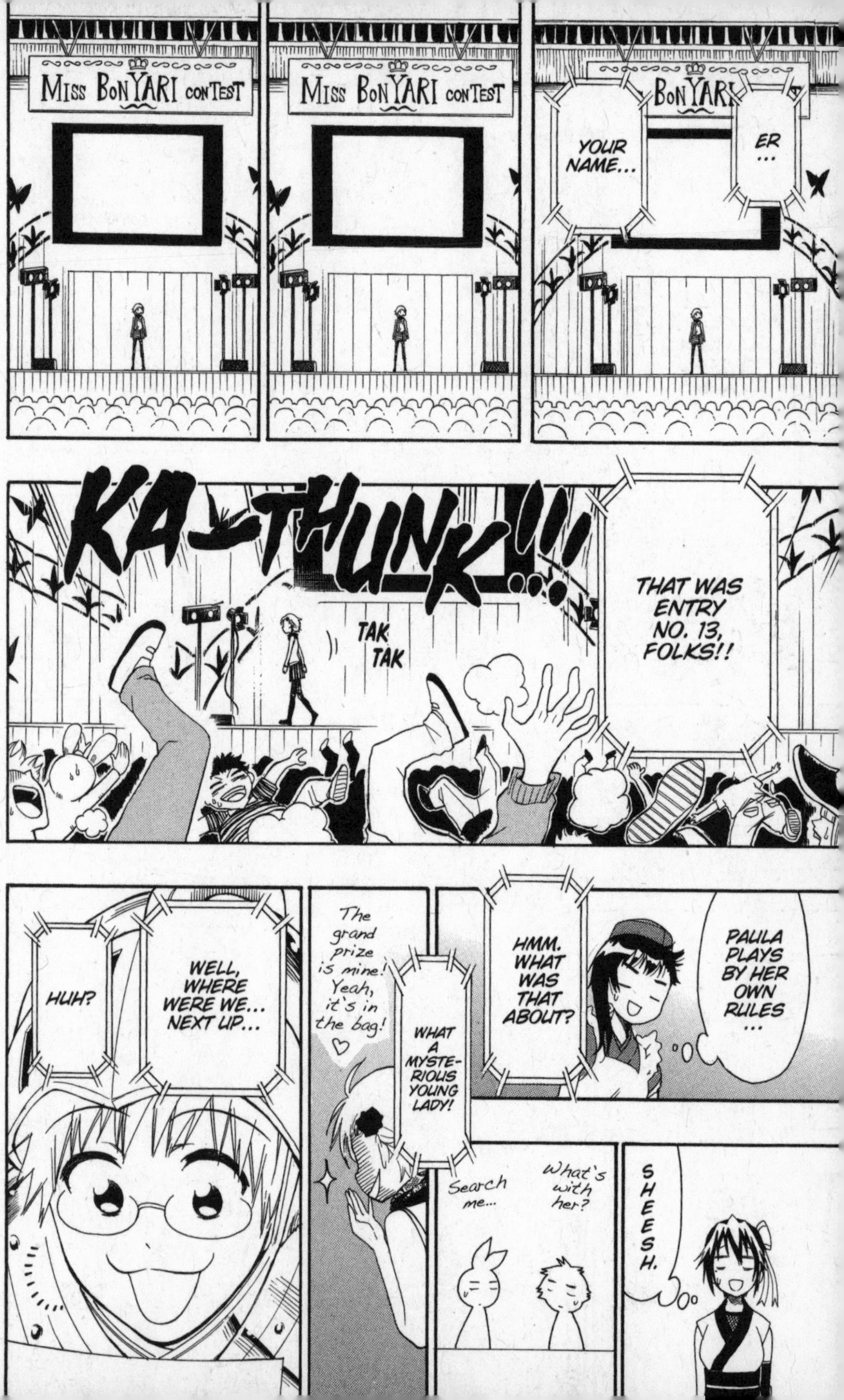
BONYARI
YOUR NAME...
ER...
MISS BONYARI CONTEST
MISS BONYARI CONTEST
THAT WAS ENTRY NO. 13, FOLKS!!
KA-THUNK!!!
TAK TAK
PAULA PLAYS BY HER OWN RULES...
HMM. WHAT WAS THAT ABOUT?
SHEESH.
What's with her?
Search me...
The grand prize is mine! Yeah, it's in the bag! ♡
WHAT A MYSTERIOUS YOUNG LADY!
WELL, WHERE WERE WE... NEXT UP...
HUH?

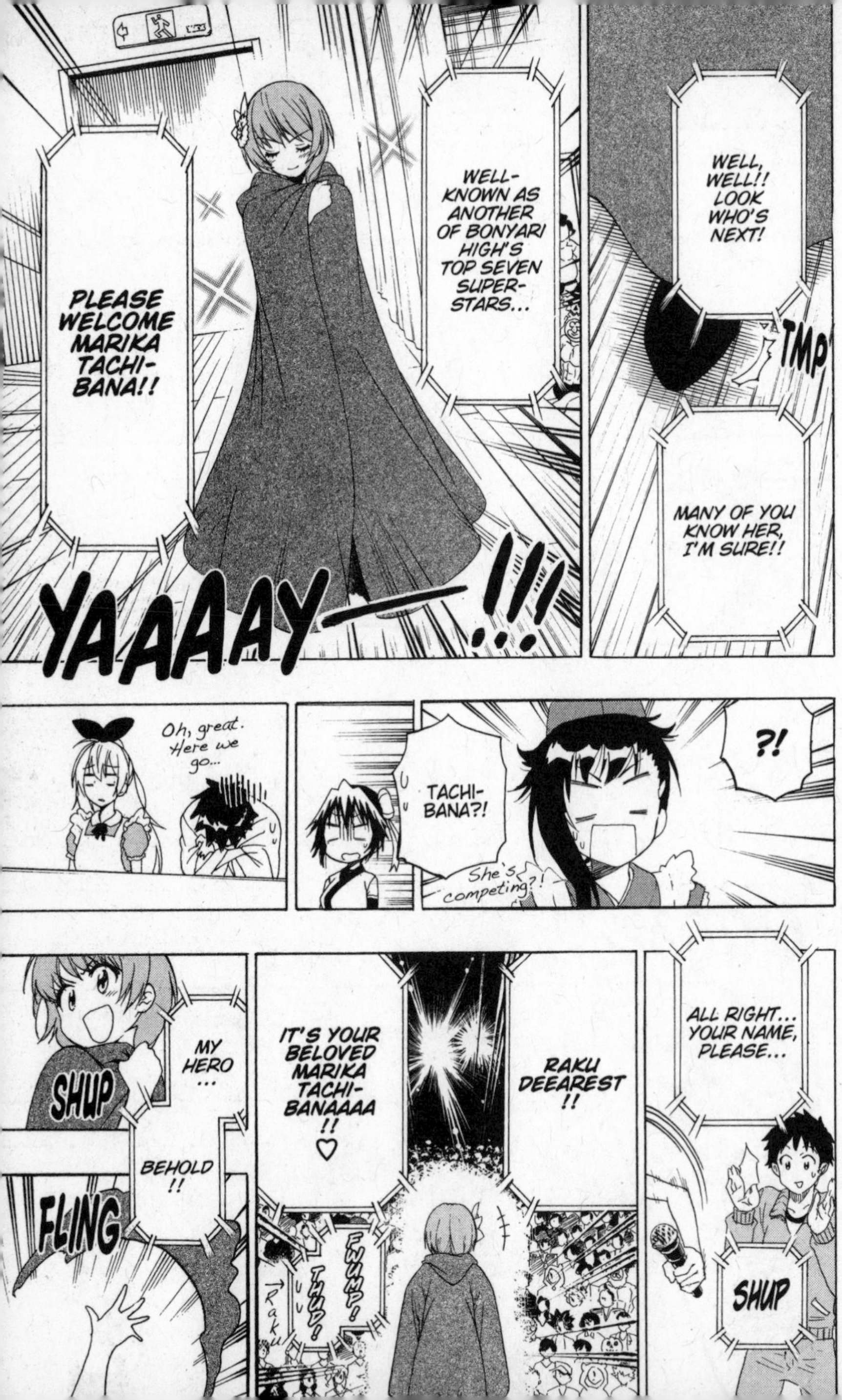
WELL, WELL!! LOOK WHO'S NEXT!
TMP
MANY OF YOU KNOW HER, I'M SURE!!
WELL-KNOWN AS ANOTHER OF BONYARI HIGH'S TOP SEVEN SUPER-STARS...
PLEASE WELCOME MARIKA TACHI-BANA!!
YAAAAY—!!!
?!
TACHI-BANA?!
She's competing?!
Oh, great. Here we go...
ALL RIGHT... YOUR NAME, PLEASE...
SHUP
RAKU DEEAREST!!
IT'S YOUR BELOVED MARIKA TACHI-BANAAAA!! ♡
FWUMP!
THUD!
Raku
MY HERO...
SHUP
BEHOLD!!
FLING

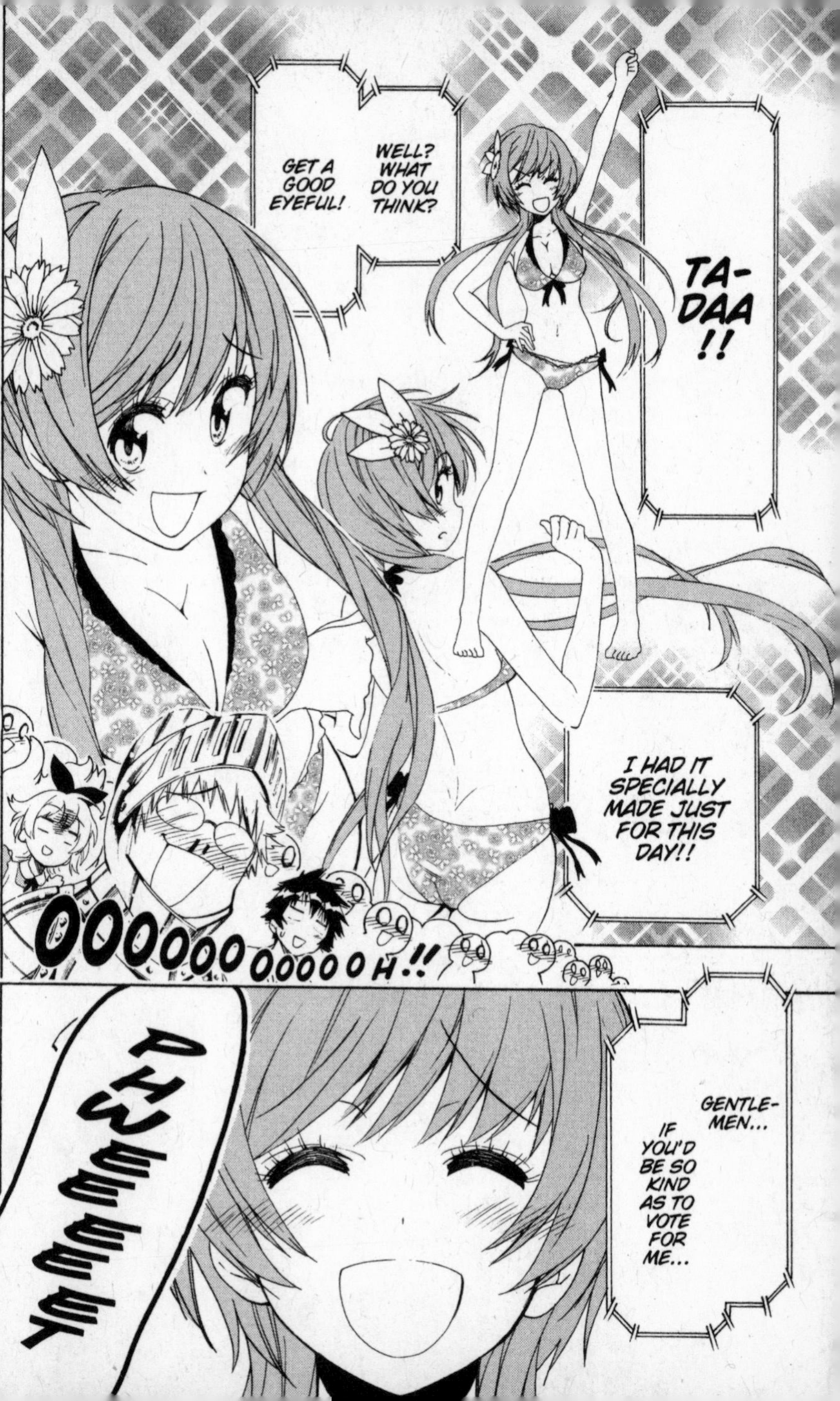
TA-DAA!!
WELL? WHAT DO YOU THINK?
GET A GOOD EYEFUL!
I HAD IT SPECIALLY MADE JUST FOR THIS DAY!!
OOOOOOOOOOOOH!!
GENTLEMEN...
IF YOU'D BE SO KIND AS TO VOTE FOR ME...
PHWEEEEEEEET

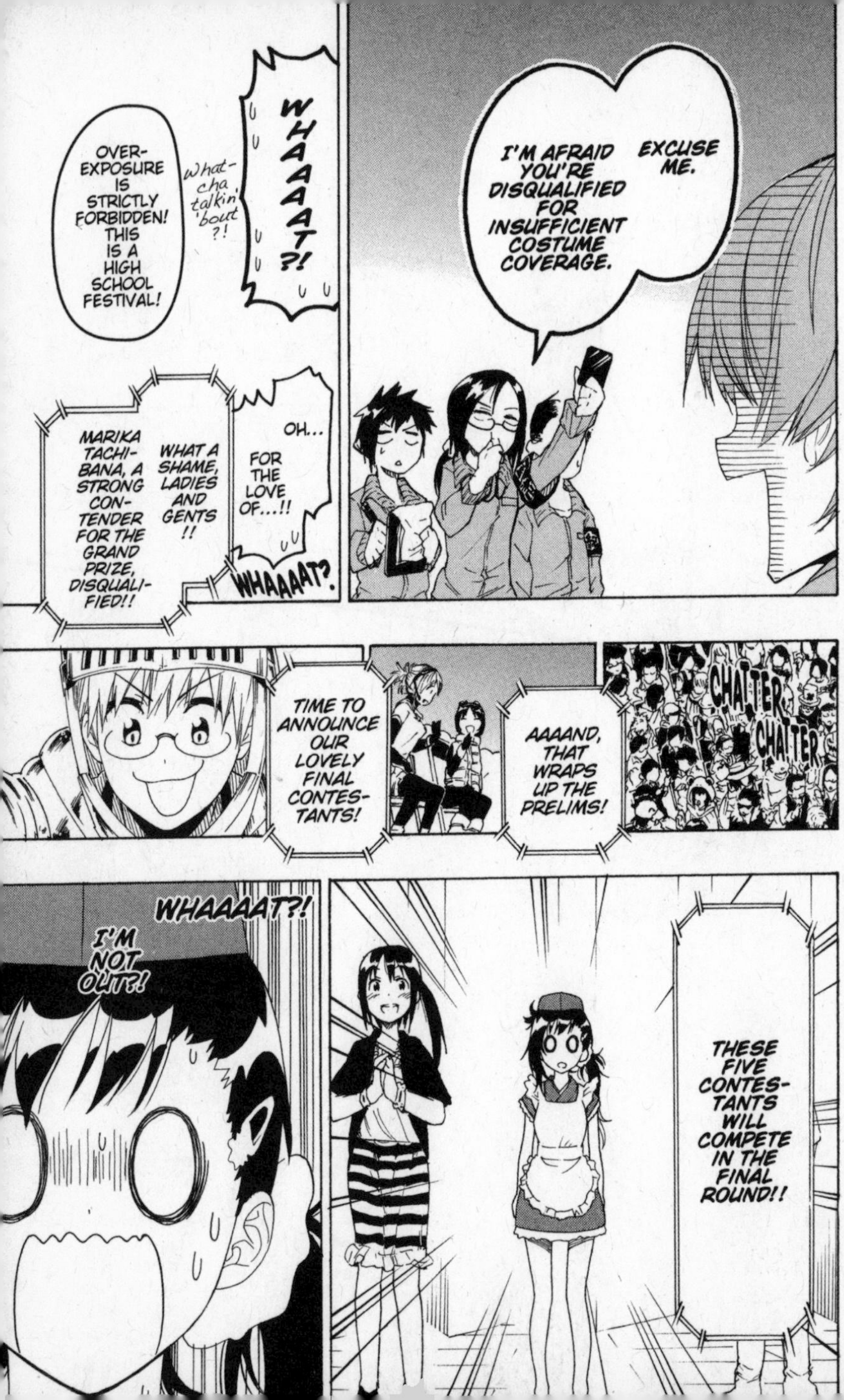
EXCUSE ME.
I'M AFRAID YOU'RE DISQUALIFIED FOR INSUFFICIENT COSTUME COVERAGE.
WHAAAAAT?!
What-cha talkin' 'bout?!
OVER-EXPOSURE IS STRICTLY FORBIDDEN! THIS IS A HIGH SCHOOL FESTIVAL!
WHAAAAT?.
OH... FOR THE LOVE OF...!!
WHAT A SHAME, LADIES AND GENTS!!
MARIKA TACHIBANA, A STRONG CONTENDER FOR THE GRAND PRIZE, DISQUALIFIED!!
CHATTER CHATTER
AAAAND, THAT WRAPS UP THE PRELIMS!
TIME TO ANNOUNCE OUR LOVELY FINAL CONTESTANTS!
THESE FIVE CONTESTANTS WILL COMPETE IN THE FINAL ROUND!!
WHAAAAT?!
I'M NOT OUT?!

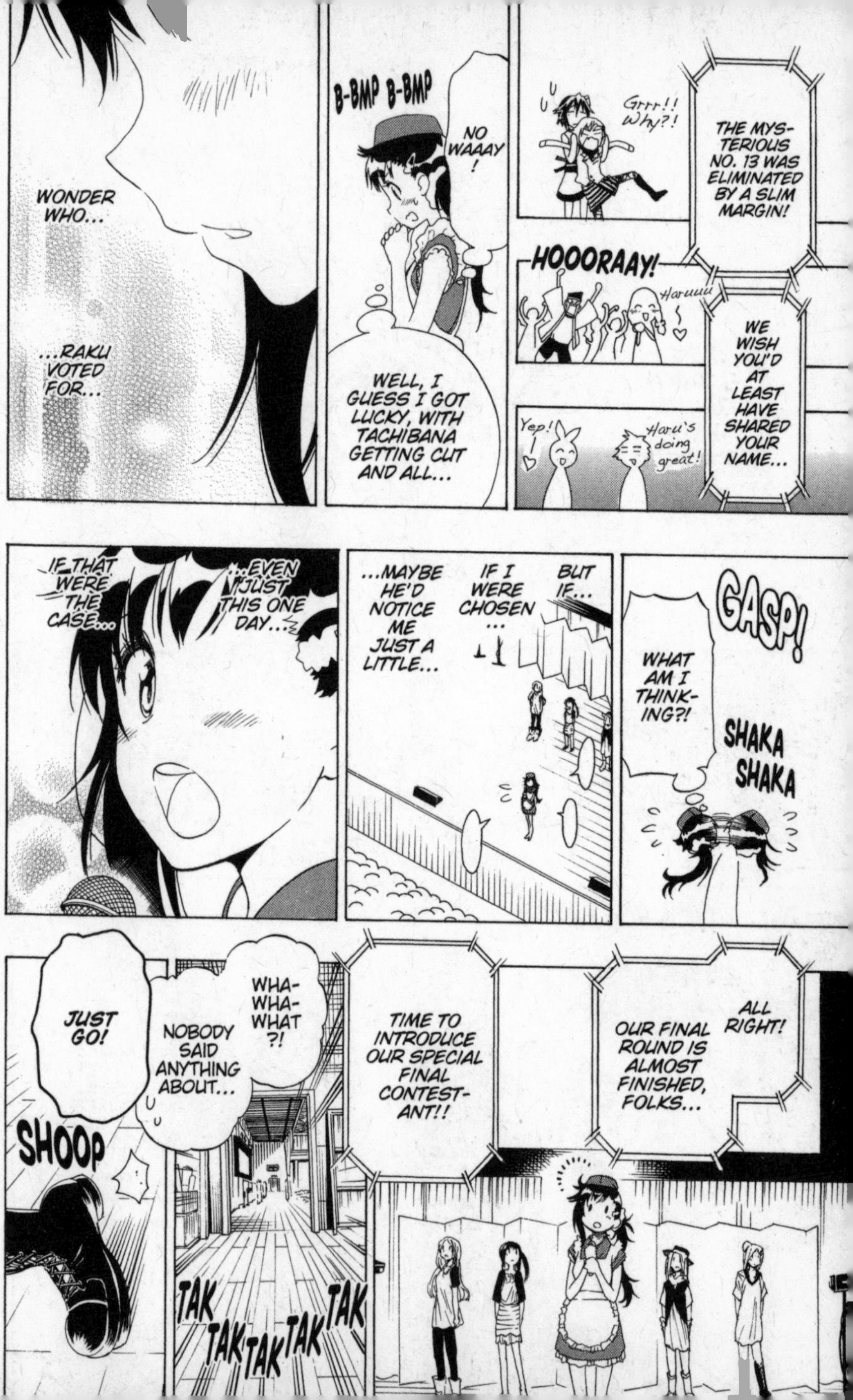
THE MYSTERIOUS NO. 13 WAS ELIMINATED BY A SLIM MARGIN!
Grrr!! Why?!
HOOORAAY!
Haruuu
WE WISH YOU'D AT LEAST HAVE SHARED YOUR NAME...
Haru's doing great!
Yep!
B-BMP B-BMP
NO WAAAY!
WELL, I GUESS I GOT LUCKY, WITH TACHIBANA GETTING CUT AND ALL...
WONDER WHO...
...RAKU VOTED FOR...
GASP!
WHAT AM I THINKING?!
SHAKA SHAKA
BUT IF...
IF I WERE CHOSEN...
...MAYBE HE'D NOTICE ME JUST A LITTLE...
...EVEN JUST THIS ONE DAY...
IF THAT WERE THE CASE...
ALL RIGHT!
OUR FINAL ROUND IS ALMOST FINISHED, FOLKS...
TIME TO INTRODUCE OUR SPECIAL FINAL CONTESTANT!!
WHA-WHA-WHAT?!
NOBODY SAID ANYTHING ABOUT...
TAK TAK TAK TAK TAK
JUST GO!
SHOOP

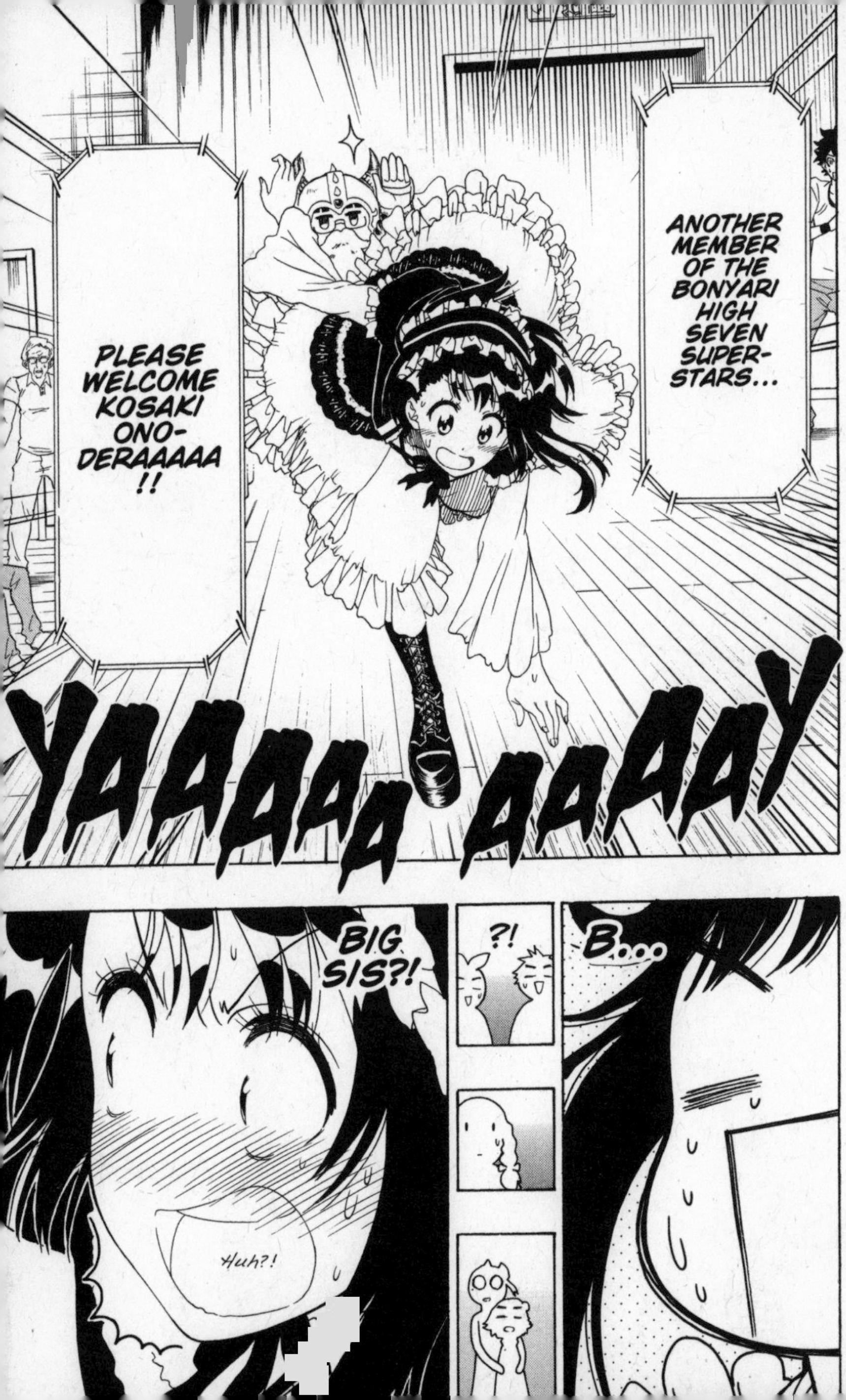
ANOTHER MEMBER OF THE BONYARI HIGH SEVEN SUPER-STARS...
PLEASE WELCOME KOSAKI ONO-DERAAAAA!!
YAAAAAAAAAAY
B...
?!
BIG SIS?!
Huh?!

Last night, 12:21 A.M.
Tee hee! Perfect...
Hee hee hee hee hee...

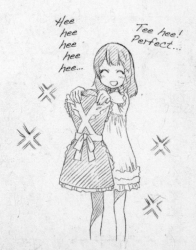

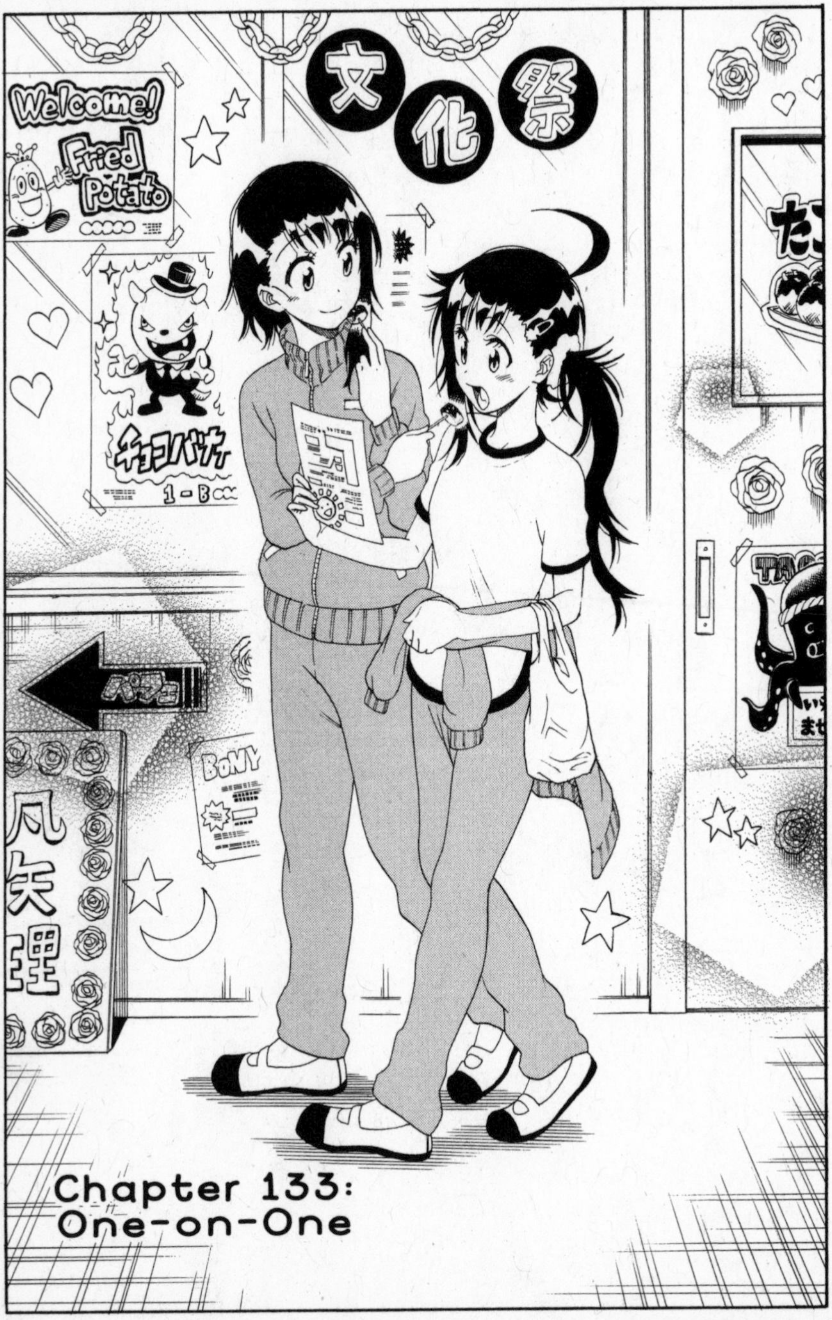
文化祭
Welcome!
Fried Potato
1-B
BoNY

Chapter 133: One-on-One

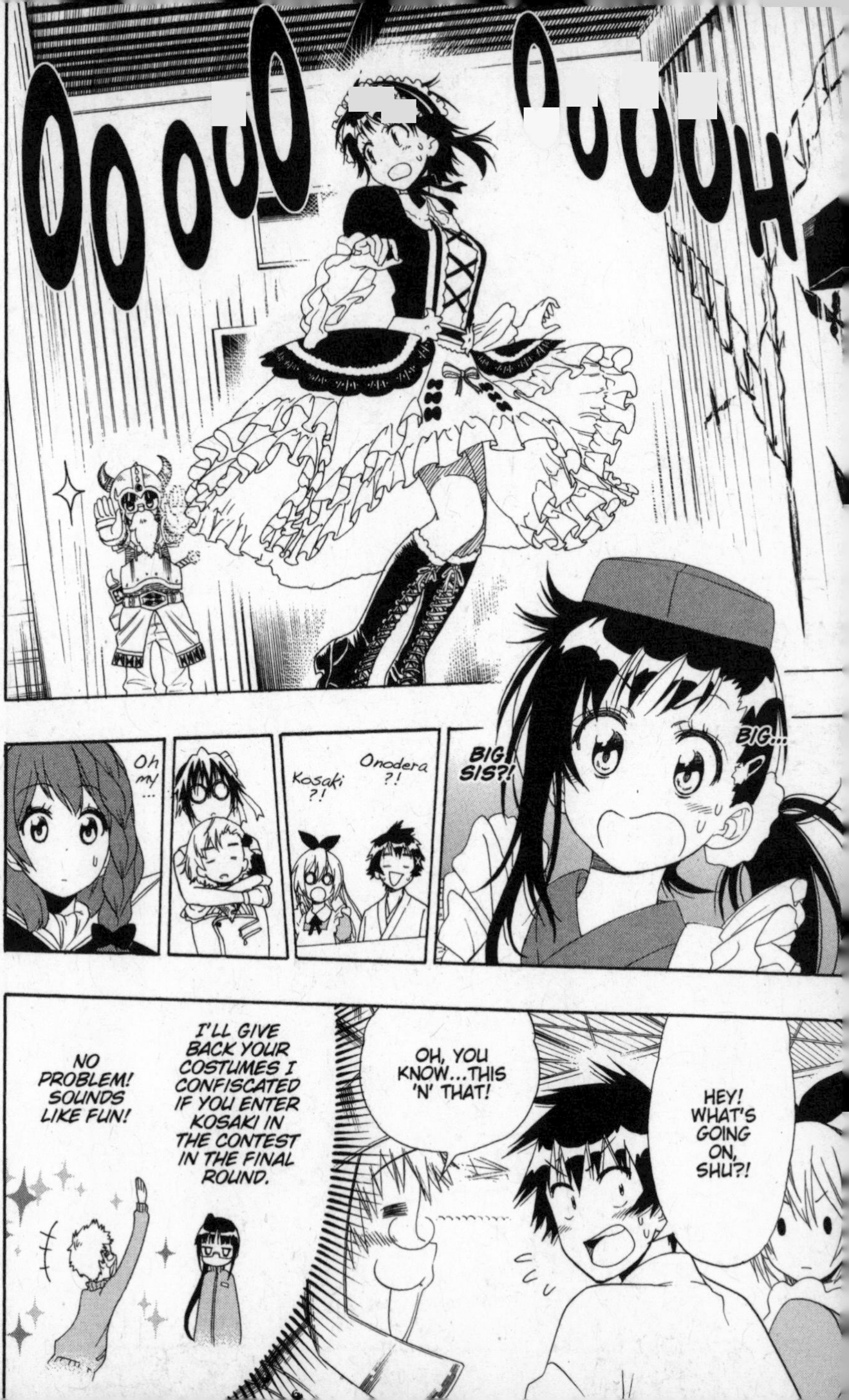

OOOOOOOOOOH
BIG...
BIG SIS?!
Onodera ?!
Kosaki ?!
Oh my ...
HEY! WHAT'S GOING ON, SHU?!
OH, YOU KNOW...THIS 'N' THAT!
I'LL GIVE BACK YOUR COSTUMES I CONFISCATED IF YOU ENTER KOSAKI IN THE CONTEST IN THE FINAL ROUND.
NO PROBLEM! SOUNDS LIKE FUN!

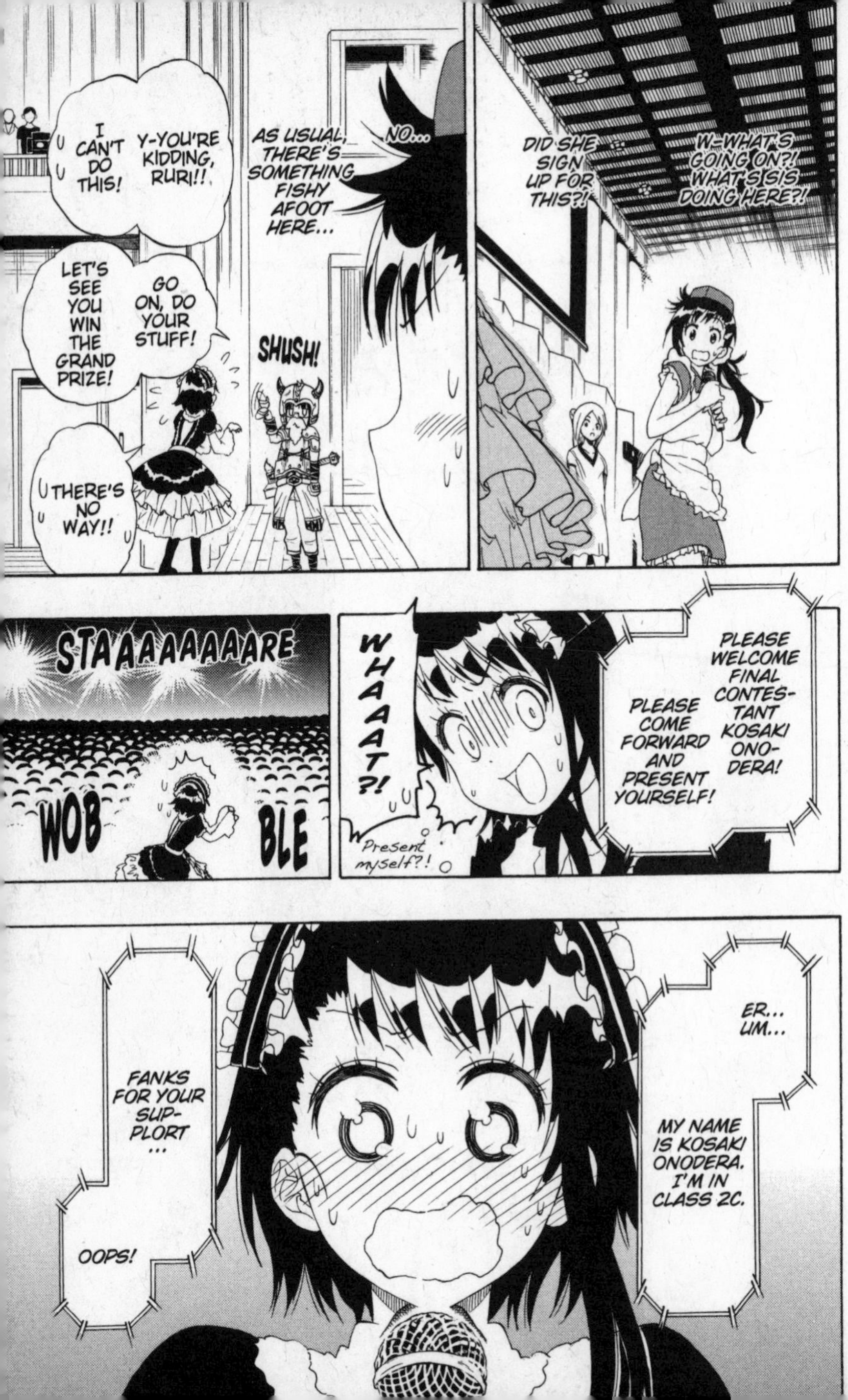
W-WHAT'S GOING ON?! WHAT'S SIS DOING HERE?!
DID SHE SIGN UP FOR THIS?!
NO...
AS USUAL, THERE'S SOMETHING FISHY AFOOT HERE...
SHUSH!
Y-YOU'RE KIDDING, RURI!!
I CAN'T DO THIS!
GO ON, DO YOUR STUFF!
LET'S SEE YOU WIN THE GRAND PRIZE!
THERE'S NO WAY!!
PLEASE WELCOME FINAL CONTES-TANT KOSAKI ONO-DERA!
PLEASE COME FORWARD AND PRESENT YOURSELF!
WHAAAAT?!
Present myself?!
STAAAAAAAARE
WOB BLE
ER... UM...
MY NAME IS KOSAKI ONODERA. I'M IN CLASS 2C.
FANKS FOR YOUR SUP-PLORT...
OOPS!

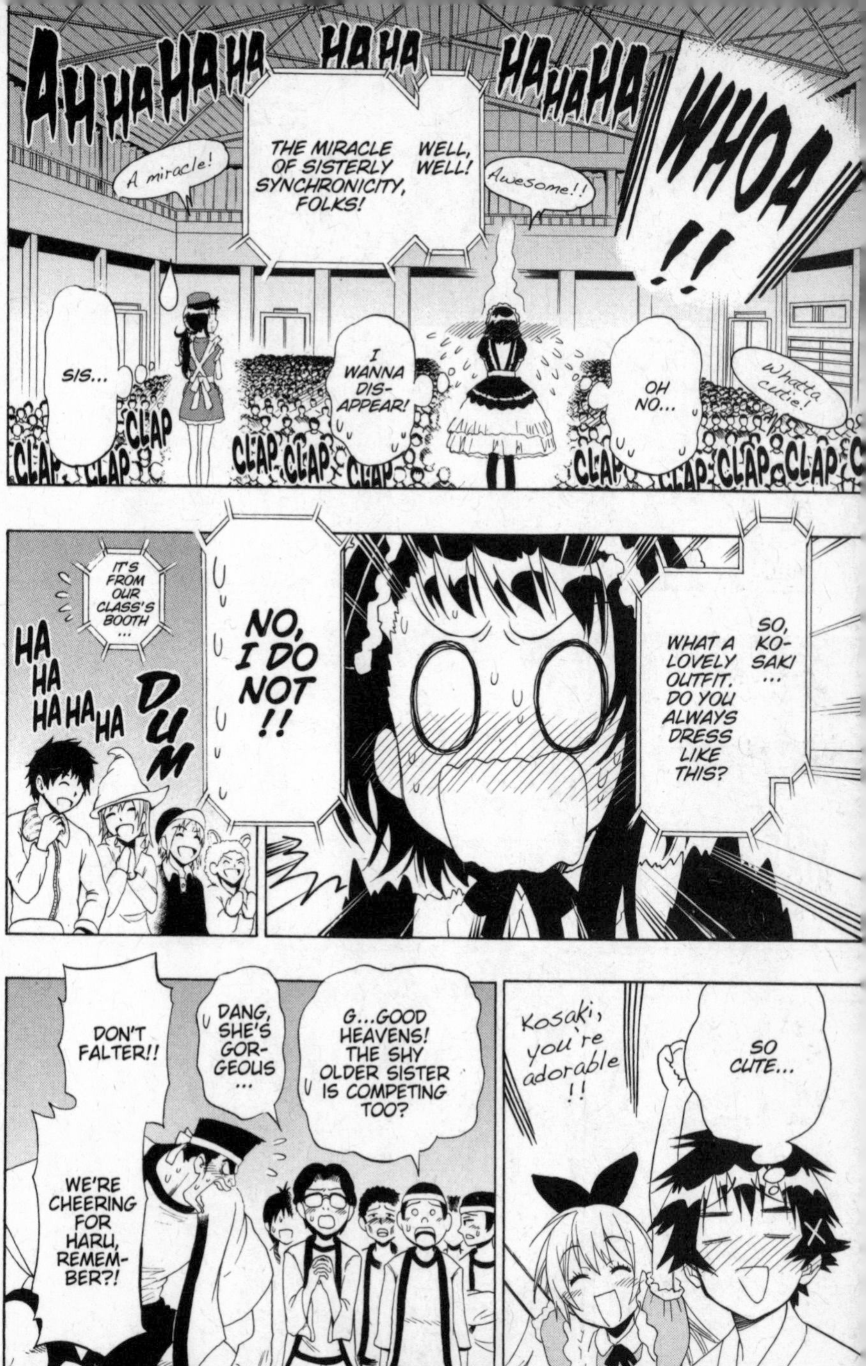
WHOA!!
HAHAHA
WELL, WELL! THE MIRACLE OF SISTERLY SYNCHRONICITY, FOLKS!
Awesome!!
HAHA
A miracle!
AHHAHAHA
Whatta cutie!
OH NO...
I WANNA DISAPPEAR!
SIS...
CLAP CLAP CLAP CLAP CLAP CLAP CLAP CLAP CLAP CLAP
SO, KOSAKI...
WHAT A LOVELY OUTFIT. DO YOU ALWAYS DRESS LIKE THIS?
NO, I DO NOT!!
IT'S FROM OUR CLASS'S BOOTH...
HA HA HA HA HA
DUM
SO CUTE...
Kosaki, you're adorable!!
G...GOOD HEAVENS! THE SHY OLDER SISTER IS COMPETING TOO?
DANG, SHE'S GORGEOUS...
DON'T FALTER!!
WE'RE CHEERING FOR HARU, REMEMBER?!

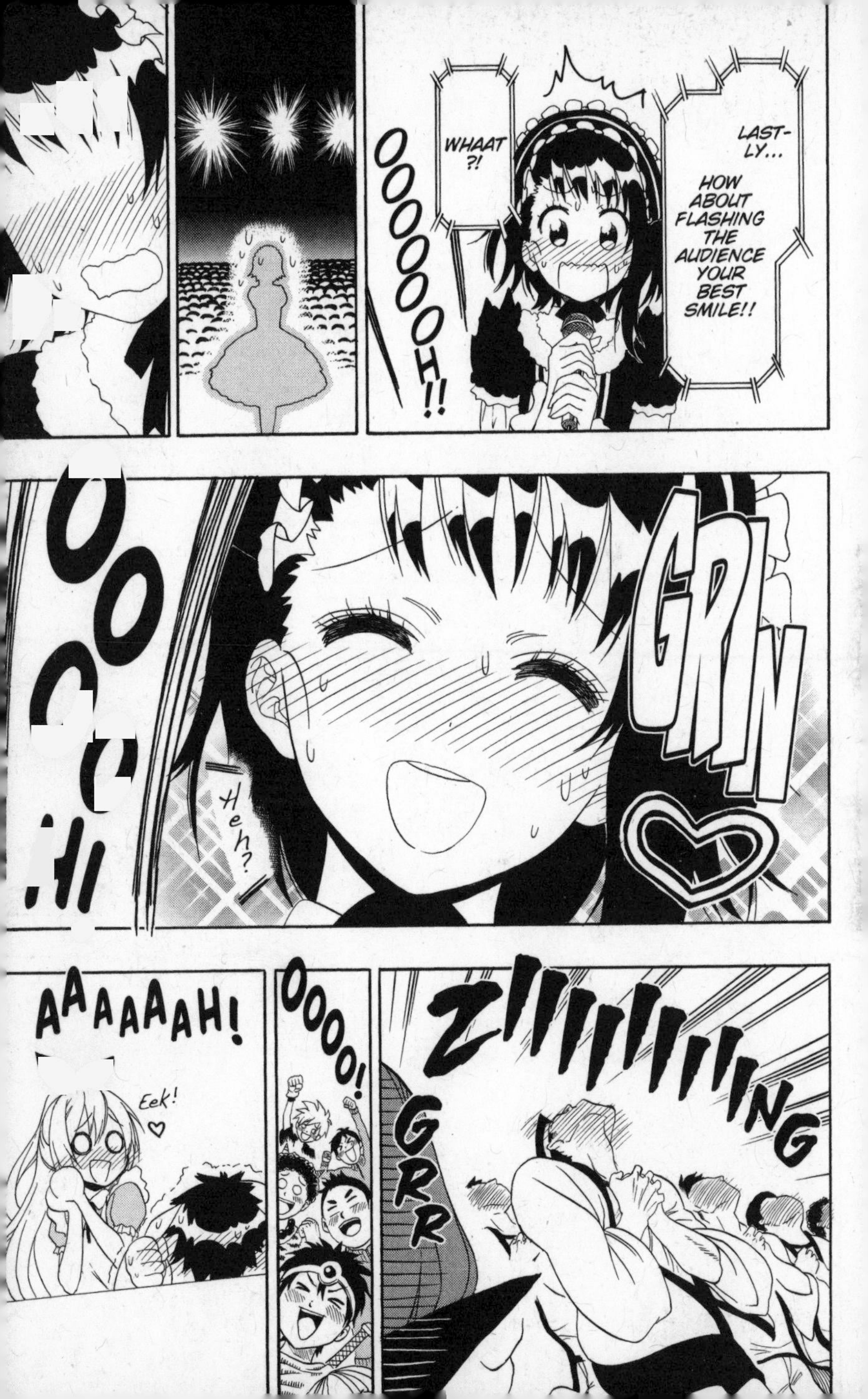
LASTLY... HOW ABOUT FLASHING THE AUDIENCE YOUR BEST SMILE!!
WHAAT?!
OOOOOOOH!!
GRIN
Heh?
ZIIIIIIIIING
GRR
OOOOO!
AAAAAAH!
Eek! ♡

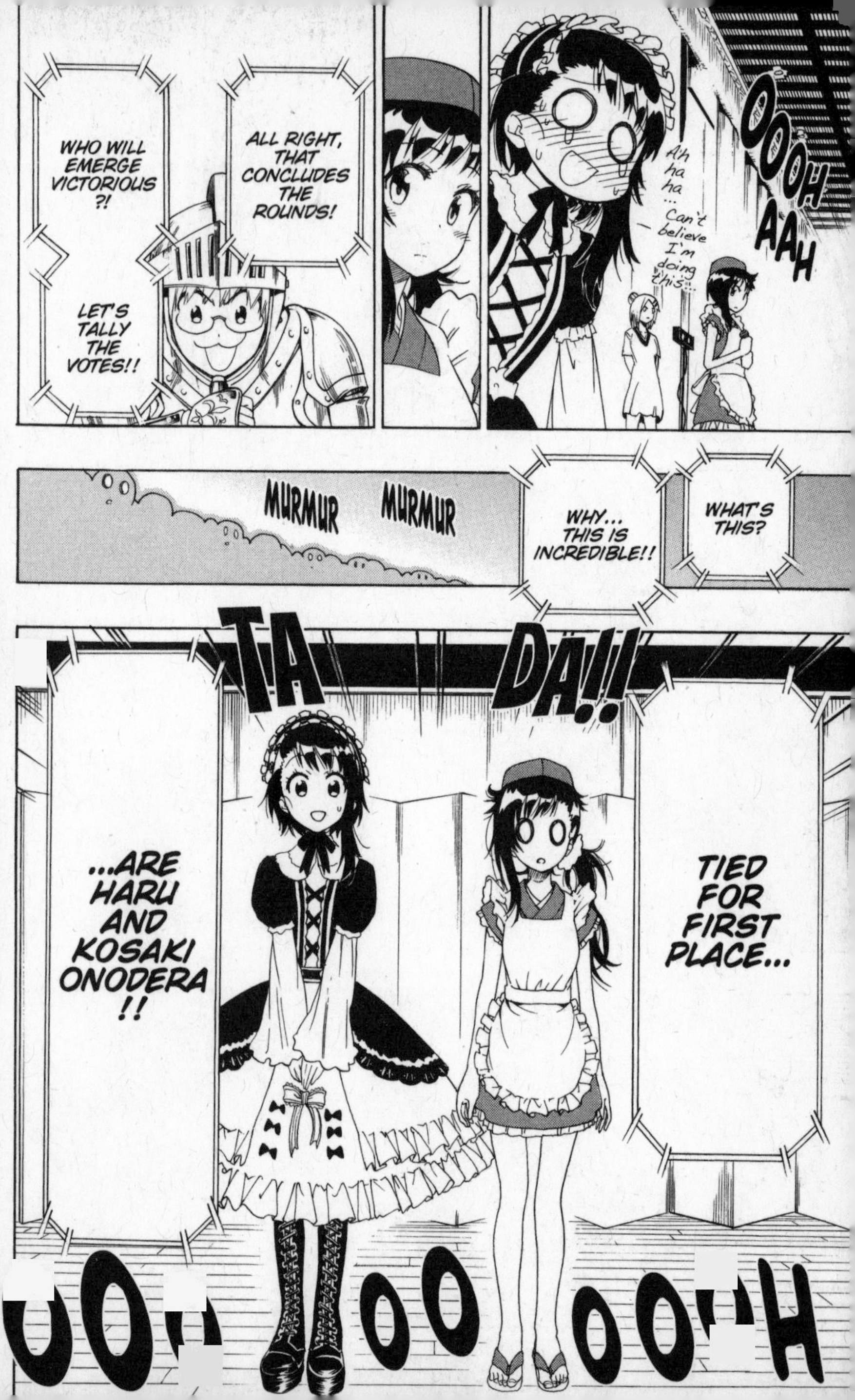
OOOOH AAAH
Ah ha ha... Can't believe I'm doing this...
ALL RIGHT, THAT CONCLUDES THE ROUNDS!
WHO WILL EMERGE VICTORIOUS?!
LET'S TALLY THE VOTES!!
WHAT'S THIS?
WHY... THIS IS INCREDIBLE!!
MURMUR MURMUR
TA DA!!
TIED FOR FIRST PLACE...
...ARE HARU AND KOSAKI ONODERA!!
OOOOOOH

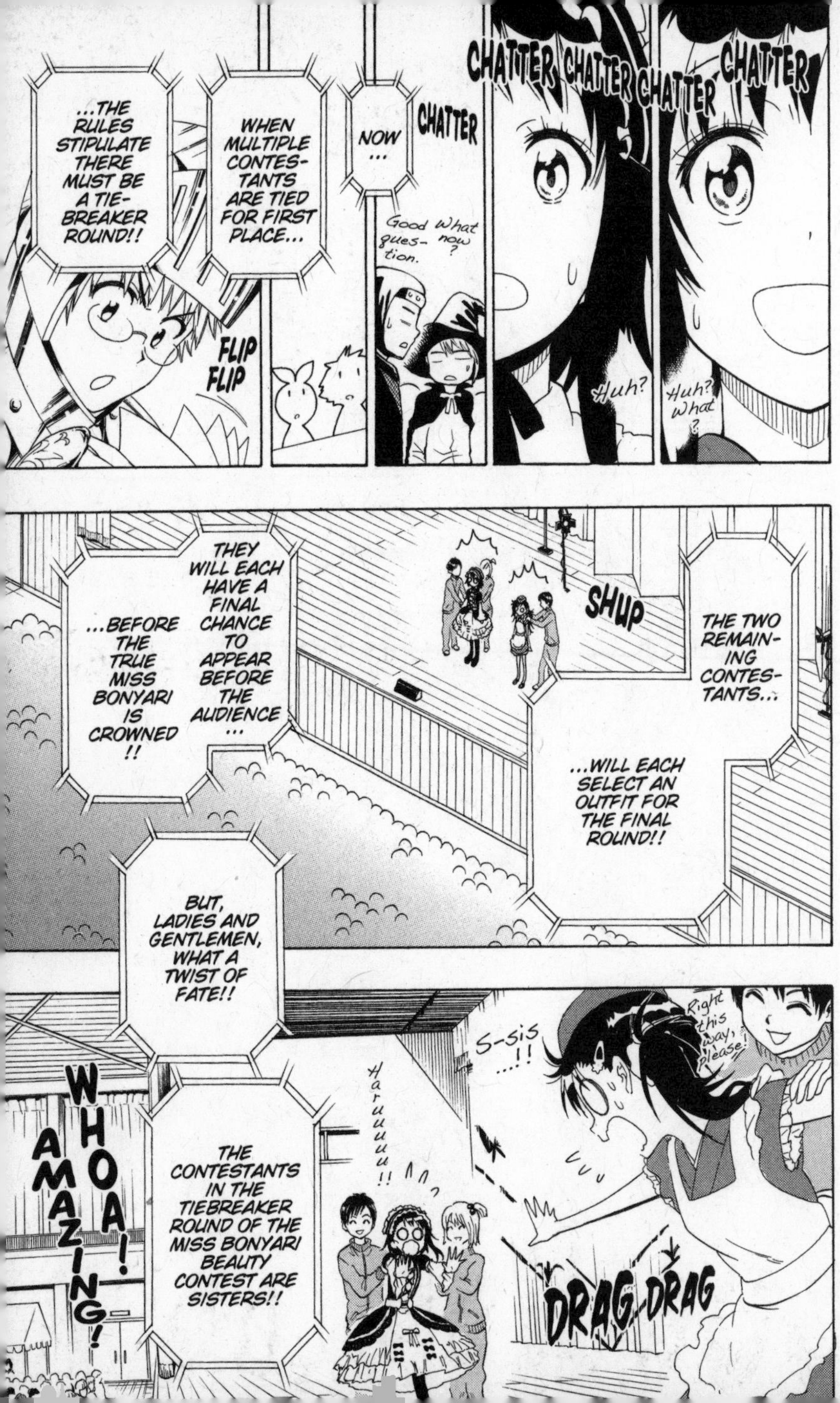
CHATTER
CHATTER
Huh? What?
CHATTER
CHATTER
Huh?
CHATTER
NOW...
What now?
Good question.
WHEN MULTIPLE CONTESTANTS ARE TIED FOR FIRST PLACE...
...THE RULES STIPULATE THERE MUST BE A TIE-BREAKER ROUND!!
FLIP FLIP
THE TWO REMAINING CONTESTANTS...
...WILL EACH SELECT AN OUTFIT FOR THE FINAL ROUND!!
SHUP
THEY WILL EACH HAVE A FINAL CHANCE TO APPEAR BEFORE THE AUDIENCE...
...BEFORE THE TRUE MISS BONYARI IS CROWNED!!
Right this way, please!
S-sis...!!
DRAG DRAG
Haruuuuu!!
BUT, LADIES AND GENTLEMEN, WHAT A TWIST OF FATE!!
THE CONTESTANTS IN THE TIEBREAKER ROUND OF THE MISS BONYARI BEAUTY CONTEST ARE SISTERS!!
WHOA!
AMAZING!

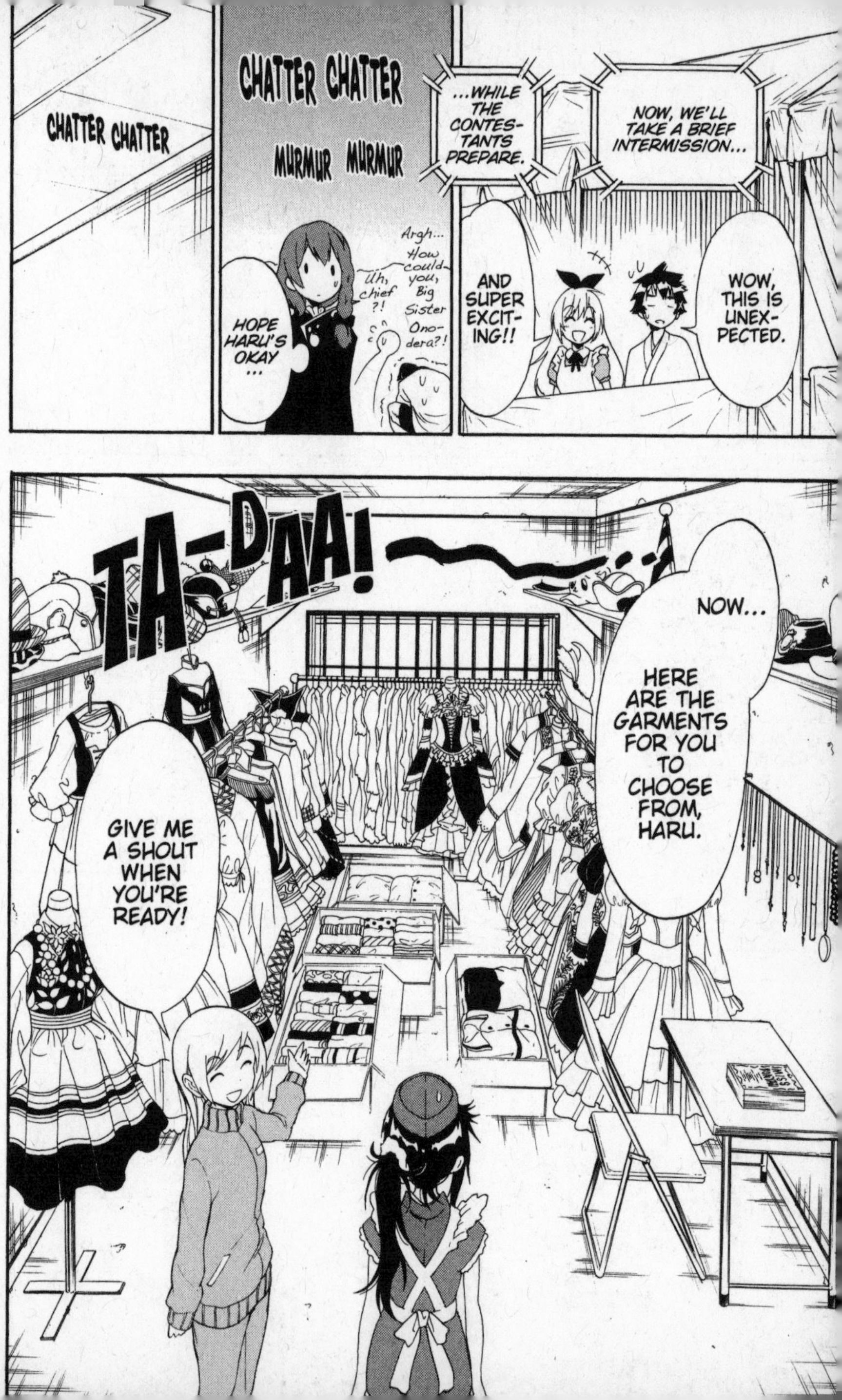
NOW, WE'LL TAKE A BRIEF INTERMISSION...
...WHILE THE CONTES-TANTS PREPARE.
WOW, THIS IS UNEX-PECTED.
AND SUPER EXCIT-ING!!
CHATTER CHATTER
MURMUR MURMUR
Argh... How could you, Big Sister Ono-dera?!
Uh, chief?!
HOPE HARU'S OKAY...
CHATTER CHATTER
TA-DAA!
NOW...
HERE ARE THE GARMENTS FOR YOU TO CHOOSE FROM, HARU.
GIVE ME A SHOUT WHEN YOU'RE READY!

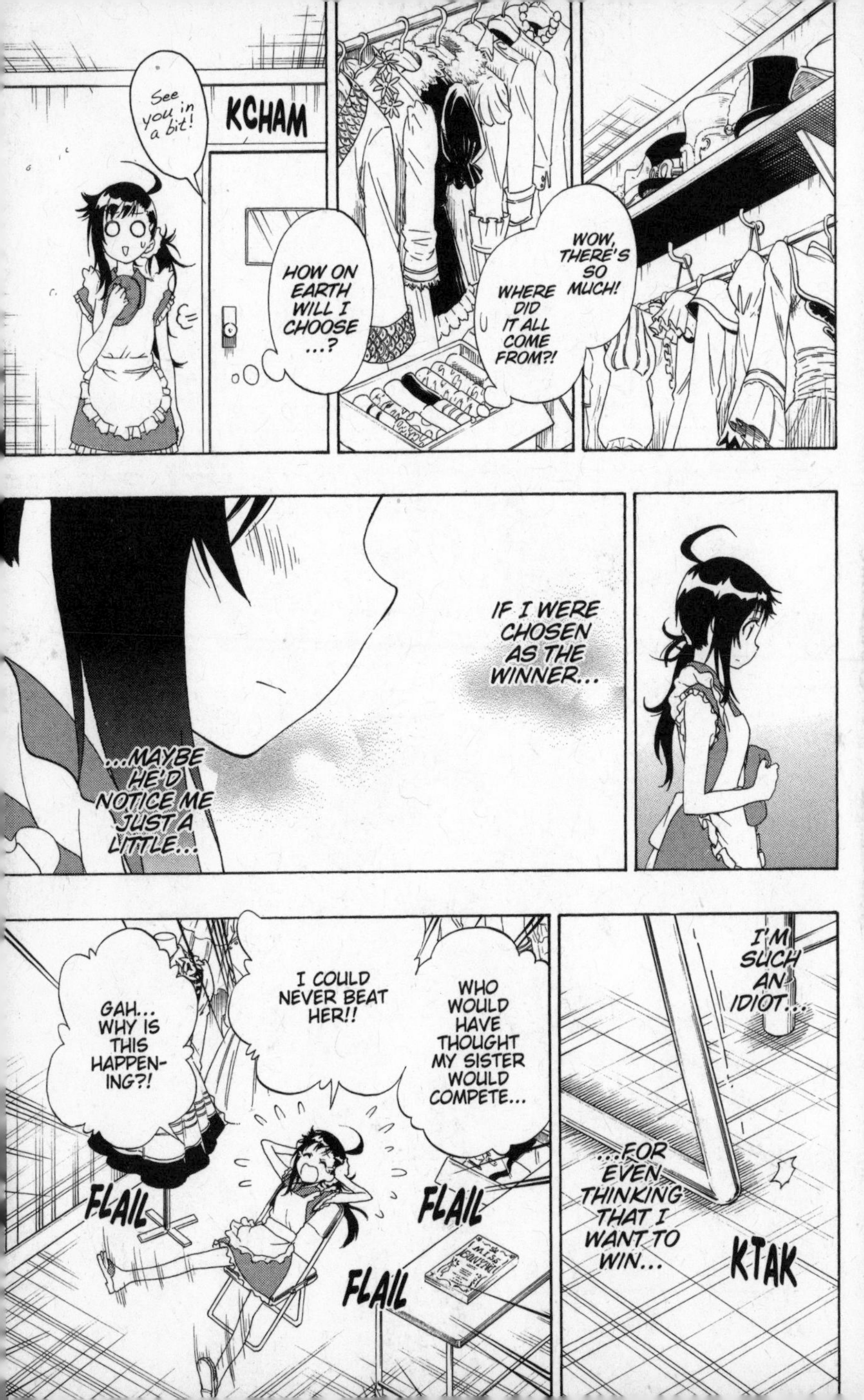
WOW, THERE'S SO MUCH!
WHERE DID IT ALL COME FROM?!
HOW ON EARTH WILL I CHOOSE ...?
See you in a bit!
KCHAM
IF I WERE CHOSEN AS THE WINNER...
...MAYBE HE'D NOTICE ME JUST A LITTLE...
I'M SUCH AN IDIOT...
...FOR EVEN THINKING THAT I WANT TO WIN...
KTAK
WHO WOULD HAVE THOUGHT MY SISTER WOULD COMPETE...
I COULD NEVER BEAT HER!!
GAH... WHY IS THIS HAPPEN-ING?!
FLAIL
FLAIL
FLAIL

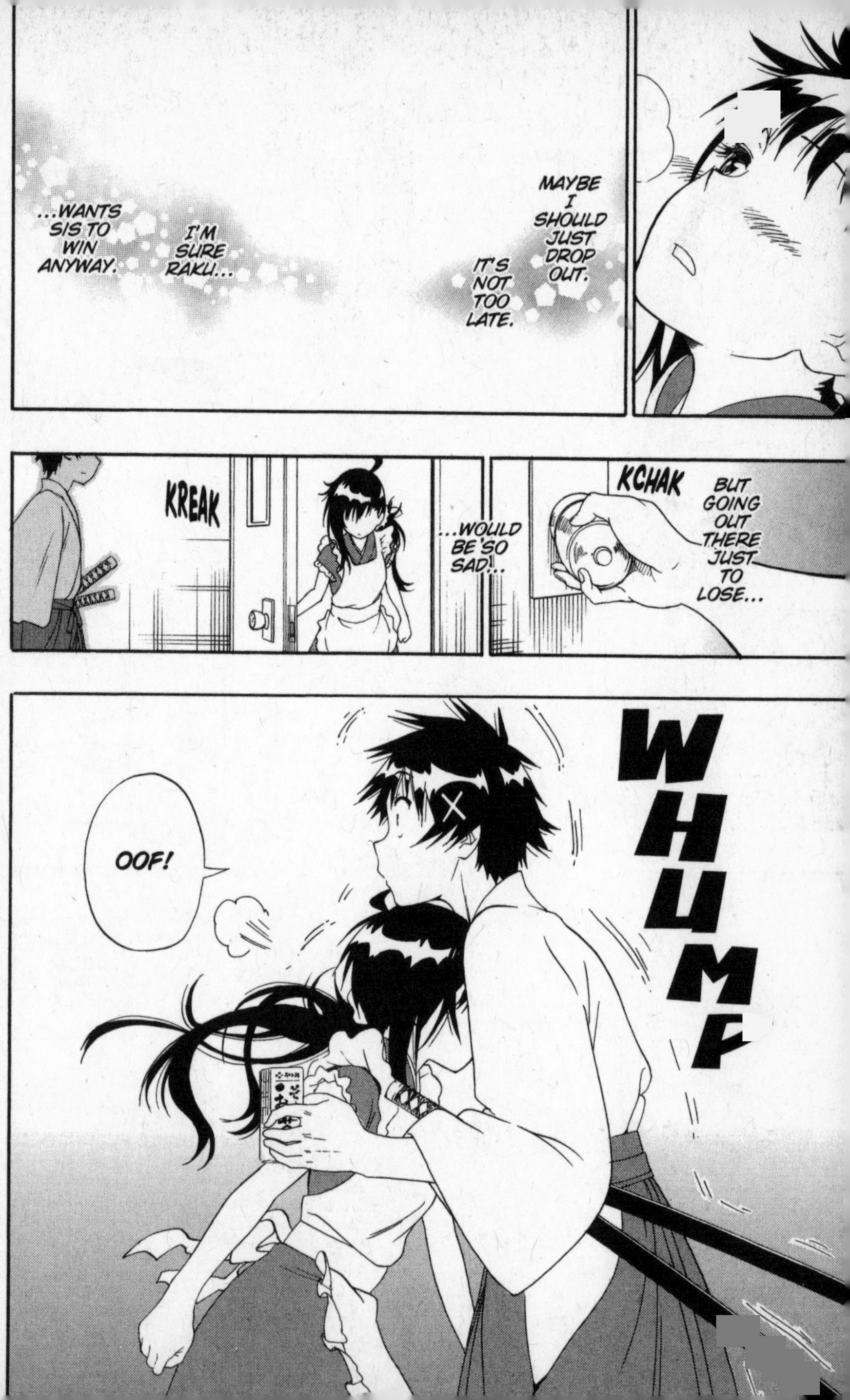
MAYBE I SHOULD JUST DROP OUT.
IT'S NOT TOO LATE.
I'M SURE RAKU...
...WANTS SIS TO WIN ANYWAY.
KCHAK
BUT GOING OUT THERE JUST TO LOSE...
...WOULD BE SO SAD...
KREAK
WHUMP
OOF!

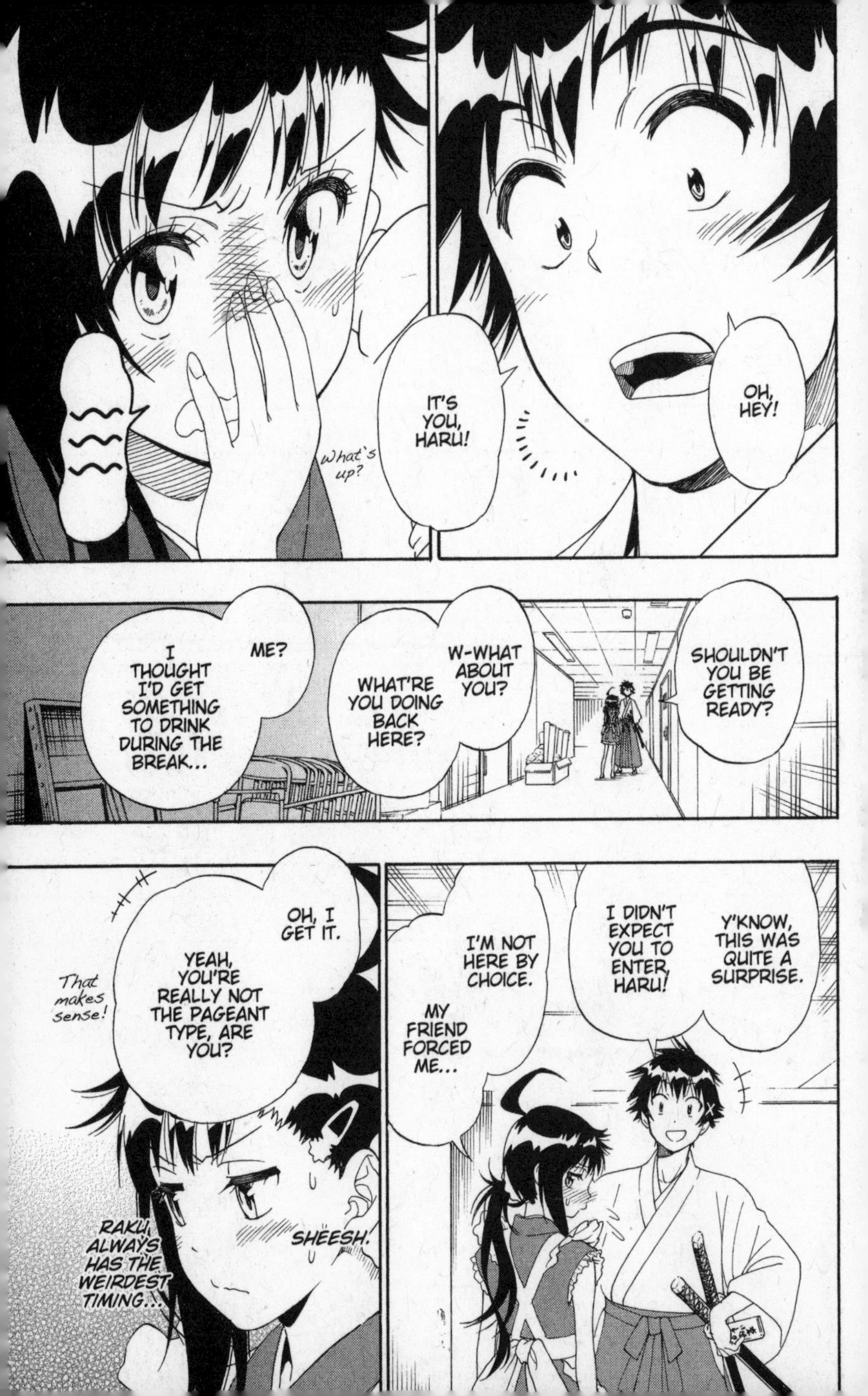
OH, HEY!
IT'S YOU, HARU!
What's up?
SHOULDN'T YOU BE GETTING READY?
W-WHAT ABOUT YOU?
WHAT'RE YOU DOING BACK HERE?
ME?
I THOUGHT I'D GET SOMETHING TO DRINK DURING THE BREAK...
Y'KNOW, THIS WAS QUITE A SURPRISE.
I DIDN'T EXPECT YOU TO ENTER, HARU!
I'M NOT HERE BY CHOICE.
MY FRIEND FORCED ME...
OH, I GET IT.
YEAH, YOU'RE REALLY NOT THE PAGEANT TYPE, ARE YOU?
That makes sense!
SHEESH.
RAKU ALWAYS HAS THE WEIRDEST TIMING...

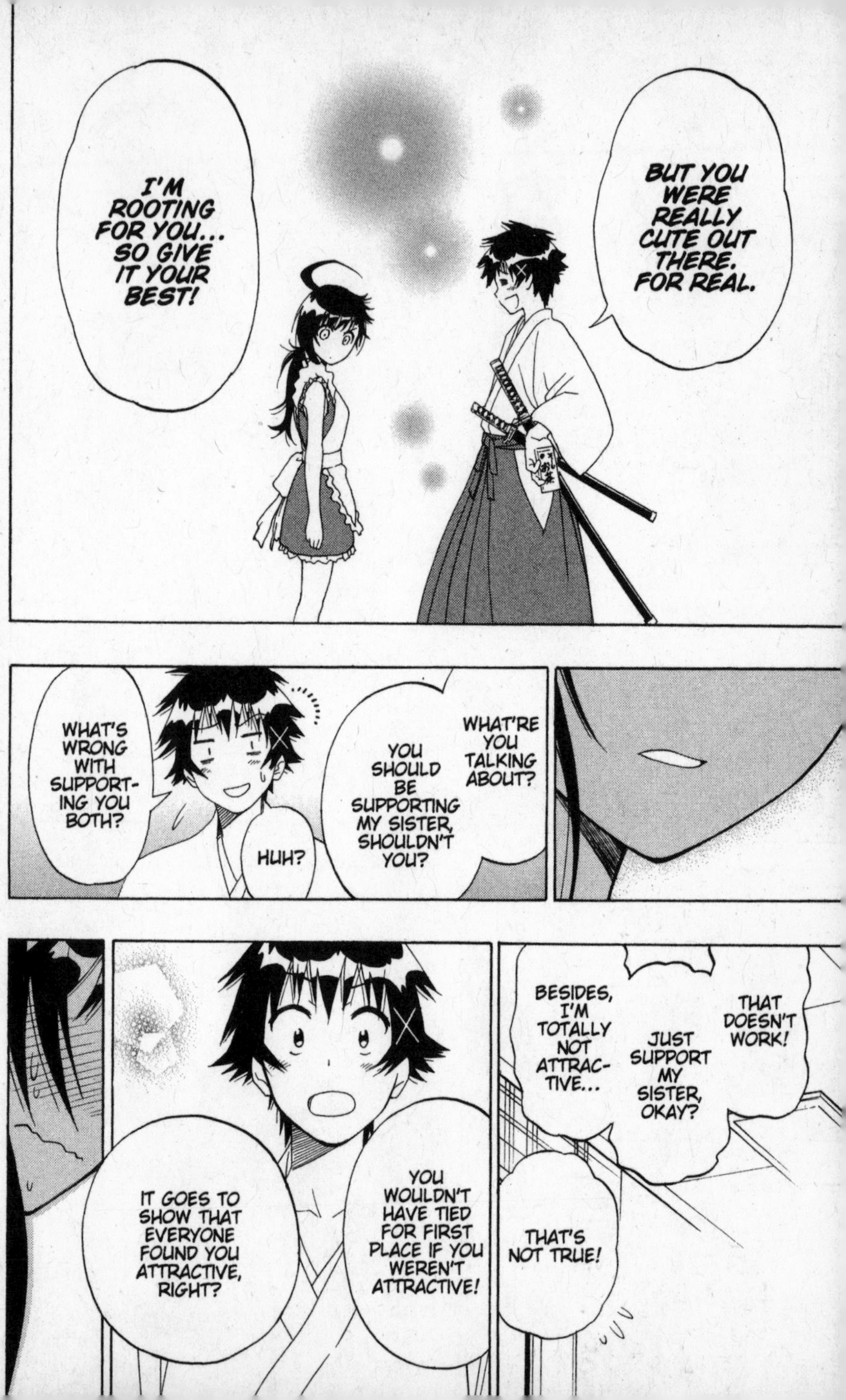
BUT YOU WERE REALLY CUTE OUT THERE. FOR REAL.
I'M ROOTING FOR YOU... SO GIVE IT YOUR BEST!
WHAT'RE YOU TALKING ABOUT?
YOU SHOULD BE SUPPORTING MY SISTER, SHOULDN'T YOU?
HUH?
WHAT'S WRONG WITH SUPPORTING YOU BOTH?
THAT DOESN'T WORK!
JUST SUPPORT MY SISTER, OKAY?
BESIDES, I'M TOTALLY NOT ATTRACTIVE...
THAT'S NOT TRUE!
YOU WOULDN'T HAVE TIED FOR FIRST PLACE IF YOU WEREN'T ATTRACTIVE!
IT GOES TO SHOW THAT EVERYONE FOUND YOU ATTRACTIVE, RIGHT?

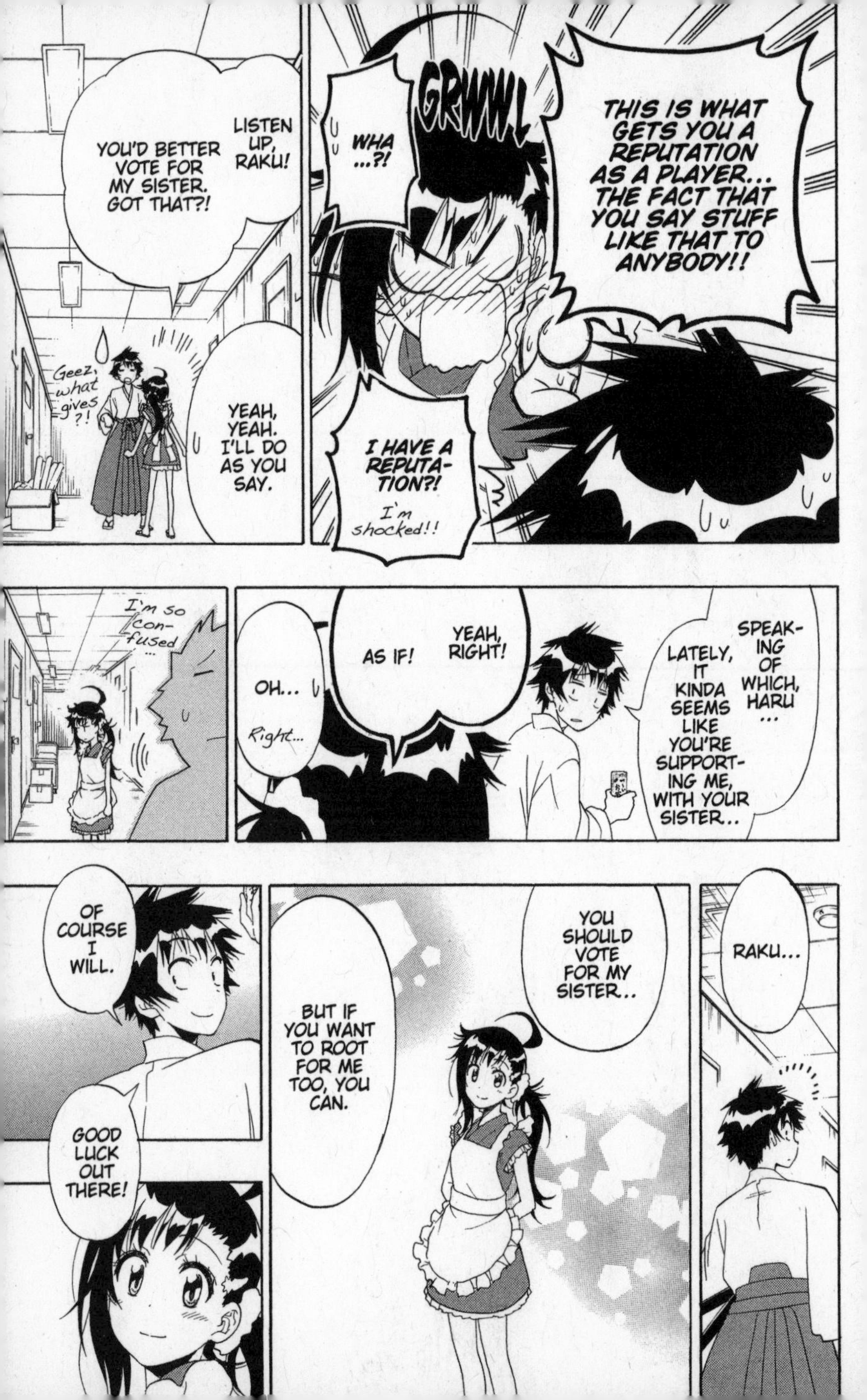
GRWWL
THIS IS WHAT GETS YOU A REPUTATION AS A PLAYER... THE FACT THAT YOU SAY STUFF LIKE THAT TO ANYBODY!!
WHA ...?!
I HAVE A REPUTATION?!
I'm shocked!!
LISTEN UP, RAKU!
YOU'D BETTER VOTE FOR MY SISTER. GOT THAT?!
YEAH, YEAH. I'LL DO AS YOU SAY.
Geez, what gives?!
SPEAKING OF WHICH, HARU...
LATELY, IT KINDA SEEMS LIKE YOU'RE SUPPORTING ME, WITH YOUR SISTER...
YEAH, RIGHT!
AS IF!
OH...
Right...
I'm so confused...
RAKU...
YOU SHOULD VOTE FOR MY SISTER...
BUT IF YOU WANT TO ROOT FOR ME TOO, YOU CAN.
OF COURSE I WILL.
GOOD LUCK OUT THERE!

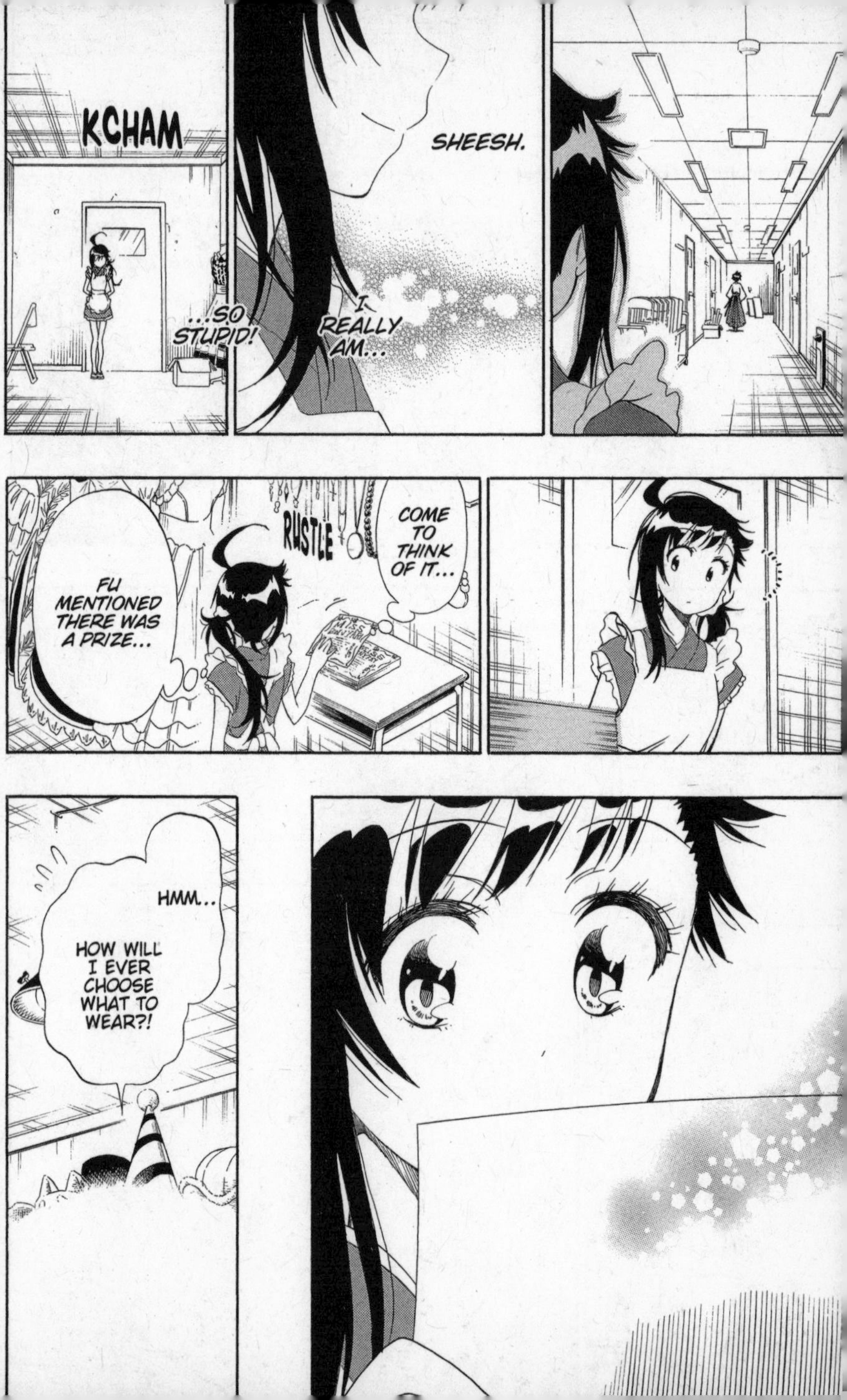
SHEESH.
I REALLY AM...
...SO STUPID!
KCHAM
COME TO THINK OF IT...
RUSTLE
FU MENTIONED THERE WAS A PRIZE...
HMM...
HOW WILL I EVER CHOOSE WHAT TO WEAR?!

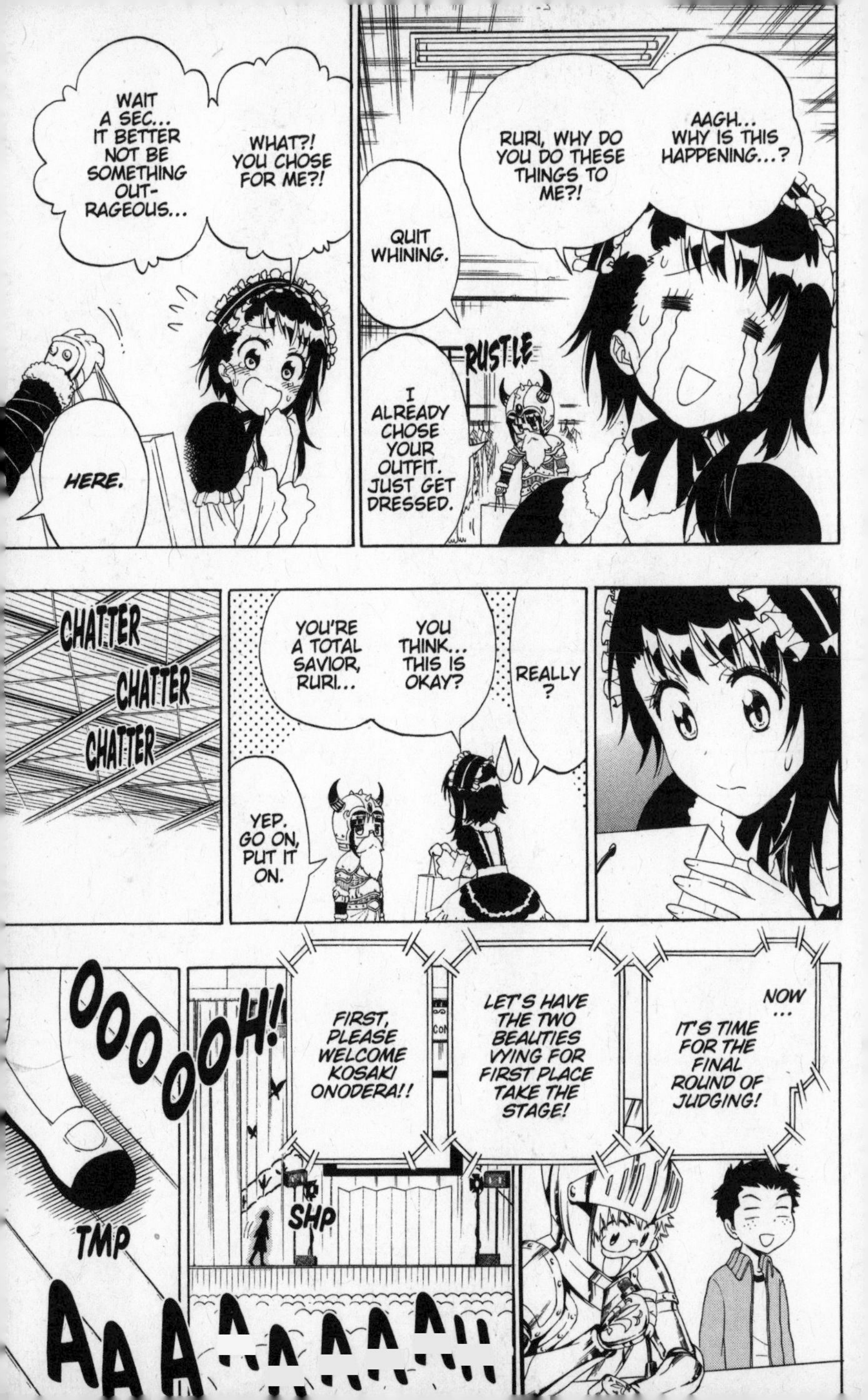
AAGH... WHY IS THIS HAPPENING...?
RURI, WHY DO YOU DO THESE THINGS TO ME?!
QUIT WHINING.
RUSTLE
I ALREADY CHOSE YOUR OUTFIT. JUST GET DRESSED.
WHAT?! YOU CHOSE FOR ME?!
WAIT A SEC... IT BETTER NOT BE SOMETHING OUT-RAGEOUS...
HERE.
REALLY ?
YOU THINK... THIS IS OKAY?
YOU'RE A TOTAL SAVIOR, RURI...
YEP. GO ON, PUT IT ON.
CHATTER
CHATTER
CHATTER
NOW ...
IT'S TIME FOR THE FINAL ROUND OF JUDGING!
LET'S HAVE THE TWO BEAUTIES VYING FOR FIRST PLACE TAKE THE STAGE!
FIRST, PLEASE WELCOME KOSAKI ONODERA!!
SHP
OOOOOH!
TMP
AAAAAAAH

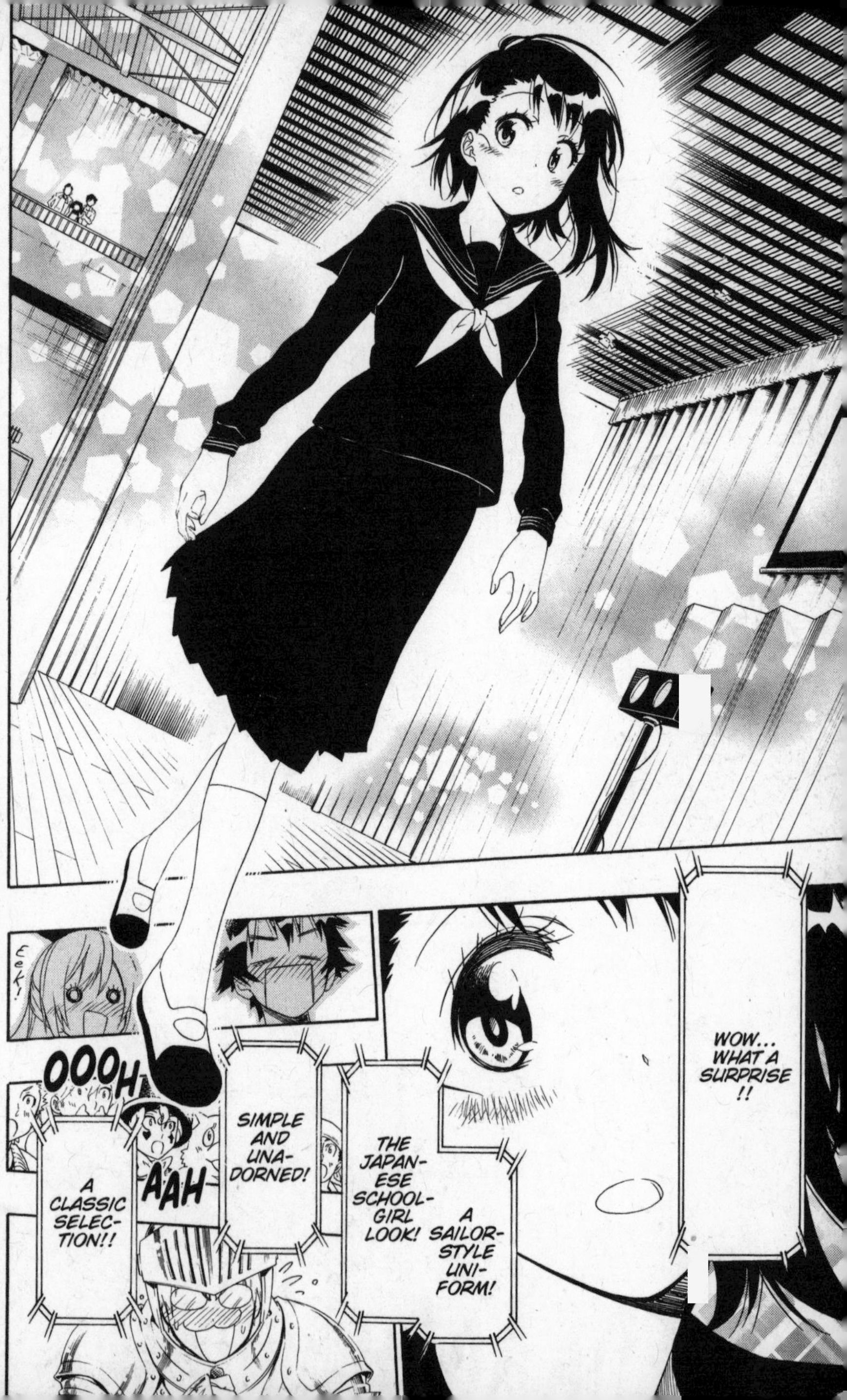

WOW... WHAT A SURPRISE!!
A SAILOR-STYLE UNIFORM!
THE JAPANESE SCHOOLGIRL LOOK!
SIMPLE AND UNADORNED!
Eek!
OOOH
AAH
A CLASSIC SELECTION!!

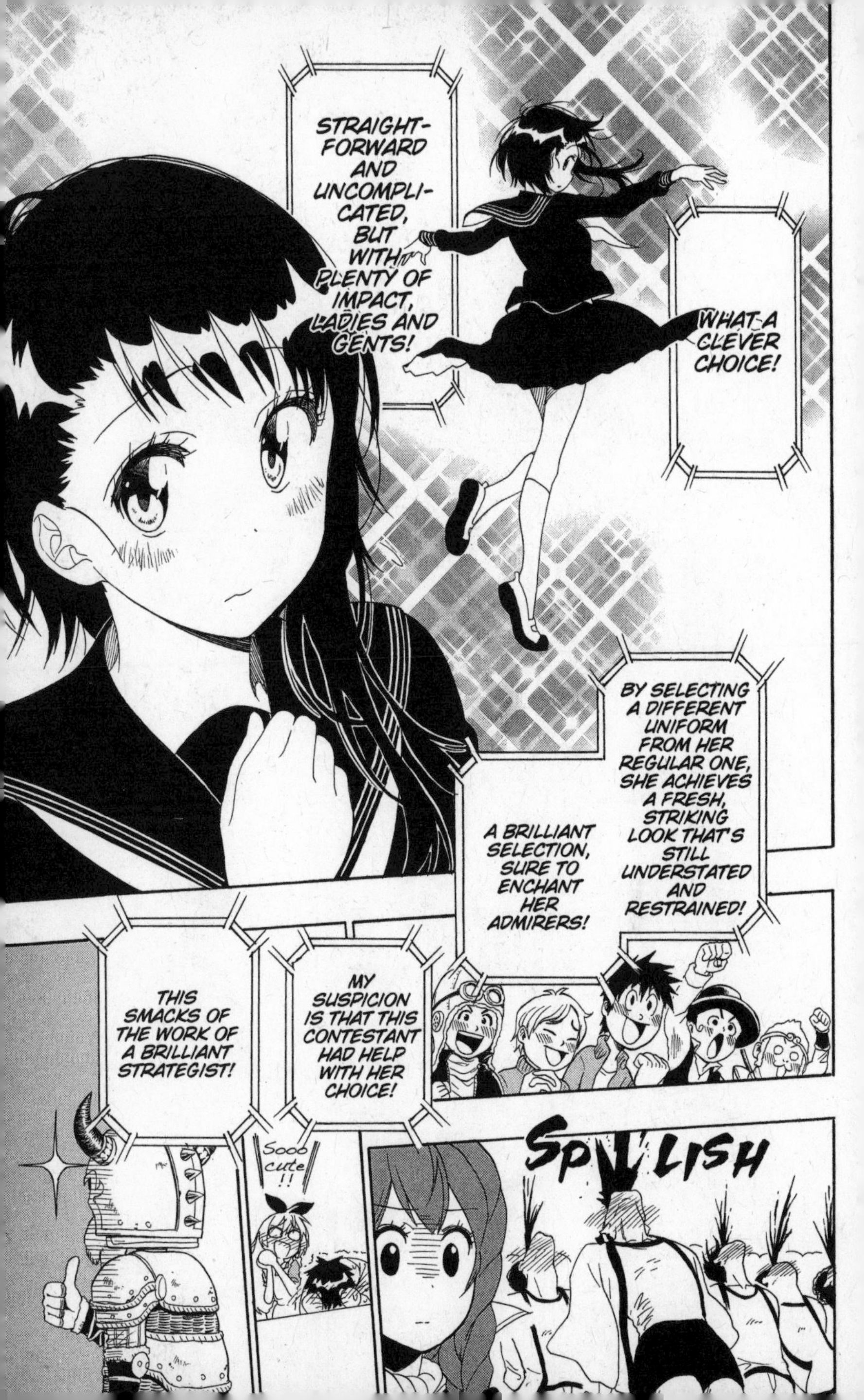
WHAT A CLEVER CHOICE!
STRAIGHT-FORWARD AND UNCOMPLI-CATED, BUT WITH PLENTY OF IMPACT, LADIES AND GENTS!
BY SELECTING A DIFFERENT UNIFORM FROM HER REGULAR ONE, SHE ACHIEVES A FRESH, STRIKING LOOK THAT'S STILL UNDERSTATED AND RESTRAINED!
A BRILLIANT SELECTION, SURE TO ENCHANT HER ADMIRERS!
MY SUSPICION IS THAT THIS CONTESTANT HAD HELP WITH HER CHOICE!
THIS SMACKS OF THE WORK OF A BRILLIANT STRATEGIST!
SPLISH
Sooo cute!!

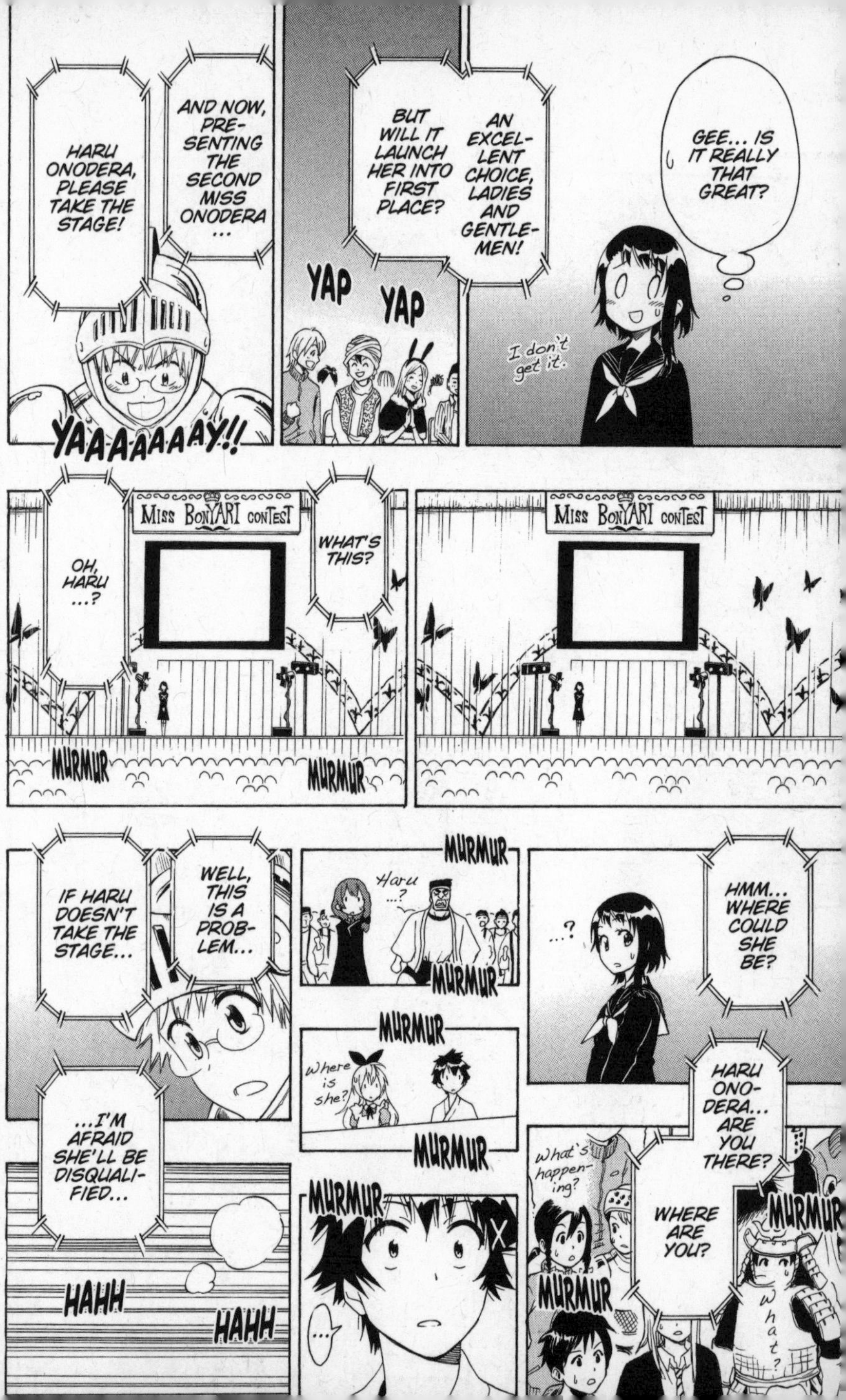
GEE... IS IT REALLY THAT GREAT?
I don't get it.
AN EXCELLENT CHOICE, LADIES AND GENTLEMEN!
BUT WILL IT LAUNCH HER INTO FIRST PLACE?
YAP
YAP
AND NOW, PRESENTING THE SECOND MISS ONODERA...
HARU ONODERA, PLEASE TAKE THE STAGE!
YAAAAAAAY!!
MISS BONYARI CONTEST
MURMUR
MURMUR
MISS BONYARI CONTEST
WHAT'S THIS?
OH, HARU...?
MURMUR
MURMUR
HMM... WHERE COULD SHE BE?
...?
HARU ONODERA... ARE YOU THERE?
WHERE ARE YOU?
What's happening?
MURMUR
MURMUR
What?
MURMUR
Haru...?
MURMUR
MURMUR
Where is she?
MURMUR
MURMUR
...
WELL, THIS IS A PROBLEM...
IF HARU DOESN'T TAKE THE STAGE...
...I'M AFRAID SHE'LL BE DISQUALIFIED...
HAHH
HAHH

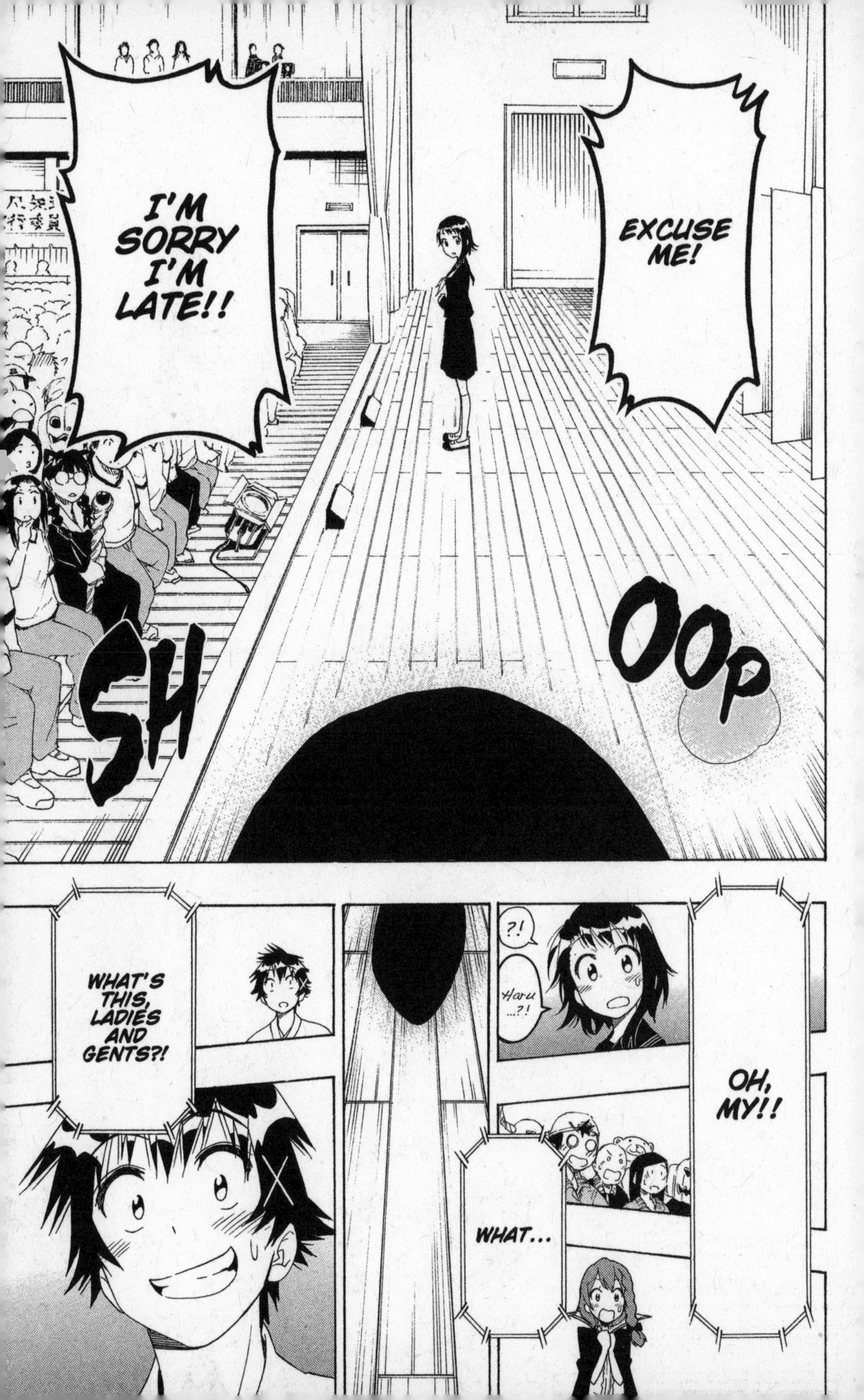
EXCUSE ME!
I'M SORRY I'M LATE!!
SH
OOP
?!
Haru ...?!
OH, MY!!
WHAT...
WHAT'S THIS, LADIES AND GENTS?!

Wow...

Gee... I was cute?

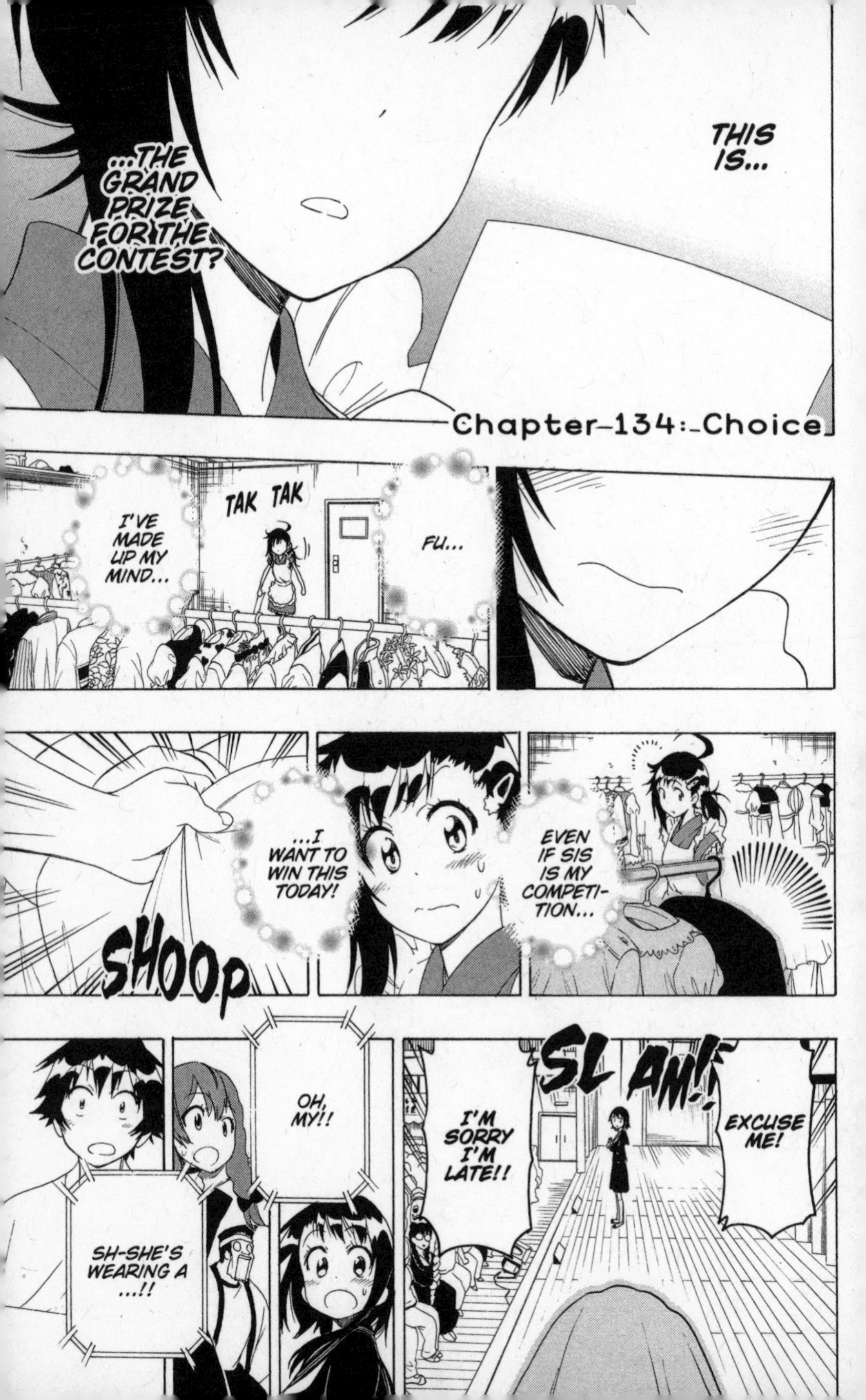
THIS IS...
...THE GRAND PRIZE FOR THE CONTEST?
Chapter 134: Choice
FU...
TAK TAK
I'VE MADE UP MY MIND...
EVEN IF SIS IS MY COMPETITION...
...I WANT TO WIN THIS TODAY!
SHOOP
EXCUSE ME!
SLAM!!
I'M SORRY I'M LATE!!
OH, MY!!
SH-SHE'S WEARING A ...!!

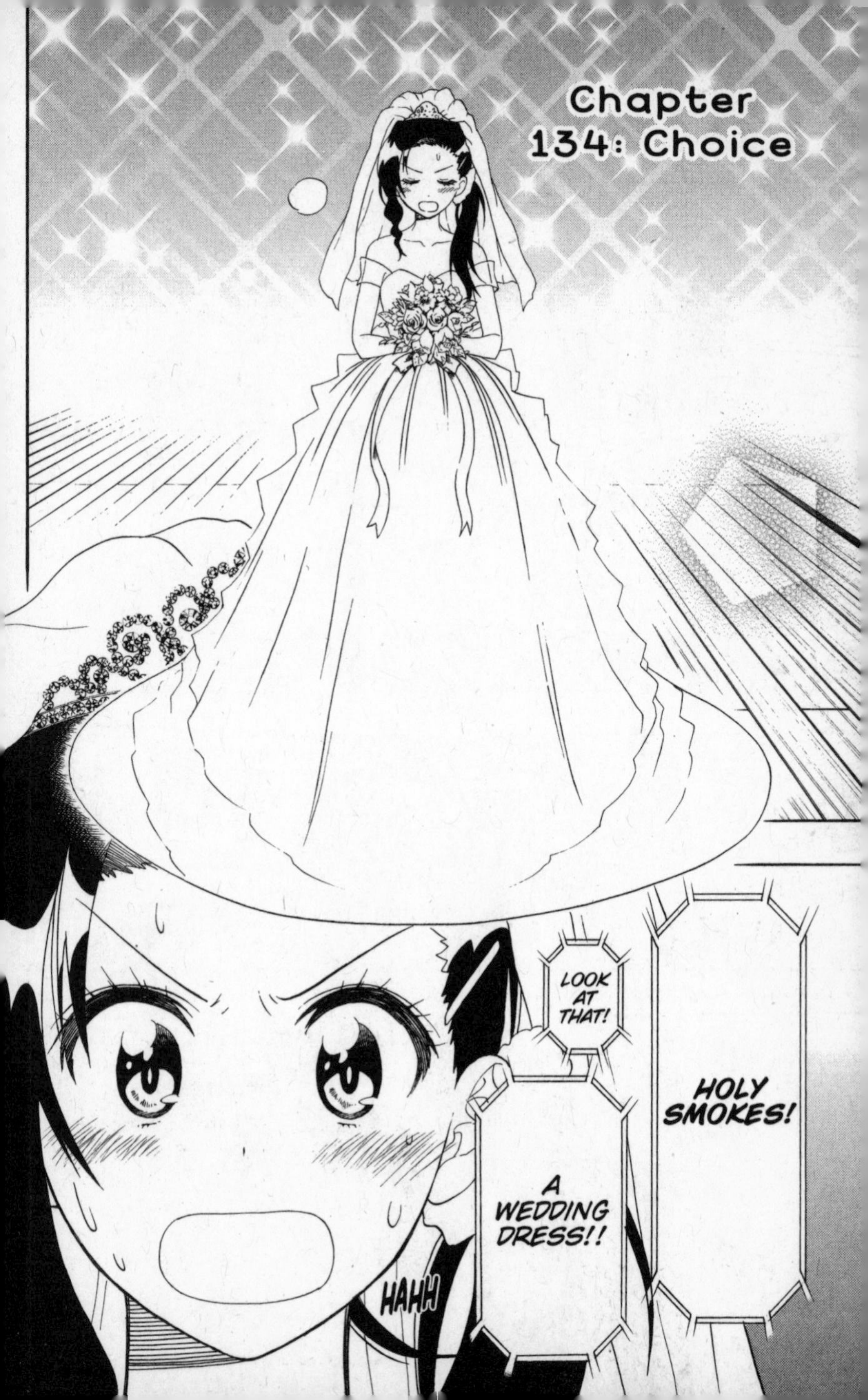
Chapter 134: Choice
HOLY SMOKES!
LOOK AT THAT!
A WEDDING DRESS!!
HAHH

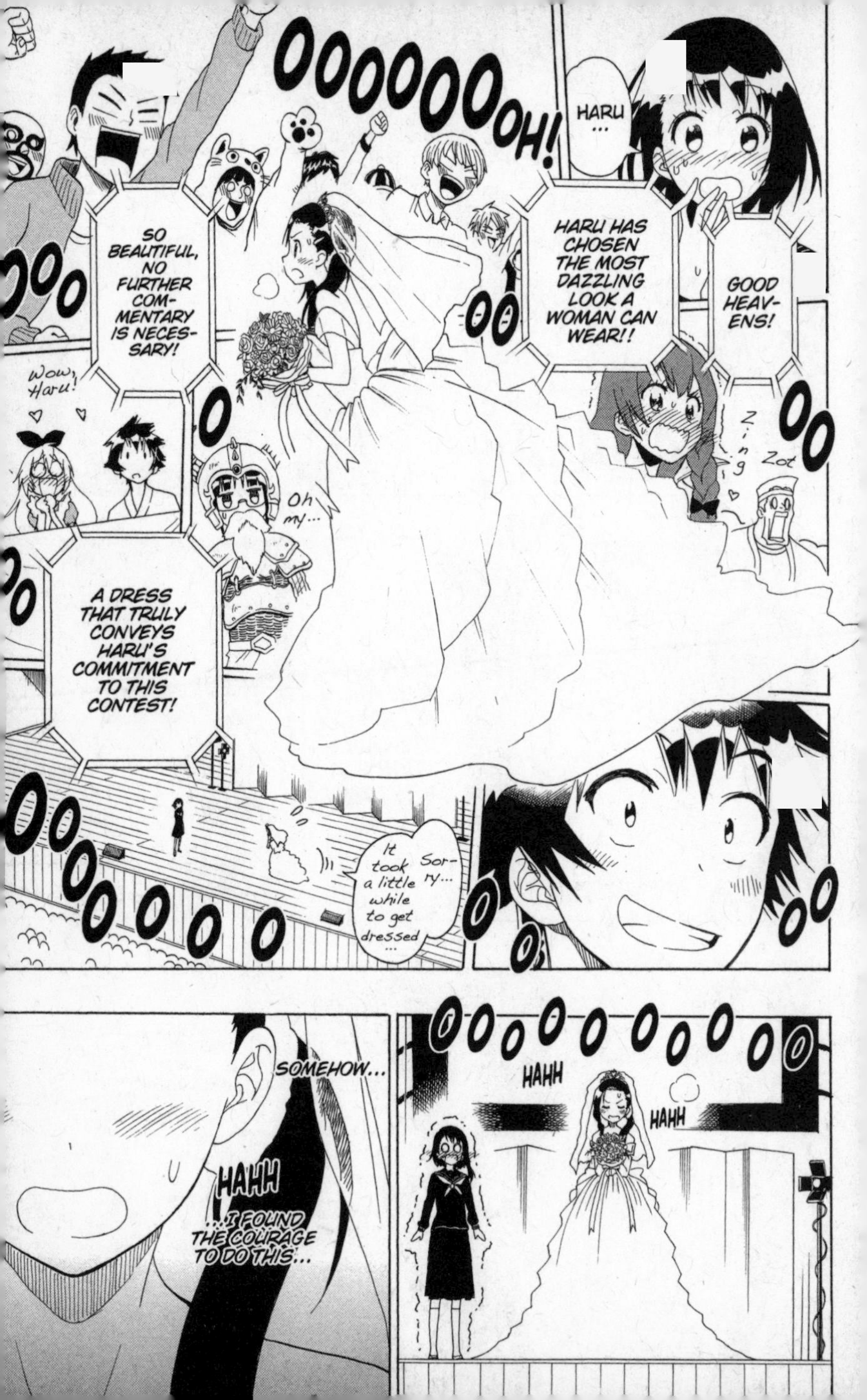
HARU ...
OOOOOOOOOH!
HARU HAS CHOSEN THE MOST DAZZLING LOOK A WOMAN CAN WEAR!!
GOOD HEAVENS!
Zing
Zot
SO BEAUTIFUL, NO FURTHER COMMENTARY IS NECESSARY!
Wow, Haru!
Oh my...
A DRESS THAT TRULY CONVEYS HARU'S COMMITMENT TO THIS CONTEST!
OOOOOOOOO
OOOO
Sorry...
It took a little while to get dressed...
OOOOOOOOOOOO
HAHH
HAHH
SOMEHOW...
HAHH
...I FOUND THE COURAGE TO DO THIS...

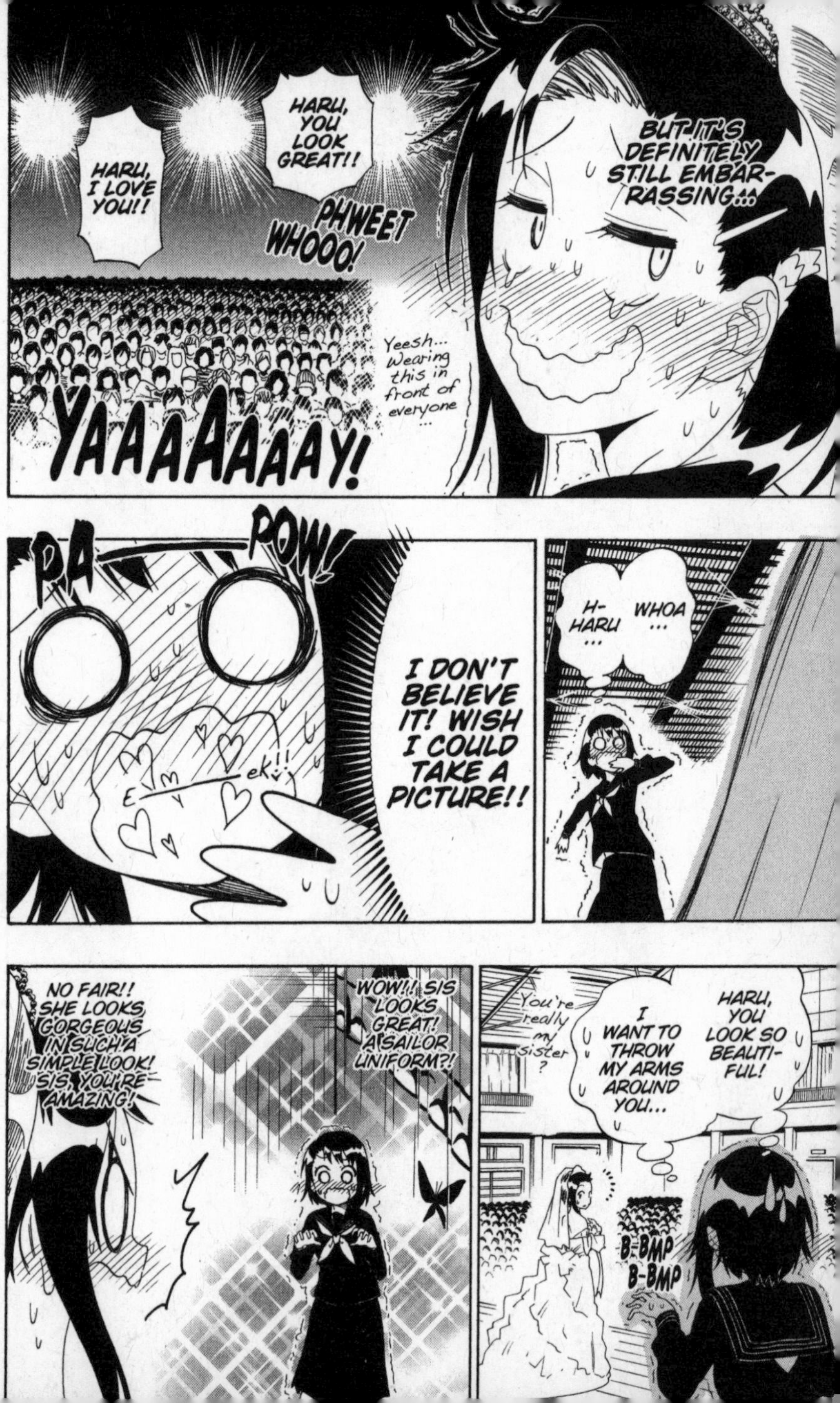
BUT IT'S DEFINITELY STILL EMBARRASSING...
Yeesh... Wearing this in front of everyone...
HARU, YOU LOOK GREAT!!
PHWEET WHOOO!
HARU, I LOVE YOU!!
YAAAAAAAY!
WHOA...
H-HARU...
I DON'T BELIEVE IT! WISH I COULD TAKE A PICTURE!!
PA—POW!
Eek!!
HARU, YOU LOOK SO BEAUTIFUL!
I WANT TO THROW MY ARMS AROUND YOU...
You're really my sister?
B-BMP
B-BMP
WOW!! SIS LOOKS GREAT! A SAILOR UNIFORM?!
NO FAIR!! SHE LOOKS GORGEOUS IN SUCH A SIMPLE LOOK! SIS, YOU'RE AMAZING!

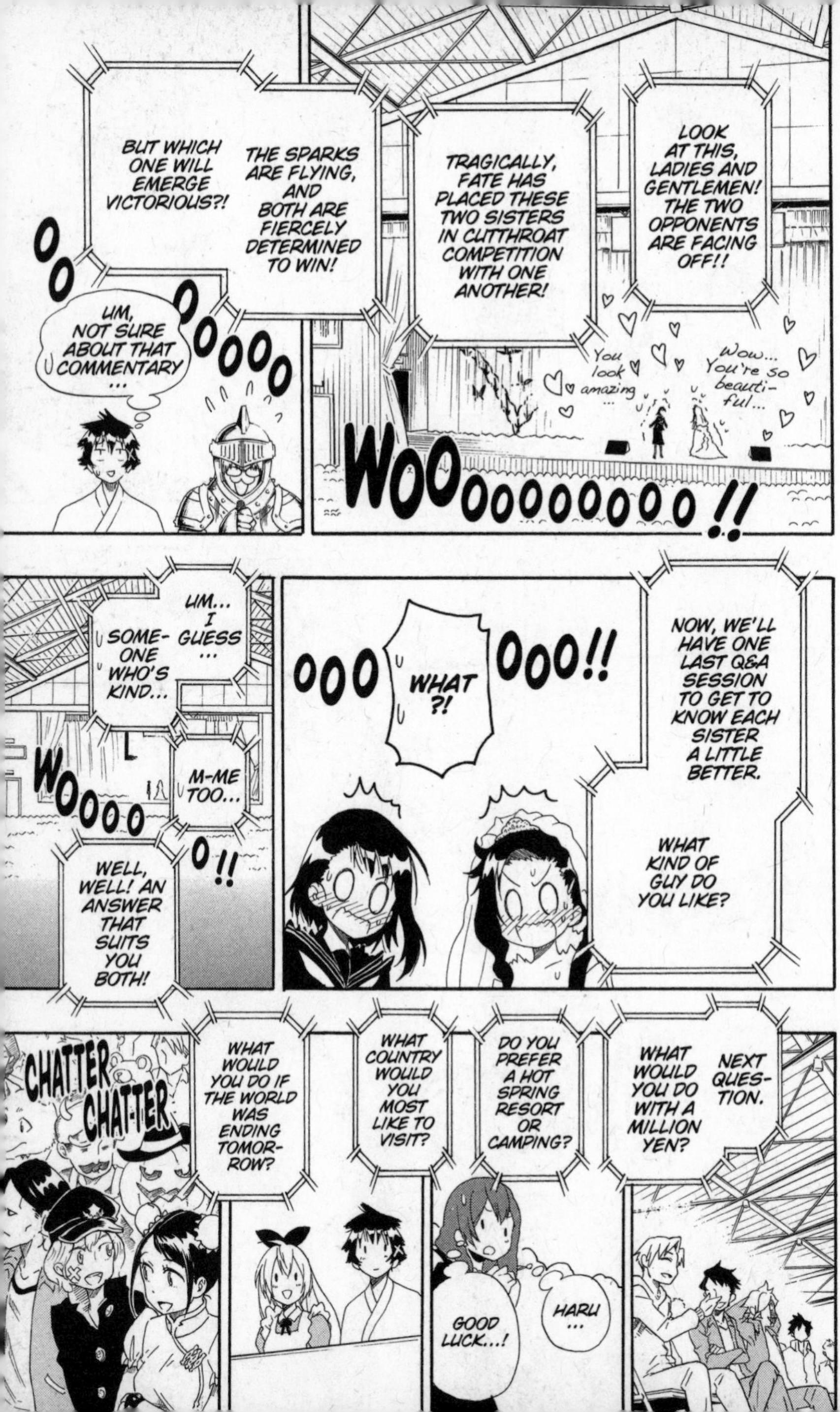
LOOK AT THIS, LADIES AND GENTLEMEN! THE TWO OPPONENTS ARE FACING OFF!!
TRAGICALLY, FATE HAS PLACED THESE TWO SISTERS IN CUTTHROAT COMPETITION WITH ONE ANOTHER!
THE SPARKS ARE FLYING, AND BOTH ARE FIERCELY DETERMINED TO WIN!
BUT WHICH ONE WILL EMERGE VICTORIOUS?!
Wow... You're so beautiful...
You look amazing...
WOOOOOOOOOOOOOOOOOOO!!
UM, NOT SURE ABOUT THAT COMMENTARY...
NOW, WE'LL HAVE ONE LAST Q&A SESSION TO GET TO KNOW EACH SISTER A LITTLE BETTER.
WHAT KIND OF GUY DO YOU LIKE?
OOOOOO!!
WHAT?!
UM... I GUESS...
SOME-ONE WHO'S KIND...
M-ME TOO...
WOOOOO!!
WELL, WELL! AN ANSWER THAT SUITS YOU BOTH!
NEXT QUES-TION.
WHAT WOULD YOU DO WITH A MILLION YEN?
DO YOU PREFER A HOT SPRING RESORT OR CAMPING?
WHAT COUNTRY WOULD YOU MOST LIKE TO VISIT?
WHAT WOULD YOU DO IF THE WORLD WAS ENDING TOMOR-ROW?
HARU...
GOOD LUCK...!
CHATTER CHATTER

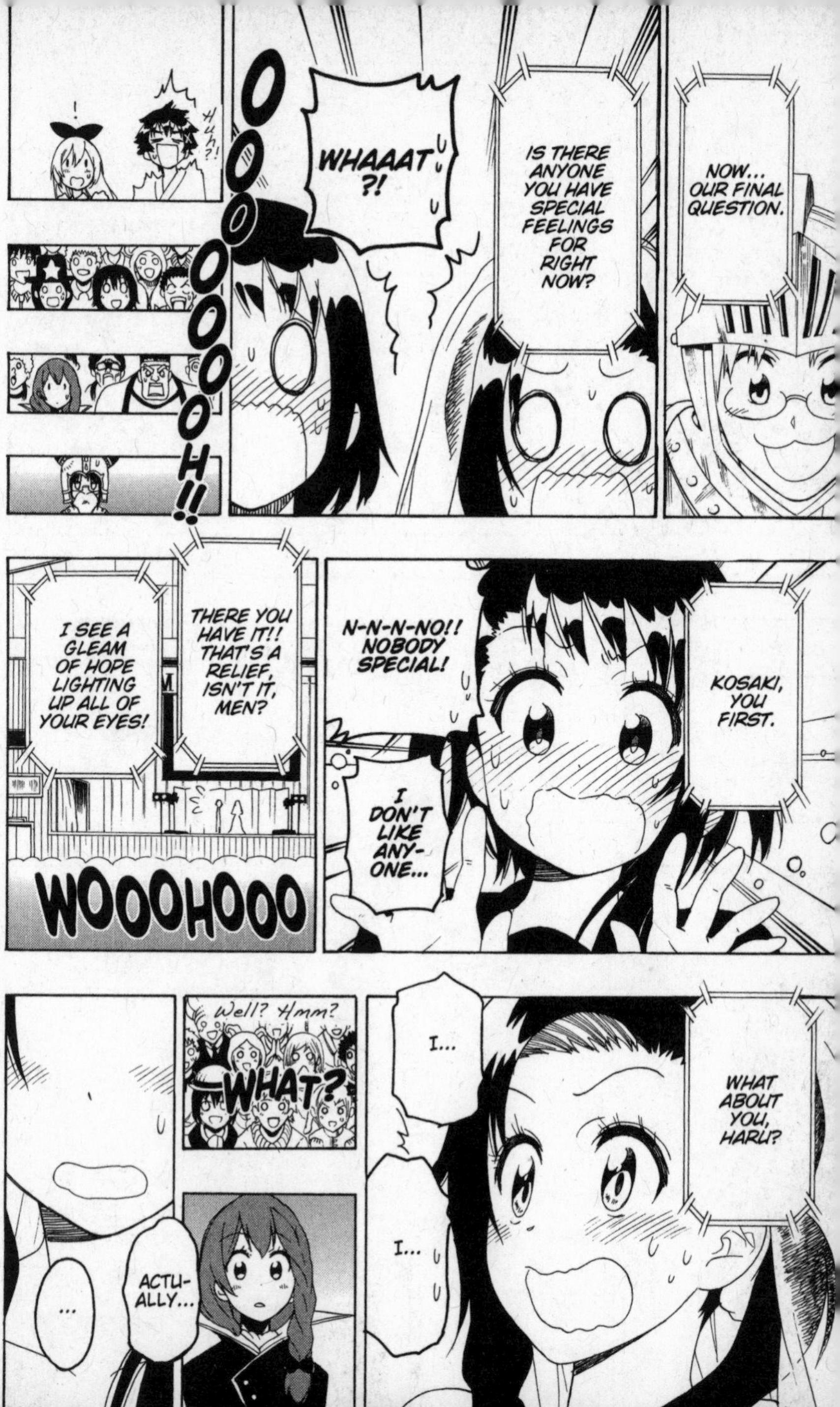
NOW... OUR FINAL QUESTION.
IS THERE ANYONE YOU HAVE SPECIAL FEELINGS FOR RIGHT NOW?
WHAAAT?!
OOOOOOOOOH!!
!
Huh?!
KOSAKI, YOU FIRST.
N-N-N-NO!! NOBODY SPECIAL!
I DON'T LIKE ANY-ONE...
THERE YOU HAVE IT!! THAT'S A RELIEF, ISN'T IT, MEN?
I SEE A GLEAM OF HOPE LIGHTING UP ALL OF YOUR EYES!
WOOOHOOO
WHAT ABOUT YOU, HARU?
I...
I...
Well? Hmm?
WHAT?
ACTU-ALLY...
...

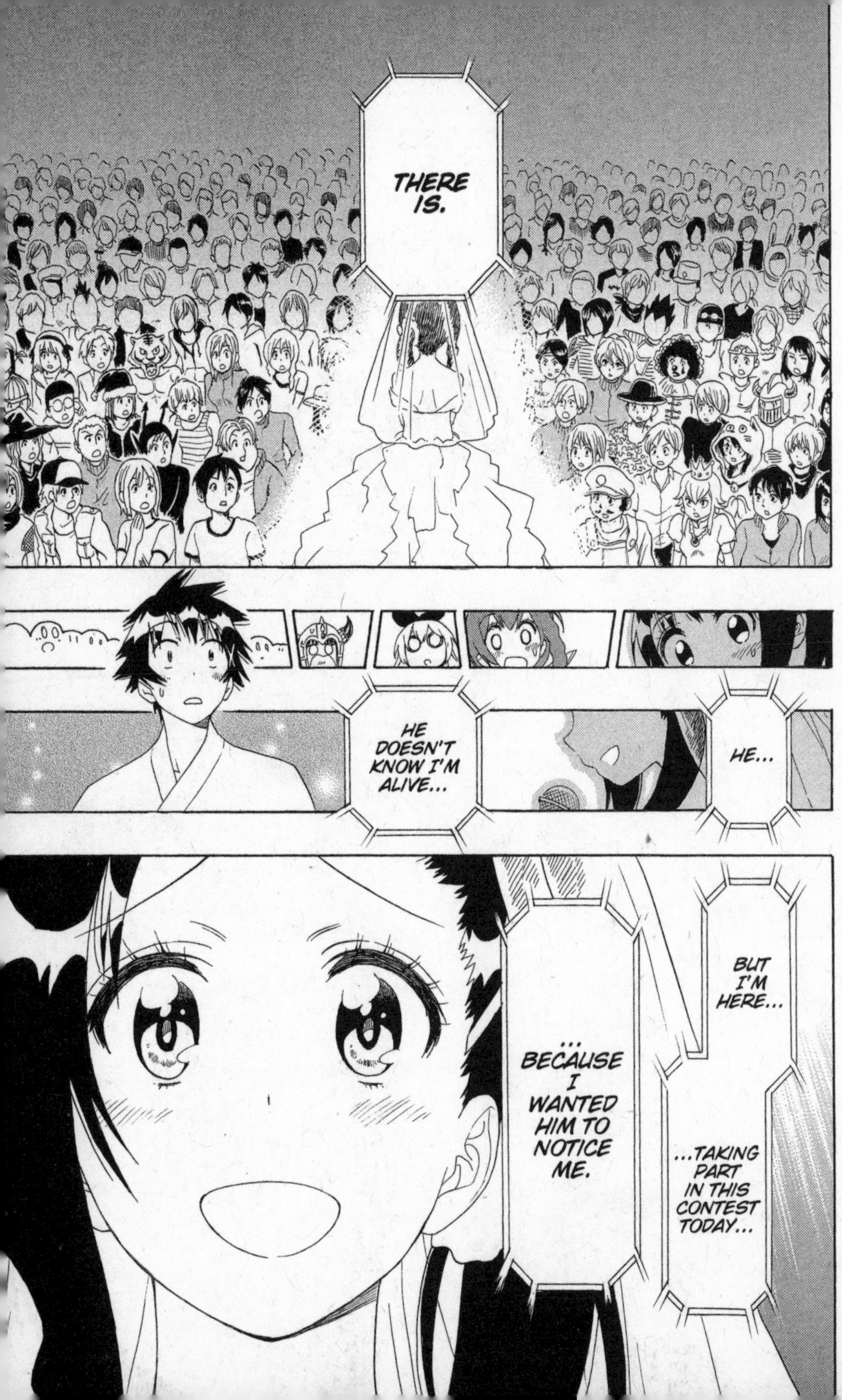
THERE IS.
HE...
HE DOESN'T KNOW I'M ALIVE...
BUT I'M HERE...
...TAKING PART IN THIS CONTEST TODAY...
...BECAUSE I WANTED HIM TO NOTICE ME.

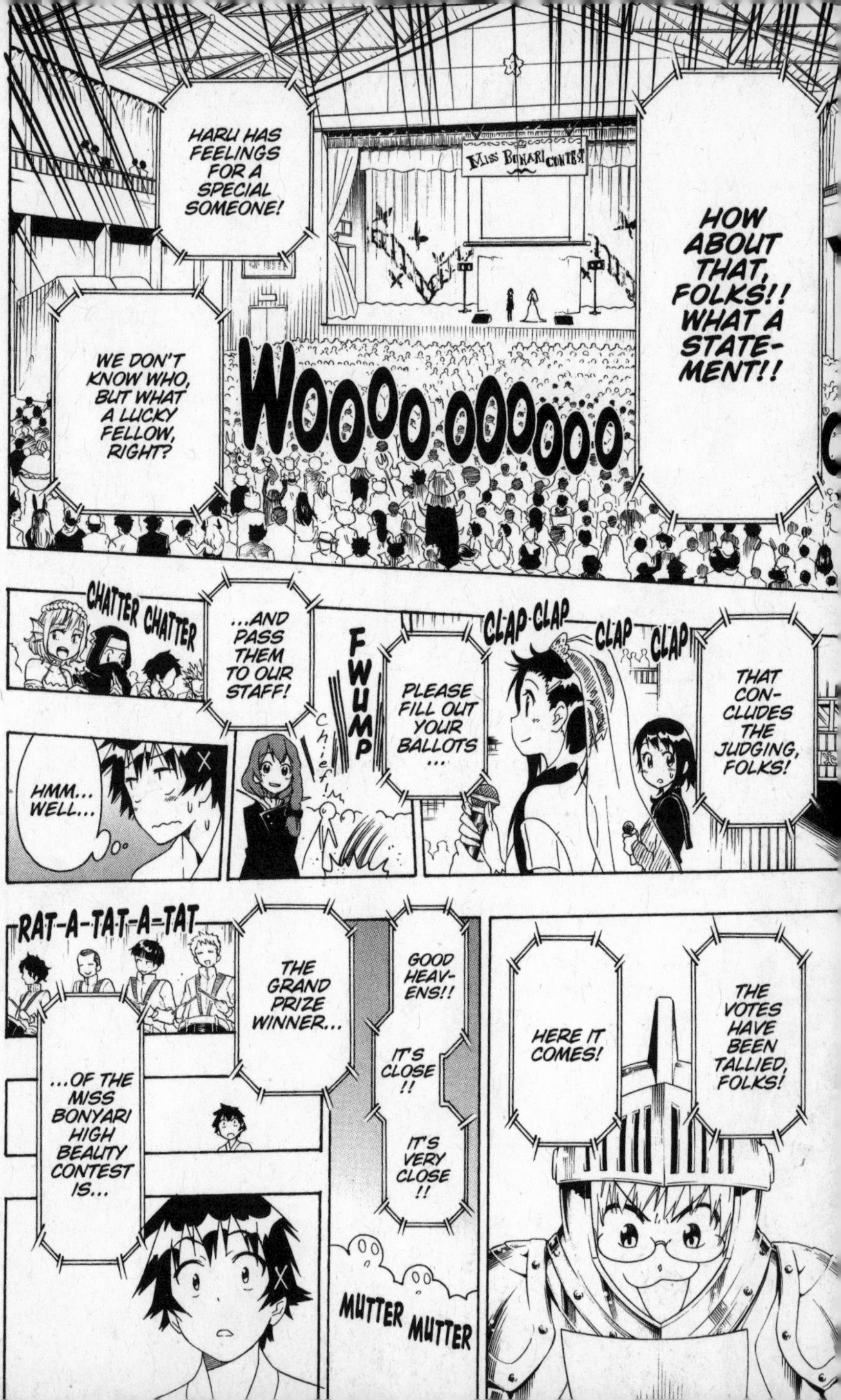
HOW ABOUT THAT, FOLKS!! WHAT A STATEMENT!!
HARU HAS FEELINGS FOR A SPECIAL SOMEONE!
MISS BONARI CONTEST
WOOOOOOOOOO
WE DON'T KNOW WHO, BUT WHAT A LUCKY FELLOW, RIGHT?
THAT CONCLUDES THE JUDGING, FOLKS!
CLAP CLAP
CLAP CLAP
PLEASE FILL OUT YOUR BALLOTS...
...AND PASS THEM TO OUR STAFF!
CHATTER CHATTER
FWUMP
Chief!!
HMM... WELL...
THE VOTES HAVE BEEN TALLIED, FOLKS!
HERE IT COMES!
GOOD HEAVENS!!
IT'S CLOSE!!
IT'S VERY CLOSE!!
MUTTER MUTTER
THE GRAND PRIZE WINNER...
RAT-A-TAT-A-TAT
...OF THE MISS BONYARI HIGH BEAUTY CONTEST IS...

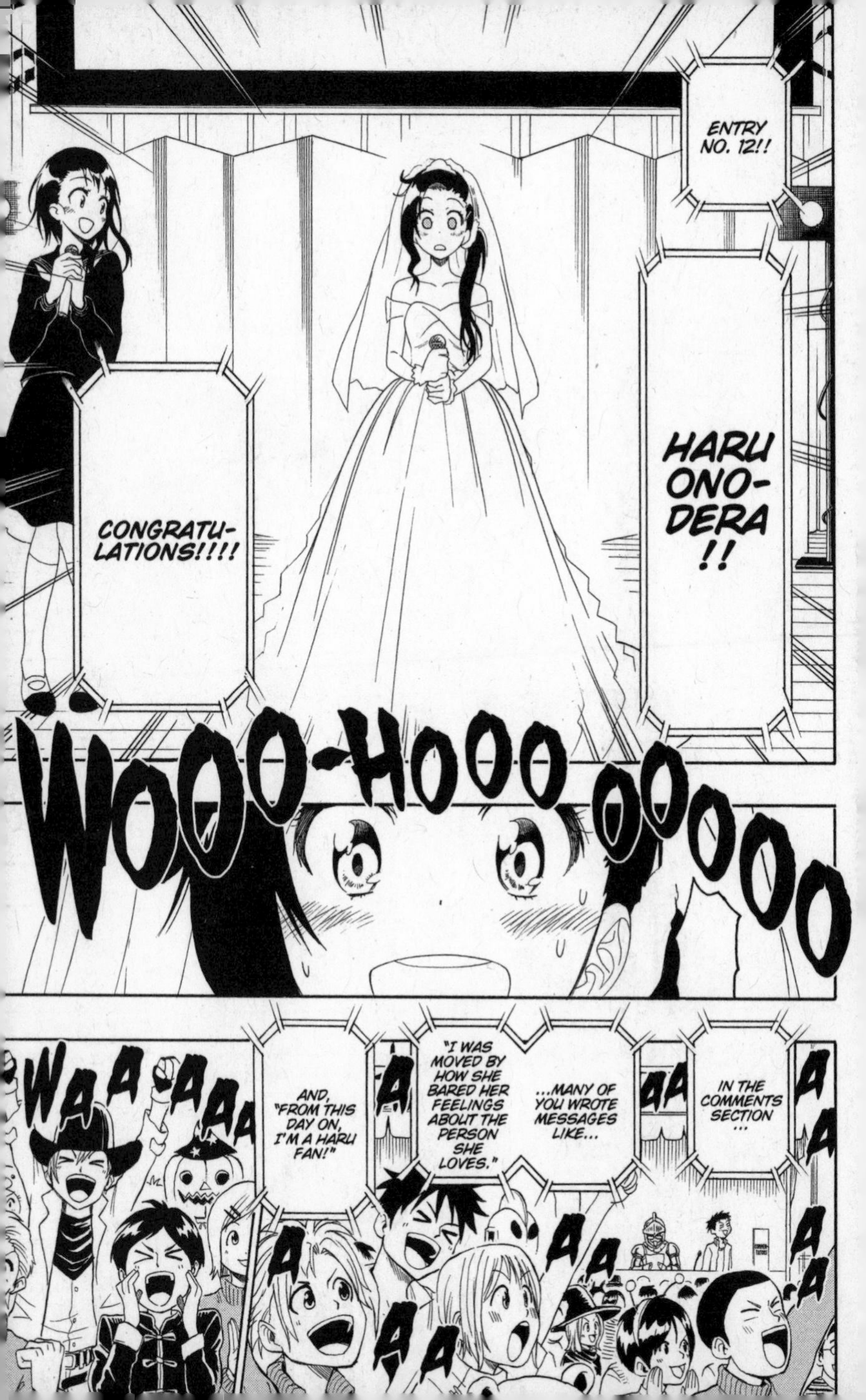
ENTRY NO. 12!!
HARU ONO-DERA!!
CONGRATU-LATIONS!!!!
WOOO-HOOO OOOOO
IN THE COMMENTS SECTION...
...MANY OF YOU WROTE MESSAGES LIKE...
"I WAS MOVED BY HOW SHE BARED HER FEELINGS ABOUT THE PERSON SHE LOVES."
AND, "FROM THIS DAY ON, I'M A HARU FAN!"
WAAAAA

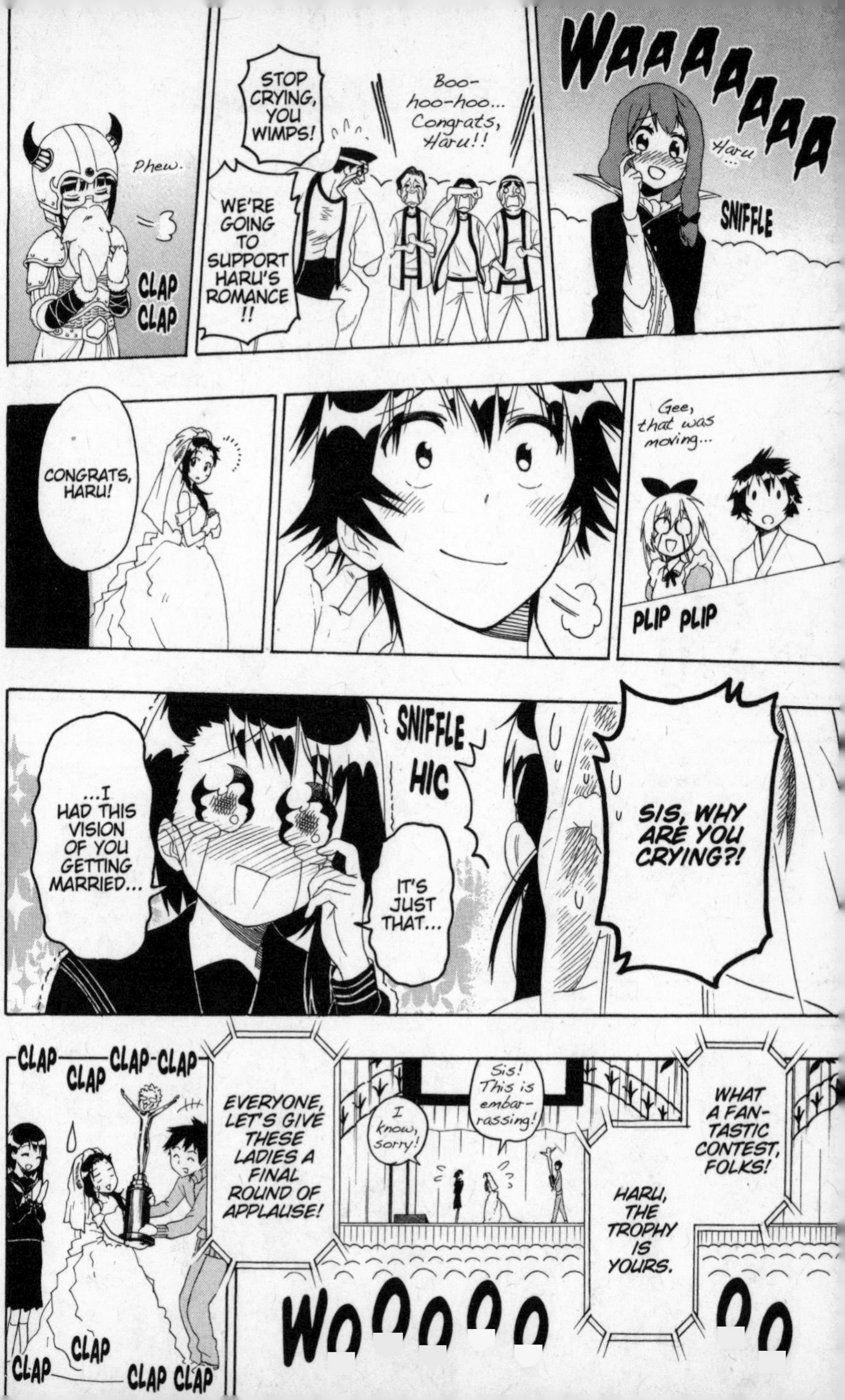

WAAAAAAAA
Haru...
SNIFFLE
Boo-hoo-hoo... Congrats, Haru!!
STOP CRYING, YOU WIMPS!
WE'RE GOING TO SUPPORT HARU'S ROMANCE!!
Phew.
CLAP CLAP
Gee, that was moving...
PLIP PLIP
CONGRATS, HARU!
SIS, WHY ARE YOU CRYING?!
SNIFFLE HIC
IT'S JUST THAT...
...I HAD THIS VISION OF YOU GETTING MARRIED...
WHAT A FAN-TASTIC CONTEST, FOLKS!
HARU, THE TROPHY IS YOURS.
Sis! This is embar-rassing!
I know, sorry!
WOOOOO OO
EVERYONE, LET'S GIVE THESE LADIES A FINAL ROUND OF APPLAUSE!
CLAP CLAP CLAP-CLAP
CLAP CLAP CLAP CLAP

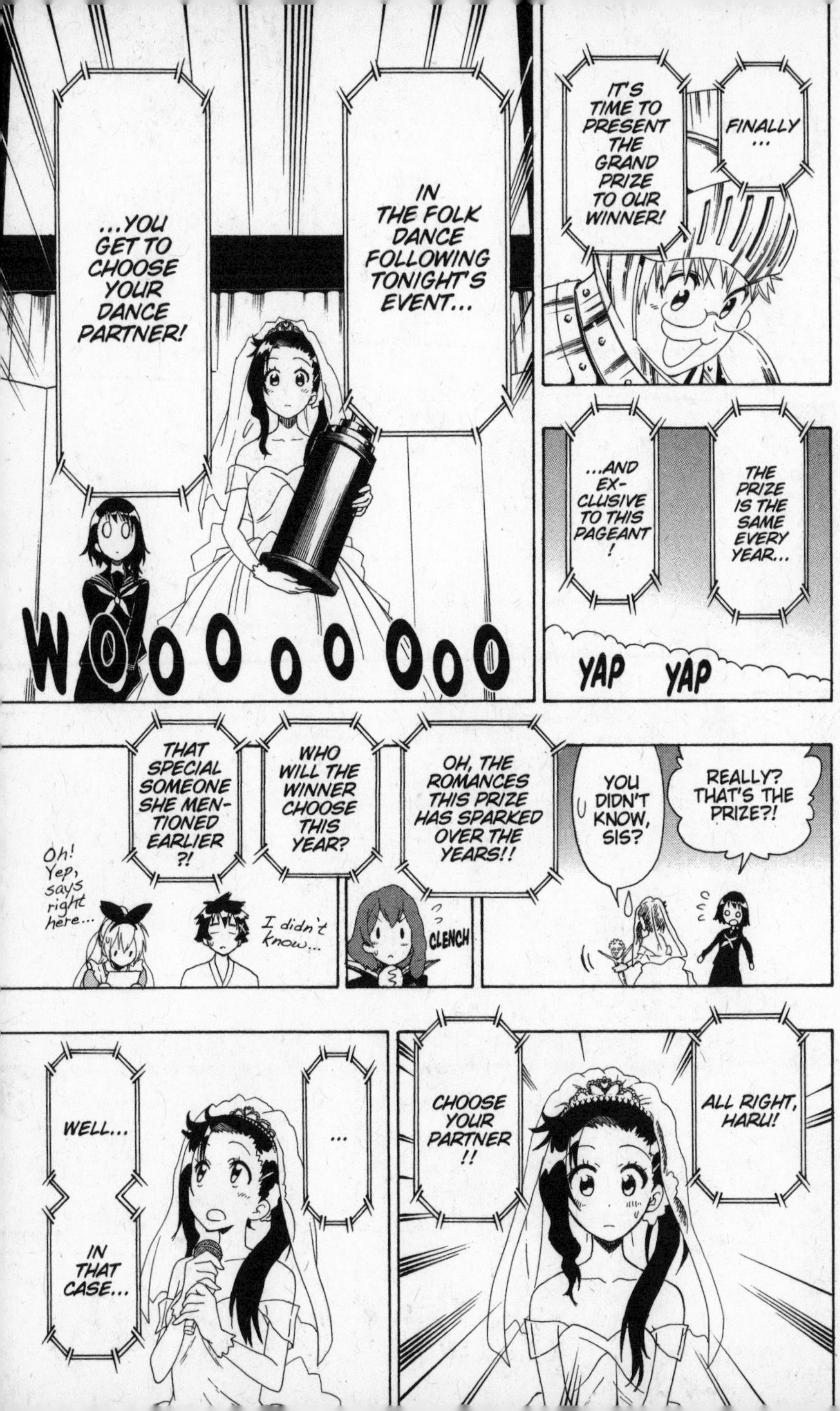
FINALLY...
IT'S TIME TO PRESENT THE GRAND PRIZE TO OUR WINNER!
THE PRIZE IS THE SAME EVERY YEAR...
...AND EX-CLUSIVE TO THIS PAGEANT!
YAP YAP
IN THE FOLK DANCE FOLLOWING TONIGHT'S EVENT...
...YOU GET TO CHOOSE YOUR DANCE PARTNER!
WOOOOOOOO
REALLY? THAT'S THE PRIZE?!
YOU DIDN'T KNOW, SIS?
OH, THE ROMANCES THIS PRIZE HAS SPARKED OVER THE YEARS!!
CLENCH
WHO WILL THE WINNER CHOOSE THIS YEAR?
THAT SPECIAL SOMEONE SHE MEN-TIONED EARLIER?!
I didn't know...
Oh! Yep, says right here...
ALL RIGHT, HARU!
CHOOSE YOUR PARTNER!!
...
WELL...
IN THAT CASE...

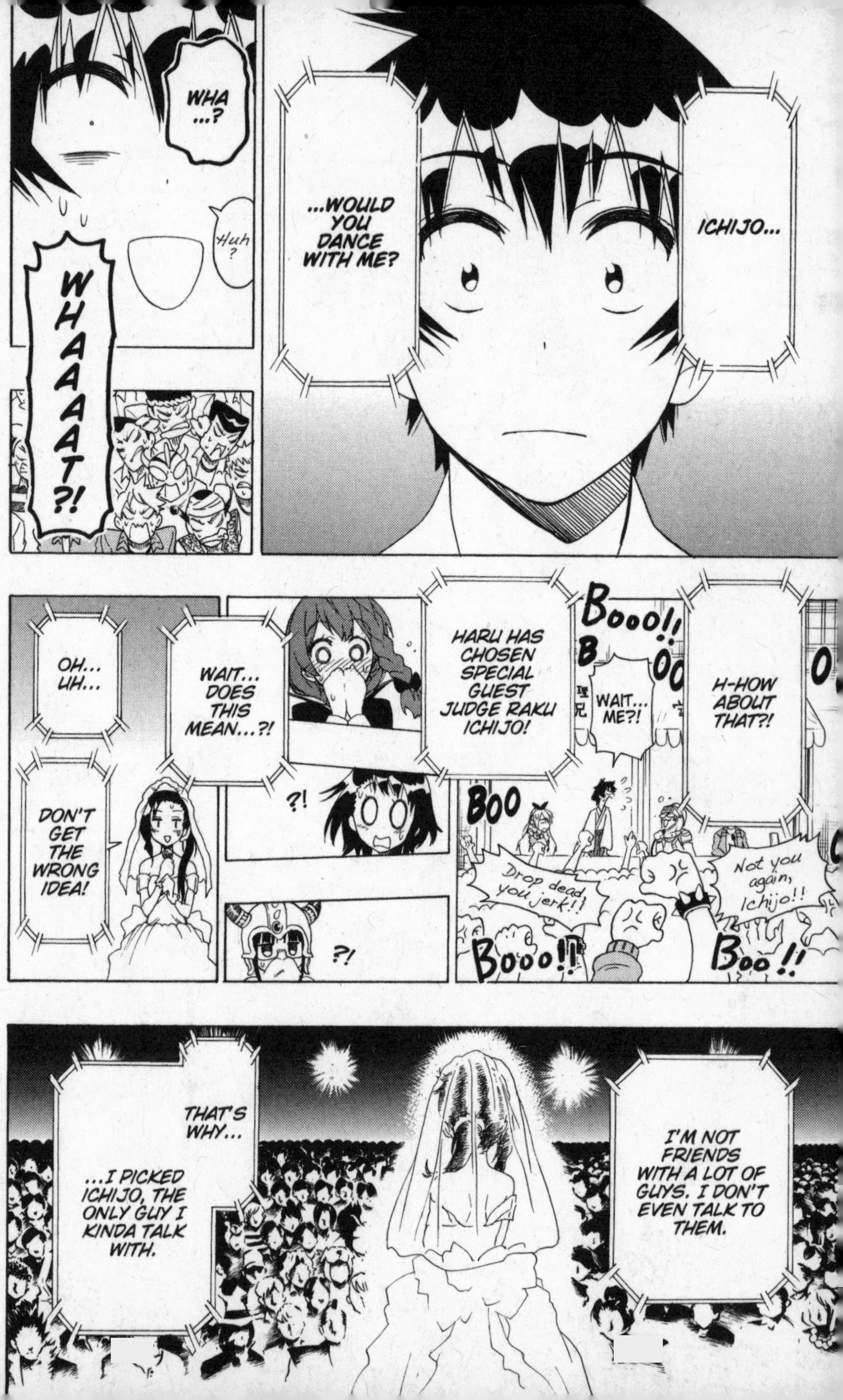
ICHIJO...
...WOULD YOU DANCE WITH ME?
WHA ...?
Huh?
WHAAAAAT?!
H-HOW ABOUT THAT?!
BOOO!!
WAIT... ME?!
HARU HAS CHOSEN SPECIAL GUEST JUDGE RAKU ICHIJO!
BOO
Not you again, Ichijo!!
Drop dead, you jerk!!
Booo!!
Boo!!
WAIT... DOES THIS MEAN...?!
?!
?!
OH... UH...
DON'T GET THE WRONG IDEA!
I'M NOT FRIENDS WITH A LOT OF GUYS. I DON'T EVEN TALK TO THEM.
THAT'S WHY...
...I PICKED ICHIJO, THE ONLY GUY I KINDA TALK WITH.

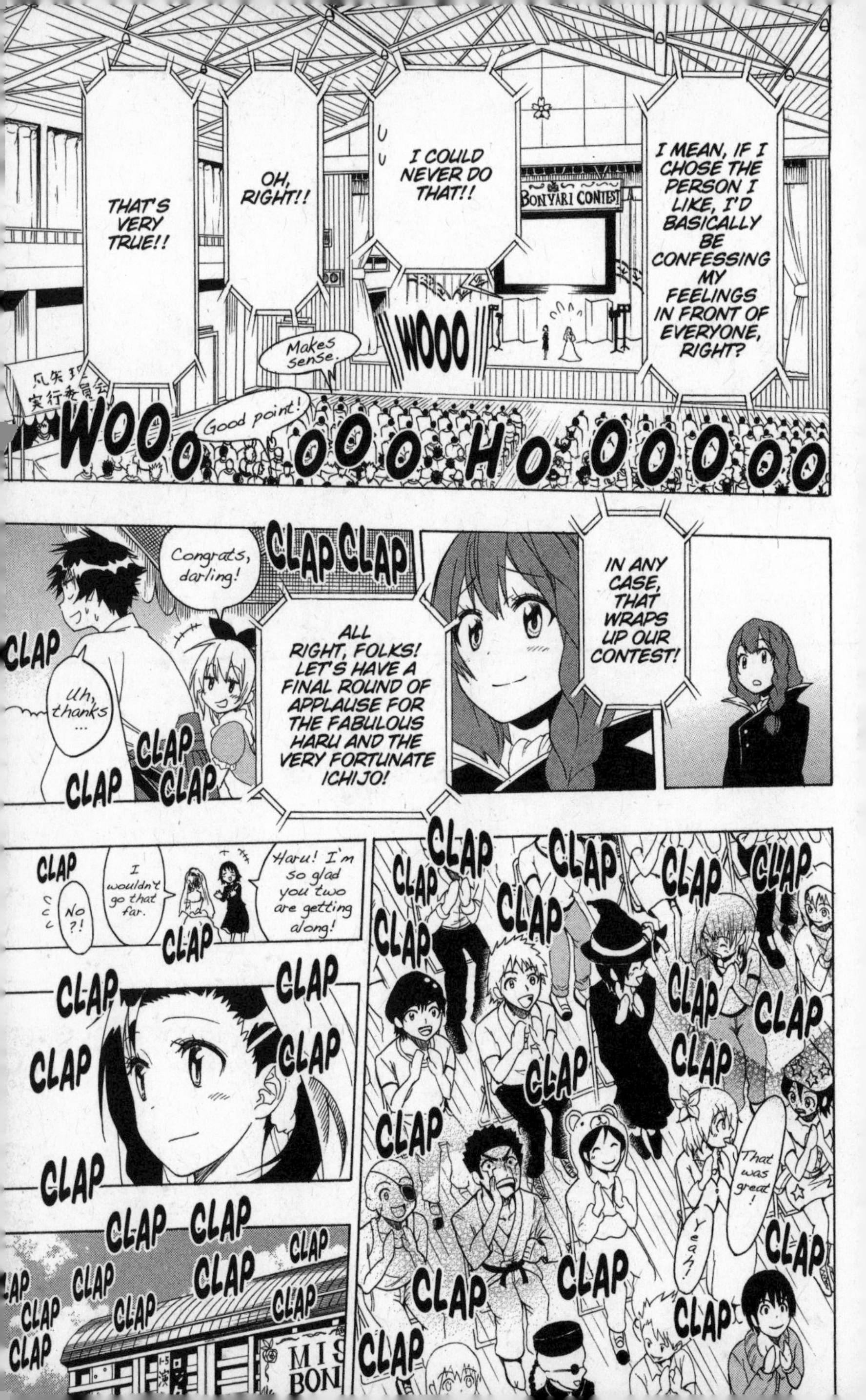
I MEAN, IF I CHOSE THE PERSON I LIKE, I'D BASICALLY BE CONFESSING MY FEELINGS IN FRONT OF EVERYONE, RIGHT?
BONYARI CONTEST
I COULD NEVER DO THAT!!
OH, RIGHT!!
THAT'S VERY TRUE!!
WOOO
Makes sense.
Good point!
WOOOOOOHOOOOOO
IN ANY CASE, THAT WRAPS UP OUR CONTEST!
ALL RIGHT, FOLKS! LET'S HAVE A FINAL ROUND OF APPLAUSE FOR THE FABULOUS HARU AND THE VERY FORTUNATE ICHIJO!
CLAP CLAP
Congrats, darling!
CLAP
Uh, thanks...
CLAP CLAP
CLAP
CLAP CLAP CLAP CLAP CLAP CLAP CLAP
That was great!
Yeah!
CLAP CLAP CLAP CLAP CLAP CLAP
Haru! I'm so glad you two are getting along!
I wouldn't go that far.
No?!
CLAP
CLAP
CLAP CLAP CLAP CLAP CLAP
CLAP CLAP CLAP CLAP CLAP CLAP CLAP CLAP CLAP
MIS
BON

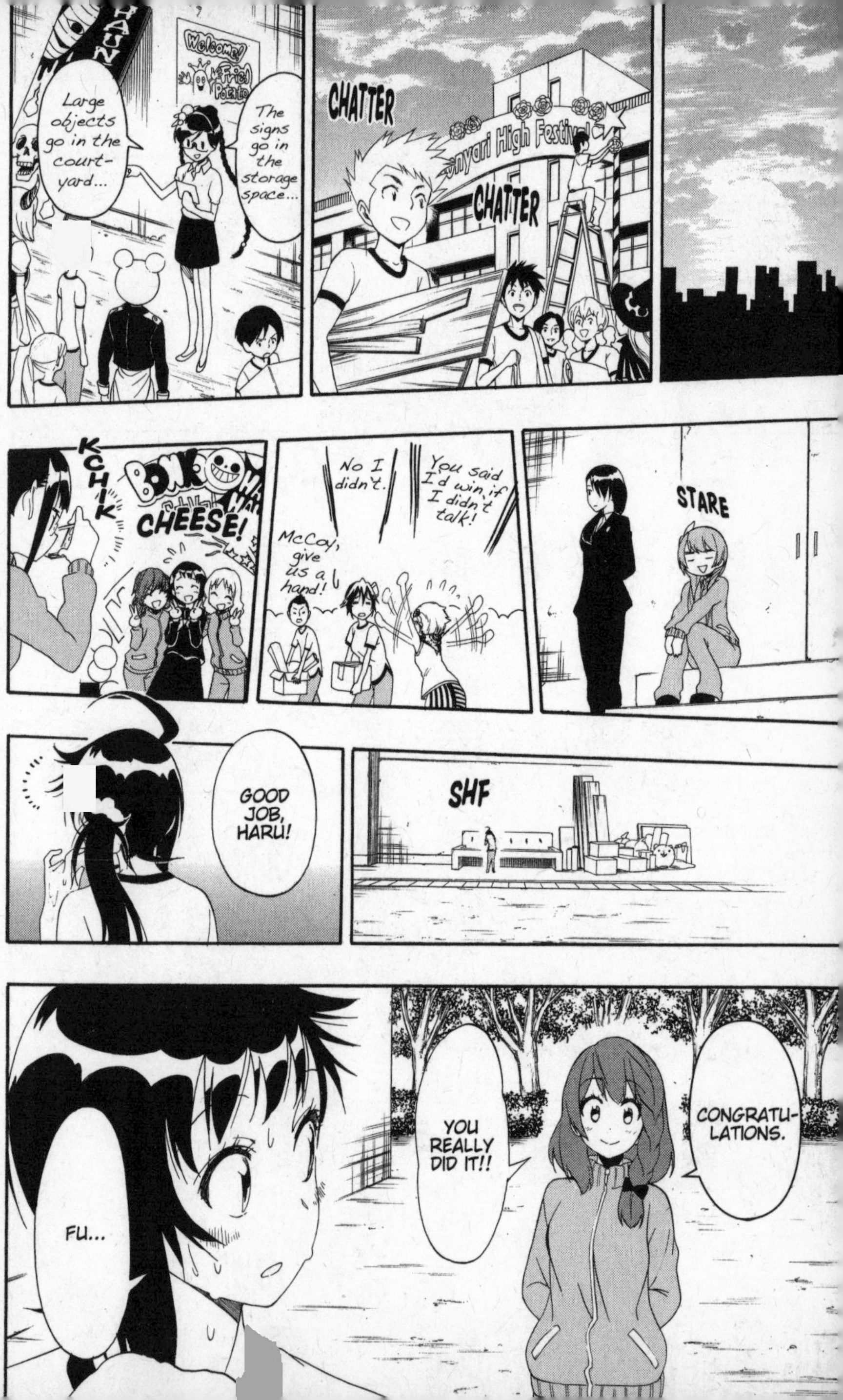
CHATTER
nyari High Festival
CHATTER
Welcome!
Fried Potato
The signs go in the storage space...
Large objects go in the courtyard...
STARE
You said I'd win if I didn't talk!
No I didn't.
McCoy, give us a hand!
KCHIK
CHEESE!
SHF
GOOD JOB, HARU!
CONGRATULATIONS.
YOU REALLY DID IT!!
FU...

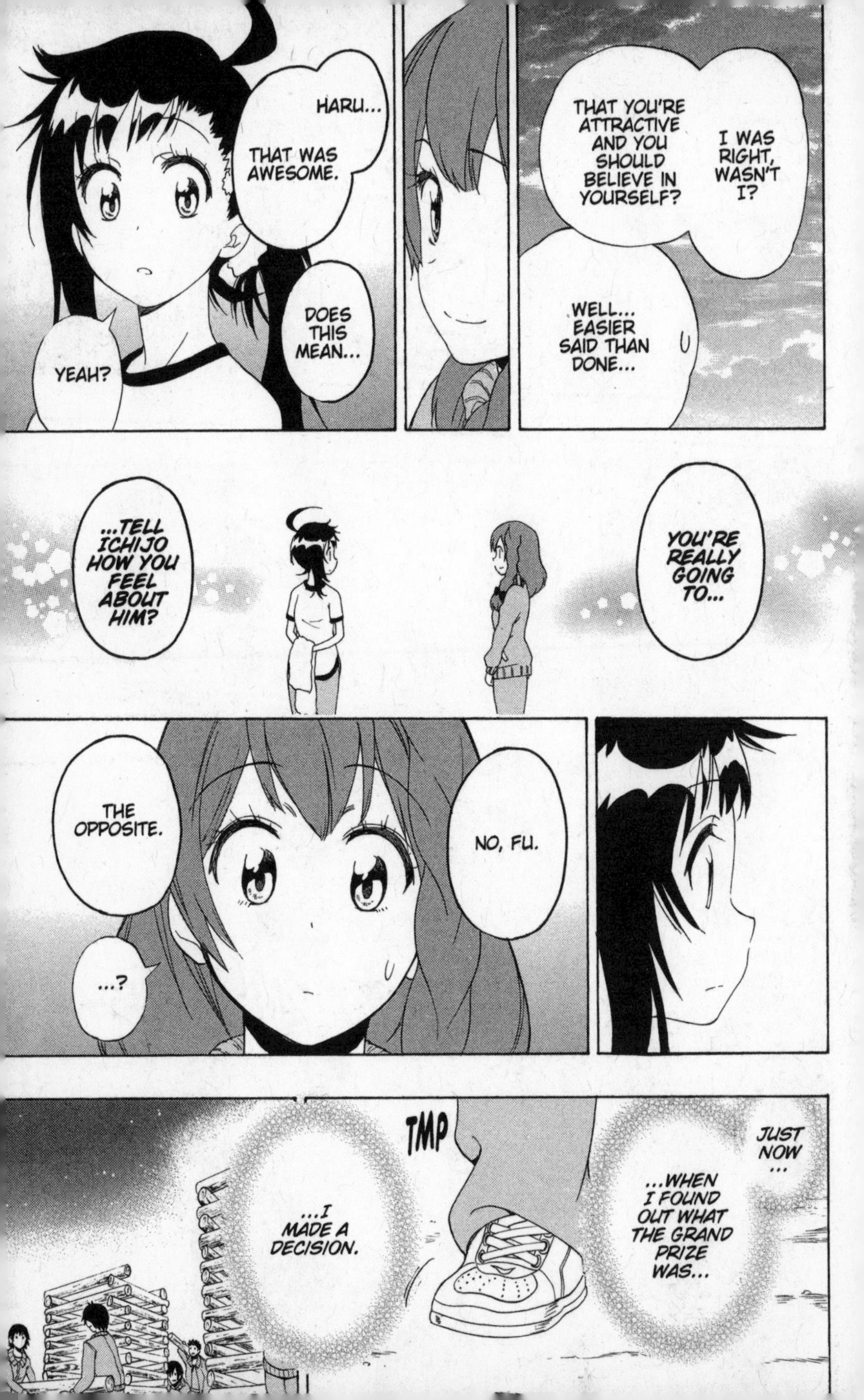
I WAS RIGHT, WASN'T I?
THAT YOU'RE ATTRACTIVE AND YOU SHOULD BELIEVE IN YOURSELF?
WELL... EASIER SAID THAN DONE...
HARU...
THAT WAS AWESOME.
DOES THIS MEAN...
YEAH?
YOU'RE REALLY GOING TO...
...TELL ICHIJO HOW YOU FEEL ABOUT HIM?
NO, FU.
THE OPPOSITE.
...?
JUST NOW...
...WHEN I FOUND OUT WHAT THE GRAND PRIZE WAS...
TMP
...I MADE A DECISION.

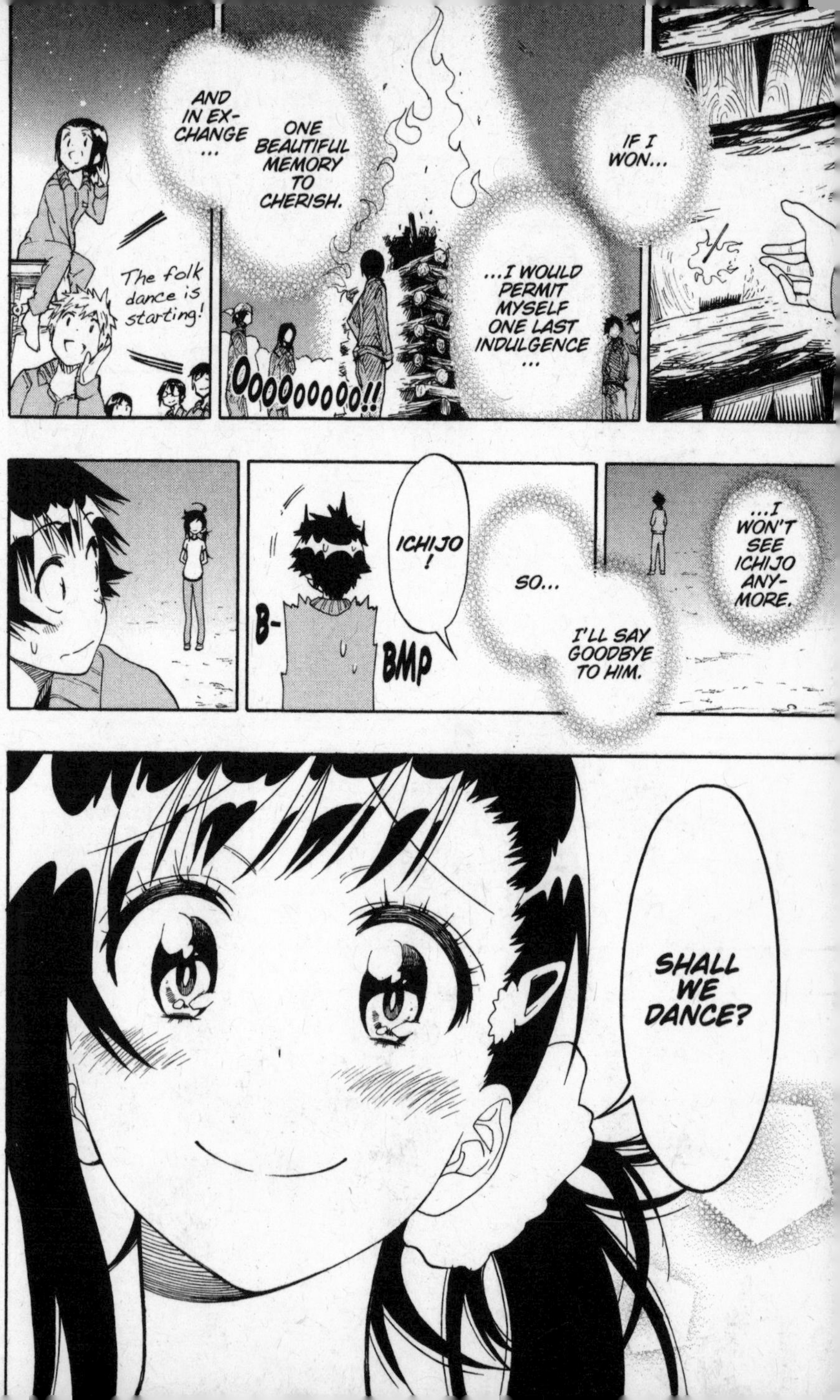
IF I WON...
...I WOULD PERMIT MYSELF ONE LAST INDULGENCE...
AND IN EX-CHANGE...
ONE BEAUTIFUL MEMORY TO CHERISH.
OOOOOOOOOO!!
The folk dance is starting!
...I WON'T SEE ICHIJO ANYMORE.
SO...
I'LL SAY GOODBYE TO HIM.
ICHIJO!
B-BMP
SHALL WE DANCE?

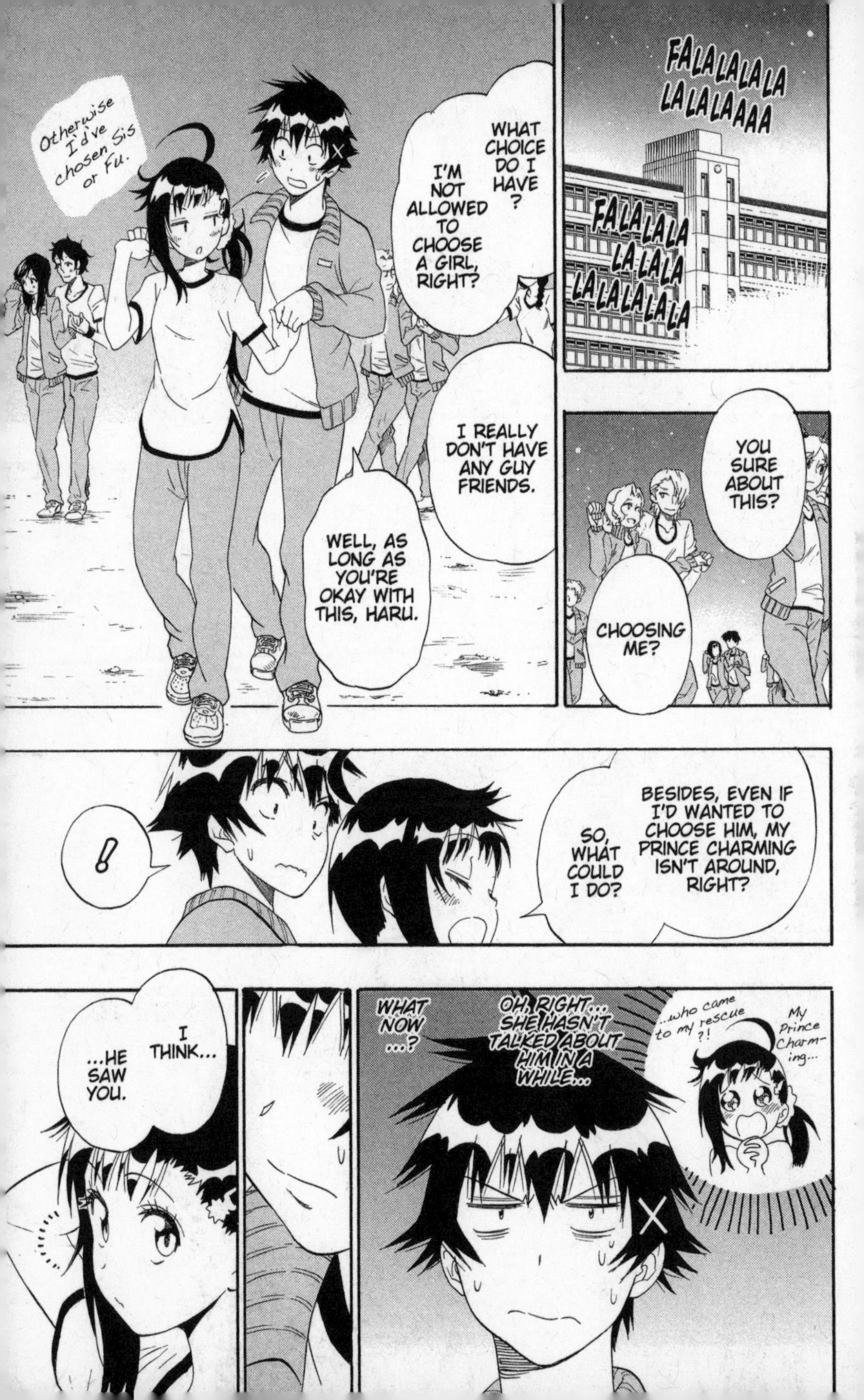
FALALALALA LALALAAAA
FALALALA LALALA LALALALALA
YOU SURE ABOUT THIS?
CHOOSING ME?
WHAT CHOICE DO I HAVE?
I'M NOT ALLOWED TO CHOOSE A GIRL, RIGHT?
Otherwise I'd've chosen Sis or Fu.
I REALLY DON'T HAVE ANY GUY FRIENDS.
WELL, AS LONG AS YOU'RE OKAY WITH THIS, HARU.
BESIDES, EVEN IF I'D WANTED TO CHOOSE HIM, MY PRINCE CHARMING ISN'T AROUND, RIGHT?
SO, WHAT COULD I DO?
!
My Prince Charm-ing...
...who came to my rescue?!
OH, RIGHT... SHE HASN'T TALKED ABOUT HIM IN A WHILE...
WHAT NOW...?
I THINK...
...HE SAW YOU.

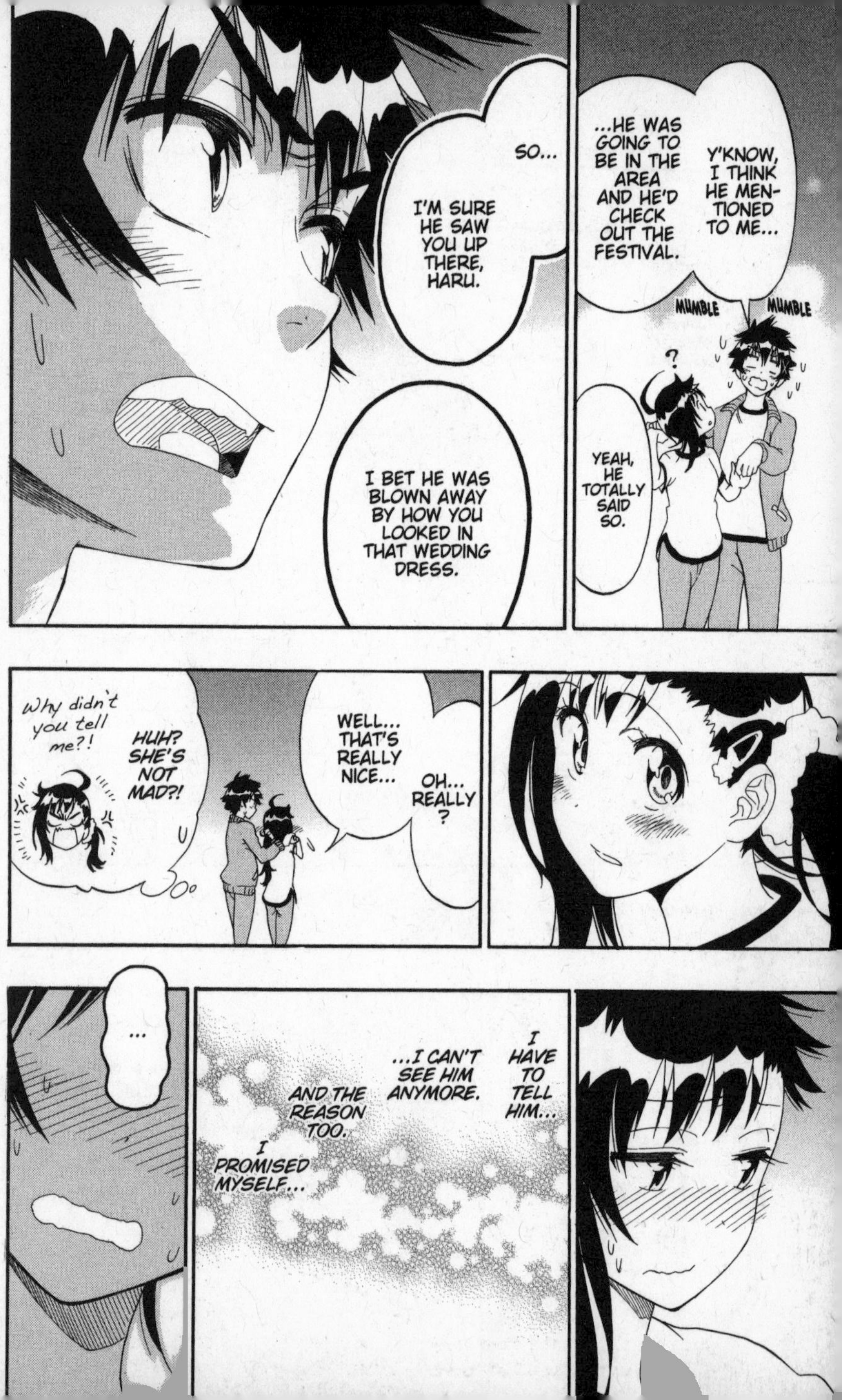
Y'KNOW, I THINK HE MENTIONED TO ME...
...HE WAS GOING TO BE IN THE AREA AND HE'D CHECK OUT THE FESTIVAL.
MUMBLE
MUMBLE
?
YEAH, HE TOTALLY SAID SO.
SO...
I'M SURE HE SAW YOU UP THERE, HARU.
I BET HE WAS BLOWN AWAY BY HOW YOU LOOKED IN THAT WEDDING DRESS.
OH... REALLY?
WELL... THAT'S REALLY NICE...
HUH? SHE'S NOT MAD?!
Why didn't you tell me?!
I HAVE TO TELL HIM...
...I CAN'T SEE HIM ANYMORE.
AND THE REASON TOO.
I PROMISED MYSELF...
...

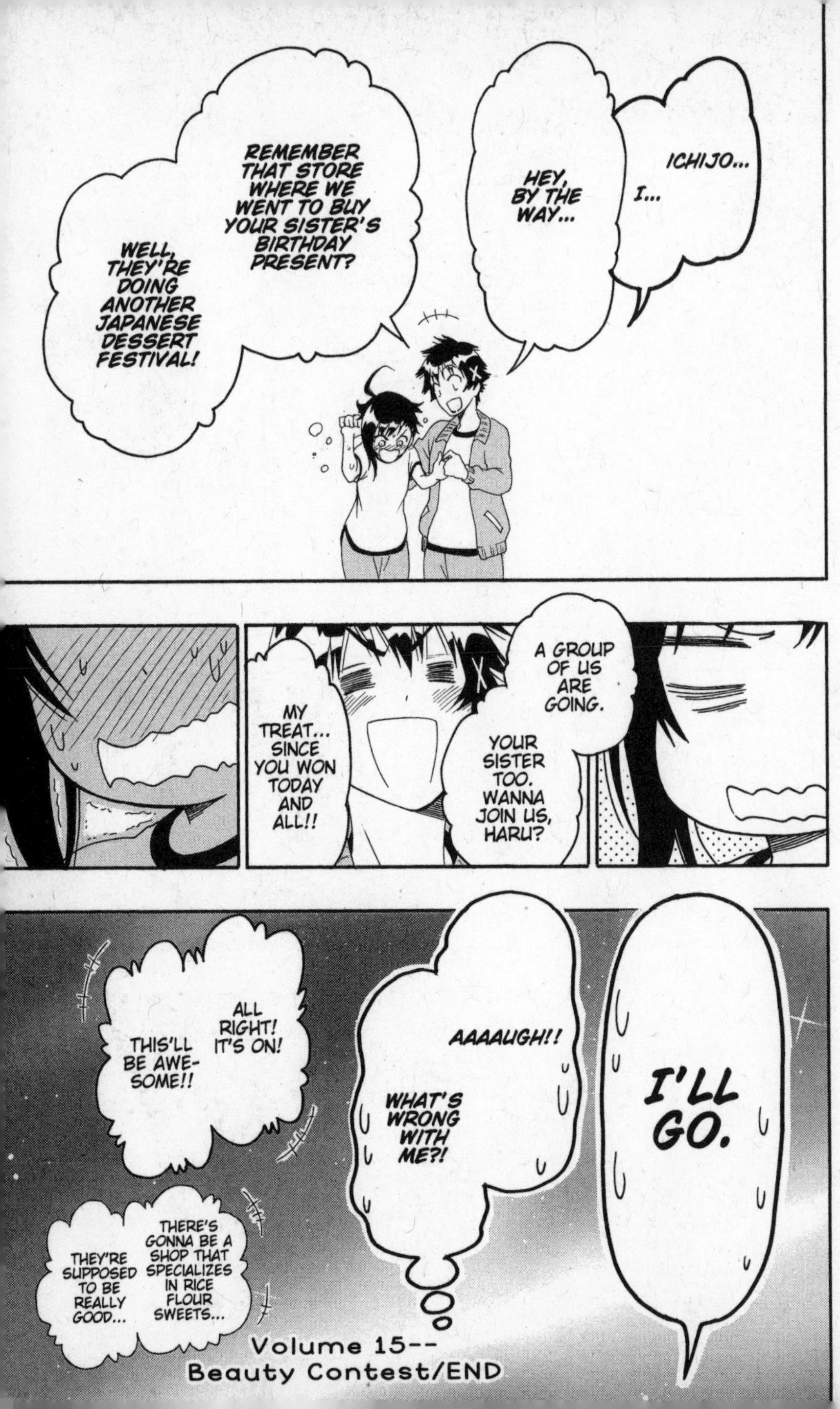
ICHIJO... I...
HEY, BY THE WAY...
REMEMBER THAT STORE WHERE WE WENT TO BUY YOUR SISTER'S BIRTHDAY PRESENT?
WELL, THEY'RE DOING ANOTHER JAPANESE DESSERT FESTIVAL!
A GROUP OF US ARE GOING.
YOUR SISTER TOO. WANNA JOIN US, HARU?
MY TREAT... SINCE YOU WON TODAY AND ALL!!
I'LL GO.
AAAAUGH!!
WHAT'S WRONG WITH ME?!
ALL RIGHT! IT'S ON!
THIS'LL BE AWE-SOME!!
THERE'S GONNA BE A SHOP THAT SPECIALIZES IN RICE FLOUR SWEETS...
THEY'RE SUPPOSED TO BE REALLY GOOD...
Volume 15--
Beauty Contest/END

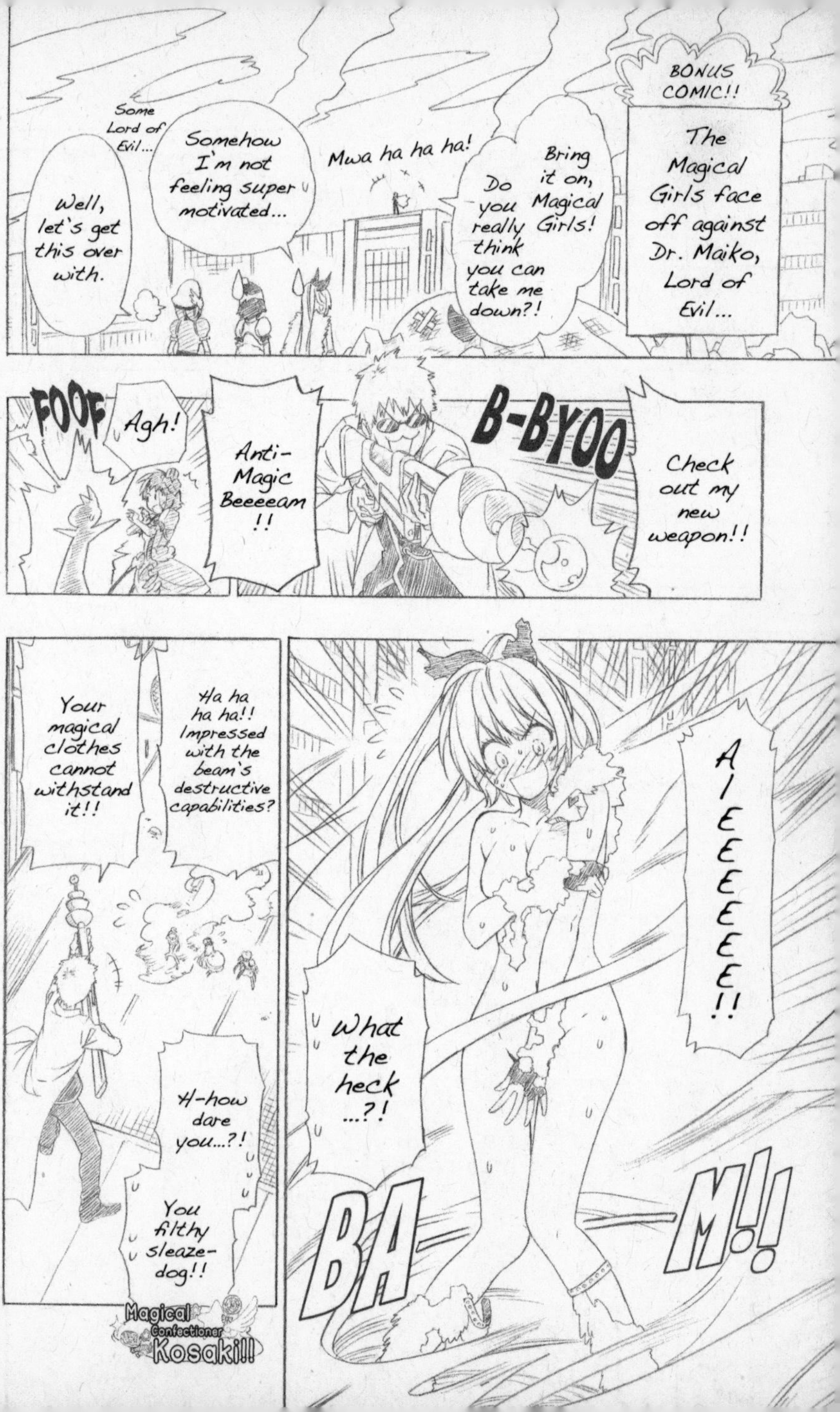
BONUS COMIC!!
The Magical Girls face off against Dr. Maiko, Lord of Evil...
Bring it on, Magical Girls!
Do you really think you can take me down?!
Mwa ha ha ha!
Somehow I'm not feeling super motivated...
Some Lord of Evil...
Well, let's get this over with.
Check out my new weapon!!
B-BYOO
Anti-Magic Beeeeam!!
Agh!
FOOF
AIEEEEEEEE!!
What the heck...?!
BA-M!!
Ha ha ha ha!! Impressed with the beam's destructive capabilities?
Your magical clothes cannot withstand it!!
H-how dare you...?!
You filthy sleaze-dog!!
Magical Confectioner Kosaki!!

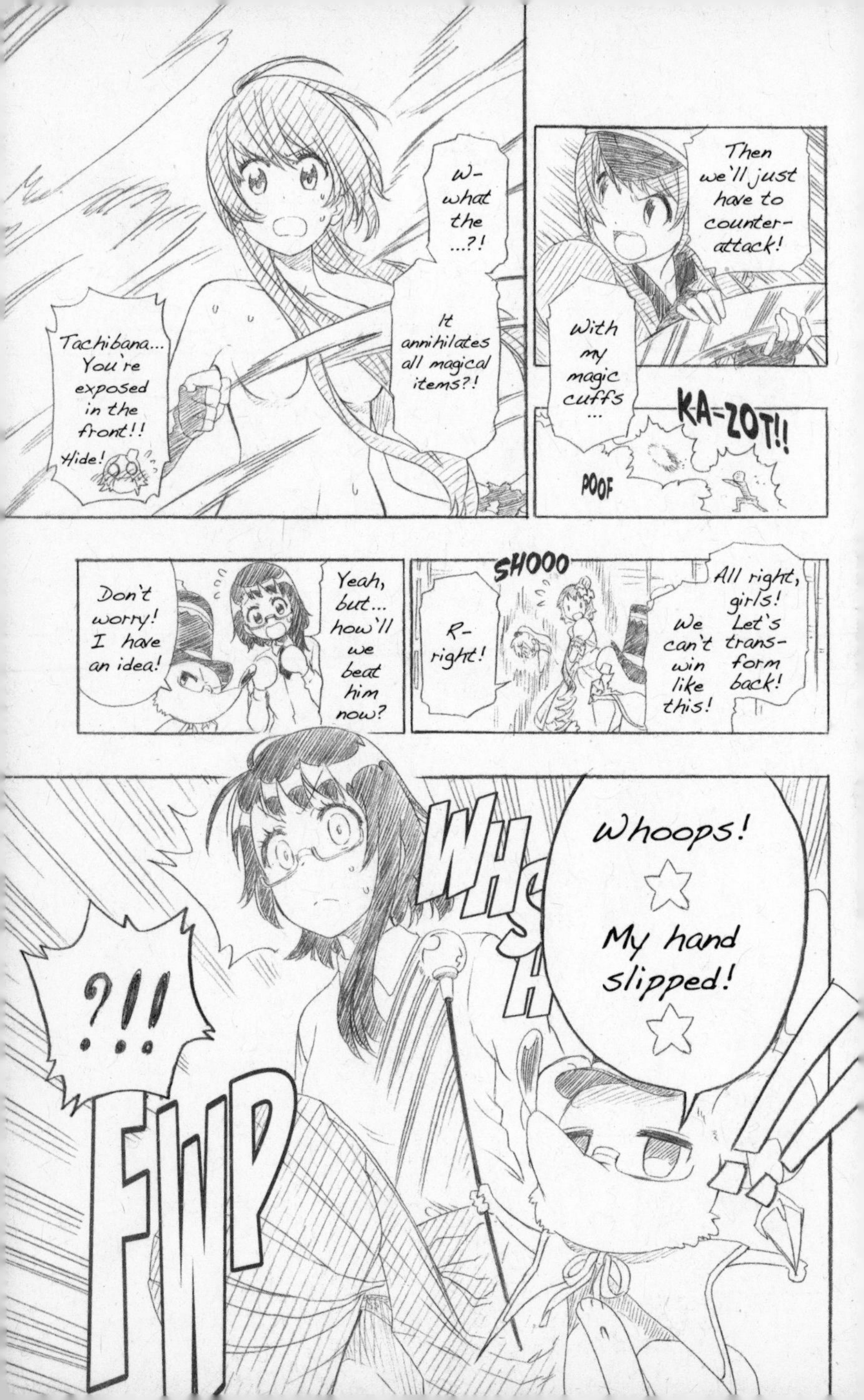
Then we'll just have to counter-attack!
With my magic cuffs...
KA-ZOT!!
POOF
W-what the ...?!
It annihilates all magical items?!
Tachibana... You're exposed in the front!! Hide!
All right, girls! Let's transform back!
We can't win like this!
SHOOO
R-right!
Yeah, but... how'll we beat him now?
Don't worry! I have an idea!
Whoops! ☆ My hand slipped! ☆
?!!
FWP

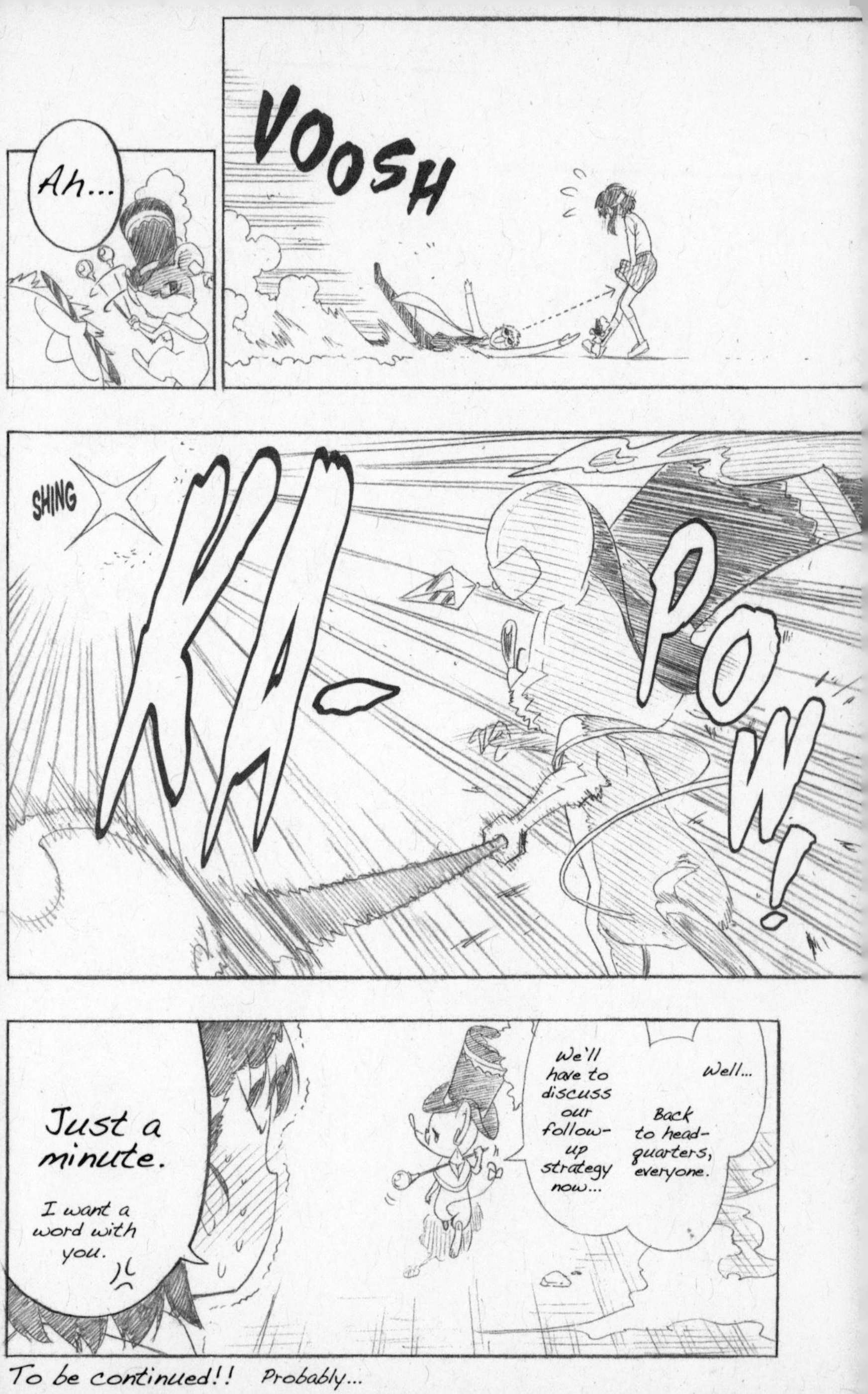
VOOSH
Ah...
SHING
KA-POW!
Well...
Back to head-quarters, everyone.
We'll have to discuss our follow-up strategy now...
Just a minute.
I want a word with you.

To be continued!! Probably...

You got off easier than us, Leader.
You have a point...

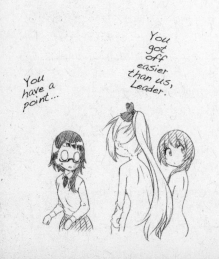

You're Reading the WRONG WAY!

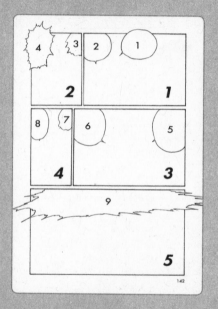

NISEKOI reads from right to left, starting in the upper-right corner. Japanese is read from right to left, meaning that action, sound effects, and word-balloon order are completely reversed from English order.